ORGANIZING BRONZE AGE SOCIETIES

The Mediterranean, Central Europe, and Scandinavia Compared

The Bronze Age was a formative period in European history when the organization of landscapes, settlements, and economies reached a new level of complexity. This book presents the first in-depth, comparative study of household, economy, and settlement in three microregions: the Mediterranean (Sicily), central Europe (Hungary), and northern Europe (south Scandinavia). The results are based on ten years of fieldwork employing similar documentation, and scientific analyses were used in each of the regional studies, making controlled comparisons possible. The new evidence demonstrates how differences in settlement organization and household economies were counterbalanced by similarities in the organized use of the landscape in an economy dominated by the herding of large flocks of sheep and cattle. The eight chapters in this book provide a new, contextualized understanding of the social and economic complexity of the Bronze Age. Its innovative theoretical and methodological approaches are of relevance to all researchers of landscape and settlement history.

Timothy Earle is Professor of Anthropology at Northwestern University. His scholarship focuses on the emergence of chiefdoms, and he has conducted field research in Hawaii, the Andes, Denmark, and Hungary. He is the author of several books, most recently *Chiefdoms: Power, Economy, and Ideology*, *How Chiefs Come to Power*, and *Bronze Age Economics*.

Kristian Kristiansen is Professor of Archaeology at the University of Gothenburg. He is an honorary Fellow of the Society of Antiquaries of Scotland, the Society of Antiquaries of London, and the European Association of Archaeologists, which awarded him the European Archaeological Heritage Prize in 2005. He is the author of *Europe before History*, *Social Transformations in Archaeology* (with Michael Rowlands), and *The Rise of Bronze Age Society* (with Thomas B. Larsson), which was awarded best scholarly book in 2007 by the Society for American Archaeology.

Organizing Bronze Age Societies

THE MEDITERRANEAN, CENTRAL EUROPE, AND SCANDINAVIA COMPARED

Edited by

Timothy Earle
Northwestern University

Kristian Kristiansen
University of Gothenburg

CAMBRIDGE UNIVERSITY PRESS
Cambridge, New York, Melbourne, Madrid, Cape Town, Singapore,
São Paulo, Delhi, Dubai, Tokyo, Mexico City

Cambridge University Press
32 Avenue of the Americas, New York, NY 10013-2473, USA

www.cambridge.org
Information on this title: www.cambridge.org/9780521748353

© Cambridge University Press 2010

This publication is in copyright. Subject to statutory exception
and to the provisions of relevant collective licensing agreements,
no reproduction of any part may take place without the written
permission of Cambridge University Press.

First published 2010

Printed in the United States of America

A catalog record for this publication is available from the British Library.

Library of Congress Cataloging in Publication data

Organizing Bronze age societies : the Mediterranean, Central Europe, and
Scandinavia compared / edited by Timothy Earle, Kristian Kristiansen.
 p. cm.
Includes bibliographical references and index.
ISBN 978-0-521-76466-7 (hardback) – ISBN 978-0-521-74835-3 (pbk.)
1. Bronze age – Italy – Sicily. 2. Bronze age – Hungary.
3. Bronze age – Scandinavia. 4. Land settlement patterns,
Prehistoric – Italy – Sicily. 5. Land settlement patterns,
Prehistoric – Hungary. 6. Land settlement patterns, Prehistoric – Scandinavia.
7. Sicily (Italy) – Antiquities. 8. Hungary – Antiquities. 9. Scandinavia –
Antiquities. I. Earle, Timothy K. II. Kristiansen, Kristian, 1948– III. Title.
GN778.22.I8074   2011
936'.01–dc22   2009051655

ISBN 978-0-521-76466-7 Hardback
ISBN 978-0-521-74835-3 Paperback

Cambridge University Press has no responsibility for the persistence or accuracy of
URLs for external or third-party Internet Web sites referred to in this publication and
does not guarantee that any content on such Web sites is, or will remain, accurate or
appropriate.

Cover drawing by Brigitta Kürtösi

In memory of Ildikó Poroszlai

Contents

List of Illustrations		*page* ix
List of Tables		xv
Preface		xvii
1	Introduction: Theory and Practice in the Late Prehistory of Europe Timothy Earle and Kristian Kristiansen	1
2	The Palaeo-Environments of Bronze Age Europe Charles French	34
3	Regional Settlement Patterns Timothy Earle and Michael J. Kolb	57
4	Settlement Structure and Organisation Magnus Artursson	87
5	Households Marie Louise Stig Sørensen	122
6	Subsistence Strategies Maria Vretemark	155
7	Technology and Craft Joanna Sofaer	185
8	Organising Bronze Age Societies: Concluding Thoughts Timothy Earle and Kristian Kristiansen	218
Appendix 1	Participating Institutions	257
Appendix 2	Doctoral Dissertations Based on the Projects	258
Appendix 3	Selected Publications Related to the Four Projects	259
Bibliography		263
Index		295

Color plates follow page 136.

List of Illustrations

FIGURES

1.1. The articulation of local versus foreign, closure versus openness in the operation of Bronze Age society. *page* 5
1.2. The articulation of scale in settlement analysis. 7
1.3. Model that shows the dialectic relationship among materiality, materialisation, and materialism, where arrows suggest how social praxis relates to the three theoretical concepts. 13
1.4. The three pillars of Bronze Age economies: the ritual, the political, and the domestic economy. 16
1.5. Model of basic material and institutional components of Eurasian societies of the third millennium BC. 17
1.6. Model of changing social formation during the second and first millennia BC in central Europe. 21
1.7. Europe, showing the locations of the project. 23
1.8. **a**. Bronze Age cairn from eastern Sweden, typically situated at higher elevations with a view over the sea, and visible as a landmark from the sea as well; **b**. Bronze Age barrows in Denmark, typically situated at higher altitudes. 25
2.1. Summary pollen diagram from Thy, Denmark. 37
2.2. Detailed pollen diagram from Hassing Huse Mose, Denmark. 37
2.3. The geology of the Chuddia River valley, western Sicily, delineating alluvial fans, bedrock, a thrust fault, and the location of the main archaeological sites. 51
3.1. Local territorial divisions between Early Bronze Age farmsteads from As, southeastern Thy. Squares

represent farmsteads, and dots, barrows, which are assumed to demarcate the infield/outfield boundary. 64
3.2. Model of Late Bronze Age settlements in southeastern Thy, and the transition to the early Iron Age, when Bronze Age farms were left and people moved into newly formed villages. Probable settlements are based on test excavations, and assumed settlements on surface indicators. 66
3.3. Settlement pattern of the Benta valley in the Early Bronze Age. 73
3.4. Settlement pattern of the Benta valley in the Middle Bronze Age. 75
3.5. Settlement pattern of the Benta valley in the Late Bronze Age. 77
3.6. Settlement pattern of the Salemi area in the Late Bronze Age. 79
3.7. Settlement pattern of the Salemi area in the Early Iron Age. 80
3.8. Classical/Hellenistic settlement pattern of the Salemi area. 81
4.1. Settlement at Bejsebakken, northern Jutland, Denmark. 90
4.2. Settlement at Limensgård, Bornholm, Denmark. **a.** Phase 1, 2050 to 1950 BC, **b.** Phase 2, 1950 to 1850 BC, **c.** Phase 3, 1850 to 1700, BC. 91
4.3. Settlement at Almhov, Scania, southern Sweden. The position for each Late Neolithic farmstead is marked with grey shading. 92
4.4. Settlement at Højgård, southern Jutland, Denmark. **a.** Phase 1, 1700 to 1600 BC, **b.** Phase 2, 1600 to 1400 BC, **c.** Phase 3, 1300 to 1100, BC, **d.** Full extent of individual farmsteads. 93
4.5. Settlement at Apalle, eastern middle Sweden, scale 1:2500; houses marked by grey shading are Phase 4. 95
4.6. Reconstruction of farmhouse at Bjerre Enge, Thy, Denmark. 97
4.7. Reconstruction of tell-house Százhalombatta-Földvár. 107
4.8. Late Bronze Age settlement at Dunakeszi, north of Budapest, Hungary. Earlier phase houses are marked in black. 111
4.9. Excavated structures at Mokarta, western Sicily. 116
4.10. Reconstruction of the merchant's house at Monte Polizzo. 117

5.1. Plan of Early Bronze Age longhouses from western Denmark.	131
5.2. Reconstruction of large Early Bronze Age house (House IV).	131
5.3. Distribution of fine and coarse ware at House II Fragtrup, Denmark.	134
6.1. Decrease in cattle from Early Bronze Age to Late Bronze Age settlements in south Scandinavia.	157
6.2. At most Scandinavian sites, the amount of young calves among the slaughtered animals is quite high, similar to Apalle or Ängdala. The pattern at Kirkebjerg, on the other hand, where the calves are missing, suggests a continuous disposal of juvenile cattle away from the settlement in an exchange system.	159
6.3. Percentage of cattle at Százhalombatta was higher during the Early Bronze Age, before 2000 BC.	165
6.4. Sheep kill-off patterns changed around 2000 BC, indicating increased wool production.	167
6.5. Red deer was the prime wild animal hunted in Bronze Age and Early Iron Age Europe. Antlers and distal parts of metapodials, cut off like the ones in the picture, dominate the assemblages.	169
6.6. Distribution among domestic animals across Monte Polizzo.	175
6.7. Red deer fragments differ between the acropolis and waste from the households at Monte Polizzo.	175
6.8a. Macro-botanical remains from Monte Polizzo. Carbonised plant remains from the Elymian (E) and Medieval (M) settlements at Monte Polizzo. **a, b.** Triticum dicoccum (emmer, E), **a.** caryopsis, **b.** spikelet, **c.** Triticum aestivum-type (bread wheat, M) rachis, **d.** Hordeum vulgare (barley, E) caryopsis, **e.** Vicia faba (faba bean, E) seed, **f.** Vitis vinifera (grape, E) seed, **g.** Prunus spinosa (sloe, E) stone.	180
6.8b. Charcoal remains from Iron Age Monte Polizzo. **a, b, c.** Olea europaea (olive tree), **d, e, f.** Ulmus sp. (elm), **g, h, i.** Quercus sp. (deciduous oak), **j, k, l.** Quercus sp. (evergreen oak).	181
7.1. Material culture indicating craft activities from Thy, Denmark: **a.** Early Bronze Age vessel from Egshvile, V. Vandet parish, **b.** Late Bronze Age vessel from Højbjerggård, Vesløs parish, **c.** Early Bronze Age	

bifacial sickle from Bjerre 6, **d**. Late Bronze Age heavy blade knife from Bjerre 1, **e**. oak timber from Bjerre 6, **f**. roof support from Bjerre 6 showing cut marks from a bronze axe similar to that shown.	187
7.2. Material culture indicating craft activities at Százhalombatta, Hungary: **a**. cup, **b**. cooking vessel, **c**. urn, **d**. jug, **e**. sickle blades, **f**. shafthole axe, **g**. cattle phalange 'burnisher,' **h**. double point, **i**. ornamented horse harness, **j**. posthole packed with debris, **k**. layers of plaster on a house wall.	193
7.3. Material culture indicating craft activities at Monte Polizzo, Sicily: **a**. carinated cup, **b**. dente de lupo bowl, **c**. jug, **d**. capeduncola, **e**. hewn limestone walls from House 1.	203
8.1. Maritime rock-art scene from Torsbo, Kville, in western Sweden showing a fleet of ships setting out on a sea journey. The number of paddlers was typically around 20.	228
8.2. Map showing the appearance of identical rock-art ships from the Early Bronze Age along the Scandinavian coastline, testifying to the importance of long-distance maritime trade and sea journeys along the Scandinavian coastline. Similar networks must have connected other maritime regions, such as the Atlantic seaboard.	229
8.3. **a**. A reconstruction of traditional farmhouse at Bjerre, Thy, **b**. The twin chiefs' farm at Legård, Thy. They demonstrate the differential access to and control over resources, from timber to cattle.	232
8.4. **a**. Two pairs of decorated antler cheek pieces found in a pot in the largest house at the tell site of Százhalombatta, **b**. Reconstruction of the use of horse harness from Danubian tell sites.	235
8.5. Greek Ionian, Corinthian, and colonial tableware from the merchant's house.	237
8.6**a**. Distribution of foreign swords connecting south Germany and Denmark.	240
8.6**b**. Distribution of Nordic full-hilted swords.	241
8.7. Capaduncola pot from the merchant's house.	243
8.8. Model of a decentralised Bronze Age chiefdom of northern Europe, at times also expanding into central Europe.	246

8.9. Model of a centralised Bronze Age chiefdom of southeast-central Europe, at times also expanding into west-central Europe. 247
8.10. Dynamic historical model of the potential transformation of gift obligations into tribute and slavery. 251
8.11. Long-term model of the rise and decline of the Bronze Age farm, compared with changes in metal supplies and ecology. 253

PLATES

1.1. **a, b.** The tell site seen from the south with the steep sides due to recent clay-taking for a brick factory. 27
1.2. The landscape of Monte Polizzo. 29
2.1. The Bronze Age shoreline in Tanum, Sweden. 41
2.2. View of the Benta stream and floodplain north of Sóskút, Hungary, today. 44
2.3. The soil profile at Érd site 4 in Benta valley, Hungary, with Bronze Age features defined at the base and Roman features at the top of the profile just below the modern plough soil. 45
2.4. Inferred view of the Benta valley for the Early-Middle Bronze Age in the lower Benta valley, Hungary. 46
2.5. Inferred view of the Benta valley for the Late Bronze Age in the lower Benta valley, Hungary. 47
5.1. Example of narrow strait between Middle Bronze Age house is from Százhalombatta-Földvár with demarcated house walls and storage pits. 137
5.2. Typical oven feature located in most houses from Százhalombatta-Földvár. 142
5.3. Adjacent specialised oven from Százhalombatta-Földvár. 143
5.4. Plan of the terminal phase of House 1 at Monte Polizzo. House was destroyed by fire. 147
8.1. Fortified tell site at Fidvár, Slovakia. Ground plan of house clusters and fortifications based on magnetic prospection, shown in section. 221
8.2. Reconstruction drawing of the tell site at Százhalombatta at its height. 233
8.3. Reconstruction of the merchant's house at Monte Polizzo. 236

Color plates follow page 136.

List of Tables

2.1. Schematic summary of major palaeo-environmental events in Scandinavia, Hungary, and Sicily during the Bronze Age and later prehistoric to early historic times. *page* 54
3.1. Comparison of settlement evidence for the Salemi, Benta, and Thy microregions. 83
4.1. Changing longhouse sizes in southern Scandinavia during Late Neolithic I to Bronze Age period VI. 89
4.2. General picture of the settlement structure and organisation in southern Scandinavia from Late Neolithic I to Bronze Age period VI. 89
4.3. Settlement structure and organisation in Thy, northern Jutland, Denmark, from Late Neolithic I to Bronze Age period VI. 96
4.4. Settlement structure and organisation in northern Bohuslän, Sweden, from Late Neolithic I to Bronze Age period VI. 99
4.5. Settlement structure and organisation in the Benta valley, Hungary, from the Early to Late Bronze Age. 102
4.6. Settlement structure and organisation in Sicily, Italy, from the Early Bronze Age to the Early Iron Age. 115
4.7. Comparison of the settlement structure and organisation from three regions in Europe. 119
5.1. Outline of analytical elements of households. 124
5.2. Various estimates of the size of the average household in the three study areas. 127
5.3. Some salient differences in household characteristics across the three areas. 152
6.1. Bronze Age crops in Thy, Denmark. 160

6.2. Bronze Age crops in southern Sweden and Iron Age crops in Tanum. 163
6.3. Bronze Age crops at Százhalombatta. 171
6.4. Early Iron Age crops in Western Sicily. 177
7.1. Investment levels in different crafts at Thy, Százhalombatta, and Monte Polizzo. 208
7.2. The organisation of production for different crafts at Thy, Százhalombatta, and Monte Polizzo. 210
7.3. Cross-craft relationships at Thy, Százhalombatta, and Monte Polizzo. 215

Preface

This book results from the combined effort and collaboration of eight universities in Europe and the United States; the National Danish and Swedish Heritage Boards; the superintendenze in Trapani in Sicily; local museums in the areas of the field projects in Denmark, Sweden, Hungary, and Sicily; and a large number of students who received archaeological training and experience in international cooperation (participating institutions in Appendix 1). The philosophy and history of the projects therefore are told in this Preface, because they represent the conditions facing archaeological research projects now and in the future.

Although research often is considered an individual project, in archaeology it is always based upon the combined efforts of many people. Archaeological excavation projects cannot be carried out by single individuals; whereas in the early days of archaeology the director of excavation was often considered solely responsible for executing and publishing the results, such practice is unwarranted and unrealistic today. Modern field projects are so demanding in their organisation and integration of diverse skills, from documentation to complex scientific analyses, that they demand teamwork, not only among individuals from different fields of knowledge, but also among institutions. Today, very few, if any, departments in the world cover all the skills needed in modern archaeological field projects. This was the archaeological raison d'être behind the joint organisation – the first pillar of the project.

The second pillar of the project, which followed from this realisation, was to assemble a group of scholars and students who shared the same vision and approach to archaeology, because when you are in the field, mutual respect and cooperation are a first condition, and from that follows good discussions and other enjoyable side effects of social interaction. However, I also looked for diversity among the participants, as innovation often originates in confronting different research and fieldwork traditions. It took time and negotiations to overcome some differences, mostly those grounded in different excavation traditions, but others were immediately realised, such as the plough-sampling strategy employed in the Thy project in Denmark, or the micromorphology analysis employed in Hungary and Sicily.

The third pillar of the project was to integrate undergraduate honours, master's degree essays, and doctoral projects into the project, as this vitalises work and helps get results analysed and published (doctoral projects are listed in Appendix 2). I believe that joint projects should be interdisciplinary, multinational, and balanced with respect to gender and junior versus senior researchers to create a dynamic environment. A sociological analysis was done at one point in the project's history in Sicily, but we did not intend to analyse the results ourselves, but rather preferred to work collaboratively and let the results speak for themselves.

The fourth pillar of the project was to integrate local museums into the individual field projects, and the national archaeological heritage organisations, because they represent cutting-edge skills in archaeological documentation, and because it secured similar documentary standards between all field projects. We used the newly developed digital documentation system from the National Swedish Heritage, Intrasis, in all three projects in Tanum, Százhalombatta, and Monte Polizzo, and staff from the rescue divisions in Sweden took part in all three projects to maintain and teach the system, even as they carried out separate subprojects. For many students, this provided important skills that qualified them for the archaeological job market.

The fifth pillar was funding. Inviting different institutions to participate brought in funding from different sources, sometimes in the form of student labour, sometimes in the form of skilled archaeologists, sometimes in the form of money for scientific analyses, which levelled out fluctuations on a year-to-year basis. Although most funding was national and institutional, we also obtained a European grant from the European Union's (EU's) 6th Framework Programme during the last four years of the project, which financed a number of PhD scholarships and some postdoctoral research. This helped greatly to integrate the research programmes into the larger project.

During the same period, a generous grant from the Swedish Riksbankens Jubileumsfond provided funding for most of the natural science analyses in the projects. Likewise, generous grants from the National Science Foundation of the United States provided funding for both the original Thy project and the field surveys in Hungary and Sicily.

After this presentation of the ideals behind the project, let me tell the story of its realisation, which, of course, never is as smooth and well planned as it may look upon completion. I shall begin by citing my old friend and museums inspector from the Thy museum, Jen-Henrik Bech. When asked about his experiences from the Thy project, which served as a model for the subsequent projects, he answered: 'If I had known all the difficulties that an international project were to involve, I never would have done it, and that would have been the biggest mistake of my life.'

The first project was carried out in Thy, a peninsula in northwestern Jutland, which borders the rough North Sea to the west and the quiet Limfjord to the east. It started in 1990, and by this time I was director of the archaeological heritage division in the National Agency for Nature Conservation and Forestry, Ministry of the Environment. The project originated out of two strands of research: At the time we were running a national program of pollen diagrams in collaboration with the Geological Survey of Denmark, which hosted the department for palaeo-botanical research headed by Svend Thorkild Andersen. We had already done interesting regional pollen diagrams from southern Jutland and Djursland, but I wanted to do one for Thy, as this was the area with the densest distribution of preserved Bronze Age barrows in Denmark. Through research by Klavs Randsborg and myself, Thy was known as one of the richest areas in burial wealth from the Early Bronze Age. By period 3, swords deposited in burials were heavily worn on their hilts, and after that time, bronzes nearly disappeared from the burial record there. It was thus an enigmatic region in Bronze Age research that deserved to be studied in a field project. I had completed a draft manuscript of my book and felt the need to test some of its hypotheses in field research.

The pollen diagram turned out to be one of the most dramatic in northern Europe (Chapter 2, Figures 2.1 and 2.2). It showed a massive forest clearance around 2700 BC providing grazing lands for herds of animals. This clearance created an open landscape, and during the Early Bronze Age most of the remaining forest was taken away, basically creating the open landscape that is known today, although the medieval period took away the last few stands of trees. We now decided to establish a field archaeological project within the catchment area of the regional pollen diagram. It encircled a 10-km-wide area in Thy with a dense barrow landscape around Lake Ove and the parish of Sdr. Hå (Chapter 1, Figure 1.7).

We further decided to create a project that placed natural science and archaeology on equal footing. To accomplish these ambitious goals, Jens-Henrik and I realised we needed the skills and supplementary funding of international partners. I contacted my good friend Tim Earle, who, at the time, was running a project in Peru that was under increasing pressure from a local insurgency in the region where he worked. He therefore readily accepted my invitation and brought a whole set-up of new ideas and field procedures. When confronted with the Danish tradition of large-scale stripping of plough soil with machines to get to the house plans, he pointed out that we were taking away all ploughed-up cultural information from underlying houses. Together with his graduate student, John Steinberg, we designed a plough soil-sampling program that provided much new information to the project and was used in John's PhD; an award-winning article in *Antiquity* in 1996 presented the methodological approach. Together we worked out systematic procedures for field walking, procedures for excavation, and sampling procedures for macro-botanical evidence, which later became a PhD by Kristina Kelertas. Soon I also invited my old friend Michael Rowlands from University College London, who came with his graduate student at the time, Nick Thorpe; he carried out much of the field walking with English students.

Over the years, the project joined forces with two remarkable rescue projects of Bronze Age farms, in Bjerre Enge in northwestern Thy, and in Ås, close to the Limfjord. Some of Tim's high demands had to give way because of the nature of the landscape in Denmark, but during trial and error we ended up with a research design that became the model of the subsequent three projects in Sweden, Hungary, and Sicily (Chapter 1). It also included the joint multinational teamwork that had been so productive, although not without heated discussions when different research and field traditions – and sometimes different personalities – clashed. However, that provided innovations in our research design and in our thinking. It was also a central aspect of the project that students and project leaders lived together and shared meals and other daily practicalities.

We also practised our anthropological knowledge of feasting by creating a feasting tradition for each project. In Thy, it was the eel party with snaps and beer (eels were, strangely enough, foreign to many American students but most of them learned to appreciate them). In Sicily, it was the midsummer party, with snaps and herring, to which all friends of the project in town were invited and at which we raised a Swedish midsummer pole and danced around it; in Hungary it was a goose-liver dinner at a traditional restaurant.

The Thy Archaeological Project (TAP) was concluded in 1997. By that time, I had been professor at University of Gothenburg since 1994 and brought students to participate in the project. I had also started up a new Bronze Age project linked to the rock-art of Bohuslän in Tanum, western Sweden, where I met Christopher Prescott from Oslo, who later became my field director in Sicily. However, in 1996, two completely independent things happened that proved to be decisive. Through one of my graduate students, Marco Montebelli, who visited Sicily for his PhD research, I received an invitation from Sebastiano Tusa, then at the soprintendenza of Trapani, to come down and start a joint project. I met with him during an international conference in Forlì that same year and realised we could work well together, as we shared a modern theoretical approach to archaeology. Later at the conference in London, which started the Bronze Age Campaign, I met Ildikó Poroszlai, then director of the Matrica Museum in Százhalombatta, south of Budapest. I told her I had always wished to do a modern excavation of a Bronze Age tell, and she answered that she – or rightly, her museum – owned one. They had just bought the land where the tell was situated at the Danube, where she had started to excavate some years before, but had stopped because of financial and other constraints. Both Sebastiano and Ildikó were keen to add natural science analyses to their excavations, as well as modern documentation procedures. One thing led to another, and after having visited both sites during 1997, we agreed to get started, but on the condition that I could invite colleagues from other universities to participate on equal terms, and on the condition that we applied similar documentation procedures and a similar research design in the two projects, which became three when we added Tanum in western Sweden.

We could never have carried out the projects without the goodwill and support provided by Sebastiano and Ildikó and their colleagues. They paved the way for the projects in multiple practical ways, so that we could concentrate on the archaeology.

Also of fundamental importance to the projects was the goodwill of the Swedish National Heritage Board to let their rescue units (the division called UV) take part in the projects and provide the digital documentation, which later became the Intrasis system. It was tested under diverse foreign conditions, but it also helped students achieve skills they could use later when applying for jobs. Of equal importance was having two colleagues on board from the very beginning, Tim Earle in Hungary and Christopher Prescott in Sicily. In Sicily, we also had Michael Kolb from Northern Illinois University to conduct the field survey (and later he also developed his own projects), and we soon added Michael Shanks and Ian Morris from Stanford University. Although Michael soon moved on to new projects, Ian Morris stayed on and conducted excavations on the acropolis during the whole period, aided by his assistants Emma Blake and Trinity Jackson, as well as Brien Garnand. I was lucky to have good assistant directors in Christian Mühlenbock in Sicily and Claes Uhner in Hungary, both of whom took their PhDs on material from the project. Sebastiano Tusa also brought in excavation teams from Sicily, which meant that we soon numbered close to a hundred.

In Hungary, we were likewise lucky to have good partners in Marie Louise Stig Sørensen from Cambridge, who brought in Joanna Sofaer, newly appointed in Southampton, just as Ildikó and her invaluable assistant, now director of the museum, Magdi Vicze, invited a group of talented Hungarian graduate students, several of whom took their PhDs in the project. Charly French supervised the students on landscape history and soil micromorphology, while Tim Earle completed the field survey of the project in collaboration with Magnus Artursson from the Swedish Heritage.

In the Tanum project, our partner became my old friend Felipe Criado and his team from Santiago de Compostela in Spain. In this project, new innovative excavation methods around the rock-art sites were developed and exchanged. Lasse Bengtsson and, later, Johan Ling were the principal field directors. The results of that work are available separately.

During the nine years of the projects, hundreds of students from Scandinavia, the United Kingdom, Hungary, Slovakia, Germany, Sicily, Canada, and the United States met and learned to collaborate internationally, as well as learning to cope with cultural differences. I consider this a major achievement of the project at a time when national and local archaeologies predominate. Excursions to visit the sites and museums of the regions were a steady ingredient

As the mayor of Salemi cuts a cake decorated with flags of all participating nations, he is surrounded by the project leaders Michael Kolb, Ian Morris, Bengt Westergård, Kristian Kristiansen, and Chrisopher Prescott, as well as local friends of the project.

in the projects. The students also learned how to adapt to a foreign country, just as they experienced the hospitality and support of local people and politicians, most notably in Sicily, where the municipality of Salemi furnished a huge building to house the project and its participants. In the illustration above, you see the mayor of Salemi cutting a huge layer cake decorated with the flags of all participating nations. The project leaders, Ian Morris, Kristian Kristiansen, and Chrisopher Prescott are, for the occasion, decorated with laurels. The photo epitomises the spirit of the projects.

To integrate the three projects, we had planning meetings every January in Rome, at the Swedish Institute, followed by dinner at our favourite restaurants. We named the project 'The Emergence of European Communities,' a name that alluded to both the present and the past. After getting the projects off the ground through rather modest funding during the first three or four years, I received a generous four-year research grant in 2002 from the Swedish Riksbankens Jubileumsfond that enabled us to employ natural scientists to conduct the osteological and macro-botanical work for all three projects, carried out by Maria Vretemark and Hans-Peter Stika, just as it paid for the Swedish participation. Parallel to this, we received an EU grant within the Marie Curie program, called 'research training networks.' It paid for six PhD grants and two or three postdoctoral positions in the project during a four-year period, just as it enabled us to arrange specialist seminars within the project. The PhD grants enabled a generation of talented graduate students who had worked for the project to do their PhD work in another country, and thus supported international integration of research. Finally, the National Science Foundation of the United States provided extensive funding for the original Thy project, the field surveys in Hungary and Sicily, and one PhD project.

This book summarises the nine years of joint efforts from all participating institutions between 1998 and 2006, and its completion rather soon after the termination of the project, in 2009, is a testimony to the collaborative spirit of the project. It was decided to leave out the ritual aspects of the project, as a separate book on the rock-art research in Tanum and Galicia is in print.

No project is without shocks, but it was a nearly unbearable tragedy for all of us in the Százhalombatta project when the inspiring and charming project leader and museum director Ildikó Poroszlai suddenly died at the age of 50 in February 2005, in the middle of an active and prosperous life. The feeling of loss is still with me, and I dedicate this book to her memory.

Finally, I wish to thank all participants, named and unnamed, who made these nine years one of the most productive and exciting experiences of my life, and contributed to its success. Most of all I wish to thank my co-editor, Timothy Earle, for many years of friendship and cooperation, and for carrying a huge workload in the completion of this book. The project started, symbolically, in 1998, when I hosted the annual meeting of the European Association of Archaeologists (EAA) at our university in Gothenburg in my last duty as president. To be able to practise in the project what I had worked for during the previous ten years during the formation of the EAA has been a gratifying experience. We all had a great time, and I do think the intellectual inspiration radiates from the pages of the book.

Kristian Kristiansen

1

Introduction: Theory and Practice in the Late Prehistory of Europe

Timothy Earle and Kristian Kristiansen

We propose to integrate dialectically processual and postprocessual theory to interpret later European prehistory. We approach this daunting task with a comparative, contextualised study of selected microregions from northern Europe to the Mediterranean. Our data derive from fieldwork projects carried out between 1990 and 2006 in Thy in Denmark, Tanum in Sweden, Százhalombatta in Hungary, and Monte Polizzo in western Sicily, supplemented by relevant data from the wider regions (see Preface). Our period encompasses the third to first millennia BC, which saw major transformations that encompassed most of Eurasia (Kristiansen and Larsson 2005; Kohl 2007). Our concern is with the local constructions of these transformative changes, which should provide a new platform for understanding the operation of basic social and economic mechanisms. We wish to transcend the dichotomies between local and global, and external and internal forces of change. Our approach is materialist and multiscalar. The materialist position simply underlines the fact that most of our data were linked to the social and economic reproduction of society, as is apparent from the content of the chapters. Symbolic and ideological forces are, for the time being, given less priority, although they were treated in several works from the project (Oma 2007; Streiffert 2006), and they constantly reverberate in our interpretations. A multiscalar approach implies that we analyse social and economic activities on scales from individual activities within the household, to settlements, to regional polities that are further imbedded in broad international interactions. Although each component, representing a chapter in the book, is analysed on its own terms, we explain operations at one level in terms of the contexts and components of the larger and smaller scales. We seek to integrate results from the three regions into a framework to understand common processes and local histories. It demands theoretical elaboration and conceptualisation, tasks we undertake in the next section.

Our research is comparative, but comparative on two distinct levels of contrast. In his earlier work that eventually led to Europe, Earle compared long-term developments in three historically independent cases (Polynesia, the Andes, and northern Europe). An empirical observation from this work was that the dynamics of each macroregion were historically quite specific. Although the basic processes were common, within each world region, the political actors (chiefs) pragmatically structured their political economy and power strategies, creating dissimilar patterns of 'how chiefs came to power' (Earle 1997). In a seminal study of Polynesia, Sahlins (1958) used 'controlled comparison,' looking at different outcomes within one macroregion. He examined, side by side, the historically close Polynesian societies to understand how political economies and social stratification resulted from differences in overall island productivity. By controlling for historical differences in culture and technology held in common within this single macroregion, Sahlins was able to unravel the intricacies of historic processes.

Now, we focus on the single macroregion of Europe and attempt to understand long-term political trajectories from the perspective of microregional studies. With such historically controlled comparisons, we hope to lay out how contrasting local patterns made a difference to the well-studied macroregional patterns of European prehistory. We believe these comparisons lay bare the driving forces of change that are so difficult to see from the macropatterning.

The field projects in Scandinavia, Hungary, and Sicily were based upon a comparative historical/archaeological perspective on the formation of regional polities in Europe. The focus of the microregional projects was on the organisation of households and settlements, and the formation of political systems in a long-term perspective. The processes of the economic use of the landscape and of integrating exchanges were a major point of departure for our work.

A central issue must be to unravel how small-scale, yearly changes in economy and environment affect and are affected by large-scale historical changes in social and political organisation. Within an Annales framework (Bintliff 1991), we explore the relationship between structure and agency, intentional and unintentional forces of historical change, and the material threads that weave together the fabric of history. We have set our time period from the beginning of the Bronze Age to the beginning of historical Europe – a period of 2000 years – in order to allow the study of long-term change. After 300 BC, the expanding Roman Empire formalised the division between empire and so-called barbarian peripheries – Celtic and Germanic societies; however, the necessary social, economic, and political building blocks for this development were created during the preceding millennia. Already from the second millennium BC, urban societies in the east Mediterranean interacted with well-organised Bronze Age societies in central and northern Europe, and we may here see the beginning of an early form of colonialism that unfolded with the advent of the Iron Age (Gosden 2004; chapter 4). It is further suggested that the processes of these interactions have roots even back into the third millennium BC (Kristiansen and Larsson 2005).

The crucial historical questions are: Why did regional political systems develop so early in many areas of Europe when population densities were so incredibly low (Zimmerman 1999) and why was Europe so resistant to subsequent urbanisation and state formation despite the fact that the necessary building blocks were in place? To answer such world-historical questions, we believe it is necessary to study over time and in scale 1:1 the changing processes, interactions, and institutions organising household, settlement, and political territories, sometimes also called community areas (Kuna and Dreslerova 2007). Such studies allow us to draw conclusions about long-term changes and compare regional differences in organisation, as well as interregional interactions and their effects on regional developments. Only then can we begin to unravel and perhaps explain the historical dialectic between short-term political forces of change and long-term, accumulating forces of change between structure and agency.

TOWARDS A MULTISCALAR AND INTEGRATIVE THEORY OF SOCIAL ORGANISING

The effort to integrate theory and practice demands that interpretative concepts are developed to match the specific archaeological material at hand. Employing a multiscalar approach demands a corresponding theoretical elaboration of scale. We shall, therefore, begin by situating our materialist approach in terms of scale and in relationship to present theoretical approaches. Our goal is to capture the active linkages in societies among economy, identity, and politics – linkages that help us understand how human action results in broad social transformations. Over the past 20 years, materialism as a theoretical touchstone has developed (a greater concern with the active role played by material culture in social practice), and we illustrate how a changing understanding of material approaches can help one understand developments across later prehistory in Europe. In the next section, we illustrate how this integrative, material approach can be accomplished with the data at hand.

Work on material culture begins with the household, the locus of everyday life and the producer of most of the activities and things that archaeologists recover. Understanding the social significance of artefacts (social things) requires a firm understanding of context and variation, and the household is an ideal unit for analysis. Since *The Early Mesoamerican Village* (Flannery 1976), the analysis of households and domestic space has developed as a concern in anthropological archaeology (Netting and Wilk, 1984). The initial concern focused on the organisation and integration of activities in the spaces associated with households. With *The Domestication of Europe* (Hodder 1990), the symbolic meaning of space came into play as well.

However, these new theoretical and analytical concerns with household have not been systematically applied in European Bronze Age research, and we want to elaborate upon a few recent and notable exceptions (Arnoldussen and Fokkens 2008; Ullen 1994; Gerritsen 1999; Roymans 1999). Among our excavations, houses in Bjerre Enge (Denmark), Százhalombatta (Hungary), and Monte Polizzo (Sicily) produce preserved house floors that allow for the detailed analysis of context, with material sometimes sealed in place by burning or drifting sand. Attempts can thus be made to see how spaces articulate with each other – inside to out, one room to the next, and different parts of the rooms with specific associations to doors and features. With this material we can begin to understand how activities involving specific objects were played out. Contrasts among different settlements can then be related to social differentiation, economic specialisation, and a range of power relationships – a starting point, for example, for understanding the social and political role of a central settlement such as Százhalombatta or Monte Polizzo.

Of prime importance in our concern with social and political institutions is to understand the linkages among space, boundaries, and the construction of private and political identities. During

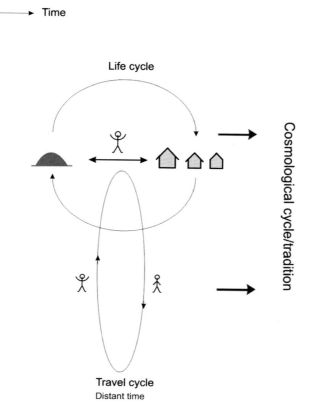

Figure 1.1.
The articulation of local versus foreign, closure versus openness in the operation of Bronze Age society.

the Neolithic and into the Bronze Age, two apparently contradictory developments marked both local distinction and international connection (Figure 1.1). Locally, the investment in built landscape included permanent farmstead and larger settlements, burial and ceremonial monuments, and cleared landscapes and field systems. These built landscapes were coupled with a material culture of everyday life (especially domestic pottery) that suggests local distinctiveness and closure. Internationally, however, the expansion of long-distance exchange networks in metalwork and other luxury items appears to emphasise openness and connection. How can we explain the dual nature of Bronze Age society – the dynamic between openness and closure? Forms of local and regional identities in material culture are thought to signal a symbolic demarcation of political and perhaps ethnic identities linked to the formation of more hierarchical and bounded forms of political power (Kristiansen 1998:chapter 8.2), and raise theoretical and comparative questions regarding ambiguity in personal and political identity (Diaz-Andreu et al 2005).

We accept the possibility that identity and ethnicity take on new forms. Present discussions circle around the concepts of the fluid and the stable (Jones 1997; Bürmeister and Müller-Schessel 2007; Kristiansen and Larsson 2005:chapter 1.2; Fernández-Götz 2008). Ethnicity may be fluid in the movements and incorporation of people, but stable in its material symbolism. Or it may be socially and demographically stable, but fluid in its material symbolism, such as incorporating foreign 'ethnic' elements (Fuhrholt 2008). The comparative evidence of the project may give some clues towards addressing questions of the use of material cultural in identity formation. With differences in gender, leadership, and social spheres of action, closure and openness in social action may exist together within different spheres of a society.

Throughout our book, social and political spheres of action will be working simultaneously, and we must understand how a person's place in society was always contingent on context. We thus ground our work firmly in the specific levels in which humans acted. However, a danger always exists that our theoretical concepts may impose a western notion of hierarchy that may not be able to fully grasp the specific character of actions and transactions that, in the past, transmitted power between people and households. The multiscalar debate in historical archaeology provides a good case in point (Hauser and Hicks 2007). In a commentary, Dan Hicks called for 'flatter, more ethnographic conceptions of scale, that seek to recognize how both small and large scale emerge from complex networks of human and material enactments' (Hicks forthcoming). Although we share this point of departure, we also recognize that constraints guide the way we construct archaeological materials (methodologies) and interpretative concepts (theory). Households, settlements, and regional polities were the multiscales of human action and of our archaeological data recovery (Lock and Molyneaux 2007). Although important differences must exist between past and present perceptions, the exercise of power and exploitation remains universal in its effects. In Figure 1.2 we illustrate theoretically how different scales are connected by opposing forces of social integration and exploitation that may lead to the rise of internal contradictions. In the concluding chapter, we explore in archaeological detail how such forces materialised in the archaeological record, leading to different historical scenarios in our three study areas.

In order to understand how economies work from households to regional and interregional systems, we introduce the concept of a political economy. The reproduction of the physical landscape, its

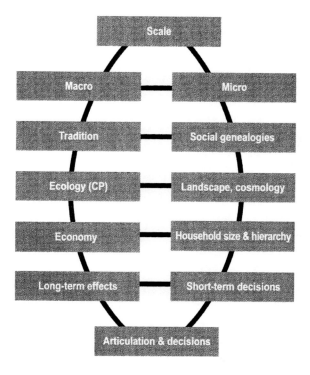

Figure 1.2.
The articulation of scale in settlement analysis.

settlements, burials and households, and broader social relations depends on the political organised economy (Earle 2002). 'The political economy is the material flows of goods and labour through a society, channelled to create wealth and to finance institutions of rule' (Earle 2002:chapter 1). This is an arena for social and political competition, which may lead to the formation of unequal access to productive resources, as some were included and others excluded through property relations in productive lands and symbolic things. At the local level, this may be reflected in different sizes of farms, or specialisation of production between settlements and communities at large, elements that can be analysed and studied in the archaeological and environmental record. Finally, the deposition of prestige objects in burials and hoards represents a ritualised aspect of how to study unequal access to wealth and its disposition or consumption.

In the political economy, institutions with a set of rules that govern the production and distribution of resources and wealth integrate domains of power The use of material culture in the expression of institutions is a prerequisite for obtaining and maintaining power (Kristiansen and Larsson 2005:chapter 1.2), while, at the same time, it regulates and constrains individuals' attempts to increase power.

Institutions are thus the building blocks of society. Their rituals legitimised the power of office holders, whether ritual chiefs or war chiefs, through visible performance and participation that engaged and integrated society's members in its reproduction. Institutions are literally built up materially through the construction of landscape features, including houses and monuments, and the gifting of objects, including items of display and identity. Thus, one makes a family by building a house or makes a political alliance by giving a special sword. The importance is that the institutions are built materially in addition to symbolically, and the process of making involves intentional actions by participants.

Agency is critical here. It has been used to make objects vital in social action (Gell 1998; Dobres and Robb 2000). DeMarrais, Castillo, and Earle (1996) introduced the concept of materialisation to account for the active role played by material culture in social strategies and as a framework in the formation and reproduction of institutions. Others have stressed the materiality of lived experiences, the role of bodily experience, and expression (Treherne 1995; Sørensen and Rebay 2008; Shanks 1999; Meskell and Joyce 2003). Here we encounter the relationship between the formation of the self through a social identity and its dialectical relationship with collective identities (from social groups or classes to polities and ethnicity).

To use this approach successfully, however, we adopt an understanding of agency that relates to the expanded material world. In his book *Art and Agency*, Alfred Gell (1998) defines agency as being social and relational. That definition includes, also, material objects and art, which are ascribed agency once they are immersed into social relationships as exemplified by religious idols and style. Animation, divinity, and power can thus be ascribed to specific objects that have undergone special rituals or are decorated in a certain way. Gell turns an abstract western concept of agency into a useful theoretical tool in a specific interpretative context. The transformation of anthropological knowledge about material culture into a modern understanding demands a series of interpretative steps: agency = abstract western concept of intentionality; symbolic meaning = western interpretation of material culture as meaningfully constituted; and socio-material relation (materialisation) = contextualised non-western interpretation of material culture as animated and empowered. Agency can be said to be at work in symbolic meaning and in materialisation, but in the latter, a more holistically complete understanding exists of the relationship between the social and the material (Tilley et al 2006). Some objects can be ascribed with innate religious power and personality that act back upon people. Therefore, in the past, symbolic meanings were imbedded in relations of meaning, power, and agency among humans, animals, and material culture (Oma 2007).

To this can be added the concept of biography to understand how objects can be used for symbolic construction and reproduction of social relations (Appadurai 1986; Kopytoff 1986). Each object has a long history of making, transfer, and use that encapsulates specific social histories of work, events, and social connection. We can begin to delineate a more systematic theoretical framework for the interplay between domestic and public space, social and ritual space, and their changing meaning by attempting to reconstruct the history of objects. We employ Gell's theoretical framework to discuss how, in the Bronze Age, personal identity was constructed through relationships to a specific object (the sword) and how that linked the individual into the political economy.

MATERIAL THREADS: SPACE, OBJECT, AND LABOUR; BIOGRAPHY AND IDENTITY

Our theoretical position is part of an ongoing change in theoretical focus within archaeology. It represents an interpretative journey from broader evolutionary concerns with prehistoric societies towards a narrower phenomenological concern with negotiated social praxis and embodiment. More than a theoretical movement from processualism to postprocessualism, it attempts to get into the otherness of the past through a change of focus and interpretative strategy and therefore corresponds well with a postcolonial discourse (Gosden 2004; van Dommelen 2006).

Subsequently, a number of theoretical concepts illustrate the rather massive change of perspective during the past 25 years, summarised as a movement from the outside to the inside of society:

From social typology ⟶ to social complexity
From materialism ⟶ to materiality
From function ⟶ to context
From representation ⟶ to praxis
From social identity ⟶ to personhood

From experience ⟶ to embodiment
From pattern ⟶ to path
From settlement ⟶ to dwelling

However, we wish to argue that many of the listed concepts are dialectically intersected into each other. By employing an updated version of a materialist approach to multiscalar interpretation, we propose to integrate levels of the lived experience in the past and its materialisation in social institutions from households to regional polities. In doing so, we emphasise the way that materials act to integrate processes through laboured transformations, flows of goods, and their embodiment; and how the material record gives a direct record for observation and interpretation. This dialectic between observation and theoretically informed interpretation, between theory and praxis, must be anchored in specific contexts.

We pursue our theoretical endeavour to integrate contexts of different scales by proposing that materialism, materialisation, and materiality represent interconnected theoretical domains of material culture with an interpretative potential to account for both individual and society (on materiality: DeMarrais, Gosden, and Renfrew 2004; Taylor 2008). We illustrate our theoretical approach by studying the Bronze Age sword. First is the history of the sword's production and use; this takes place as part of political economies that linked together international relations and regional political systems. At the individual level, the sword symbolised warriorhood; it was an inalienable object acting as the embodied materiality of the fierce fighter of the Bronze Age world. Sword and warrior in this way became one. The sword also identified the warrior as a member in good standing of a social institution, defined by certain rules and social etiquette and also by a number of recurring material accoutrements, including dress, weapons, musculature, and scarred body. He was thus a member of a larger brotherhood that empowered its members. We call this an institutional materialisation of warriorhood. Finally, the warriors' martial actions, from cattle raiding to long-distance trading and raiding, to property enforcement and defence of his chieftain, contributed to the political and economic reproduction of a stratified society, and therefore belong under the theoretical umbrella of materialism, imbedded in the social relations of production.

Materialism in the Marxist tradition states that the production and reproduction of the material conditions of life are necessary, but not sufficient, conditions for understanding the relationship between people and things. In capitalist society, this relationship tended to mask the real conditions of power. Ideology mystified and naturalised power, and only by dissolving these mystifications through historical analysis and laying bare the real conditions of economic exploitation could the working class be mobilised and liberated by concrete political action. Production, circulation, and consumption of goods were the basic analytical tools employed in the Marxist analysis of the political economy (Marx 1973), coupled with an analysis of labour, value, and accumulation in capital (Marx 1975). This framework was employed to analyse the dynamic between ideology and economy in social anthropology and archaeology during the 1970s and 1980s (Friedman and Rowlands 1977; Godelier 1978; Gilman 1981; Kristiansen 1984b). More recently, Marx's concept of value and commodity was employed by Colin Renfrew to characterise the political-economic changes that accompanied the Bronze Age (Renfrew 2001), thereby granting the political economy of the Bronze Age a historical status closer to our own time. This proposal had also earlier been forwarded by Steve Shennan (1993), and was later employed by Kristiansen and Larsson (2005:figure 38).

Using the concept of biography of things, the history of an object can be analysed to uncover its social life, reproducing the interpersonal and power relationships of society. An analysis of a sword's biography provides clear support for a materialist analysis of class relationships in the Bronze Age. The sword's history starts as a complex commodity chain; copper and tin are mined from distant places and smelted within a complex socio-political world of resource ownership and labour organisation. Some level of social hierarchy and stratification is often observed near the metal source, suggesting that control over the mining procedures results in unequal access to sources of wealth and power. Then the metal must be transported, often over great distances. The traders were, in most cases, probably warriors who could guarantee the safety of the wealth, and the differential value between source of origin and place of final production would be returned to the trader. Moving along routes of trade and political alliances, such as the river Danube with its line of forts, local leaders could easily demand gifts in return for freedom of movement, although rules of guest friendship probably also were widespread. Some economic advantage would clearly return to those in-place chieftains. Finally, received by, for example, a local chieftain in Scandinavia, who traded for export commodities such as cattle hides, amber, or perhaps slaves, the metal could be transformed by an attached craftsman (Brumfield and Earle 1987), likely supported by the local chieftain. The swords and other items could then be given in formal ceremonies to the chief's retinue of supporters, but swords could probably also be acquired on journeys to distant allies and brought home. The particular flows and production transformations of the sword imbedded it within a particular world of economic control used to support a local leader's ambition (Earle 2004).

During the 1980s, this foundation version of materialism as developed for capitalist societies did not fully account for the way material culture was employed in precapitalist societies. Here, oral and symbolic traditions in material culture served to reinforce social and political institutions, gifts transactions replaced monetary transactions, just as economic surplus was replaced by social and cultural capital that could be converted into political power, tributary relations, and exploitation. Through the performance of ceremonies, rituals, travels, and other activities, material culture entered into an institutional and symbolic field of action, where myth and other symbolic meanings linked persons and material culture together. This relationship was termed materialisation (DeMarrais, Castillo, and Earle 1996). Essentially, the processes that created cultural meaning were imbedded within the political economy such that different media could be used differentially by segments of a society (Earle 2004). Kristiansen and Larsson (2005) employed the concept to develop a methodological strategy to identify institutions through their material culture. Although inspired by *Symbols in Action* (Hodder 1982), these papers went one step further by linking symbolic meaning to institutional fields of power (Bourdieu 1977). The framework for performing and executing power was considered to be rooted in symbolically and mythically loaded institutions that could be reconstructed, at least in part, through an analysis and interpretation of their material culture. In this way it could be demonstrated how material culture, when activated by holders of chiefly and priestly offices, acquired the power to convert symbolic power into political power.

From here, the step was rather short to the concept of materiality. Once we delimit symbolically fields of forces or institutions, questions of the formation of social and personal identity, personhood, and agency become pertinent. Here, a theoretical discourse from psychology and philosophy that examined personhood and embodiment met with a theoretical discourse in anthropology and archaeology that examined their social and cultural conditions (Strathern 1988; Gell 1998). This theoretical trajectory employs materiality to account for the cultural construction of body, self, and their embodied praxis (Shanks 1999; Treherne 1995). Other theoretical approaches to materiality were developed in *Metaphor and Material Culture* (Tilley 1999) and *Rethinking Materiality: the Engagement of Mind with the Material World* (Renfrew, DeMarrais, and Gosden 2004). Because materiality is constructed through social relations, it should not be equated with a modern perception of the individual, according to some researchers (Brück 2006), whereas others maintain that personhood in the Bronze Age was closer to a modern perception of the concept, as it was linked to membership of an social group or institution that provided a bounded identity with rules for its realisation. It materialises in stable regional rules of ritual etiquette and body adornments in burials over long time periods (Kristiansen and Larsson 2005:chapter 5). The materialisation of the materiality of objects and personhood is bound up with the reproduction of institutionalised power, which, in the end, comes down to the social relations of production. The conditions for personhood and self-realisation are thus ultimately dependent on a proper analysis of materiality, materialisation, and materialism forming an interconnected field of interpretation.

Figure 1.3 summarises the theoretical and explanatory relations among materiality, materialisation, and materialism, and delimits how these concepts empower social identity, social institutions, and society through processes of agency, political practice, and relations of production.

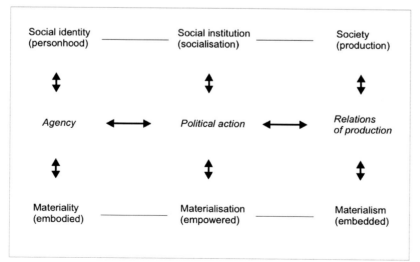

Figure 1.3. Model that shows the dialectic relationship among materiality, materialisation, and materialism, where arrows suggest how social praxis relates to the three theoretical concepts.

We propose that materiality cannot be understood or explained as an isolated theoretical concept. It needs to enter into a dialectical relationship with related concepts that add social meaning, political power, and economic direction. Other theoretical perspectives would, of course, relate it to more concepts, whether in psychology, cognition, or sociology; however, we consider the relationships among materiality, materialisation, and materialism to be fundamental to archaeology.

Having stated our basic framework, we proceed to the problem of bridging a modern theoretical understanding with a contextualised understanding of the otherness of the past. In our understanding, it demands more that a hermeneutic mediation between the two. In addition to relevant comparative readings in history and anthropology, it demands a conceptualisation of the interpretative route taken.

During the Bronze Age, social identity was constructed through material objects that were used in social action and ritual performance among the living and the dead. The warrior and his sword illustrate the dialectic between objects and individual in the formation of personhood, institutions, and interaction. What is a sword without a warrior, and what is a warrior without a sword? They constitute each other in ways more intricate and personal than can be deduced by pure social and technological logic. Their biographies constitute each other, read in the scars and disfigurations of the warrior and from the wear and repairs of the sword. Archaeology can retell the biographies of multiple generations of anonymous warriors by studying the use wear, damages, and repairs on the thousands of well-preserved Bronze Age swords and, when skeletal preservation allows, also the bodily damage to the warriors themselves (Kristiansen 1984a, 2002; Molloy 2007; Sofaer 2006).

Bronze Age weapons, especially the sword, represent the emergence of a system of martial arts that defined the warrior as an institution. It included rules of etiquette and behaviour, from training programmes and the conduct of combat to the rituals of the dead warrior and his weapons. One could bury a sword in Bronze Age Europe in two ways: it could be given as a gift to the gods, as a ritual hoard, or it could accompany the dead into the afterlife. These represent two situations of social and ritual action within the cycle of raids and combat: death of the warrior or chief versus defeat or victory in combat. In both cases, tales of heroic deeds would accompany the deceased, but the sword could always be retrieved; it remained a physical reality to be reckoned with. This duality of deposition characterises the whole Bronze Age; sometimes, hoarding takes precedence and other times, deposition is in burials. It testifies to a landscape of ritualised memory, in which natural sanctuaries for hoarding were just as important as visible burial monuments. These two practices were part of a strategy to 'keep while giving,' to use the terminology of Weiner (1992). The deposited prestige goods (giving) would remain in the landscape (keeping) and retain their power, and thus empower its chiefly lineage. This is the Bronze Age way of giving while keeping, and ultimately the objects and their power could be retrieved, whether by an enemy to destroy them or, in bad times, when needed to defend the lineage.

Depositions were part of an ongoing dialogue, an exchange of powers between gods and mortals, living and dead (ancestors). Gods and ancestors were active agents in the landscape and in the lives of their lineages. In the tell societies in Hungary, genealogies were, in a similar way, linked to the ongoing accumulation of households throughout centuries, turning the tell settlement into a monument of social genealogies and memory. Likewise, the barrows and cemeteries were linked by heroic tales of ancestors, of the social genealogies in the barrows and ritual sanctuaries, just as ritual performance by chiefly priests disguised as gods upheld time and cosmos. However, ritual ceremonials were upheld not only by the gods but also by the domestic economy. Tell settlements and chiefly farmsteads depended on producers who supplied their chiefly house and supported their warriors. In addition, although they may 'produce' honour and, importantly, cattle by their raids, warriors also reinforced the flow of metal by travelling and trading, sometimes taking service with foreign chiefs. Bronze Age economies were thus based upon three intertwined institutions: the ritual, the political, and the domestic economies, and they were kept in motion by the flow of tribute and labour, cattle, and warriors (Figure 1.4). An economy based on trade in staples rather than metal and prestige goods alone would emerge with the Iron Age, although there were early beginnings among the tell societies in Hungary, as we shall see.

TRANSFORMATIONS IN EUROPEAN PREHISTORY

We consider now the major social and economic transformations in the ritual, the political, and the domestic economies from 3000 to

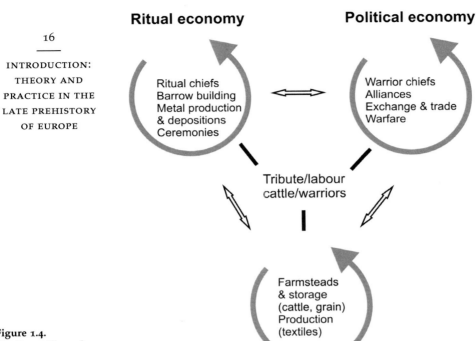

Figure 1.4.
The three pillars of Bronze Age economies: the ritual, the political, and the domestic economy.

500 BC to help situate historically our three case studies within the macroregional prehistory of western Eurasia.

The origins of the family, gender divisions, and mobile property

We propose that the monogamous family, gender divisions, and related property divisions originated in the social transformations of western Eurasia from the late fourth millennium BC into the third millennium BC and became the foundation for later developments. This cultural transformation, named Corded Ware and Battle Axe cultures in central and western Europe and Yamna cultures in the Pontic steppe, altered concepts of family, property, and inheritance, and facilitated the formation of a mobile, agro-pastoral society from the steppe region across Europe (Koryakova and Epimakhov 2007; Kohl 2007; Vandkilde 2006; Harrisson and Heyd 2007). It focused on the monogamous extended family as a central social and economic unit, probably based on patrilineal Omaha kinship (Kristiansen and Larsson 2005:chapter 5.5), favouring the accumulation of mobile wealth through networked expansion and exogamous alliances, and transmission of that wealth across generations. The individualised *tumulus* burials, furnished with these same symbols of wealth, ritually instituted these new principles, now also transferred to the land of death. They correspond to a specific religious cosmology that developed into a complex religious system by the second millennium BC and then was described in written sources (Kristiansen and Larsson 2005:chapter 6).

Figure 1.5 presents a model of this social organisation and its basic components, comprising the family barrow or tumulus that was the ritual extension of the new kinship system, in which the transmission of mobile property (animals) was crucial. The barrow ritually defined the free man, his family, and his property, and it defined the male warrior as chieftain (Vandkilde 2006). Male and female gender were strictly demarcated in burial ritual through the orientation of the body, laying on left or right side, and this structure was unchanging throughout Eurasia. No doubt gender became essential, balancing relations between the sexes in burial. Mobile herding societies often exhibit a gendered division of labour with males as tribal fighters, and this we see reproduced in burial rituals throughout the third and second millennia in Eurasia. Although cereal farming was

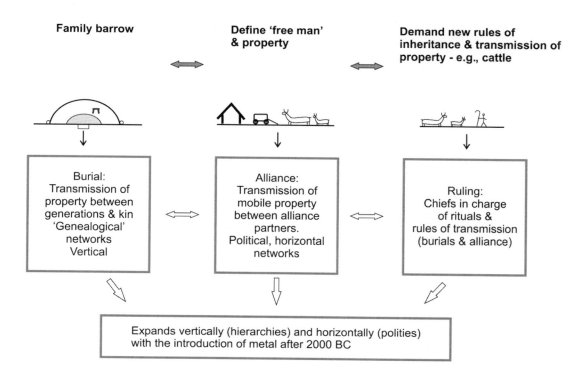

Figure 1.5. Model of basic material and institutional components of Eurasian societies of the third millennium BC.

certainly part of the economy, herding was dominant, especially in central and northern Europe. In an agro-pastoral society, property in animals and their products determine rights and pathways of transmission and inheritance. With the political significance for new mobile wealth, emerging chiefs could assert and maintain these rules to benefit leadership. Their new position became materialised in the ubiquitous, carefully executed war axe in precious stone, copper, silver, or gold. We begin to see the contours of a more complex division of social roles and institutions (Müller 2002). Specialists, such as the metalsmith, can be identified in burials, and ritualised, priestly functions are also indicated in grave goods. A complex society of warriors, priests, specialists, and herder/farmers is emerging, albeit in embryonic form.

Expansion of the agro-pastoral economy was rapid and sometimes dramatic. During the Early and Middle Neolithic, large forest reserves remained in Europe, although mainly on lighter soils. During the third millennium BC, however, these areas were colonised by expanding pastoral herders and warriors (the secondary products revolution, in Andrew Sherratt's terminology), who rapidly cleared the forests for grazing lands (Kremenetski 2003; Kristiansen 2006b; Shishlina 2001). They practiced some cultivation of cereals, but much of the economy rested on wool, milk, hides, draft animals, and meat produced for trade (Sherratt 1997).

From the late third millennium, a maritime/riverine counterpart complemented the land-based society of the Corded Ware, Single Grave, and Battle Axe cultures. The Bell Beaker cultures expanded along the western Mediterranean and the Atlantic façade before moving inland along major rivers as far east as Hungary. According to recent strontium isotope analyses of teeth and bone (Price et al 2004; Heyd 2007), the Bell Beaker expansion was carried by migrating people, evidently with the metallurgical knowledge of skilled smiths, in addition to the boat skills of traders. The beginning of the second millennium saw the integration between these two social and cultural traditions, supplemented by a new bronze technology able to mine and distribute large quantities of metal throughout Europe (Harrison and Heyd 2007).

To summarise, during the third millennium BC, a new social, economic order emerged in Eurasia. Widespread travel, seasonal transhumance, and some migrations accompanied these changes. By the mid third millennium BC, common ritual and social institutions existed from the Urals to northern Europe (Kristiansen 2006b; Prescott and Walderhaug 1995) and laid the foundation for later developments in social and economic complexity during the first half of the second millennium BC (Kohl 2008). After 2000 BC, this social formation developed, linked to a new metal technology and the emerging, integrated system of trade that linked Europe's dispersed political economies.

METAL PRODUCTION, LONG-DISTANCE TRADE, AND WARRIOR ARISTOCRACIES

Across Europe and into Asia, the Bronze Age initiated systematic and wide political connections and travels and trade between emerging urbanized centres with constant demands for raw materials and their peripheries with demands for precious goods and knowledge from the centres. A new and dynamic process was under way, which, after 2000 BC, was to transform Europe. Following an economic setback in the Near East in the late third millennium BC, a new expansion and search for tin, gold, and copper began. For the first time, explorations turned westward and contacts were established with central Europe and the western Mediterranean, leading to the tin mines of Cornwall in southern England and the Erzgebirge in Germany. A metallurgical explosion took place in Europe; within a few generations, large-scale mining and mass production of tin bronze reached high levels. From new centres of production, bronze ingots in the hundred thousands were distributed throughout Europe, creating networks of interdependency and desires for metallurgical skills. Amber and tin ended up in the east Mediterranean. Similar amber necklaces found in the distant rich graves of Wessex and Mycenae testify to newly established connections (Kristiansen 1998:figures 192 and 196). Recent works (Bertemes 2000; also Strahm 2002; Vandkilde 2007) summarise changing economies, technologies, and social organisation that characterise Europe after 2000 BC:

Society: the introduction of new status and prestige goods (daggers/swords, lances, ornaments, metal cups, etc.) and the first appearance of 'princely graves' symbolised the emergence of a new institution of chiefly leadership and a division between elite and commoners.

Religion: new burial rituals included single graves and family groups in large cemeteries, aristocratic burials in barrows, new ritual depositions, and new symbols and iconography. New gods such as the 'Divine Twins' symbolised horses and chariot and their role in warfare as well as in carrying the sun.

Settlements: divisions emerged among open villages in the lowlands, fortified hilltop settlements, and ritual sites. In temperate northern Europe, large farm halls of the chiefly lineages were built, evenly spaced across the landscape.

Economy: division of labour and specialisation, commoditisation of metal, weights and measures, intensification of mining, and expansion of long-distance trade in finished and unfinished products all emerged.

Technology: tin bronze, specialised workshops, complex casting techniques, and specific alloys for specific artefacts became evident. New skills in boat building and in the construction of chariots and wagons advanced communication, trade, and raiding at sea and over land.

The emergence of a more complex, stratified society penetrated all social spheres. A new aristocratic leadership emerged on top of the traditional clan-based organisation of farmsteads and hamlets. It was sustained by a new political organisation based upon elite warriors commanded by chieftains. With the introduction of the chariot, the composite bow, the long sword, and the lance, warfare took on a new social, economic, and ideological significance from the beginning of the second millennium BC. This was reflected, for instance, in burial rituals in which chiefly barrows became a dominant feature of the cultural landscape. Master artisans came to build chariots, breed and train horses, and produce and train warriors in the use of new weapons. The packages of skills were so complicated that it must have demanded, at first, the transfer of artisans, horses, and warriors. The warrior aristocracies and their attached specialists transformed Bronze Age societies throughout Eurasia and the Near East.

In terms of settlements and domestic economies, two competing systems appeared: one based upon unfortified individual farmsteads and hamlets spread evenly in the settled landscape, and the other, upon an agglomeration of people in larger, mostly fortified settlements, whether villages or larger semi-urban settlements. The expansion of nucleated, fortified tells characterised the Hungarian-Carpathian region; with this expansion came large cemeteries and the introduction of cremation as the dominant burial treatment, linked to new perceptions of body and individual. The cemetery is the ritual equivalent of the village and the tell settlement (Sørensen and

Rebay 2008). We propose that these different settlement forms and burial rituals represent distinct social formations that cycled throughout the Bronze Age (Figure 1.6); however, the two forms coexisted during long periods as diverging trajectories between northern and central/southern Europe into the Iron Age.

During the Bronze Age, stable and stratified societies developed that, in northern Europe, constructed a landscape of barrows and large and smaller farmsteads regularly spaced in an organised landscape of fields and pastures, intersected with tracks that connected all settlements. In eastern central Europe, this settlement system gave way to an organised system of large fortified tell settlements surrounded by open settlements and connected by rivers and inland tracks. On Sicily, fortified settlements developed mainly in areas in contact with Mycenaean traders, whereas traditional settlements were simply hamlets.

To summarise, we trace three world historical changes in later European prehistory. First is the expansion of a new social and economic form of agro-pastoralism after 3000 BC, creating the open landscapes of Europe and introducing a new kinship system and new perceptions of mobile property. Second is the systematic introduction of bronze technology around 2000 BC and the concomitant development of a trading-based political economy and increasing

Figure 1.6.
Model of changing social formation during the second and first millennia BC in central Europe (from Kristiansen 1998:figure 224).

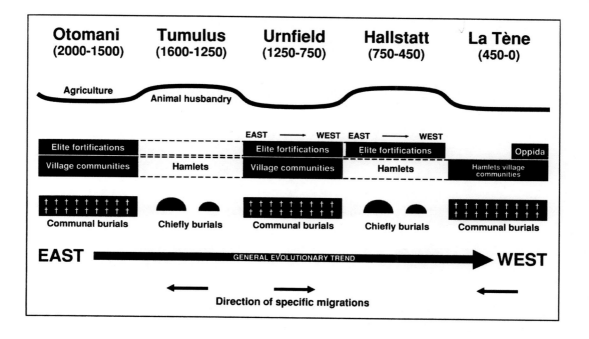

social stratification that integrated Europe. Third is the development of the trade-based imperial systems of the Phoenician and Greeks, whose colonisation of the west Mediterranean dramatically impacted trade, urbanization, and social complexity into central Europe.

THREE EUROPEAN REGIONS DESCRIBED

The three projects are to be understood within a regional framework – in the present linked to specific research traditions, in the past linked to their role in regional developments during the Bronze Age (Figure 1.7). Chronologically, the regions employ different systems. In Scandinavia, the period from 2300 to 1750 BC is called the Late Neolithic or Dagger Period, although copper and bronze axes became numerous after 2000 BC. Early Bronze Age starts 1750 and lasts until 1150 BC. The Late Bronze Age continues until 500 BC. In Hungary, the period 2300 to 1750 BC is called Early Bronze Age, followed by the Middle Bronze Age that lasts until 1300 BC, when the Late Bronze Age begins and lasts until 750 BC, when the Iron Age starts. In Sicily, the scheme is similar to that in Hungary. In our project, we attempted to cover the whole period from 2300 BC until 500 BC in our surveys, although the excavations covered different slices of this long period. The change in Sicily from Bronze Age roundhouses to the proto-urban Iron Age settlement at Monte Polizzo took place sometime after 1000 to 800 BC.

South Scandinavia

Southern Scandinavia is a world of low, rolling hills and water, where the coast is never far away. Whereas south Scandinavia is made up of hilly fertile moraine, western Jutland and northwestern Germany formed a more flat and less fertile plain outside the last glaciations. The Baltic Sea, in conjunction with the many straits and fjords, made maritime connections of prime importance. To the west, connections were among Norway, Jutland, and northwestern Europe, with the river Elbe as an entry to central northern Europe. To the east, the Baltic Sea connected south Scandinavia with the Baltic coastal plains and central Europe via the river Oder and, farther to the east, Vistula.

The Nordic region entered metal exchange networks with central and southern Europe during the early second millennium and flows intensified after 1750 BC. By 1500 BC, an original Nordic culture emerged, linked to a new more hierarchical organisation of society and landscape. It persisted for 1000 years, producing outstanding examples of metalwork and dramatic rock-art. The transformation of society and landscape has been documented and analysed in metalwork (Vandkilde 1996), and it became the topic for the Thy Archaeological Project that was the model for this project (Earle et al 1998). The settlement structure was based upon single farms, raising comparative questions as to the causes of the more nucleated settlements to the south versus these dispersed settlements (Chapters 3 and 4). Marking south Scandinavia, and especially Denmark and Scania, are the tens of thousands of Bronze Age barrows constructed during a rather short time period between 1500 and 1150 BC (Figure 1.8). They still dominate the landscape in many areas, especially in Thy.

Figure 1.7.
Europe, showing the locations of the project.

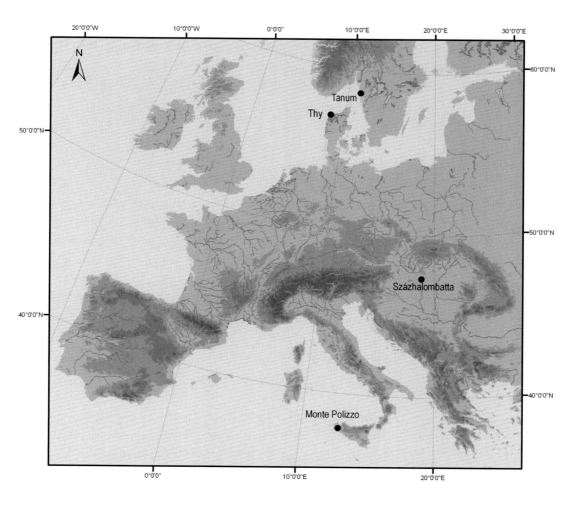

The landscape of Bohuslän is a rocky coast of small islands, dramatic headlands, and embayment and interior farmlands and forest. Because of land upheaval since the end of the last glaciations, the Bronze Age coastal landscape was much more of an archipelago than the present. In this landscape of sea, rocky islands, and more fertile inlets, cairns were constructed on top of the rocky islands and at the high points of the coast line (Figure 1.8), whereas settlements were concentrated more inland, where there was some fertile land for farming.

The Tanum project aimed at identifying and excavating the Bronze and Early Iron Age sites of the World Heritage Site in Tanum to reconstruct the environment of the rock carvings. The project has, during the first three seasons, identified many sites and test-excavated three or four settlements and ritual spaces in front of rock carvings, and produced a pollen diagram demonstrating intensive land use from the Bronze Age onwards. The settlement patterns reveal a continuum of activities in the landscape, from ritual activities in front of rock-art sites to seasonal sites. At present, settlement evidence is rare, but large burial stone cairns at the coast and barrows to the interior suggest a social pattern closely linked to the broader Scandinavian society.

Hungary

The landscape of Hungary is dominated by large river systems, especially the Danube, the extensive central plain, the Carpathian Mountains, and the rolling loess hills of Transdanubia. The Danube divides Hungary from north to south. To the west and south is fertile moraine; to the east, the large Eurasian steppe plains reached their western border and connected Hungary, the river Tisza, and the Carpathian plains with western Eurasia. The Danube linked the Black Sea with central Europe, and, before it turns west into central Europe, the long north–south passage through Hungary became a bottleneck for the movement of goods and people to be controlled by a system of fortified tells during the Bronze Age (Gogaltan 2005).

In central Europe, the Danube was the main east–west communication channel, in some periods serving much the same transport role as the Mediterranean. With the rich ore depositions in the Carpathians, Bronze Age communities in Hungary developed rapidly from

THREE EUROPEAN
REGIONS DESCRIBED

Figure 1.8.
a. Bronze Age cairn from eastern Sweden, typically situated at higher elevations with a view over the sea, and visible as a landmark from the sea as well; b. Bronze Age barrows in Denmark, typically situated on higher altitudes (photo from Eve Melheim and Kristian Kristiansen).

the earlier second millennium BC onwards. From the Early to the Middle Bronze Age, a complex settlement system grew here, centered around fortified tell settlements with specialised functions in production and trade, ranging from the Black Sea to Slovakia. Despite similarities in settlement structure and metalwork, distinct local and regional cultures developed. We wish to trace this development from small-scale village societies to a more hierarchical society transmitting influences between the Black Sea and Scandinavia (*Bronzezeit in Ungarn* 1992).

Although several tell sites had been partially excavated, excavations have not expanded laterally to describe settlement structure, nor have they been integrated into a surveying program of regional contemporary settlements. Our aim was to describe the tell settlement and establish its relation to the local social and economic environment.

The Százhalombatta site is a tell site built on a westerly bluff of the Danube, south of Budapest (Plate 1.1). It contained well-preserved occupation layers (3–5 m thick) across 800 years, from ca. 2300 to 1500 or 1400 BC. Later settlements during the Late Bronze Age Urnfield period and Early Iron Age did not produce similar thick accumulating layers, probably because of a different tradition of house construction. It is a fortified semi-urban settlement with central functions, and an internal division between a supposed acropolis and the village. Enlarged during the Early Iron Age, a large fortified settlement covered the whole site and was protected by a major fortification. To this Early Iron Age component belonged a large, tumulus cemetery, with several well-excavated burials. Environmental archaeology has been produced (pollen diagram) pointing to heavy exploitation and opening of the landscape in the Bronze Age (Chapter 2). The survey in the Benta valley further provided evidence of a dense settlement system of sites, and a fixed distance between tells (Chapters 3 and 4). The tell site itself has been partly destroyed by removal of clay to the nearby, now-closed brick factory.

Sicily

In the central Mediterranean, Sicily bridged between Mycenaean/Greek culture and settlements, Italian–central European influences, and local cultures during the Bronze and Early Iron Age (Leighton 1999). We wished to explore the specific dynamic between foreign and indigenous settlements and cultural traditions. Whereas in central and northern Europe, foreign influences were transmitted through long-distance relationships, on Sicily, from the later second millennium onwards, local populations and eastern colonists developed a close symbiosis. This contrast allows historical comparisons between different types of interaction and their implications for boundary formation and social development in Europe.

Our main site, Monte Polizzo, is situated on a mountain ridge 730 m above sea level in western Sicily (Plate 1.2). It provided a view of

(a)

(b)

Plate 1.1. a, b. The tell site seen from the south with the steep sides due to recent clay-taking for a brick factory (photo from Claes Uhner).

the whole coastal plain from Palermo bay to the north; the western shores, with the Phoenician settlement of Mozzia; to the south coast, with the Greek settlement of Selinunte. The fertile rolling landscape of western Sicily provided an ideal place for agriculture, which soon became contested with the arrival of, first, Phoenician and, later, Greek settlers on the coastal plains. On western Sicily, Bronze Age indigenous settlements of roundhouse tradition and the Iron Age semi-urban settlements of rectangular houses were situated on easily defended plateaus, while the fertile lowlands were cultivated with an extensive economy, which gradually intensified during the Iron Age.

In Sicilian archaeology, as in Hungary, we have good, partially excavated settlements but rather few inland sites of indigenous type, just as the local settlement system is missing (Leighton 2005). Therefore, a goal was to establish the relation between the local formation of nucleated, semi-urban settlements and their environment and trade connections during a period of transformation and colonisation. The settlement of Mokarta, which dates from the Late Bronze Age, came to represent the conclusion of a long Bronze Age tradition of roundhouse settlements, which came to an apparently abrupt end with the beginning of semi-urbanised settlements, represented by Monte Polizzo (Tusa 2000).

Monte Polizzo, the focus of our excavations, was an urban, fortified settlement that has remained untouched since antiquity. It dates from 700 to 500 BC and has unusually good preservation, in contrast to most other Elymian settlements. A network of roads (surveyed during the first two seasons) covered the site, linking the entrances of the settlement with the water supply and the different parts of the acropolis. Mokarta, a neighbouring site previously excavated, covers the later second millennium, and the project carried out supplementary archaeological and scientific work there as well (Tusa 1998). Archaeological work was also carried out in Salemi, where the project had its headquarters, whenever new construction gave opportunities to excavate.

Monte Polizzo was located with a clear eye to defence, overlooking the landscape of western Sicily. The development from Late Bronze Age Mokarta to Monte Polizzo demonstrates the major change that accompanied the beginning of the Iron Age and the colonisation of Sicily by Phoenicians and Greeks. Colonisation had a major impact upon indigenous populations and their settlement organisation (Streiffert 2006; Mühlenbock 2008).

OUR RESEARCH DESIGN

A multiscalar research design and methods

To achieve a sound empirical foundation for the historical and theoretical questions of the project, we concentrated our studies in intensively analysed microregions that allowed us to produce archaeological and environmental data of high quality – that is, of high resolution and detail. The research design had to be similar across all three regions to allow comparisons, and it had to use the most modern archaeological and scientific methods. Our objective for the coordinated microregional studies has been to develop a flexible approach that collects spatial, artefactual, and environmental data at three nested scales – the region, the settlement, and the household. This objective required the introduction of new approaches to each area studied at the same time it required the adoption of archaeological traditions specific to the regions. To give an example, in

Plate 1.2.
The landscape of Monte Polizzo (photo from Christian Mühlenbock).

Hungary there still exists a tradition of hand drawing and colouration of archaeological features, which was carried out parallel to the digital recording of the features using total station.

THE REGIONS

The regional scale of archaeology required a reconstruction of the prehistoric environments and their resource conditions and a description of the distribution of prehistoric settlements across those landscapes. Based on a tradition of Scandinavian research, our work combined paleo and environmental work (Chapter 2). Methods included standard procedures for paleo-pollen recovery in low, wet locations and for micromorphological sampling from prehistoric soil horizons in archaeological contexts. These procedures allow modelling regional plant communities and soil regimes. Thin-section micromorphology, now an acknowledged descriptive and interpretative tool in archaeological investigation, proved to be an excellent tool to describe prehistoric landscapes. The analyses of buried soils aided in environmental sequencing of a landscape as well as identifying major and minor transformations influenced by combined natural forces and human activities. We were able to reconstruct the main productive resources available to human settlements across time and identify how economic uses of the landscapes transformed and often destabilised them.

Systematic field walking across each microregion provided the basic information on settlement distribution, size, density, and date. It followed a standard procedure of line walking fields with 10 m intervals, counting the finds. Prospective settlements were then walked intensively and all finds collected. In each region, the specific nature of the land surface and settlement visibility required the adjustment of field methods (Chapter 3). In Sicily, relatively high densities of prehistoric ceramic remains allowed for normal procedures for total coverage, as developed in regional archaeological surveys (Sanders, Parsons, and Santley 1979). These procedures had also been used successfully in the 1970s to inventory settlements in Hungary, where we also conducted systematic shovel testing across surfaces of varying visibility from forests to grasslands and fields with standing crops. In Scandinavia, systematic line walking and shovel testing proved essential to get systematic descriptions of artefact densities needed to define settlements; the low densities of litchis and a virtual absence of pre-Iron Age ceramics on the surface make settlements hard to recognize and define. Here settlements could often be confirmed only with patterned machine clearing.

SETTLEMENTS

Once a prehistoric settlement is recognized, the first objective is to map the distribution of houses and other activities across its surface (Chapter 4). If settlements have been ploughed, the standard procedure in Scandinavia has been to remove the plough soil rapidly, by machine, to reveal the pattern of features preserved in the subsoil. With the famous work of Carl Johan Becker starting in the 1960s, these methods allowed the description of both house forms and settlement structure in detail. The assumption has been that, because the plough soil was disturbed, it can be removed to allow such broad-scale excavations. Although the results of such research were visually dramatic, we realised that because the prehistoric land surface had been ploughed, most artefacts indicative of settlement activities were included in the plough soil and their removal by machine destroyed our ability to look at potential patterns in settlement structure. Our goal was thus to develop methods to recover and describe artefactual patterns across a settlement surface by systematically sampling the plough soil by machine or small-scale test excavations (Chapter 3). This so-called Phase II research is meant as a rapid assessment of artefact remains that retain substantial spatial pattern despite ploughing. Machine clearing has become a standard for rescue excavation, often based on the rapid and low cost of results, but we emphasise that, along with surface mapping of preserved features and subsurface mapping with various remote-sensing devices, plough soil work can be conducted rapidly and provides an excellent alternative for mapping settlement structure.

INTENSIVE EXCAVATIONS OF HOUSEHOLDS

As described in Chapter 5, our objective has been to recognize and excavate preserved house structures to provide detailed information on household archaeology. Houses are treated as social contexts for everyday activities, and the analyses of their artefactual remains provide a detailed means to look at the household's subsistence economy, craft production, and spatial variation in gender and status activities, both within and between households. To accomplish these goals, we needed broad-scale excavations, covering the activity areas within and outside of houses. Our procedures included recovery of artefacts with detailed contextual information regarding their association with features and other artefacts. We excavate with great care, recording locations of finds according to a meter grid system and find spots. All soils were routinely screened and sampled by flotation to recover a light fraction of macro-botanicals and a heavy fraction of micro-artefact and zoo-archaeological remains. In addition, routine sampling for micromorphological analyses allows recognition of construction techniques, floor surfaces, and surface use, as well as the postdepositional processes. Although such procedures are time consuming and cannot be applied universally, they proved highly productive, as they allowed a hitherto unseen botanical and osteological resolution of analysis, when compared to traditional excavation methods without screening (Chapter 4).

Documentation became central to our excavations, allowing horizontal reconstruction of activity areas and features associated with particular household activities. Our documentation system was based upon the total station, using The Swedish National Heritage Board (UV) newly developed database integrated with GIS, named Intrasis. All documentation, from feature drawings to sites, was recorded in digital format, allowing ongoing computer analysis, presentations, and comparisons.

The macro-botany and zoo-archaeological remains were recovered and analysed in accordance with the research design of the project. To give an example, it is important to distinguish between patterns of production and consumption in both cereals and animal bones, as it may reveal division of labour, social differences in consumption, and other aspects of the household and settlement economies. We have, therefore, given special attention to the formulation of research in osteology and in macrofossil analysis, in which we expect to be able to trace long-term changes as well as internal changes linked to the division of labour and contrasting patterns of production and consumption in households and settlements.

Preliminary results using our systematic methodology suggest contrasting patterns of everyday life, sociability, and political formation among the three regions of study. In Sicily, Monte Polizzo was a truly compact urban settlement with few settlements around, competing and interacting with Greek and Phoenician coastal settlements. In the Benta valley of Hungary, a proto-urban tell settlement was situated on the Danube within a dispersed regional settlement system of dual hierarchies of fortified and open settlements. Thy and

Tanum, in contrast, consisted of unfortified farmsteads spread across the landscape. The aforementioned represent some of the original formulations of the research objectives and the corresponding research design we developed. As should become apparent from the substantial chapters to follow, many doctoral projects and senior participants from different countries energized discussions, debate, and new syntheses that emerged from regular seminars and annual meetings. The creative energy of the project's many participants should be apparent in this book's substantive chapters that seek to open up discussion of archaeological methods and the resulting statements regarding European late prehistory.

2

The Palaeo-Environments of Bronze Age Europe

Charles French

With contributions by Chad Heinzel, Pal Sumegi, and Johan Ling, Gianna Ayala, Sandor Guylas, Michael J. Kolb, Gabriella Kovács, and Chris Severa

During the third millennium BC, a rapid and intentional destruction of forests took place over wide regions of Europe to allow a new agricultural economy, often dominated by animal husbandry. By the second millennium BC, these open landscapes were evidently managed to maintain productivity. Much investment was made in infrastructure, from farm buildings and field systems to trackways. In opposition to a landscape enclosed by forests, these new open landscapes provided new avenues of visibility and interconnectivity, and with innovative uses of chariots, wagons, and ships, easier and faster communications opened up. Monumental barrows and large settlements had a dramatic visual impact that could easily have defined property rights and a more visible settlement hierarchy as people moved across the landscape.

However, a more permanently open landscape also introduced concerns of maintaining productivity. Soil, especially the light soils, became more prone to erosive forces as well as nutrient depletion, especially when no longer sustained by forest regeneration. Instead, fertility had to be maintained by other cultural practices, including fallow, application of manure, and forest management. Despite such care, ecological crises sometimes would strike, as happened in the heavily settled and exposed landscape of Thy on the North Sea coast of Jutland. The dominant herding economy and the demands for timber for large farm buildings led to a near-extinction of proper forests, peat was used for heating, and driftwood was sometimes used in house construction. In contrast in both central Hungary and western Sicily, agricultural intensification led to soil erosion, certainly from later Bronze Age times and increasing in intensity and scale over time. Thus the extensive agricultural environments of the Bronze Age introduced the potential for overexploitation of the land and different human responses to this, as exemplified in our case studies.

Each project in Scandinavia, Hungary, and Sicily had several subprojects investigating subregional environmental sequences and the development of the Holocene landscape as well as the forms of cultural impact on these different landscapes. Significant issues and processes have been addressed in each subregion, particularly the nature of earlier Holocene woodland development and the associated processes of soil formation, trajectories of woodland clearance, and the impact of human settlement and agricultural activities on the vegetation and soil complex. The main chronological focus is the second and first millennia BC.

These investigations help situate Bronze Age settlement with respect to contemporary land use and associated economic development in microregions. The combination of new subregional palynological investigations and the study of soil development sequences is a powerful research methodology to investigate past landscapes (French 2003:59). This project afforded the chance to use such methods in close association with archaeological survey and excavations. Indeed, this approach is fundamental to make inferences about the scale and variation of landscape change through time.

Extensive palynological and soil studies for the Thy region of North Jutland, Denmark, and to a lesser extent for the Tanum area of Sweden, provide a clear picture of vegetation change in the later Neolithic and Bronze Ages. New geoarchaeological survey and soil analyses were undertaken in the lower Benta valley of central Hungary just south of Budapest to set in context the Százhalombatta tell site and the smaller Bronze Age sites from its hinterland. These studies enable the forming of a relatively complete picture of palaeo-environmental changes in each microregion. For the Sicilian study area, new and associated geoarchaeological studies in western and central Sicily, as well as existing palynological studies from Lake Pergusa, tell a good part of the Holocene landscape story for the Monte Polizzo area.

The second and first millennia BC of each microregion exhibit strong landscape change, but particularly occurring in the later Bronze and Iron Ages, although with variation over time. Overarching palaeo-environmental themes evident in each microregion include extensive pre-Bronze Age deforestation and the predominance of grassland over arable land until the end of the Bronze Age and into the mid to late first millennium BC, when arable cultivation gradually became more extensive. Similarly, from the later Bronze Age onward, increasing signs of disruption in those landscapes include peat growth, river channel avulsion, and soil erosion and soil aggradation in valley systems.

SCANDINAVIA

The Thy region, northwest Denmark

Extensive palynological investigations have indicated that a once well-forested landscape with small clearings had been transformed to an extensively open and grassland landscape by the end of the second millennium BC. Nonetheless, there is much evidence for the management of the surviving woodland, but this diminishing resource must have had a real impact on human settlement activities and, indeed, the first millennium BC sees more disturbance indicators associated with fire and arable cultivation.

Today, large areas of west and north Thy are covered by windblown sands, but these dune systems were not created until much later – from the early thirteenth century AD (Hansen 1957) – although some sand drifting had probably begun as early as the Middle Neolithic (Liversage 1987). In contrast, central and eastern Thy are mainly covered by sandy and clayey tills. This area of northwestern Jutland has abundant palaeo-vegetation data, mainly thanks to the extensive palynological work of Andersen (1989, 1990, 1992, 1992–93, 1994–95, 1996–97; Andersen and Rasmussen 1996). These analyses have provided both site-specific (from buried soils beneath Neolithic and Bronze Age barrows) and more subregional pollen data from lakes, bogs, and small wetland hollows.

The story of the postglacial vegetation record begins about 9000 BC with an earlier Holocene tree succession similar to other pollen sequences from Denmark and represents dense, stable forest (Andersen 1992–93, 1989) (Figure 2.1). A birch–pine forest gave way to hazel woodland by about 6600 BC, then developed into a lime–elm–oak–hazel–alder forest between about 6600 and 3400 BC. About 3400 to 2900 BC, the first signs of human intervention really become evident in this forested landscape. This consisted of minima of lime and

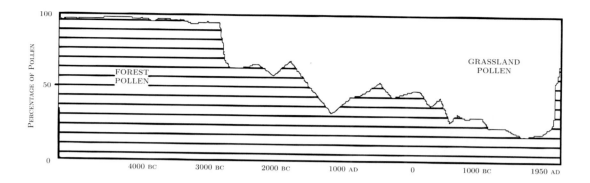

maxima of more light-demanding tree species, such as hazel and alder, with the occurrence of wild grasses, open-ground herbs, and bracken, accompanied by abundant charcoal dust. These changes resulted from slash and burn or landnam phases of human activity in the forest in the middle to later Neolithic. Arable fields were present at this time. Then, in the early third millennium BC, there was extensive forest clearance, perhaps the most massive in northern Europe, which essentially created an open grassland landscape across Thy.

Turning to the more specific and detailed record from the Hassing Huse Mose profile in the Thy region (Figure 2.2), human interference with the once fully forested landscape becomes very evident from about 2640 BC (Andersen 1992–93). Although both elm and

Figure 2.1.
Summary pollen diagram from Thy, Denmark (after Andersen in J. M. Steinberg 1997).

Figure 2.2.
Detailed pollen diagram from Hassing Huse Mose, Denmark (after Andersen in J. M. Steinberg 1997).

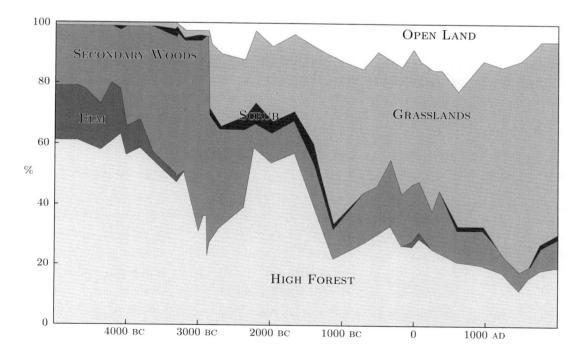

lime already were much reduced in the previous Neolithic period, tree pollen suddenly decreased from 91 percent to 69 percent over about 30 years and the percentages of trees stayed low (69–59 percent) throughout the Late Neolithic–Early Bronze Age period from 2640 to 1650 BC. Also, the tree pollen curves change markedly, with local populations of hazel, birch, and alder being cut away, although some coppice stands may have remained. Wild grasses and herbs of open ground (e.g., mugwort, sheep sorrel, goosefoot family, and ribwort plantain) increase dramatically, and cereal pollen (barley-type) became more common. Thus there would appear to be substantial cleared areas in an increasingly opened-up woodland, with both pasture for grazing land and bare ground for arable cultivation available. Indeed, ard marks from ploughing have been observed in the buried soils beneath Bronze Age barrows such as those at Bjergene 1 and 2, Visby, and Damsgard (Andersen 1996–97).

Deforestation continued in a stepwise manner in the Early Bronze Age, and again at about AD 500 and AD 1000 (Andersen 1992–93). Between about 1650 and 1200 BC in the Early Bronze Age, tree pollen halved, from 69 percent to 33 percent. With comparison to the present landscape with stands of trees and no forests, but with trees accounting for approximately 15 percent in the pollen diagram, it suggests a landscape without substantial forests towards the end of the Early Bronze Age. Although coppice is still present (represented by oak fern and bracken), as are birch, pine, ash, and oak, wild grasses have increased strongly, from 26 percent to 54 percent, and herb plants of open ground have increased somewhat. This would appear to represent increased grazing pressure as well as some cultivation. Kristiansen (1998) suggested that the Bronze Age settlement pattern was composed of barrows with surrounding pasturelands on higher ground, with settlements and fields nearby, but on the lower slopes and often near water.

From the Late Bronze Age (1100 BC) to the Roman Iron Age (AD 485) trees again decrease slightly, although birch, ash, and oak remained important in the landscape (Andersen 1992–93). Herbs of open ground became much more frequent, and beginning in about 500 BC, sheep sorrel increased, indicative of open and disturbed ground, as well as barley-type cereal and the introduction of oats. Much charcoal dust implies further vegetation clearance by fire. Finally, as in some other areas of Denmark, heath vegetation was scarce and patchy until after 200 BC. Elsewhere in Thy at Bjerre, blown sand began to blanket the Late Bronze Age field systems (Earle et al 1998).

This subregional pollen record for Thy is augmented by pollen records from buried soils beneath a number of Early Bronze Age barrows in the same area that reveal a similar picture of human impact on the vegetation record but with greater clarity (Andersen 1996–97). By the time many of the barrows were built, trees remained a scarce resource in the landscape, with relics of coppiced wood in the vicinity, and evidence for both pasture with variable intensities of grazing and some limited arable land. Trees became more or less absent from this more mosaic landscape by the later Bronze Age (say 1000 BC), and grazing pressure increased.

A relatively similar picture pertains for the Neolithic and Bronze Age periods in other areas of Denmark. This pattern of dramatic opening up of the woodland in the early third millennium BC was also repeated in western Jutland. In southern Scandinavia, however, deforestation and the creation of extensive grassland took place later, in the mid to later third millennium BC, and in eastern Scandinavia from the Late Bronze Age (Bergund et al 1991; Kristiansen 1998; Rasmussen 1996). For example, in the Vroue area to the south of Thy in western Jutland (Andersen 1994–95; Odgaard 1994), the clearance of lime-dominated woodland in the Neolithic was associated with evidence of burning, coppicing, grazing, and patches of heathland, providing a high level of landscape diversity. In the Naesbyholm Storskov area of Zealand, southeast Denmark, the Bronze Age witnessed a landscape with multiple uses of the remaining open woodland, open ground for grazing and hay crops, as well as the presence of some cereals and damp to wet ground (Andersen 1989). Similarly, elsewhere in north and east Denmark, the earlier Neolithic (3800–3500 BC) lime-dominated woodland had given way to a highly diversified landscape with swidden rotation agriculture in the middle Neolithic (3300–3100 BC), which was becoming quite treeless and grassland-dominated by the later Neolithic (2400–2000 BC) (Andersen 1992; Andersen and Rasmussen 1996).

Thus, hand in hand with an extensively developed archaeological landscape of burial monuments and settlements, the landscape became ostensibly open over the late third and second millennia BC, although with varying degrees of openness and exploitation for managed woodland, grassland, and arable crops. Significantly, soil degradation (in terms of acidification and leaching) and the advance of heathland-type vegetation do not appear to have been a major factor affecting the Bronze Age landscape on any great scale until later prehistoric and historic times, particularly in the Thy region. Thus, these highly human-modified landscapes remained relatively stable in later prehistoric and, especially, Bronze Age times.

The loss of forest trees would have been a significant problem for the procurement of both fuel and building material. By the Late Bronze Age, households at Bjerre in Thy were relying on peat, and timbers were of increasingly poor quality.

TANUM, NORTHERN BOHUSLÄN, SWEDEN

In contrast to Thy in the Early Bronze Age, against a backdrop of falling sea level caused by eustatic land uplift, the landscape of the Tanum study was deforested, heathland had expanded, and arable cereal crops were apparently grown in a more mixed economy. Grassland became more extensive in the later Bronze Age, associated with an expansion in human activities evident in settlements, graves, and rock-art.

In the early twentieth century, about 50 percent of the coastal area of northern Bohuslän consisted of bare rock, 20 percent heath, 8 percent forest, and about 22 percent arable and meadowland (Bertilsson 1987). Two recent studies of shore displacement recently were carried out in northern Bohuslän (Påsse 2001 and 2003) and Tanum (Berntsson 2006) areas. In the Tanum study, the shoreline was about 16 to 17 m asl around 1800 to 1700 BC, falling closer to 14 m asl by 1300 BC and about 11 to 10 m asl by about 500 BC (Plate 2.1). These dates fit quite well with the shore displacement curve describing the uplift of northern Bohuslän. These studies imply that about 30 percent of the currently available low arable land was covered by the sea during the Bronze Age, and that sea levels dropped roughly six meters between the beginning and end of the period (Ling 2008). Thus, only about 20 percent of the current coastal areas of northern Bohuslän could have been available for cultivation during the Bronze Age (Ling 2008).

Palynological studies from the coastland of northern Bohuslän display a similar chronological pattern of deforestation and expansion of heathland. These related events seem to have had their first general impact from about 1800 BC (Freis 1951; Svedhage 1997; Påsse 2004; Ekman 2004a, b). There are two different phases of vegetative

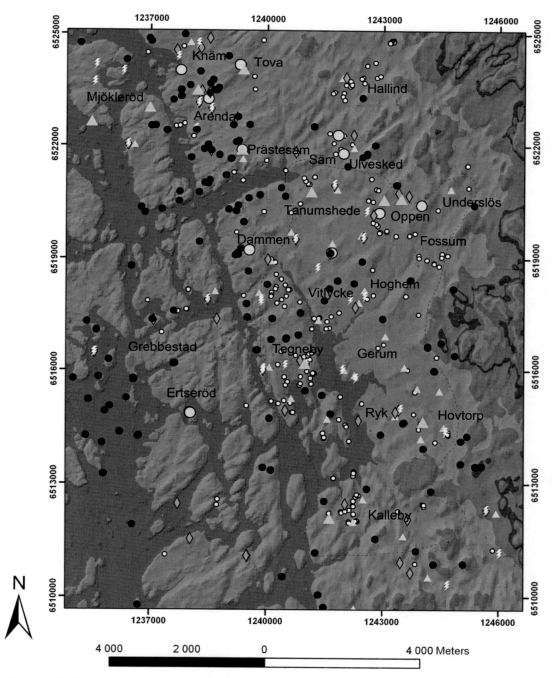

Plate 2.1. The Bronze Age shoreline in Tanum, Sweden, and the distribution of cairns (black dots), rock art sites (red dots), cupmark sites (white dots), settlement sites (large triangles), settlement indicators (small triangles), metal finds (yellow dots), flint daggers (blue rhombs), and flint sickles (white flashes). It shows the strong maritime orientation of cairns and rock art, the rock art sites defining places for gathering and harbors.

growth in the Bronze Age. About 1840 to 1400 BC, indications of herbs, heath, and wild grass increased, suggesting more grazing land in the area during the later Neolithic to Early Bronze Age. Indeed, grazing land expanded greatly by about 1500 BC. An apparent predominance of a pastoral economy in the earlier half of the Bronze Age then lessened from 1500 to 500 BC as remains from the settlement sites reveal the use of cereals such as barley, naked wheat, and emmer (Munkeberg 2006; Streiffert 2004, 2005; Bengtsson and Strid 2005).

In the Iron Age, about 600 to 250 BC, herbs and wild grasses increased significantly, which suggests an extensive expansion of grazing land. A majority of rock-art sites from northern Bohuslän apparently peak at this time. The increase of rock-art, settlement, and graves and the increase of culture-indicative vegetation suggest that this phase was the most intensive period of human expansion and vegetation change for the region.

A mixed pastoral/arable economy must not be viewed in isolation without considering other food resources that could have been exploited. In the northern Bohuslän area, in addition to cattle, sheep, and pig (Jonsson 2005), fish bones dated to the Bronze Age often outnumber bones from domestic or wild mammals. For instance, at excavations adjacent to a house structure from the Bronze Age on the island of Orust, fish bones comprised mainly large fragments of pollack, though there were also some fragments of cod, herring, and mackerel present. This region was heavily maritime in its orientation, probably throughout the sequence.

Although no geoarchaeological survey has been carried out in this landscape, the hard and relatively impermeable and acidic geology associated with the coniferous woodland would have led to acidic brown earth development. Deforestation and associated arable farming and manuring activities would have served to ameliorate these acidic soils somewhat. But if poorly managed or subject to increased rainfall or rising groundwater tables, this landscape quickly could have become subject to localized podzolisation and heathland development. This would have made these areas suitable for only occasional grazing activity. Consequently, this landscape could be seen to become more marginal in terms of supporting human agricultural activities over time, and more easily subject to soil and vegetational change with its lower inherent resilience.

SZÁZHALOMBATTA AND THE LOWER BENTA VALLEY, CENTRAL HUNGARY

Charles French, Pal Sumegi, Sandor Guylas, and Gabriella Kovacs

The coincident archaeological investigations of the Bronze Age tell site at Százhalombatta (Poroszlai and Vicze 2004) and the associated smaller settlement sites in the lower Benta valley (see Chapter 3) have allowed a unique insight into the earlier prehistoric environment in central Hungary. Most importantly, good contexts of palaeo-environmental survival were discovered in the recent projects beneath archaeological sites, eroded loessic and colluvial deposits, and within relict river channels. After extensive clearance of the loessic landscape earlier in the Neolithic, the Early-Middle Bronze Age witnessed a lengthy period of stable grassland conditions associated with animal husbandry, including a well-developed floodplain edge woodland. From the Late Bronze Age (from 1200 BC) this landscape became more erosion prone and gradually cleared. This was associated with a greater frequency of arable agriculture, a trend that increased through later prehistory and history.

Palaeosols

Chernozems are the modal soil type in this part of Hungary (Fuleky 2001). During the earlier-mid-Holocene, forest brown earths had largely become stable grassland or chernozem soils with a high organic component. Well-developed examples occur beneath the tell site at Százhalombatta overlooking the Danube (Fuleky 2001, 2005; Fuleky and Vicze 2003; Kovacs 2005).

In addition, a new study of the palaeosols and palaeo-vegetation has just been completed as part of the lower Benta valley archaeological project (Chapter 3) (Plate 2.2). Despite extensive field surveys, augering, and test pitting, only a few examples of brown earth profiles with clay enrichment and good structure have been observed, especially between Érd and Sóskút. These reddish brown sandy loam soils are characterised by an organic A horizon over a B horizon that exhibits some clay accumulation in the lower part of the profile. Much more common are well-developed chernozem soils that have a substantially thick A horizon and subsequently received silt-size material suggestive of a loess component, whether derived from wind-blow or hillwash processes.

There is little doubt that by later prehistoric times (first millennium BC) eroded loess (or fine calcareous silt) was on the move both in the air and downslope in a largely cleared landscape, and was especially being deposited on the lower slopes of the valley, on the floodplain itself, and in former channel meanders. The loess-derived colluvial deposits are rarely more than 30 to 80 cm in thickness, as evident at Érd (up to 80 cm thick), about 2 km upstream from the Százhalombatta tell (Plate 2.3). These aggrading deposits have accumulated on a disturbed and thin brown earth (likely already transformed from a forest brown earth through human activities), probably during the last millennium BC, and at Érd site 4 are certainly sandwiched between the later Bronze Age and Roman occupations. Farther upstream, thinner loess (<75 cm) deposition was observed over a well-preserved chernozem near Sóskút and at two test pit locations just to the east of Sóskút, and thicknesses of 40 to 50 cm of loessic silt are repeatedly found in the upper third of relict palaeo-channel fills in the floodplain.

Plate 2.2.
View of the Benta stream and floodplain north of Sóskút, Hungary, today (C. French).

Palynology

A detailed palynological record now exists for the lower Benta valley from five profiles from relict palaeo-channel deposits located between Lake Bia and Érd, over a distance of about 20 km upstream from the Százhalomabatta tell site (Sumegi and Bodor 2006) (Plates 2.4 and 2.5).

The following sequence is presented. Between about 4900 and 3500 BC, there was a scant but increasingly prevalent mixed deciduous woodland composed of common oak, alder, and willow, with lime and hazelnut on the margins emerging in the Benta valley. Pine and spruce conifers were some distance away, and declining, whilst the elevated loessic and more barren calcareous areas were covered by grasses, especially *Poa arvensis*. Goosefoot (*Chenopodium*) was on the wetter soils closer to the floodplain, with evidence of shallow water and marshy margins in the floodplain. Importantly, the appearance and expansion of *Plantago lanceolata* (ribwort) and *P. major/media* (plantain) indicate trampling, and the presence of *Filipendula* suggests larger open areas suitable for grazing.

Plate 2.3.
The soil profile at Érd site 4 in Benta valley, Hungary, with Bronze Age features defined at the base and Roman features at the top of the profile just below the modern plough soil (C. French).

Between 3500 and 1200 BC, there was river channel migration, incision, and infilling, especially in the first half of this period. This suggests greater rainfall and runoff, or at least greater runoff associated with clearance activities, leading to an expansion of wet habitats. A general increase in softwood gallery forests and woodland vegetation occupied the alluvial floodplain and its margins, with a significant expansion of beech and hornbeam as well as increases in small-leaved lime, common oak, alder, willow, birch, and hazelnut. This was coincident and indicative of greater rainfall, a decrease in mean summer temperatures accompanied by an increase in mean winter temperatures, and a decrease in mean annual temperature fluctuations. In contrast, elm frequencies dropped drastically, probably indicating human-activity related and disease factors at work.

At the same time, an increase in hazelnut may also reflect the opening up of woodland on the slopes and its encouragement through greater light availability and human gathering activities. Moreover, the appearance of walnut (*Juglans*) may also be associated with deliberate exploitation by humans. These same slope areas beyond the valley margins now witnessed a significant expansion

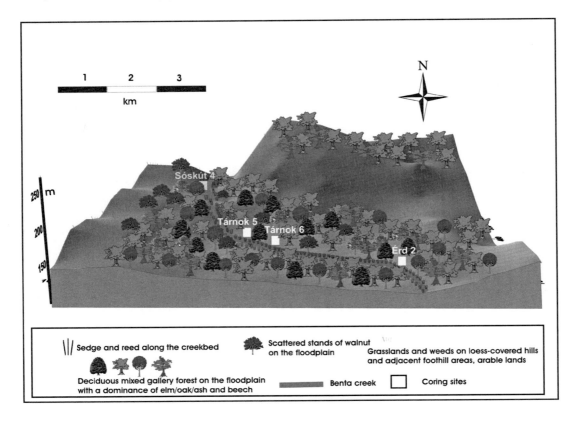

Plate 2.4.
Inferred view of the Benta valley for the Early-Middle Bronze Age in the lower Benta valley, Hungary (P. Sumegi / S. Guylas).

in *Artemisia*, as well as a number of signs of increasing agricultural activities (i.e., animal husbandry and crop cultivation) as indicated by pigweed (*Polygonum*), pearlweed (*Sagina*), prince's feather (*Amaranthus*), rib-grass (*Plantago lanceolata*), and plantain (*Plantago major/media*). But the generally subordinate amount of cereal pollen does strongly suggest the dominance of grassland and animal husbandry on the opening slopes of the valley. This is corroborated by the abundant domesticated faunal remains assemblaged from the Százhalombatta tell site excavations, which are indicative of livestock husbandry on an extensive scale throughout the Bronze Age (Chapter 6).

Between about 1200 and 1100 BC, there was a major period of soil erosion leading to the aggradation of eroded soil in the upper one-third of the palaeo-channel fill sequences. It is hard to avoid the conclusion that the uptake of former grassland for arable land use in the later Bronze Age was responsible for this, as well as severe exploitation or disruption of the woodland on the margins of the floodplain.

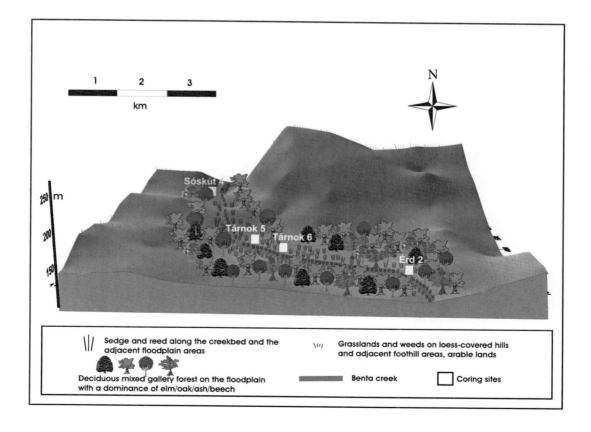

Plate 2.5.
Inferred view of the Benta valley for the Late Bronze Age in the lower Benta valley, Hungary (P. Sumegi/S. Guylas).

At about 1100 BC, an abrupt change happened with the formation of peat with associated reeds and sedge growth in the palaeo-channel sequences. This is indicative of a sluggish and relatively inactive floodplain, perhaps even the ponding of freshwater in the valley and reduced outfall into the Danube. Strikingly, the quick succession of erosion and peat signatures in the landscape appears to be coincident with the demise of the small-site occupation tradition, and perhaps the beginning of burial of these sites by hillwash-derived eroded soil material.

Between 1000 BC and AD 1000, a retreat in hazel and common oak was accompanied by a significant advance of beech, and conifers in more distant areas. Fresh and increasing pasturelands are marked by *Chenopodium bonus-henricus* overcoming *C. murale*, as well as the appearance and growth of weeds like *Artemisia*, prince's feather, and hogweed, along with barley (*Secale*), indicating an advance of crop cultivation from late Iron Age times onwards and the decreasing importance of animal husbandry. Beech, an important fuel wood in metal smelting, also decreases towards the end of this time. This picture of increasing disruption of woodland, the expansion of open-ground herbaceous vegetation, and arable exploitation has been observed elsewhere in later prehistoric and earlier historic times in Hungary at sites such as Kis-Mohos To and Bátorliget in northeastern Hungary and Sarret in central Hungary near Lake Balaton (Willis 1997; Willis et al 1998), and is generally consistent with the main period of hillwash and valley infilling such as seen in the lower Benta valley.

This more comprehensive pollen and soil study suggests that at least four landscape zones existed, each with slightly different vegetation trajectories in this landscape – the floodplain itself, the floodplain/lower slope margins, the slopes and the hills beyond. Prior to the second millennium BC, the wider landscape was substantially open and dominated by grassland for a considerable time. The woodland remaining along the floodplain edge was the last to be cleared, probably implying that it was managed as a valuable long-term resource. Settlement was located just above that woodland/floodplain edge margin, and was primarily associated with a pastoral economy. This long-term landscape stability seems to have ended abruptly between 1200 and 1100 BC when active floodplain changes were associated with greater runoff and erosion. At the same time, loessic sediment derived from the slopes with the increasing uptake of grassland for arable land was able to get into the river channel system and lead to sediment accumulation, channel avulsion, and channels being cut off to become their own micro-environments. Then, after a century of landscape instability, the system again slowed and reestablished, as is evident in the growth of peat in the palaeo-channel system and an inactive floodplain with reeds and sedge growth at about 1100 BC. Whatever else, this dramatic change in the landscape must have been associated with wider socio-cultural and economic factors, not just changes in rainfall and runoff. From this point on, there was an increasing emphasis on and importance of cereals, and once into historic times there was a combination of renewed peat growth in the floodplain and an absence of any substantial accumulations of eroded soil and loess in the system, which is indicative of long-term landscape stability.

THE CHUDDIA VALLEY AND MONTE POLIZZO, WESTERN SICILY

Landscape change was dominated by episodic soil erosion and valley infilling set against a trend towards increased aridity after about 5500 BC. Towards the end of the Bronze Age and into the Iron Age, when first Mokarta and then Monte Polizzo were flourishing, major valley alluviation had begun, associated with an intensifying semi-arid climate, more extensive use, and occupation of the steep valley sides. An essentially open landscape, it certainly had some evidence for cereals and other arable crops, weeds, vines, and fruits, but with patches of older woodland surviving in the immediate hinterland.

During the earlier Holocene, the local climate is believed to have been much moister, especially between about 7000 and 5200 BC (Heinzel et al 2004; Heinzel and Kolb in press), as has been observed for many other areas in the southern Mediterranean region at this time (French 2003, 2007; Castro et al 1998, 1999). This probably enabled the development of oak woodland in the Monte Polizzo area from about 8700 BC, as in the rest of Sicily, although this has not yet been confirmed for the Chuddia valley specifically. At this time, high lake levels at Lago di Pergusa also suggest moister conditions.

Associated with the growth of the earlier Holocene woodland, it was sufficiently moist to support woodland development and, with limestone weathering, to enable the concurrent development of brown forest soils. For example, in the Chuddia valley, a well-developed palaeosol was observed beneath the Armata alluvial fan dated to before about 6500 BC. Here, a 50-cm-thick soil profile comprised a brown forest soil (after Bridges 1970), which implies well-drained, stable, vegetated and more temperate conditions of soil development.

Beginning about 5550 to 5250 BC, climatic conditions became gradually more semi-arid/xeric (Heinzel and Kolb in press), coincident with the opening up of a once mixed deciduous and evergreen forested landscape (Leighton 1999:16, 17, and 57) through settlement, deforestation, and agriculture, and consequent landscape destabilization. Although it is unknown when the olive tree (*Olea*) was first introduced, its spread was, in part, enabled by increased aridity. During the Early-Middle Bronze Age (2000–1200 BC), this landscape had become its driest in the Holocene. By the seventh to sixth centuries BC, major landscape change had begun to occur that was associated with widespread erosion and sediment deposition as alluvial fan sedimentation in Chuddia valley (for example Figure 2.3). Interestingly, the first occupation at Monte Polizzo appears to have occurred during a period of slightly increased rainfall with periodically intense rainfall events, followed by a return to moderately dry conditions. Subsequently, during the fourth to sixth century AD, there was a second major phase of landscape change, erosion, and sediment deposition in Chuddia valley. An important feature of the Chuddia valley landscape was its multiple natural springs that occur at mid- and toe-slope locations on Monte Polizzo and Montagna Grande. Without these, it is unlikely that the large and established sites of Monte Polizzo and Mokarta could have flourished as they did.

For the past 2200 years, the area has been relatively arid, with one notable exception. This occurred in the Archaic period 'Little Ice Age' (500–350 BC), which was a period of increased rainfall, accompanied by slightly cooler temperatures, probably by as much as 1.5 degrees centigrade. There was palaeosol development associated with this phase of cooler and wetter climate, as well as soil erosion and increased accumulation of alluvial sediments. Conditions suggest bare, de-vegetated and unstable slopes affected by rainfall events, undoubtedly coincident with increasing aridity, particularly in later prehistoric times. Eroded material comprised the pediments and fans on mountain slopes in the Chuddia valley system. First there were clastic sediments (limestone, meta-limestone, and gravel) from Montagna Grande, quartzitic gravel from Monte Polizzo, alluvial fan deposits of mainly clast-supported gravels with moderate imbrication, and mainly matrix-supported conglomerates forming pediment surfaces of Monte Polizzo itself, with average slope of

12 degrees and depths of 4 to 6 m. Certainly much of this sediment was on the move from Neolithic times onwards; for example, the Lentini alluvial fan was associated with a series of stacked channel sediments with pottery from the mid–later Neolithic to Copper Ages.

In addition, a number of other studies of pollen, plant macrofossils, wood charcoal, and soils from the structures at Monte Polizzo have provided complementary data. The pollen studies by Hjelle (2004a and 2004b) conducted from House 1 and the adjacent Chuddia valley and the Stretto Partanna basin, about 17 km south of the site, generally corroborate and amplify the geoarchaeological research. Despite variable preservation and no long-term pollen sequences, any deciduous and evergreen woodland that had developed in the

THE CHUDDIA VALLEY AND MONTE POLIZZO, WESTERN SICILY

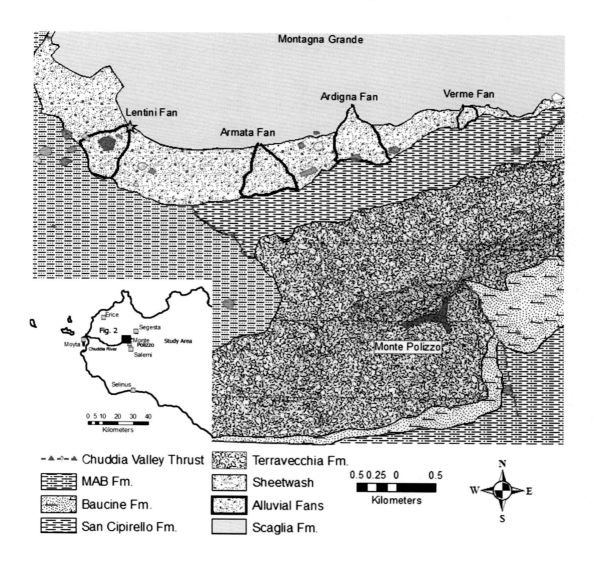

Figure 2.3.
The geology of the Chuddia River valley, western Sicily, delineating alluvial fans, bedrock, a thrust fault, and the location of the main archaeological sites (C. Heinzel).

earlier Holocene had long since disappeared and the landscape was dominated by grasses and Compositae. New palynological data are forthcoming from nearby Selinunte at Mazaro del Vallo (Chapter 6) and would indicate considerable subregional variation in woodland survival with both open and arable ground. The charcoal analyses of the Monte Polizzo structures suggest, for example, that the wooden structural beams were made of evergreen and deciduous oak, probably of local origin. This indicates some very tall trees from the undisturbed climax vegetation in the vicinity, and these trees may well have survived at higher elevations, possibly growing on the northern slopes of Monte Polizzo. Nonetheless, in the first millennium BC, remaining woodland was progressively cleared for cereal, fruit, and vine cultivation, all of which are undoubtedly associated with increased aridification and erosion signatures in the valley systems around Monte Polizzo. Indeed, the plant macrofossil and charcoal remains from the excavated structures at Monte Polizzo provide good evidence for the presence of cereal crops of hulled multirowed barley, emmer, and free-threshing wheat, as well as field beans, flax, fig, almond, and grapevines. The first millennium BC landscape of the Monte Polizzo area was essentially open with some evidence of cereals with other arable crops, weeds, and fruits, but with patches of older woodland survival in the immediate hinterland.

Soil micromorphology from selected house structures at Monte Polizzo and Bronze Age Mokarta revealed prepared earthen floors, their repeated repair or resurfacing, hearths, the deposition of wood ash, and a general level of cleanliness in the structures prior to their destruction (French and Lee 2006). Unfortunately, very few data were revealed about the pre-site soil environment.

THE UPPER TROINA VALLEY

Similar combined trajectories of increasing aridity and deforestation and erosion began in a localised manner in the fifth millennium BC, intensifying in the Bronze Age and in Roman, historic, and modern times, probably as major episodic events.

Although the upper Troina valley is some distance away to the east of the Monte Polizzo area, it is the only other area of Sicily with a comparable geoarchaeological survey (French 2003; Ayala and French 2003, 2005). Three major phases of valley sedimentation were recognized in the Holocene in this valley in the Nebrodi Mountains.

At mid-slope in the mid fourth millennium BC, scattered Neolithic farmstead sites were situated on thin colluvial slope deposits (e.g., at Casa Sollima), which, in this case, were subsequently buried between the mid fourth millennium and Hellenistic (mid first millennium BC) times (French 2003).

Major periods of hillwash and valley sedimentation, channel incision and avulsion, and alluvial terrace formation followed in three subsequent phases. These were in the earlier second millennium BC and the later Roman period (dated by thermo-luminescence of pottery and optically stimulated luminescence of valley fill sediments), and again more recently in the latter half of the twentieth century AD. Deforestation of much of the oak woodland on the valley slopes was probably associated with the first two phases of instability, undoubtedly involving intensive animal husbandry and wood exploitation, especially the tall oak trees in the Nebrodi Mountains to the north for naval timber in Roman times (as mentioned by Diodorus, IV.8.4.1–2 and Silius Italicus, XIV.237). Finally, the most recent and ongoing phase of erosion and valley sedimentation is apparently associated with the uptake of pastureland for arable crops, a situation exacerbated by European Community agricultural subsidies.

DISCUSSION

Although available palaeo-environmental data are variable among the projects, there are a considerable number of palaeo-vegetational data for the Danish, Swedish, and Hungarian case study areas, and a range of palaeosol and sedimentary data for the Danish, Hungarian, and Sicilian studies. Some common threads appear relevant to the development of these landscapes in the Bronze Age (Table 2.1).

First, there are good indications of Early Holocene woodland development associated with soil formation and generally more moist and warm palaeo-climatic conditions. The brown forest soils occurring in earlier Holocene and Neolithic contexts in Denmark, Hungary, and Sicily would have been inherently quite stable, well drained, and supportive of woodland. Once disturbed and denuded, however, they would have become prone to erosion and nutrient depletion without soil and land management. In Sweden and Denmark, given the different climatic and geological conditions pertaining, soil and vegetation cover and landscape change would have been much more variable in their possible trajectories. Blown sand

Table 2.1. Schematic summary of major palaeo-environmental events in Scandinavia, Hungary, and Sicily during the Bronze Age and later prehistoric to early historic times (C. French)

Study region	Early Bronze Age	Middle Bronze Age	Late Bronze Age	Iron Age and later
Thy, Denmark	Once well-forested landscape with few small clearings and well-developed soils transformed to extensive open grassland; some arable	Open grassland	Open grassland	Further clearance; expansion of cereals; heath and peat formation
Tanum, Sweden	Deforestation and expansion of grassland; expansion of heathland	Some cereals and mixed land use	Some cereals and mixed land use	Expansion of grassland
Lower Benta valley, Hungary	Open pasture on loessic slopes; woodland on floodplain margin; well-developed soils	Open pasture on loessic slopes; woodland on floodplain margin	Soil erosion and channel avulsion, 1200–1100 BC; from 1100 BC peat formation in floodplain; expansion of grassland; some arable; changes in tree frequency and composition	Expansion in arable farming
Chuddia valley, Sicily	Soil development; episodic soil erosion and valley aggradation set against increasing aridity and gradual deforestation	Gradual deforestation and agricultural activities	Major alluvial sedimentation	In Iron Age, intensification of agricultural activities (wheat, barley, emmer, grapevines), but patches of woodland survival
Troina valley, Sicily	Intensifying clearance and erosion set against increasing aridity	Intensifying clearance and erosion	Intensifying clearance and erosion	In Roman period: intensifying clearance; erosion and valley aggradation

and impermeable hard rock areas would have seen natural trajectories of acidification, leaching, waterlogging, and blanket peat formation. Also, once deciduous woodland was cleared and disturbed by human activities throughout the Neolithic and Bronze Age periods, the forest brown earths developed during the earlier Holocene would have become increasingly susceptible to acidification and heathland development, particularly if overgrazed or overploughed without suitable manuring and nutrient replenishment. Certainly, this process had started in the later first millennium BC in some parts of Denmark, for example, and this process has rarely been reversed since then. Longer-term climatic trends to a wetter and slightly cooler environment since the Bronze Age also would have had a strong influence and been an underlying driving factor of landscape and land-use change in northwestern Europe, as would the opposite trajectory of increasing aridification since the Bronze Age for southern Europe (Castro et al 2000; Courty et al 1994; French 2007; French et al 1998).

In northwestern Denmark, the well-developed mixed deciduous woodland of the Mesolithic and earlier Neolithic periods had begun to be substantially cleared by the later Neolithic to Early Bronze Age. Clearance, grazing, and some minor arable activity led to an increasingly open countryside within the Bronze Age. Nonetheless, this landscape does not seem to have suffered any appreciable soil degradation and was sustained for at least two millennia. Cultivation on any great scale does not really begin until later prehistoric times, but ultimately was not sustainable and many areas reverted to acidic heathland and woodland in historic times. In the Tanum area of Sweden, a picture emerges quite similar to that seen in the Thy region, but it appears to be happening later within the Bronze Age and at a slower pace.

In central Hungary, human impact in the earlier Holocene led to the creation of a substantially open and grassland-dominated landscape by the Early Bronze Age. This equilibrium was sharply broken in the later Bronze Age, about 1200 to 1100 BC, with river avulsion and the downslope erosion of loessic silt deposits. This latter feature has an inescapable linkage with the intensification of arable land use, but it was short-lived. This landscape quickly restabilised after a century or so, despite the increasing importance of arable crops over grassland in later prehistoric and historic times. The implication is for long-term sympathetic land management practices within the Early-Middle Bronze Age in this region, with a predominance of grassland for grazing over intense arable cropping. This changed briefly in the Late Bronze Age (1200–1100 BC), and then stabilised after 1100 BC. Subsequently, arable intensification occurred throughout later prehistoric, Roman, and medieval times.

In western Sicily, from as early as the sixth millennium BC, strong hints in the palynological and sedimentary records suggest the beginnings of the aridification process. This process became much more severe in the last two millennia, and has been a major driver in soil erosion and valley-filling phenomena. Erosion events appear to have been episodic and punctuating a longer-term relative equilibrium, but were gathering pace and severity from later prehistoric times onwards, which is indicative of intensifying human activities, especially arable agriculture. The establishment of settlement sites such as Mokarta in the later second millennium BC and Monte Polizzo in the first millennium BC appears to be coincident with an increasing intensity and extensiveness of clearance, diminished tree resources, the presence of cereal, fruit, and vine crops, and eroded soil aggrading in associated valleys.

Thus, each microregion witnessed different soil and vegetation changes leading to landscape transformation over different time scales. But many of the processes are similar, just taking different routes and levels of intensification over time, and are often related as much to longer-term palaeo-climatic change as human impact on the landscape. Nonetheless, it is in the Bronze Age, essentially during the second millennium BC, that we see the creation of the modern landscape on a widespread scale.

ACKNOWLEDGEMENTS

The authors would particularly like to thank the McDonald Institute for Archaeological Research, University of Cambridge, Julie Boreham of the McBurney Laboratory, Department of Archaeology, University of Cambridge, and the Radiocarbon Laboratory of the University of Poznań.

3

Regional Settlement Patterns

Timothy Earle and Michael J. Kolb
With contributions by Magnus Artursson, Jens-Henrik Bech,
Martin Mikkelsen, and Magdolna Vicze

This chapter leads a three-part, multiscalar analysis of human settlement as a means to understand basic dynamics of social, political, and economic organisation. The three scales of analysis are handled in this chapter for the regional pattern of settlement distribution with respect to cultural landscapes, in Chapter 4 for the structure of individual settlements with respect to the layout of houses and other spaces, and in Chapter 5 for the character of individual households. A multiscalar approach helps explicate alternative means by which prehistoric, European populations built up their organisations by articulating modular, but variable, units of family, community, and polity. Each of these organisational levels maintained distinctive dynamics that were balanced with and against larger formations (Johnson and Earle 2000).

At the level of the microregion, we attempt to reconstruct changing patterns of settlement for the three major areas of study in Scandinavia, Hungary, and Sicily. Work involved detailed, systematic surveys in each region to identify, date, and describe settlements from late prehistory. As the surface signatures and preservation of sites varied from region to region, the particular survey methods used had to be adapted to local conditions, but our objectives were always to describe sites according to criteria that would be comparable across time and across the three regions. Using survey results, we examine how human populations spread out with respect to each other and to economic and social opportunities in the landscape in order to understand the regional organisation and economy of prehistoric society. We thus consider the size of settlements, their spacing and association, their correspondence with productive and trading opportunities, and, ultimately, how settlements were organised into political systems. The three regions document parallel developments of settlement hierarchies that suggest chiefdom-like political organisations. The centrality, scope, and openness of these systems were, however, highly variable, and we argue that the different pathways of development reflect specific conditions of regional and international political economies, the export and import of key commodities, and the control over trade in key wealth objects. Although the pieces were similar, the nature of political hierarchies proved to be quite variable, especially in the degree of centrality and their political power. Material and historic conditions appear together to determine these alternative pathways towards complexity.

Regional settlement pattern studies have a long tradition in archaeology, and continue to be robust to analyze and compare diachronic patterns of human population history. Their success lies with the fine-grained and integrative view of environment, human activity, and social landscapes, and remains a reputable technique in both Old and New World regional research (Ashmore 2002; Banning 2002; Bintliff et al 2000; Kowalewski 2008; Zorn 1994). Since their early use, settlement analyses have been carried out with the view that archaeological sites may be identified and assigned a place in an appropriate chronological framework suitable for regional synthesis. Their assumptions in turn have facilitated comparative settlement studies (Fletcher 1986; Kolb and Snead 1997; Bevan and Conolly 2002; Galaty 2005; Alcock and Cherry 2004), and contrasting regional histories are examined in tandem in order to explore variation and its impact on settlement distribution, stability, and change. Problems, however, in regional sampling and in understanding the relationship between surface finds and ancient occupations often limit the explanatory power of settlement analysis (Kowalewski 2008; Fish and Kowalewski 1990; Bevan and Conolly 2006). Such deficiencies can also limit our ability to compare regional prehistories. Settlement pattern studies are thus best used as means to construct models of prehistoric societies to be further evaluated with intensive excavations.

In this chapter, we emphasise an approach to comparative settlement analysis in order to address and mitigate these limitations by using a systematic methodology that focuses upon the variables of economy, population, and organisation. Our goal is to describe and compare long-term settlement changes in three European regions in late prehistory. Considerable environmental differences exist across the regions, ranging from oceanic temperate to continental temperate to Mediterranean subtropical. Local histories and culture characteristics also dictate specific pathways of change for the cases discussed. They were imbedded in regional trajectories of social organisation, while at the same time interactions connected each regional tradition to international systems. Despite such variation, the comparison of these regions offers a fruitful way to consider long-term settlement change that includes the evaluation of potential causes for variation, stability, and evolutionary development.

The most challenging step is to estimate population both of individual settlements and of each region for comparative purposes. Although not denying the methodological difficulties of these estimations, these calculations are essential to understand the basic social character of the societies being investigated. We, therefore, have developed first-order approximations based on explicit estimations of the key variables, each of which can be perfected with new research. Following a number of demographic models (Zorn 1999; Paine 1997; Chapter 4), we defined five levels of settlement density: (1) urban, 20 houses per hectare; (2) proto-urban, 15 houses per hectare; (3) dispersed, 8 houses per hectare; (4) highly dispersed, 4 houses per hectare; and (5) single farm, 1 house. This gradient of house density represents a spectrum of settlement arrangements that facilitates comparison for the three regions. As various field crews found and inventoried surface-find concentrations, they were routinely described according to size, density, and phase.

Regional population estimates were made by calculating densities of habitations using two nested methods: (1) dwelling-based estimates for those archaeological sites where a dwelling had actually been described; and (2) area density estimates for those archaeological sites defined by artefact scatters (Zorn 1994). The dwelling-based method first estimates the size of a family in a region based on size of the roofed area, historical analogy, and other factors (Chapter 5). Then the number of contemporary houses is counted and multiplied by that number to obtain the size estimate. In most cases, the number of houses is unknown, and so the area density method is employed using an estimate of household per square hectare, based on structure density standards established by excavations. In our cases, the density of structures is established based on experience with settlements with different ceramic densities (Chapter 4). When each settlement was described on survey, it was described according to date, size, and density of artefact scatters. Using the five levels of settlement density outlined earlier, estimating overall population is routine, but the figures derived should be considered rather rough approximations. Population estimates are essential to help understand how societies operated, but we expect to refine estimates as more precise measures of key variables become available. Our reflexive approach to comparative studies allows the strategic positioning of people upon the landscape and facilitates the physical mapping of social relationships related to property, power, sociability, and meaning.

PROBLEM FORMULATION

The goals of our settlement pattern analysis are to describe and suggest explanations for contrasting patterns of political development. We formulate the problem as how prehistoric people organised themselves with distinct and meaningful local conditions and histories. For comparative purposes, we thus describe several key variables: population density, distribution of settlements with respect to economic resources, the percentage of population in the largest settlement, the percentage of people in fortified (versus open) settlements, the organisation of settlements spatially into political units, and the estimated size of the political systems. Our methods for describing regional patterns were developed to make use of data from systematic surveys and to make possible comparative assessments across time and the regional cases that we have chosen for study. The specific methods used in survey were tailored to local archaeological and field conditions, and they are described briefly for each case. Figures are presented to give rough approximations of similarity and differences among our cases, looking for explanations of major contrasts. We wish to describe the regional structure of settlements as representing political and economic systems, and the observed patterns of similarity and contrast are striking. These variables help us propose models of political and social organisation based on settlement structure.

Descriptions of the individual cases

SCANDINAVIA
Scandinavia in the Late Neolithic and Bronze Ages was highly variable in environment and human history, but the overall pattern was

one of relatively low-density, small-scale settlements composed elementally of individual farmsteads. Our primary case material comes from Thy in northwestern Jutland, and its settlement data form the basis for our farmstead model. As discussed in Chapter 4 and Chapter 5, the variations through time and from one area to the next were in density, clustering, and sizes of individual farms. At certain moments, settlements appear to have characterised social hierarchies, while at other times the farms seem to have been almost all the same. In agriculturally rich regions, such as Scania, southern Jutland, or Thy, farm densities were apparently substantially greater than in agriculturally marginal or marine-oriented regions such as Tanum. However, within a region, the degree of social hierarchy seen in the settlements appears to increase or decline primarily according to the regions' changing connections with broad political and trade networks. No doubt, our consideration of Thy does not represent the densest or most complex settlement patterns for the whole Scandinavian region (Chapter 4), which appears to contain variations on a theme of settlement dispersal. Thy is characteristic of a general southern Scandinavian model, although its population density may have been relatively high. Such small and dispersed settlements contrast rather sharply to the more aggregated settlements in central and southern Europe discussed later. Remarkably, however, many of Thy's social and economic characteristics, including overall population density, economic relations, and polity sizes, appear to have been rather typical of Bronze Age chiefdoms described elsewhere through Europe.

THY, DENMARK

Thy is located on the extreme northwest of Jutland, with a gently rolling moraine landscape intermingled with areas of drifting sand and uplifted seabeds and some limestone ridges with high-quality flint. The region's economy has been based on mixed farming, animal husbandry, and fishing. When ranked according to gross natural productivity, the northern environment of Scandinavia had the lowest of the three regions considered here, because of the length of the growing season and the limited range of available prehistoric crops. Historically, Thy was known to be relatively productive for farming, and it would certainly have been agriculturally richer than Tanum and many other areas in Scandinavia. In the Neolithic and through the Bronze Age, animal husbandry was important in Thy both for subsistence and for export of secondary products (Earle 2002; Chapter 6).

The time period under consideration is the Danish Bronze Age (1700–500 BC), divided into an Early and Late phase. Until recently, knowledge of the Bronze Age in Thy was based primarily on the many barrows that mark its landscape; residential sites were poorly known until an increase in rescue and research investigations in the 1990s. As part of the Thy Project, we conducted a systematic field survey searching for settlements. During the winter months when fields were not under crops, we surveyed a total of 8.4 km² in three areas of Thy, using a standard procedure of line walking at 10 m intervals with detailed recording of sites within 50 x 50 m blocks. Sites were recognized by the distribution of artefacts on the surface; for the Neolithic and Early Bronze Ages, most diagnostic artefacts were stone tools and, for the Late Bronze and Early Iron Age, most were ceramics. Although 3684 surface finds were recorded in the Thy Archaeological Project database, only a small number were datable to one period. Using only the datable stone artefacts, the number of finds appears to have increased significantly from the Early to Late Neolithic Ages. Although the stone tools dated to the Early Bronze Age decline, this may reflect the relative abundance of datable stone artefacts from that period. Some Early Bronze Age sites were easily identified because their communities specialised in sickle manufacture (Chapter 7); others had relatively small numbers of undiagnostic flake tools and waste. Late Bronze and Early Iron Age settlements were fairly easy to identify based on ceramic finds. 'Sites' were defined by concentration of flakes, stone tools, ceramics, fire-cracked stones or dark charcoal-coloured patches on the ploughed field surface, and were verified by intensive plough soil excavation and screening (Steinberg 1996). Based on the occurrence of 2 or more artefacts from a specific period, the pattern of settlement growth appears clearly: 2, Early Neolithic; 6, Late Neolithic; 8, Bronze Age; and 15, Early Iron Age. The main jump in population was into the Late Neolithic, a moderately low population density continued through the Bronze Ages, and then a second growth occurred into the Early Iron Age. For purposes of our analysis, we propose a stable population during the period of focus and construct a single settlement model.

Although the evidence is still fragmentary, the Bronze Age model of settlements appears to have been based on modular farmsteads scattered across the landscape. Danish scholars agree that, in the Bronze Age, a dispersed settlement pattern of farmsteads spread across the landscape (Becker 1980, 1982; Thrane 1980, 1999; Rasmussen 1993, 1995; Adamsen and Rasmussen 1993), and this dispersed, farm-based settlement was established at least by the later part of the Neolithic when permanent longhouses were built (Nielsen 1999; Earle 2004). This long period of stable settlement then changed dramatically in the Early Iron Age, when small, nucleated village settlements became the norm (Becker 1982; Hvass 1985). The shift from dispersed to nucleated settlements in Denmark fits a broad development with local variations across southern Scandinavia (Chapter 4) and parallels settlement changes in Holland and northern Belgium (Roymann and Fokkens 1991; Arnoldussen and Fontijn 2006).

In what we call the *standard model* for the Danish Bronze Age, the modular unit of settlement was the farm. The longhouse residence and secondary structures for storage and sometimes cattle pens were in each farm (Chapter 5). Cultivated fields, fallow land, and meadows surrounded its buildings, and the resource area of a farmstead was perhaps about 1 km^2 (Poulsen 1980; Mikkelsen 1996). These farms were not defended, except perhaps by placement in the open with good visibility. Individual farms sometimes contained two residential units in the same longhouse or in adjacent houses (Mikkelsen in press; Bech and Olsen in press). Farm units were scattered across the landscape to give a fairly regular spacing with easy access to resources, evidently varying somewhat in density according to the richness of the soil and particulars of local subsistence. Clusters of houses seem to represent many phases of rebuilding for a single farm, but small farm groupings are known (Chapter 4). Generally speaking, the distance between contemporary farmsteads could be expected to be at least several hundred meters but in some cases they may have been placed closer to each other. The density of farms probably varied in particular locations through the Bronze Age, but evidence is hard to quantify now. This pattern of dispersed farmsteads may not be found everywhere in Scandinavia (Chapter 4), but it does seem to fit Thy quite well.

House distributions in accordance with the standard model are known in numerous cases, from Thy, as for example, on the Ås ridge where local farmers also specialised in flint sickle manufacture (Mikkelsen 1996, 2003) (Figure 3.1). Here, farms, sometimes with two houses, were spaced so that the density would have been one or two

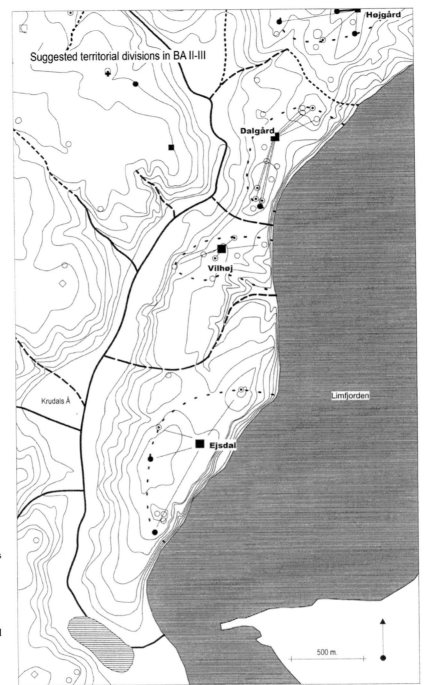

Figure 3.1.
Local territorial divisions between Early Bronze Age farmsteads from As, southeastern Thy. Squares represent farmsteads, and dots, barrows, which are assumed to demarcate the infield/outfield boundary (affer Mikkelsen 2003).

households per square kilometer. Based on general rescue archaeology and an extensive survey and excavations related to the construction of a gas pipeline and subsequent rescue and research, we know of areas within Thy where single Bronze Age houses or even groups of houses are scattered so densely in the landscape that distances sometimes do not exceed 50 to 100 m. The settlement at Bjerre Enge provides a good example of an apparent concentration of perhaps two or three farmsteads within 1 km². Here a former seabed with moist sandy sediments provided good pasture and easily arable soils that supported comparatively dense habitation through most of the Bronze Age (Bech 1997; Earle et al 1998; Bech and Mikkelsen 1999; Bech 2003). Density of sites indicates that at least in portions of the Bronze Age, the number of contemporary farms was higher than predicted by the standard model. An open question is how many farms within a particular area were contemporaneous, and whether these farms were organised within a community structure. Many houses at these settlements were probably built sequentially by a few farmsteads (Chapter 5).

Based on the evidence described earlier, we suggest that the standard model can be applied to Thy, but perhaps the settlement density should be increased locally to two farms per km². Estimating twelve persons per farm on average (Chapter 5), the population size of a region of 50 km² would have been about 600 to 1200 people, reflecting a relatively simple chiefdom controlling a low-density population probably dependent heavily on animal husbandry. A chieftain could control more people only by expanding his territory. Based on the style zones of Danish bronze (Rønne 1987), chiefdoms might have controlled at maximum about 400 km² with up to 5000 subjects. These style zones were, however, divided at most times into several autonomous polities. For a generation or so, a successful chieftain was probably able to expand based on his personal abilities, but such a large-scale polity probably was never effectively institutionalised. An Early Bronze Age chieftain in Thy probably would have organised a polity of one to two thousand.

Taken as a whole, most Danish Bronze Age longhouses do not differ very much from each other, but in the Early Bronze Age of Jutland some big houses with roofed areas of up to 500 m² were evidently chiefly residences (Ethelberg 2000; Artursson 2005a). Although substantially smaller, with roofed areas each of about 260 m², the two

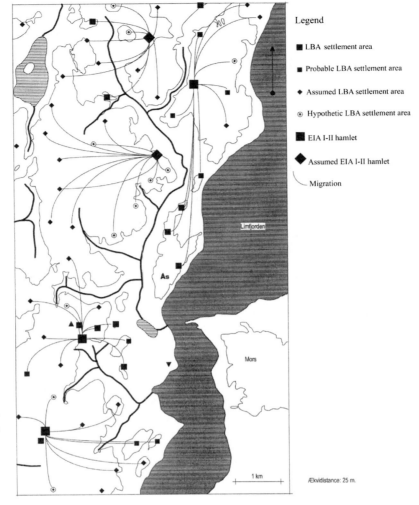

Figure 3.2.
Model of Late Bronze Age settlements in southeastern Thy, and the transition to the early Iron Age, when Bronze Age farms were left and people moved into newly formed villages. Probable settlements are based on test excavations, and assumed settlements on surface indicators (after Mikkelsen 2003).

biggest Bronze Age houses in Thy were at Legård, where they appear to have been built sequentially. They were substantially larger than all other excavated houses in Thy, and were built using the locally unusual plank construction method for the walls. Although the Legård houses cannot match the very big longhouses elsewhere, the inhabitants most probably held a higher, chiefly status. The artefacts and other finds from Legård, however, give no indications of special activities there, in contrast to other large residences where manufacture of bronze artefacts sometimes has taken place (Nilsson 1996; Ethelberg 2000). The house at Legård did, however, have evidence for animal stalls, and cattle may well have been the primary exportable wealth at this time. The amount of stone waste and number of tools at these sites were also quite limited, perhaps suggesting that most work took place away from the house, perhaps on dependent farms. We know that some settlements specialised in stone tool production, creating a regional and, in fact, interregional system of exchange among settlements (Chapter 7).

In the open, built landscape of Thy, the settlement pattern of Bronze Age farmstead was mirrored by the burial pattern for the dead. Thousands of Early Bronze Age barrows were scattered across ridges, hills, and other locations of Thy. The barrows were, by and large, built on higher locations, standing visibly above the houses in locations that had been grasslands (Chapter 2). These barrows were clustered in the landscape almost as cemeteries that may suggest a community pattern for the more isolated farmsteads. A hierarchy existed in the size of barrows, some over 9 m, others 3 or 4 m, and many lower. In conjunction with distinctions of burial equipment and in the size of longhouses just described, Thy's population appears to have been organised hierarchically in the Early Bronze Age. The main part of bronze weapons and jewelry recovered from these barrows date to the later part of the Early Bronze Age (1300–1100 BC) and show one of the highest concentrations of buried wealth in southern Scandinavia at this time (Randsborg 1974; Kristiansen 1978).

By the Late Bronze Age in Thy (1100–500 BC), the regional pattern of dispersed farms and clustered burials continued little changed (Fig. 3.2). The evidence for a social hierarchy is, however, lost. Farmhouses were perhaps a little smaller and the range in their sizes was much less (Chapter 4). Secondary Late Bronze Age burials were often placed in and nearby existing barrows, where they were clustered as small cemeteries, probably indicating social groups. No new barrows, however, were constructed, and the bodily decoration at burial included some bronze items, but these were drastically reduced in number and weight and became more standardized, although differences between burials can still be observed. It seems as if the pattern of organising the landscape by both farms and burials remained little changed, at the same time that social difference was flattened. In the Sundby site of eastern Thy, however, recent excavations have documented rather rich Late Bronze Age burials and indications of bronze casting suggesting that some social differentiation continued in Thy (Mikkelsen and Kristiansen in press). This point appears to support the general model that hierarchy may not have changed as much as it might seem, because the means for representing it changed away from the longhouses and barrow monuments. In contrast to the distinctive Late Bronze Age settlement hierarchy in southwest Fyn (Thrane 1999), southwest Seeland, and Scania (Artursson 2005b), the overall picture in many areas like Thy were characterised by only subtle differences among farmsteads and burials.

Based on the distribution of wealth in the burial, the hierarchy in size of both burial mounds and houses, and the concentration of metal production at some large houses, a hierarchical or chiefly structure existed at least locally in the Early Bronze Age of Jutland and certainly also in the Late Bronze Age of Fyn and Seeland. The nature of this hierarchy should not be overemphasised, as it appears to have been quite fluid and changing, as opportunities and constraints for amassing wealth and distinction were quite unstable. The size and stability of these hierarchies seem to have been quite modest, with only fairly small populations involved and with the dispersed farmstead settlement as the norm. The larger houses and the construction of thousands of Bronze Age burial mounds of Thy existed for only a few hundred years, and the subsequent Late Bronze Age settlements show as yet only subtle evidence for a continuing hierarchy. The overall dispersed farmstead settlement was thus the norm, for which pulses of change occurred.

TANUM, SWEDEN

Tanum was a rocky and highly irregular coastal zone during the Bronze Age. Some pockets of good soil certainly were farmed, but it appears the primary economic orientation was towards the sea. Few Bronze Age settlement structures have been investigated to date in northern Bohuslän, and those that have been studied were almost exclusively isolated house structures. Overall, the pattern fits well with a low-density variant of the standard model. Houses and settlement finds indicative of individual houses were scattered across the landscape, located mainly within the coastal zone (Bertilsson 1987; Lindman 1997, 2004). The majority of settlements in Tanum have been found on higher areas of the plain where farming would have been ideal and on the lower plain adjacent to the sea. Close to the sea are the majority of rock-art sites (Ling 2008). The few sites that have been investigated that date 1200–500 B.C. contain single residential structures that are quite small, 13 to 24 m long (Streiffert 2004) with no apparent arrangement as a settlement hierarchy. The parish does contain the highest numbers of flint daggers and sickles known in Bohuslän. These are artefacts imported from Jutland, suggesting the region's involvement in maritime trade from the Late Neolithic through the Bronze Age (Algotsson and Swedberg 1997; Apel 2001). The burial record of the region contains contemporaneous barrows in the agricultural uplands and rock cairns overlooking the sea at point of passage (Ling 2008). The monumental burial of the dead, therefore, suggests two clear identities, one associated with local farming and the other with a maritime world involving trading and raiding.

Bronze Age household economies in northern Bohuslän suggest a sparse settlement with intriguing organisational linkages. We can propose a very low-density, dispersed pattern of households that would have involved farming, fishing, and seafaring. Households would undoubtedly have formed networks of dispersed local communities with close association to the rock-art sites. Although no evidence exists now for an established political hierarchy in house sizes, the opportunities for distinction gained in foreign trading and raiding existed for local wealth accumulation. The large stone cairns on the coast could attest to such distinctions. Although the region was distant from the developed social hierarchies in the richer agricultural zones of Scania and Denmark, the presence of both flint and metal wealth and the stylistic references in the rock-art suggests that these seafaring people were part, perhaps as specialised mariners, of the broad Scandinavian social development, especially during the Late Bronze Age. Future systematic surveys, excavations, and analyses are needed to clarify the picture of these sites and their uses during the Bronze Age of Tanum.

HUNGARY

In the Bronze Age, Hungary had a varied settlement history across its mountain valleys, rolling loess hills, Great Plain, and major river systems. Much of the region had soils under forests or grasslands suitable for cereal farming and animal herding. The network of rivers provided routes for trade in metals and commodities. Because central Hungary is environmentally variable, the Benta valley cannot be considered generally representative of Hungarian prehistory. As a microregional study, our work can be used as a model against which to evaluate the likely variability in local developments that will emerge with future work.

Based on existing research, the overall pattern of central Hungary in the Bronze Age was one of moderate settlement density with sites that ranged from fortified central places (quite large permanent tells) to small open settlements (Chapter 4). Permanency, size, and hierarchical arrangements of settlements probably reflected microregional variation in agricultural productivity and the locales' articulations with emerging trade networks. Our case material from the Bronze Age Benta suggests intermediate-scale chiefdoms economically based on cereal agriculture, on animal herding, and, increasingly, on trade. The social hierarchy seen in settlement sizes and fortification appears to increase through time, probably reflecting the area's potential for agriculture, for the production of animal products for trade, and for the control of long-distance trade along the Danube.

The main section of the Benta stream that we studied flows from Lake Bia, through rolling loess-covered hills and limestone ridges to the Danube. It contains roughly 50 km^2 of territory. During the Early and Middle Bronze Age, the Benta witnessed a period of stable grassland, floodplain, and woodland that suggests mixed cereal cultivation and animal herding (Chapters 2, 6). This landscape became increasingly cleared and more erosion prone in the Late Bronze Age, probably with a shift to more intensive agriculture. Historically, it was known to be productive for both dry farming and animal husbandry, being most likely the second most productive region in our European sample.

In the Benta valley, the Hungarian MRT had inventoried all sites and conducted a systematic survey of the microregion (Dinnyés et al 1986). We evaluated the quality of its survey by visiting all known sites and surveying selected areas where no settlements had been found. We concluded that their survey was comprehensive and that all sites of any size had been located. The MRT listed thirty-four sites with Bronze Age ceramics (Vicze et al 2005), and we investigated these by shovel testing to define the extent of settlement and systematic small test excavations to date occupation phases. We then classified the sites into an established typology based on defensiveness and size, and dated them to phase (Chapter 4). Defensive versus open settlements was determined by site placement on easily defended topographic positions (ridges, hills, and cliffs) and evidence for fortification (trenches and ramparts) versus placement on gradual sloping soils without evidence of fortification. Within each category, sites were further described regarding residential population based on area extent and density. Density of occupation for each time period was calculated for each quarter-hectare area based on the numbers of sherds of that period recovered in test excavation: low, 7–14; medium, 15–50; high, 51–100; and very high, >100. Population of a site was estimated as follows: low densities areas are believed to represent highly dispersed settlements with about four houses per hectare, medium to high density as dispersed with eight houses per hectare, and very high densities are believed to represent proto-urban settlements with an average of fifteen houses per hectare. The size of a house unit is tentatively set at six persons (Chapter 5).

Results of our field survey show more than a tripling of residential area and presumably of population from the Early Bronze Age (5 sites with 9.0 ha, 510 people) to the Middle Bronze Age (13 sites with 31.25 ha, 1692 people). Then the region's population appears to have declined into the Late Bronze Age (13 sites with 26.5 ha, 1026 people). The densities of regional population show a corresponding marked growth from ten persons per km^2 in the Early Bronze Age to $34/km^2$ in the Middle Bronze Age then declining to $21/km^2$ in the Late Bronze Age. According to the establish chronology, a gap exists between the Middle Bronze Age Vatya settlements and the Late Bronze Age settlements that have Urnfield ceramics associations (Chapter 4). The continuity in occupation at almost all Vatya settlements into Urnfield phases, however, suggests no such abandonment and reoccupation.

SETTLEMENT PATTERN CHANGE IN THE BENTA VALLEY DURING THE BRONZE AGE

The settlement record shows that, based on population size, political hierarchies developed across both fortified and nonfortified settlements through the Bronze Age. Based on the association of settlements with landscape conditions, finance in the political economy apparently was balanced as a mix between mobilisation of staple goods and control over trade in wealth, and the relative mix affected the resulting political system. Through the Bronze Age, the balance of staple versus wealth finance appears to have shifted increasingly towards control over wealth.

Five Nagyrév settlements from the Benta valley have been identified as dating from the Early Bronze Age (Figure 3.3). Total population was quite small – about 500 – 38 percent of which lived within fortified settlements. The population was roughly divided into what we believe were two polities, associated with separate and apparently co-dominant central places – the fortified Százhalombatta-Földvár tell (27/2) and the dense open Sóskút settlement (26/4); 95 percent of the population lived in these two settlements. The lower valley was dominated by the fortified tell, with an estimated 2 ha of occupation (190 people) that sat high on a bluff overlooking the Danube, north of the Benta. The site's position was ideal for monitoring trade along the Danube; in contrast, it was ill placed for agriculture because the river truncated its catchment area. Unfortified settlements in the lower valley included small hamlets or farms at Tárnok 31/1, located on a low slope above a side stream, and Érd 9/4, located on a bench just above the Benta floodplain. Both settlements were positioned within good loess soils. The locations of these secondary settlements were probably chosen to emphasise agriculture and herding.

In the upper valley, the substantial open settlement at Sóskút contained 4.75 ha of dense occupation (300 people). It sat on rolling loess soils above the stream, in an area ideal for farming and herding. The site appeared similar to a tell, but apparently it was unfortified (Chapter 4). Another settlement in the upper valley was a very small site 1/26 (0.25 ha; perhaps only a single farm) on the hilltop, and it later became a hillfort. In the two small polities of lower and upper valley segments, virtually all people lived in the primary village site, and no substantial settlement hierarchy existed. These Bronze Age polities were not of the political scale or organisation complexity typical of chiefdoms. The locations of their co-equal centers suggests the two polities had contrasting economic opportunities that, in the subsequent period, would combine to form a composite political economy that supported the emergent valley-wide chiefdom.

Thirteen Vatya settlements are known to have existed in the Benta valley by the Middle Bronze Age (Figure 3.4). Estimated population more than tripled to 1700, 36 percent of which lived within fortified settlements. By this time the microregion had apparently been united into one chiefly polity, as documented by a new hierarchy of

SETTLEMENT PATTERN CHANGE IN THE BENTA VALLEY DURING THE BRONZE AGE

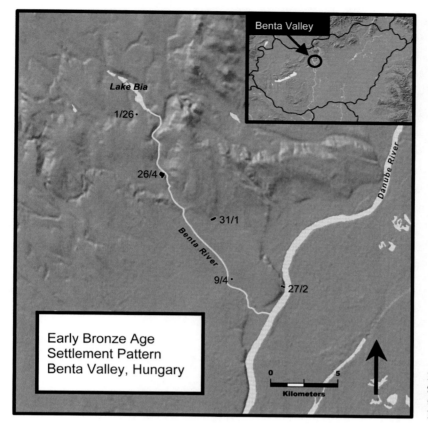

Figure 3.3.
Settlement pattern of the Benta valley in the Early Bronze Age.

intervisible, fortified settlements. Four, or perhaps five, forts were placed strategically through the valley. These included the original Százhalombatta-Földvár tell (now 5.5 ha; 310 people); a new tell (27/14; 2.0 ha with 140 people) positioned just south of the Benta on the Danube's cliffs; the small Sóskút hillfort in mid-valley (1 ha; 50 people); and the substantial Bia hillfort (2.5 ha; 100 people) located at the top of the valley. A fifth, undated fortification (1/3) also existed in the upper valley; although without evidence of habitation, like the Sóskút hillfort, it was paired with an undefended settlement (1/4). These fortified sites were placed on high ground so that they could be seen one from the next.

Based on size of estimated population, a clear hierarchy existed for the fortified sites. The largest was more than twice the size of the next two, and two others have only small resident populations. The main forts were positioned on the valley's peripheries, apparently to protect against external threats and along the rivers where any commerce could have been monitored and controlled. The chain of forts also overlay the open settlements, over which they could have maintained political domination. Here, a warrior elite might have been in residence and exerted control over staple production at hinterland settlements at the same time they could monitor trade in wealth along the Danube and Benta. Analysis of ceramics from all settlements shows a significant concentration of cooking jars on the fortified sites, perhaps documenting the mobilisation of staples to support the fortified groups (Klehm 2006). At the main tell, the density of bone remains suggests that this central place received animals from outlying settlements (Chapter 6).

The importance of the fortified settlements, however, should not be overemphasised. Most population (64 percent) lived in unfortified settlements, some of which were of considerable size. The dominant open site was Tárnok (31/1), with an estimated 12.5 ha of settlements and 550 residents. This large village was located in the lower central valley on good agricultural land, and it was apparently larger than the main tell. Five additional smaller villages (9/3, 9/4, 26/7, 26/4, and 1/4) were spread along the first bench or lower slopes of the Benta valley, where they would have maintained immediate access to prime agricultural and grazing land. These villages were each 2 to 3 ha in size with a range of 80 to 120 residents. Three much smaller settlements (hamlets or farms) were scattered here and there along the stream, also close to agricultural field areas.

A pattern of open settlements formed a clear site hierarchy, dominated by the large central village of Tárnok, which contained an estimated population equivalent to all other open settlements. As a whole, they appear to be involved primarily with crops and animal production. Could the large settlement of Tárnok (rather than Százhalombatta-Földvár) have been the center of power for the valley chiefdom? Intriguingly, excavations at tell settlements show little evidence of social differentiation in housing, seeming to represent a fairly equal segment of the population (Chapter 5). The overall pattern of consumption on the sites and within the cemeteries suggests a common, corporate identity that did not emphasise differences (Chapter 5). Despite this apparent equality, the position of fortifications suggests that warriors were critical to Middle Bronze Age society and that Százhalombatta-Földvár was probably the main central place. Perhaps, however, it was dominant only in its sphere of power, reflecting control over emerging luxury trade. The paired

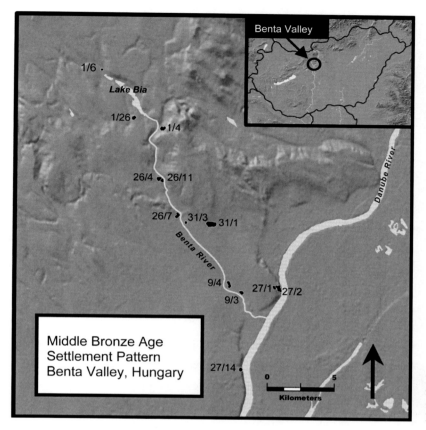

Figure 3.4.
Settlement pattern of the Benta valley in the Middle Bronze Age.

SETTLEMENT PATTERN CHANGE IN THE BENTA VALLEY DURING THE BRONZE AGE

central Middle Bronze Age settlements of Százhalombatta-Földvár and Tárnok may represent a continuation from the Early Bronze Age of two distinctive bases of power in staple production and luxury trade. Thus, the new Middle Bronze Age Benta chiefdom could well be an amalgam, a heterarchical structure incorporating within a single polity different sources of power and finance. Thus, Tárnok could have dominated the agricultural communities producing staples and animal products in the valley, and Százhalombatta-Földvár could have dominated the hierarchy of forts, providing warrior protection at the same time that it controlled movement of wealth and other commodities.

In terms of the pattern of cemeteries that placed the dead with respect to the living, Middle Bronze Age cremation urn cemeteries have been located in many locations through the valley. Although additional research is needed, cemeteries appear to have been located near settlements, but separated by some distance and topographic division such as a ravine (Vicze 1992, 1993, 2001, 2008). Urn cemeteries are known near the two tells and at several other locations through the valley. In the Middle Bronze Age, the Vatya population of the Benta was relatively dispersed both as the living and as the dead.

In the Late Bronze Age, thirteen Urnfield settlements are known from the Benta valley (Figure 3.5). The warrior segment of the Urnfield chiefdom that spread across the valley appears to have strengthened control, emphasising more dispersed settlements and a dominant central fort (Chapter 4). Estimated now at 1000, population was less sizeable. The percentage of population living within the fortified settlements was unchanged (37 percent), and population was further concentrated in the lower part of the valley. As in the preceding phase, the hierarchy of fortified sites continued, but the dominance of a main fortified settlement (a former tell) increased substantially. The emergence of Százhalombatta-Földvár as the dominant settlement reinforces the conclusion that control over trade in wealth was increasingly the main source of power. Three, or perhaps four, forts date to this period: Százhalombatta-Földvár (expanded to 7.75 ha and 310 people), the Bia hillfort (reduced to 1.5 ha and 40 people), the Sóskút hillfort (remaining small at 0.5 ha and 20 people), and the undated, fortified enclosure of 1/3. The secondary Middle Bronze Age tell (27/14) was abandoned.

The pattern of open, Late Bronze Age Urnfield settlements was very similar to that of the Vatya, although lower densities of habitations suggest that their overall population sizes declined (Chapter 4). The dominant settlement continued to be Tárnok, with a reduced area of 7.5 ha and an estimated 210 inhabitants. The five smaller villages (1/4, 9/3, 9/4, 26/4, 26/7) all continued to be occupied with similar areas (2–3.75 ha) and estimated numbers (70–110). Four additional smaller settlements (hamlets or farms) were also noted, two of which continued from the previous period.

Using the settlement pattern data from the Benta valley, we can construct a model of Bronze Age society that proposes the formation and transformation of a Bronze Age chiefdom. Early Bronze Age Nagyrév settlements suggest local corporate groups with a minimum of regional structure and social hierarchy. During the subsequent Middle Bronze Age Vatya society, a hierarchy of forts was created across the valley. Assuming the forts were associated with a warrior hierarchy, this segment probably came to dominate an

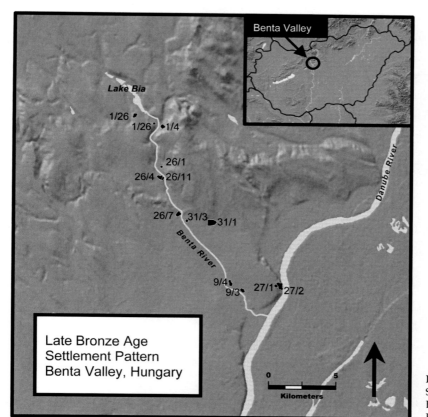

Figure 3.5.
Settlement pattern of the Benta valley in the Late Bronze Age.

overarching political structure critical for defence. The fortification may well reflect intensive, interpolity warfare, and the documented Middle Bronze Age massacre at village site 9/4 dramatically illustrates the risks of living in an unfortified settlement (Chapter 4). The importance of fortified settlements should, however, not be overemphasised. Most people lived in open settlements. In the Early and Middle Bronze Age, the single largest open village contained the largest residential group, and, assuming that settlement size measures political significance, these must have been important central places.

We envision two sources of wealth and finance in the Bronze Age society of the Benta Valley: dispersed agricultural production of animal products and food and channelled luxury trade in metals and other commodities. Based on the comparative sizes and placement of settlements, the balance, as a measure of the relative significance of the alternative sources of power, apparently shifted. In the

Early Bronze Age, the largest settlement was an open village surrounded by prime agricultural land in the central valley. In the Middle Bronze Age, two settlement hierarchies exist for fortified and open settlements. One hierarchy focused on the routes of movement (especially the Danube) and the other, on the central valley agricultural land. In the Late Bronze Age, however, population shifted increasingly down valley, suggesting a greater dependence on wealth derived from extraction from and participation in the luxury trade.

SALEMI, SICILY

The Salemi region incorporates mountainous terrain punctuated by well-drained valleys with fertile soils. In Sicily generally, detailed settlement pattern studies are sporadic (Leighton 1999). Settlement densities appear to have been low through the Bronze Age, and, at this time, the area may have been used largely for animal herding. The initial emergence of complex societies in Sicily may have been based on the control of animals raised for export, but by the Iron Age crop production became central. A fairly stable, grassland landscape in the Bronze Age and then some instability in the Iron Age fit this subsistence reconstruction (Chapters 2 and 6). Historically, the Salemi region was known to be highly productive agriculturally, probably the most productive in our sample of European regions. These valleys form three distinct drainage systems that surround Salemi's most impressive archaeological sites: the hilltop settlements of Montagna Grande (Poggio Roccione), Monte Polizzo, Monte Rosa (Salemi), and Cresta di Gallo (Mokarta). Settlement research in this region has tracked long-term economic and political changes in the first millennium BC associated with Greek and Phoenician contact and coastal colonies.

Results of our field survey show an eightfold increase in residential area and presumably of population from the Late Bronze Age (eleven sites with 8.3 ha) to the Early Iron Age (twenty-two sites with 29.8 ha). Then, during the Classical/Hellenistic Period, the region's population appears to have stabilized but became more concentrated (twelve sites with 25.6 ha). Our survey methodology (Kolb and Tusa 2001; Kolb 2007) included an intensive pedestrian survey of 339 freshly plowed fields (35 km² with 33 percent average visual coverage), and detailed surface collection (100 percent visual coverage) of each identified artefact scatter. Nearly 43,000 artefacts

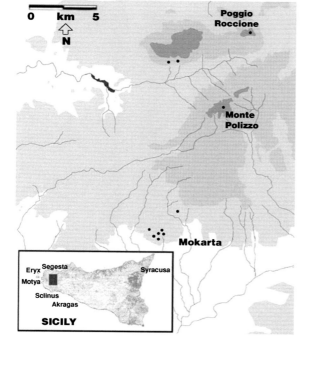

Figure 3.6.
Settlement pattern of the Salemi area in the Late Bronze Age.

were identified, sorted, and counted in the field, and just over 3000 diagnostic artefacts were collected for laboratory analysis. We identified both settlement sites associated with higher-density artefact distribution and some scattered nonresidential activities with low-density artefact scatters.

During the Late Bronze Age, population density was quite low, at 24/km^2, and settlements clustered at two defensive locations (Figure 3.6). Seven of the Late Bronze Age sites were located on or near Cresta di Gallo (366 m asl), most probably consisting of a single community. One of these sites is the small village or hamlet of Mokarta, an archaeologically excavated site possessing ten round stone houses and covering about 1 ha in area. Each settlement was unfortified, but was located high enough to possess an excellent vantage point of the surrounding Grande River valley and a definite defensive advantage. The other three sites, perhaps a second community, were located at lower elevations in the Chuddia River valley to the north and had easy access to agricultural land. Based upon a general population of 100/ha (dispersed housing with ten individuals per household and ten houses per hectare), the Cresta di Gallo region had an estimated population of about 650 people, whereas the Cuddia River valley

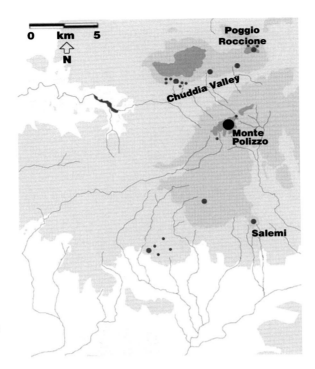

Figure 3.7.
Settlement pattern of the Salemi area in the Early Iron Age.

settlements had about 200 people. If combined, these two communities could have formed a very small chiefdom.

During the Early Iron Age, population grew substantially, attaining an estimated population density of 112/km². Several large and fortified proto-urban settlements dominated the region's settlement hierarchy, which also included some small, open settlements (Figure 3.7). The largest Iron Age settlements were placed defensively and further protected by fortification walls. The most dominating site is located on Monte Polizzo (713 m asl), a trefoil peak with a commanding vista of most of western Sicily. The site is approximately 11.8 ha in size and consists of a ceremonial acropolis surrounded by house clusters that lack a standardized urban geometry. This large proto-urban settlement served as a central place in the settlement system. Two other hilltops were used as contemporaneous settlements as well. Salemi (440 m asl) represented the second largest settlement, at 3.9 ha, and Poggio Roccione (653 m asl) had three separate household concentrations totaling 2.2 ha. Each of these major sites was evidently a separate community. Other settlements were unfortified, small, and scattered sites located in the Chuddia and Grande river valleys proximal to arable land and convenient spring water. These

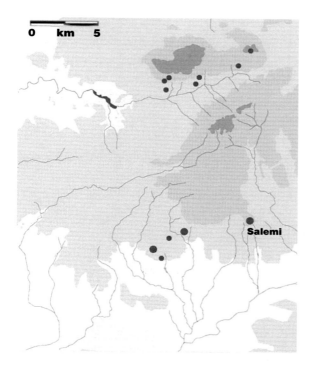

Figure 3.8.
Classical/Hellenistic settlement pattern of the Salemi area.

smaller settlements appear to be satellite hamlets directly associated with the larger hilltop settlements. Based upon a general population of 150/ha (proto-urban housing with ten individuals per household and fifteen houses per hectare), the total hilltop settlement would be approximately 2700 people (Monte Polizzo with 1800, Salemi with 600, and Poggio Roccione with 300). The dispersed valley sites represent about 1200 people.

After the abrupt abandonment of Monte Polizzo around 475 BC, Salemi becomes the predominant settlement during the subsequent Classical/Hellenistic period (Figure 3.8). With a dense network of houses filled with a high proportion of imported Hellenistic and Punic ceramics, Salemi was a prosperous settlement that was completely incorporated into a broader island economic sphere. The remaining nine sites of this period are dispersed throughout the countryside, again near arable land and convenient water sources. Based upon a general population of 200/ha (urban-style housing with ten individuals per household and twenty houses per hectare), Salemi would have a population of 800 people and the other nine dispersed valley sites, a population of 2300 people. This resulted in an overall population density of $89/km^2$. The percentage of population living within fortification decreased substantially to 26 percent of the total, and we can suggest that the region had established a comparatively peaceful political structure, perhaps tied to Hellenistic hegemony.

Based upon the available data, we propose a model for the development of urban societies due to increasing articulation with coastal colonies. During the Late Bronze Age, a fairly small chiefdom (total population of about 850) apparently emerged, loosely concentrated around Cresta di Gallo. The majority of residential hamlets were located at fairly low elevation, in and near the agricultural fields, but given the area's fairly low population density, herding may have been important. By the Early Iron Age, a single polity had formed, with population increasing to about 4000 people, most probably broken into multiple communities dependent on agriculture and trading. Monte Polizzo evidently served as a primate center around which most of the other sites served auxiliary or logistical roles, perhaps including even Poggio Roccione. Most settlements were placed defensively at high elevations, well away from the valley agricultural areas. The role of Salemi at this time is curious, perhaps an independent polity rather than auxiliary to Monte Polizzo. By the Classical/Hellenistic period, the region's population decreased slightly to 3000 people and was mainly dispersed throughout the countryside, with only a quarter living within fortifications. The large number of imported fine wares and foreign coins at Salemi suggest a prosperous region that was closely allied with either the coastal Greek or Punic colonies, and the significant increase in hinterland settlement indicates a greater integration of valley productive activities. By this time, this region had probably become a supplier of agricultural produce to the coastal colonies.

III. Comparative analysis of the cases

The comparative study of economy, population, and organisation helps recognize and interpret contrasting patterns in late European prehistory. The variables considered in Table 3.1 appear to be interconnected; ranking of highest population density is mirrored by the ranks of largest site size, of the percentage of the population living in defended settlements, and of estimated polity size. Although local histories and culture characteristics were of great importance, we propose generally that two economic variables (gross agricultural productivity and spatial positioning with respect to international

Table 3.1. Comparison of settlement evidence for the Salemi, Benta, and Thy microregions

Place	Time	Population density	Largest site size	Percentage defended	Polity size numbers	Area
Salemi	LBA	26/km²	150	76	850	33 km²
	EIA	118/km²	1800	69	3900	33 km²
	Classic	89/km²	800	26	3100	33 km²
Benta	EBA	10/km²	300	38	300–500	20 km²
	MBA	34/km²	550	36	1700	50 km²
	LBA	21/km²	300	37	1000	50 km²
Thy	EBA	12–24/km²	50	0	1000+	50–100 km²

LBA = Late Bronze Age; EIA = Early Iron Age; EBA = Early Bronze Age; MBA = Middle Bronze Age
Rank order of cases based on key variables:
Population density: Salemi>Benta>Thy
Largest site: Salemi>Benta>Thy
Percentage population defended: Salemi>Benta>Thy
Size of polity: Salemi>Benta>Thy

trade) channelled long-term trajectories in population growth and political development.

First in our analysis are the two underlying economic variables. Gross agricultural productivity is generally a good predictor of social complexity for early agrarian societies, for which control over staple production provides surpluses used to finance institutions of rule. On a macro scale, productivity most directly reflects temperature and sunlight gradients increasing from north to south. For the three main cases, although each seems to have been a productive agricultural microregion within its broader area, gross productivity would rank the cases from highest to lowest as: (1) Salemi, (2) the Benta, and (3) Thy. This ranking corresponds well with the ranking of highest population densities recorded for the cases: the Salemi Early Iron Age was nearly three times greater than the Benta Middle Bronze Age, which was probably twice that of Thy in the Bronze Age. These differences in population density apparently reflect differences in the microregional potential to intensify agriculture, and the ranking translates into the potential surplus production for staple finance in emergent chiefdoms. As discussed later, this density gradient matches an increase in settlement size and probably the corporate identity of its groups.

Using only the population densities for the Bronze Age, a more complicated pattern emerges linked to the second key economic variable, positioning with respect to international trade. With one exception, Bronze Age population densities were quite similar, ranging between 10 and 26 /km², probably reflecting relatively low and quite stable populations dependent on mixed pastoral–crop subsistence economies. A weak trend to increased density from north to south probably reflects overall productivity, but variance from that trend was important. We believe that the primary variance reflects a region's specific and quite variable articulation with an emerging international trade.

Spatial position determines specifically how each region articulated with international commodity flows during the second and first millennium BC. The changing trade patterns were, themselves, an outcome of specific histories of consumer demand and the technology of transport, and correspondingly changed opportunities for wealth finance and chiefdom development. In Scandinavia, the emergence of relatively high population densities and social complexity in southern Jutland during the Early Bronze Age, for example, may have relied on control over a bottleneck in land-based transport involving animal drives and amber shipments south to the Continent. In a primary source area, such as Thy, with productive pastures and rich availability of amber, some social hierarchy emerged. During the Late Bronze Age, however, the locus of power shifted eastward to the Danish islands, especially Fünen, probably caused by changing commodities and a new transport system based on boats. The political economy of Thy and southern Jutland became marginalised and their social hierarchies withered. In Hungary the timing was different but the underlying causes similar. Through the Bronze Age, commodity flows involving metals and other wealth goods progressively channelled along major corridors where water-based transport dominated. An early balance between staple and wealth finance among many local polities shifted towards larger-scale chiefdoms controlling major river arteries. During the Middle Bronze Age, a valleywide chiefdom appears based both on staple production in the Benta and wealth movement along the Danube. This was the period of highest population density and of the largest settlements. Then, as population declined and staple finance was displaced by wealth, the transformation of chiefly structure reflected its strategic management of the river bottleneck. In Salemi, Sicily, social development was also tied to changing patterns of international trade. In the Bronze Age, trading in the Mediterranean seems to have been concentrated to the east, linked to demands by Middle Eastern agrarian states.

Some trading with Sicily certainly existed, most probably for animal products. In the Iron Age, the Greek and Phoenician trading empires were based on a string of colonies and efficient water-based transport through the western Mediterranean. These colonists were economic specialists – traders and high-end commodity producers. Salemi's location in Sicily made it close to coastal colonies, which required staples that the interior valleys provided. The development of intensive agriculture thus resulted in a spike to population density and the opportunities for managed interchange with foreign powers. In each of these cases, the primary source of finance appears to have been trade, but the specifics differed in terms of both the nature of articulation and timing.

The political economy shows a fairly dramatic gradient from north to south in terms of control over agricultural labour and staple production. Supplemental to this control was the specific patterns of trade that created local opportunities for wealth accumulation and relatively rapid changes in social complexity. Social complexity is measured fairly directly by three settlement variables that show basically the same north–south gradients, but with important contrasts in timing. First is the size of the largest settlement, which gives some idea of the degree of centrality in political power. The largest Iron Age settlement in Salemi (Monte Polizzo) was more than three times larger than the largest Bronze Age settlement in the Benta, which, in turn, was probably ten times the size of the largest Bronze Age settlement in Thy.

Second is the percentage of population protected by fortification, a rough indication of direct military control. In Salemi during the Iron Age, the percentage of the population living within fortified settlements was high (nearly 70 percent). In the Benta during the Bronze Age, the percentage living defensively was intermediate (about 36 percent), half that for Iron Age Salemi. In Bronze Age Scandinavia, settlements were dispersed and unfortified.

Third is the estimate of polity size, which we take to be a rough overall indicator of political reach. Here, the same rank order is apparent but the differences are more subtle: In Salemi, the Iron Age polity centered at Monte Polizzo had an estimated population of 3900, in comparison with the Middle Bronze Age polity of the Benta with perhaps 1700 people. The size of the chieftaincy of Thy in the Early Bronze Age was probably considerably less, perhaps a 1000 as a basal unit that increased episodically with a strong chieftain.

The four regions appear to have had polities with similar orders of magnitude in the low thousands, but each appears to be organised quite differently in spatial extent (Kristiansen 2007). The Sicilian society had a proto-urban core that controlled a relatively compact region of perhaps only 33 km²; this would have represented a centralised political system loosely allied with neighboring hilltop polities (Kolb and Speakman 2005). In the Benta, the somewhat smaller population was spread over a larger territory of perhaps 50 km², and the similar sizes of the two largest settlements suggest a dual power base for the Middle Bronze Age. In Scandinavia, with lower population densities, in order to fashion a chieftaincy of a thousand or so, the spatial extent of the polity would have required nearly 100 km² of scattered farmsteads; the control over such a dispersed population would have been fundamentally problematic. The political power appears to have increased from north to south, as population became increasingly concentrated and more easily controlled. The settlement data and their implication for political organisation and finance document Kristiansen's insight that the chieftaincies of the north were of a different, more decentralised, and more politically dynamic type than those of the south. In simple terms, this pattern reflects the gradation from a networked to a corporate political strategy (Blanton et al 1996) that changed the character of social life in the societies under consideration (Chapters 4 and 5).

4

Settlement Structure and Organisation

Magnus Artursson

With contributions by Jens-Henrik Bech, Timothy Earle, Dániel Fuköh, Michael J. Kolb, Kristian Kristiansen, Johan Ling, Christian Mühlenbock, Christopher Prescott, Chris Sevara, Sebastiano Tusa, Claes Uhnér, and Magdolna Vicze

This chapter compares the structure and organisation of settlements across Europe, bridging the chapters on regional settlement patterns and households. The settlement represents the local organisation of habitations: how households were placed with respect to each other and to common spaces for work, ceremonies, and social interaction. Important variables included the density and number of contemporaneous households, the permanence of house sites and their interrelations, the existence of defining fortifications, and internal social differentiation marking social distinction. Overall, the settlement types varied within each region and appear in each region to represent settlement hierarchies of regional polities (Chapter 3). The size and density of the largest settlements, however, show a marked trend from relatively small and informal aggregates in Scandinavia to large, proto-urban settlements in Hungary and Sicily. The larger settlements in Hungary and especially in Sicily appear to have a regular settlement structure, with houses in well-defined lots, roadways, and public spaces. In Sicily, a central, religious complex defines a new level of corporate labour investment. Although social differentiation surely existed in all circumstances, complexity varies quite markedly in its form. In Scandinavia, elite households stood out, but appear more as a part of a flexible network of changing power relationships seen also in the metal wealth and burial mounds; in Hungary, a more common, corporate group identity was signalled by apparent uniformity of houses and material culture; and, in Sicily, the formal settlement structure suggests a clear elite stratum defined by multiroom structures and international material culture evidently marking differences (Chapters 3 and 5).

SOUTHERN SCANDINAVIA

Settlements and their organisation in southern Scandinavia during the Late Neolithic and Bronze Age were heavily dependent on the significance of the individual regions and their natural resources, though some general trends seem valid for the whole area (Artursson 2005a,b; 2009). Our two case studies in southern Scandinavia focus on regions in close proximity to the sea – Thy in northwestern Jutland, Denmark (Earle 2002) and Tanum in western Sweden (Ling 2008). The Thy region, at least during the Early Bronze Age, must be considered an important part of the networks in the central Limfjord region, but Tanum was more marginal.

To get a general picture of settlement structure in southern Scandinavia, we consider material from several central regions in addition to Thy and Tanum. A great effort has been made to improve the knowledge about settlements in southern Scandinavia, and an important part of these studies has been to identify variation in the settlement structure and organisation, both within and among microregions (Björhem and Säfvestad 1989; 1993; Tesch 1993; Gröhn 2004; Artursson 2005a,b; 2009). The existing model has, for a long time, been based on the presumed existence of a 'standard' longhouse and farmstead in combination with a simple model for how the farmsteads were positioned and organised in the landscape (Chapter 3). The prevailing model states that single farms were spread out more or less evenly in the different regions of southern Scandinavia, and that the most complex settlements might have been small clusters of two or three contemporary farmsteads. The level of cooperation among individual farmsteads traditionally has been considered to have been quite low.

A NEW MODEL – VARIATION IN TIME AND SPACE

New studies of the settlements from Scania and comparative studies of material from other parts of southern Scandinavia permit a revised model for settlement structure involving the longhouse and farmsteads during the Late Neolithic and Bronze Age. Instead of using the term standard longhouse or farmstead, we must look for variation in the material, both contemporary and over time. Based on a comparative study of several hundred longhouses in which ^{14}C-datings from the individual buildings played a crucial role for establishing a

Table 4.1. Changing longhouse sizes in southern Scandinavia during Late Neolithic I to Bronze Age period VI

Time period	Absolute date	Size of longhouses (length/width)	Roofed area	Ratio of size of longhouses (smallest/largest)
LN I	2350–1950 BC	9–30 m 6–8 m	70–250 m^2	1:3.57
LN II–BA IA	1950–1600 BC	9–47 m 7–9 m	70–350 m^2	1:5
BA IB–III	1600–1100 BC	10–60 m 7–10 m	75–450 m^2	1:6
BA IV–VI	1100–500 BC	10–35 m 6–9 m	70–280 m^2	1:4

LN = Late Neolithic; BA = Bronze Age.

typology and chronology for southern Scandinavia, we can show that variation exists in size of contemporary longhouses, in a range that changes over time (Artursson 2005a, 2009) (Table 4.1; see Chapter 5).

Based on old materials and studies of recently excavated settlements, greater differences in settlement structure and organisation also are apparent (Table 4.2). The range in difference (isolated to clustered farmsteads) seems to have been closely connected with the availability of important natural resources and the centrality to long-distance networks (Artursson 2005b, 2009; Artursson et al 2005; Artursson and Björk 2007). In richer and more central regions, variation in settlement structure was noticeable with everything from single farms to more or less complex hamlets, whereas the variation in more marginal areas was more moderate. Single farms were the basic unit, but small clusters or hamlets with two or three farmsteads also existed in the more central parts of these regions.

Table 4.2. General picture of the settlement structure and organisation in southern Scandinavia from Late Neolithic I to Bronze Age period VI

	LN I–BA I; 2350–1500 BC	BA II–BA III; 1500–1100 BC	BA IV–BA VI; 1100–500 BC
Single farm	x	x	x
Cluster of farms	x	x	x
Hamlet	x	x	x
Small village			x
Fortified settlement			x
Hillforts			x

LN = Late Neolithic; BA = Bronze Age.

New evidence for the development of the building tradition and the settlement structure is, in itself, enough to talk about the presence of a subtle settlement hierarchy and a stratified society in some central regions of southern Scandinavia already existing during the Late Neolithic. In combination with a reevaluation of the archaeological material from the graves and offerings in the area, a much better picture of daily life in this society emerges (Chapter 5). When all facts are reconsidered, already from the first half of the Late Neolithic, 2350 to 1950 BC, this society must be described as stratified, with its social foundation in small- and medium-sized chiefdoms based on some form of heritable social ranking and a warrior ideology (Artursson 2009; Artursson et al 2005; Artursson and Björk 2007).

By the first half of the Late Neolithic, settlement structure became more varied in size of the longhouses and farms, at least in certain central areas of Scandinavia (Tables 4.1, 4.2) (Artursson 2005b, 2009). This complexity in settlement structure can be traced back into the Middle Neolithic B (2800–2350 BC), when, for instance, we have a few examples from the island of Bornholm in the southern part of the Baltic Sea (Lekberg 2002; Artursson 2005b, 2009). Our interpretation of the material is that both single farms and hamlets existed by at least the beginning of the Late Neolithic. A good example of small hamlets that date to the first half of the Late Neolithic includes Bejsebakken from the Limfjord area (Figure 4.1; Sarauw 2006, 2007a; see also Jensen 1973; Apel 2001; Artursson 2000).

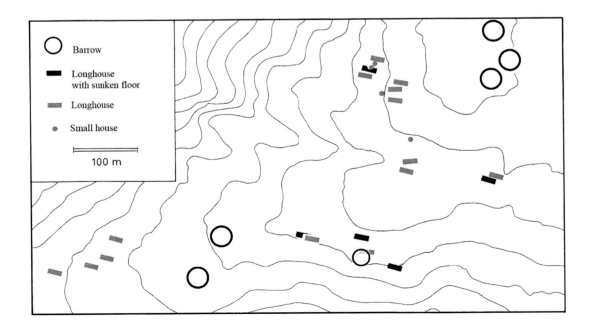

Figure 4.1. Settlement at Bejsebakken, northern Jutland, Denmark (after Sarauw 2006).

During the second half of the Late Neolithic and the Bronze Age period I, the range in size of longhouses increased to 1:5 (Table 4.1). Examples of larger and more complex hamlets also suggest a subtle settlement hierarchy in southern Scandinavia. Good examples of hamlets from the second half of the Late Neolithic and Bronze Age period I include Limensgård on Bornholm (Figure 4.2; Nielsen and Nielsen 1986; Artursson 2005b, 2009). Such aggregations of farms could be interpreted as "chiefly hamlets" (Kristiansen 2006). At Limensgård, three phases can be identified, each with a dominant farm. Inhabited from 2050 to 1700 BC, this hamlet consisted of one large farm and three medium-sized ones. The large farm remained in the same area of the settlement during the whole period, suggesting a continuity of power. At Almhov (Figure 4.3), at least five or six contemporary farms existed during the second half of the Late Neolithic and Bronze Age period I. One farm had a sequence of significantly larger longhouses during the whole time of the settlement. The farms at Almhov were placed in an oval circle with an open area in the middle (Artursson 2005b, 2009; Gidlöf, Hammarstrand Dehman, and Johansson 2006).

Then, during Bronze Age period IB–III, which had the maximum range in size of longhouses, with a ratio of 1:6, longhouse constructions shift from two-aisle to three-aisle, size of roofed area increased, and wealth included a range of metal objects, but especially weapons. Probably all these changes can be attributed to established contacts with northwestern and central Europe involving expanding trade in metal and other commodities. These changes appear to materialise the emergence of small- and medium-sized chiefdoms supported by warriors (Kristiansen 2006). The idealized identity of the warrior can

Figure 4.2. Settlement at Limensgård, Bornholm, Denmark: **a.** Phase 1, 2050 to 1950 BC, **b.** Phase 2, 1950 to 1850 BC, **c.** Phase 3, 1850 to 1700, BC (Artursson 2005b).

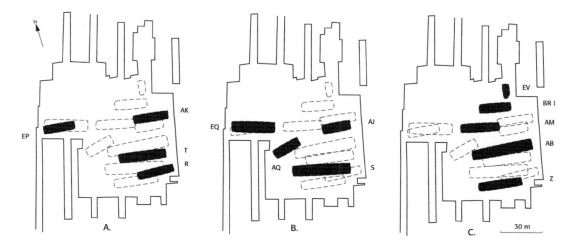

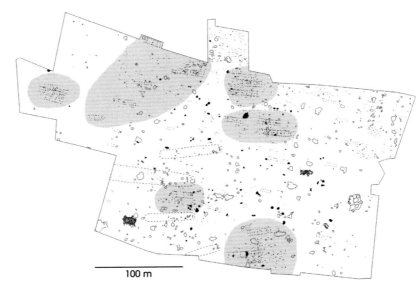

Figure 4.3.
Settlement at Almhov, Scania, southern Sweden (Artursson 2005b). The position for each Late Neolithic farmstead is marked with grey shading.

be seen in the equipment of the dead placed under huge barrows and cairns (Artursson et al 2005:502).

Several examples show the same complexity in settlement structure and organisation as during the earlier periods. At Højgård (Figure 4.4) in southern Jutland, for example, a small hamlet of three or four contemporary farms has been excavated (Ethelberg 2000; Artursson 2005b; 2009). There is no evidence of fortification during this period, but some of the largest farmsteads were placed high in the landscape, which, in itself, documents a defensive settlement (Artursson and Björk 2007:322).

From Bronze Age period III, the range in length of longhouses decreased to a ratio of 1:4. This moderation in difference also characterises the Late Bronze Age. A general decrease in longhouse size could imply that the political and social organisation had become less complex, but, according to our interpretation, this change can best be attributed to a restricted use of the longhouse as a marker of status and position. Other materials seem clearly to indicate a marked social hierarchy existed during this period in some central regions.

Evident examples of hamlets and even small villages become more and more common during the Middle and Late Bronze Age. From this time, densely populated settlements have been excavated in western Jutland, Denmark (Becker 1980, 1982) and in eastern

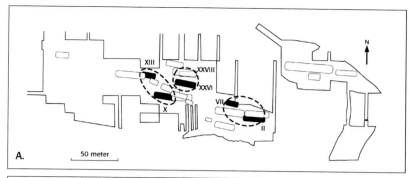
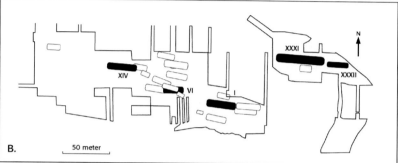
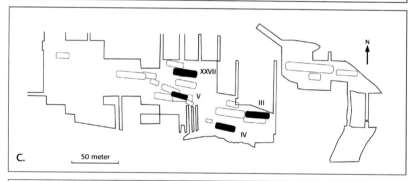
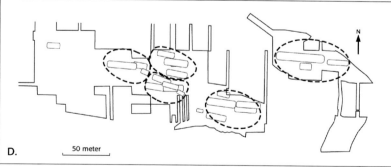

Figure 4.4.
Settlement at Højgård, southern Jutland, Denmark: **a.** Phase 1, 1700 to 1600 BC, **b.** Phase 2, 1600 to 1400 BC, **c.** Phase 3, 1300 to 1100, BC, **d.** Full extent of individual farmsteads (from Artursson 2005b).

middle Sweden as at Apalle (Figure 4.5; Ullén 2003; see also Borna-Ahlkvist 2002). During the Late Bronze Age, the character of the settlements in some areas became defensive. In eastern middle Sweden, for instance, fortified settlements and hillforts were built, and some show evidence of having been attacked and burnt (Olausson 1995). In the same area, examples of densely populated settlements with up to ten to fifteen contemporary farmsteads must be characterised as small villages (Ullén 2003). This agglomeration of people could be a response to a heightened aggression or a change in the nature of warfare.

As we have shown with this new model, the development of differences in longhouse sizes and in settlement structure that started in the Late Neolithic represent a gradual reorganisation of society. During the Late Neolithic I, social differentiation was established, with small, decentralised chiefdoms. These chiefdoms are gradually transformed into larger and more developed polities during the following time period, Late Neolithic II–Bronze Age period IA, documented, in part, by the establishment of chiefly farmsteads and hamlets. True chiefdoms with well-established hereditary transfer of power, but still with a decentralised structure based on chiefly networks, can be identified in several archaeological materials from Bronze Age periods IB to III. Large farmsteads and chiefly hamlets document relatively complex chiefdoms. During the Late Bronze Age, the general decrease in size of the longhouses could be interpreted as a less complex society, but the development of a more complex settlement structure and the continued investment in metal and large burial monuments in some central areas instead suggest a concentration of wealth and a centralisation of power to these parts of southern Scandinavia.

According to the new model, the change in centrality in the long-distance networks over time means that settlement structure and organisation changed substantially from one period to another. A central region during the Early Bronze Age, such as Thy in northwestern Jutland, was, in a couple of hundred years, transformed from a rich and wealthy region to a much more marginal position (Earle 2002). Also, changes in the local economies due to the establishment of too many farmsteads and the resulting ecological problems most likely impacted the organisation of settlements and society over time in many regions.

THE THY REGION IN NORTHERN JUTLAND, DENMARK

For southern Scandinavia, the Thy region possesses good farming soils and pasturage conditions that lay across an open and rolling landscape. Although marginal to the highest concentrations of Neolithic and Late Bronze Age populations in Scandinavia, Thy and the western Limfjord region witnessed a cultural fluorescence in the Early Bronze Age, associated with an abundance of barrow constructions and rich bronze finds (Randsborg 1974; Kristiansen 1978). We describe here the distribution of settlement structures across the Late Neolithic and Bronze Ages in Thy. Known settlements have increased rapidly during the past 20 years as a result of systematic rescue and research excavations directed by the Thisted Museum and the Thy Archaeological Project (Bech 2003; Earle 2002; Kristiansen 1998). Based on this new evidence, settlement structure appears to fit into the "classic" model of individual farmsteads and helps us understand some more details of this model (Chapter 3). Farms appear to be quite broadly distributed in an open cultural landscape (Andersen 1995, 1999), although they may cluster in some areas where promising soils or other favorable conditions attracted a more concentrated settlement (Table 4.3). A somewhat more complex social structure,

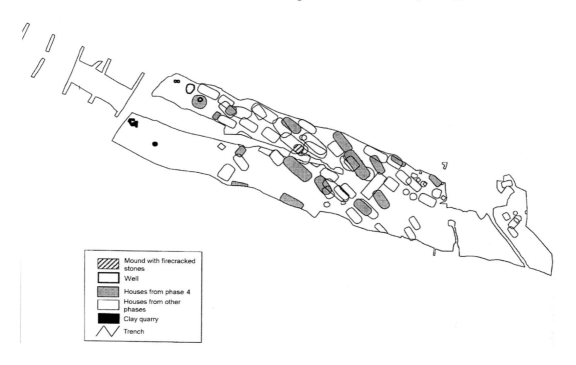

Figure 4.5. Settlement at Apalle, eastern middle Sweden, scale 1:2500; houses marked by grey shading are Phase 4 (after Ullén 2003).

Table 4.3. Settlement structure and organisation in Thy, northern Jutland, Denmark, from Late Neolithic I to Bronze Age period VI

	LN I–BA I; 2350–1500 BC	BA II–BA III; 1500–1100 BC	BA IV–BA VI; 1100–500 BC
Single farm	x	x	x
Cluster of farms	x	x	x
Hamlet			
Small village			

LN = Late Neolithic; BA = Bronze Age.

however, may have existed during the Early Bronze Age, when a few larger three-aisle houses were built, apparently for higher-status individuals.

The number of excavated houses is still quite limited dating to the Late Neolithic (2350–1700 BC). Only one house is radiocarbon dated to this period, with ten houses assigned to the Late Neolithic–Early Bronze Age period I based on construction form. The frequent and broad distribution of Late Neolithic flint daggers suggests that settlements were widely scattered farmsteads. The construction of more permanent houses starting in the Late Neolithic I suggests a new pattern of land tenure associated with established farmsteads scattered in the landscape and replacing each other, as continued in the subsequent Bronze Age (Earle 2004). Evidence for social differentiation is limited; a few houses were larger, and some burials contained particularly high-quality flint daggers and arrowheads (Sarauw 2007b).

During the Early Bronze Age (1700–1100 BC), especially by periods II and III, a rather fluid social hierarchy emerged in Thy. By period II, all houses in Thy were built according to a standard architectural form with a three-aisle structure. Were farmsteads ever clustered as discussed in the revised model presented earlier? Recent excavations at Bjerre and Ås document quite a high concentration of Bronze Age houses, most of which were probably not contemporaneous, but replaced each other in sequences of farmsteads. Figure 4.6 illustrates what the settlement at Bjerre Enge may have looked like at this time. Occasionally, paired residential units appear to have made up one farmstead. Two habitation units, each with separate cooking areas, have been identified in the opposite ends of some longhouses, and paired longhouses can sometimes lie with the same orientation only 25 m apart.

In contrast to several Danish Iron Age sites, for which direct evidence of a community structure includes the fences or ditch systems surrounding contemporary farms, no such conclusive evidence exists for Bronze Age settlement structure in Thy. The Bronze Age settlement at Bjerre Enge does provide a good example of an apparent concentration of perhaps two or three farmsteads within 1 km². Here, a former seabed with moist sandy sediments provided good pasture and easily arable soils that supported comparatively dense habitation through most of the Bronze Age (Bech 1997; Earle et al 1998; Bech and Mikkelsen 1999; Bech 2003). Density of sites indicates that at least in parts of the Bronze Age, the number of contemporary farms was higher than predicted by the standard model. Assuming that, across the Bronze Age a single farmstead could have had at least 33 sequential houses, locations with greater house densities may represent concentrated farms. Even if some close-lying farms in Thy may have been contemporary, however, their internal relations remains as yet unclear.

Evidence of social difference at Thy exists in contrasting size and impressiveness of a few large houses during the Early Bronze Age. The two largest houses, excavated at Legård, were 33 × 8 m (255 m² roofed area) and 34 × 8 m (268 m²). Although smaller than the chiefly halls of southern Jutland and southern Sweden, these large houses were still impressive (Chapter 8), similar in construction to the southern chiefly halls, despite the fact that, in Thy, the forest that could have provided the construction wood had long been cleared (Chapter 2). A few other structures in Thy were greater than 20 m long, but smaller than the Legård houses, and quite a large number of smaller longhouses probably held a less prominent group of farmers (Figure 4.6).

Was the Early Bronze Age society of Thy stratified? Bech and Olsen (in press) emphasize that the pattern suggests a prosperity range for farmers, with some being more successful than others. The two large houses at Legård were certainly distinctive and were evidently linked to the impressive houses of southern Jutland that belonged to a chiefly elite. Among the mid-sized houses, such as at

Figure 4.6. Reconstruction of farmhouse at Bjerre Enge, Thy, Denmark. Drawing by Bente Draiby.

Bjerre site 6, the addition of space may represent accrued status or simply an expansion to accommodate another family. Emphasis is on variations, but always within a common form, and the system was certainly not divided rigidly into class groupings. Independent farmers, warriors, and chieftains could rise or fall in status, a common characteristic of chieftaincies (Earle 1997). The Legård houses were unquestionably distinctive, however, more than first among equals. This variation in longhouse sizes is mirrored in barrow constructions. Some were distinctively great, standing above the others (Chapter 3). The size variation of barrows suggests a highly visible division of personal status that persisted across time in a monumentalized landscape that materialised inherited, hierarchical status. The social differences are clear, although they represent differences more in degree than in kind. The houses, farmsteads, and barrows were all quite similar, differing only in size and complexity, and the range of activities within the household economies were probably quite similar (Chapter 5).

During the Late Bronze Age (1100–500 BC), the finds from Thy show considerably less wealth, and the society appears to have become more egalitarian, although some form of social hierarchy may have continued, as it certainly did elsewhere. In comparison with the rest of Denmark in the Late Bronze Age, the documented metal finds from Thy dropped to among the lowest (Kristiansen 1978). Well-dated houses are limited, but the tendency is for decreased sizes. No exceptionally large houses have been found. Isolated farmsteads continue, and generally the structure of settlements appears to have changed little except for the loss of evidence for hierarchical distinction. The pattern of land ownership described for the Early Bronze Age may thus have continued unchanged, as evidenced by continuities in settlements and cemeteries structure. Although the structure remained, the economy no doubt failed to support differentiation in wealth and presumed power at the same level as before.

THE TANUM REGION IN NORTHERN BOHUSLÄN, SWEDEN

Tanum has an impressive array of rock-art, but, so far, lacks clear signs of a complex settlement structure or hierarchical organisation. Although perhaps only because of the lack of large excavations, the general impression is of a more egalitarian social system. One possible explanation for the lack of complex settlement structure could be

Table 4.4. Settlement structure and organisation in northern Bohuslän, Sweden, from Late Neolithic I to Bronze Age period VI

	LN I–BA I; 2350–1500 BC	BA II–BA III; 1500–1100 BC	BA IV–BA VI; 1100–500 BC
Single farm	x	x	x
Cluster of farms	?	x	x
Hamlet			?
Small village			

LN = Late Neolithic; BA = Bronze Age.

the relatively poor agricultural resources of the area (Chapter 2), but the importance of a specialised maritime economy should be considered carefully (Ling 2006, 2008). Offerings and stray finds from Tanum contain flint daggers and metal objects that must have been obtained from Thy and beyond. Tentatively, we suggest that Tanum provided maritime specialised personnel for the trading and raiding expeditions on which emergent complexity elsewhere relied, but in Tanum itself the population was less divided, as perhaps is understandable given what we know of maritime societies.

Information regarding Late Neolithic and Bronze Age settlements and household economies in northern Bohuslän is sparse so far, partially because of relatively limited excavations. However, the large number of rock-art panels, graves, and settlement finds, combined with pollen records and archaeobotanical evidence, indicate substantial activity in the region by the Bronze Age. The general knowledge of Late Neolithic, and especially the settlements and farmsteads from the time period, is almost nonexistent, but the Bronze Age settlements reveal a sparse but nonetheless quite complicated economic and social pattern. Judging from the materials recovered so far, a mixed economy based on fishing and farming seems to have been predominant during the Bronze Age.

Just a few Bronze Age settlements from northern Bohuslän have been excavated. They comprise more or less rectangular longhouses that date from 1200 to 500 BC. Their sizes range from between 13 to 24 m in length and 3 to 7 m in width (Streiffert 2005). The settlements that have yielded more comprehensive information are indicative of single farms or small clusters of farms rather than hamlets (Table 4.4). There is, however, a settlement from Uddevalla that may have been a hamlet (Lindman 1997), but its status is not as apparent as those excavated in Scania (Artursson 2005b, 2009).

The complexity of the farmsteads and the structure and organisation of the settlements excavated so far are relatively low. The single farms and small clusters of two or three farms of today suggest that the individual settlement held a population varying between six and thirty persons. The distribution of period-specific settlement indications, graves, rock-carvings, and stray finds in the Tanum area and, more generally, in the northern Bohuslän region, has revealed patterns or clusters of presumptive dwelling sites of different size and complexity from the Bronze Age (Ling 2008), which, with future systematic surveys and excavations, will increase the knowledge about the Bronze Age settlement pattern in the region.

THE BENTA VALLEY, HUNGARY

Detailed knowledge about Bronze Age settlement structure in Hungary is still quite limited, so a comparative study of settlement structure is necessarily preliminary. Although rescue work during the past 10 to 15 years provides large-scale excavations of open settlements, well-dated house remains are still rare and it is difficult to establish contemporaneity among structures on individual sites. Our phase II case study of the Benta valley is no exception, and its material gives us only a rough picture of the development in the area (Chapter 3). Here we compared briefly the Százhalombatta Archaeological Expedition, Százhalombatta, Hungary (SAX) results with excavations in the northern Hungarian Plain and Transdanubia, where large rescue projects have been carried out in connection with motorway constructions. We can conclude that, in contrast to Scandinavia, settlements tended to be larger and denser, and that this contrast probably represented a fairly sharp difference in social organisation. We describe excavations of individual settlements and then try to contextualise them within a regional context provided by the Benta valley project.

The settlements of the Hungarian Bronze Age are quite variable and clearly represent a hierarchy based on size. The largest sites, with greater than five hundred inhabitants, were an order of magnitude greater than the largest Bronze Age settlements in Scandinavia. Some settlements were small and open, probably composed of individual farms or hamlets of a few farms not unlike those in Scandinavia. Others were dense villages, sometimes of quite large size and fortified, and most people lived in these large settlements at least at certain times. The largest of these appear to have been central places.

Overall, the Hungarian settlements represent alternative ways to organise living spaces, as seen in differences in permanency, sizes, densities, and internal arrangements. We suggest a major division into fortified versus open settlements, and variation within each category according to the size and density of settlements, as follows:

I. Fortified settlements: tell settlement core (15 houses/90 persons per hectare); tell settlement edges (4–8 houses/24–48 persons per hectare); and smaller and less dense hillforts.
II. Open settlement: large village (4–15 houses/24–90 persons per hectare, up to 500 total); small village (4–8 houses/24–48 persons per hectare, about 100 total); hamlet (3–4 houses, about 20 total); and single farm (1 house/6 persons).

The distinctive settlements of Bronze Age Hungary were its fortified sites. The largest were tell settlements with densely packed houses typically placed in naturally well-defended positions, often strengthened by defensive works (Chropovsky and Herrmann 1982). The larger tell settlements are located along main waterways such as the Danube or Tisza Rivers (Bóna 1975; Kovács 1982; Vicze 2000; Sz. Máthé 1988), where they likely controlled communication and trade (Uhnér 2005). They have deeply stratified deposits that built up over considerable time, close to a thousand years in some situations. The organisation and complexity of these settlements are not well known, because excavated areas have been necessarily small (Kovács 1988). Settlement density presumably was quite high, based on the high artefact densities in deposits and on the incidence of houses identified by the excavations. Several tell settlements have evidence for more or less permanent house plots arranged around open areas or along streets and alleys, indicative of community continuity in ownership and organisation (Bóna 1992). No doubt, tell settlements represent central functions in hierarchically organised small- or medium-sized chiefdoms (Chapter 3).

The hillforts in the region are fortified defensive positions without substantial settlement constructions or deposits. They seem to complement the tell settlements' defensive functions at strategic places in the landscape, controlling important lines of communication. The numbers of houses and residents in the hillforts are hard to estimate as their inner structure and organisation are not well known, but one can presume that some kind of permanent warrior force was resident there to uphold their defensive function.

Table 4.5. Settlement structure and organisation in the Benta valley, Hungary, from the Early to Late Bronze Age

	Early Bronze Age 2800–2000 BC	Middle Bronze Age 2000–1500 BC	Late Bronze Age 1500–800 BC
Single farm	x	x	x
Cluster of farms	x	x	x
Hamlet	x	x	x
Small village	x	x	x
Village	x	x	x
Hillfort	x	x	x
Tell settlement	x	x	

The open settlements comprise everything from single farms to quite large villages with most people living in the larger settlements. This variation in size, density, and complexity is probably attributable to a difference in function and economic activities, closely connected with their position in the landscape (Chapter 3). Some were unexpectedly large and dense, with estimated populations equivalent to tell settlements, whereas others were small artefact concentrations of 0.25 or 0.5 ha that could well indicate a single farm or two. The relationship between fortified and open settlements is largely unknown, but doubtless they must have been parts of larger, regional settlement systems in which their individual functions were imbedded within a regional economic and political organisation (Chapter 3; Uhnér 2005). The relatively limited settlement space that Bronze Age tells occupy makes it most likely that basic economic activities such as agriculture and animal breeding were concentrated in the open settlements and that surplus from these farmers was mobilised by the tells (Chapter 3).

Early Bronze Age (2800–2000 BC)

The Early Bronze Age cultures of central Hungary (Chapter 1) show an emergent settlement hierarchy, later dominated by tell settlements. Two major cultural traditions are the Makó and Nagyrév. The Makó culture was in the earlier phase of the Early Bronze Age, characterised by small and briefly used settlements and cemeteries. The size of settlements is generally small, presumably a few households scattered over a relatively large area, indicating a cluster of farms rather than a village. Although limited spatially, a Bell Beaker tradition is also found in the Budapest-Csepel area, closely related to the Makó and early Nagyrév culture and connected to the Bohemian-Moravian Bell Beaker tradition. The Nagyrév culture is then a more mature phase of the Bronze Age and a direct predecessor of the Middle Bronze Age tell cultures. A rough understanding of changing settlement structure is beginning to emerge from settlement excavations and these results can be given some regional context with SAX research.

Contrasting patterns in the Early Bronze Age can be summarised according to the main cultural traditions. For the Makó culture, settlements appear to have been quite ephemeral. Their network of small settlements can be found on the fertile banks of both larger and smaller rivers and are characterised by dispersed, small farmsteads represented by scattered pits and ditches that suggest small, one-phase settlements. Containing only a limited amount of archaeological material (i.e., modest amounts of ceramics and disposed bone material), some of these, however, have produced clear evidence of bronze working (Kővári and Patay 2005). No house has been found so far, indicating structures that archaeologically do not leave clear traces (Szalontai and Tóth 2003).

The Bell Beaker groups located on the Danube and its tributaries seem to have had an economy based on both agriculture and animal husbandry, including especially horse breeding probably involving trade with local Makó and early Nagyrév settlements (Kalicz-Schreiber and Kalicz 2001:441ff). The Bell Beaker settlements were single farms and hamlets spread out along the shores of the Danube and its tributaries. Some Bell Beaker settlements were larger than others, and these differences may represent contrasting placement within regional geopolitics. Settlement sites contain boat-shaped houses and some pits. The number of houses on the excavated sites range from one to thirteen, with many pits differing in size and apparent function. Displaying a strict regularity, the form, structure, and size of houses, as well as the types of pits, are the same across sites. Each household appears to have had its own special working area, with each house also providing evidence for the cohabitation of humans and animals (Endrődi 2007). The sites are directly associated with good arable and grazing land. No defences or other demarcating feature has been observed.

In contrast, the Nagyrév settlements were more substantial and permanent, including both fortified tells and open settlements. The tell settlements of the Nagyrév culture were typically placed in naturally well-defended positions along the Danube and its tributaries, and their defences were often reinforced with ditches. Knowledge of the organisational structure of settlements is limited, but small excavations show quite dense structural arrangements of houses (Poroszlai 2000). The size of houses varies from smaller ones of 4 to 5 m width and 5 to 6 m length, to larger ones of 5 to 6 m width and 10 to 11 m length. The distance between houses varies between 1 and 5 m and built-up areas remained constant throughout the life-span of the tell (Bóna 1992; Poroszlai 2000b; Vicze 1992). From the very beginning, these sites can be safely identified as proto-urban, where individual household units have clearly defined areas at their disposal. The constant self-imposed limitations in the settlements suggest a strong descent-based community. Consistency in the built environment created a degree of familiarity, which ultimately leads to identity, where tells can become 'the physical and social expressions of continuity' (Chapman 1991:93) and communality. The open settlements of the Nagyrév culture are often situated close to streams or rivers, usually on a low hill or smaller undulation. In most places, the open settlements consist of a few pits and postholes. Some of the pits were used for clay mining, and the clay could have served for pottery or for wattle-and-daub construction, although house remains are few (Simon 2006).

This overview can be given more detail by drawing on the research in the Benta valley and its associated uplands, where Nagyrév cultural traditions dominated, but some Bell Beaker features are known. SAX focused its research on the Százhalombatta-Földvár tell (27/2), where previous excavations had recognized a long-term Bronze Age tell settlement (Poroszlai 2000). These earlier excavations document a substantial Early Bronze Age settlement built on a naturally defensible ridge above the Danube. Size was apparently about 2 ha, with nearly 200 persons, although erosion of the river cliff and clay mining associated with a brick factory make our estimate conservative (Vicze 2005). Low-density scatters of Early Bronze Age ceramics were recovered adjacent to the main tell, but test excavations did not document a major occupation. On the tell, earlier excavations had identified a few houses placed in a dense and regular pattern along streets, alleys, and open areas (Poroszlai 2000). Although the excavated area was small, it appears to represent a central part of a dense, proto-urban settlement structure. An enclosing ditch may have fortified the central tell.

Elsewhere in the Benta valley, four additional sites have been documented with Early Bronze Age ceramic finds with densities suggesting residential populations. The primary settlement was Sóskút 26/4 that sets on an undulating plain above the Benta River. It had an area of 4.75 ha with substantial amounts of Early Bronze Age ceramics, suggesting a sizeable residential population of perhaps three hundred, somewhat larger than the Százhalombatta-Földvár tell. The location is nondefensive except for a steep, natural embankment cut by the stream.[1] The settlement had a single, concentrated core of 2.25 ha with high- or very-high-density remains, suggesting a proto-urban settlement structure not unlike a tell. The cultural layer, up to 1 m, suggests a long-term occupation. Three additional Early Bronze Age settlement sites included a low-density, spotty distribution of ceramics of the period, suggesting an isolated farmstead at Érd 9/4, a dispersed hamlet at the Tárnok site 31/1, and another farmstead at what would become the hillfort site of Bia 1/26. At Érd 9/4, rescue excavations for road construction found one boat-shaped longhouse, typical of Bell Beaker style and similar to houses excavated at other sites along the Danube.

In comparison to the Nagyrév culture that contain tells, most settlements from elsewhere in Transdanubia were fairly small and less permanent. They range from single farms to hamlets and small villages. Some of these were fortified. The ditches are quite substantial, usually 5 m wide and 2 to 2.5 m deep (Honti 1996). The fortification ditches encircled the settlements in an oval shape, interrupted by narrow passes and gates. Other ditches can also be found inside the settlements.

During the Early Bronze Age, settlements through Hungary were fairly small and quite variable, according to cultural tradition and the associated economic base. At least some appear to have grown into dense, internally structured, and often fortified central places, but the regions of their domination would have been quite small. In the Benta valley, some settlement hierarchy had apparently emerged, with two settlements of dense population dominating small settlement regions with smaller, probably dependent settlements (Chapter 3). This trend sets up the pattern that peaked in the subsequent period.

Middle Bronze Age (2000–1500 BC)

During the Middle Bronze Age, societies who lived in dense and long-occupied tells spread over the central and eastern parts of present-day Hungary. The regions along the middle Danube, where the Benta valley is situated, and eastward towards the Tisza were occupied by people of the Vatya culture, which developed from the preceding Nagyrév culture (Bóna 1975:31; 1992:24; Kovács 1982:279; Vicze 2000:119). Communities were organised around central-place tells surrounded by open settlements (Chapter 3). Many of these tells were placed in naturally well-defended positions and fortified by ditches and ramparts of varying size and complexity.

The Middle Bronze Age settlements in the northern part of central Hungary are relatively well known, and its diagnostic settlement form is the tell. A developing centralisation among settlements can be detected, which indicates a clearer specialisation and stratification within the society. This settlement hierarchy seems to have been influenced by strategic locations and socio-spatial strategies. Tells occupied by the Vatya culture show more persistent inner layouts. Houses tend to be rebuilt more or less on top of previous ones, implying an increasingly planned and controlled spatial organisation (Vicze 1992, 2000). The repetition of individual domestic units leads to a concept of permanent home and ancestry. Strong senses of identity and communality, with a clear increase in population, led to a degree of socio-political evolution that is reflected in the greater variety of settlement layouts specific to this area of the Carpathian Basin (Kovács 1982; Vicze 2000). The basic construction and size of houses do not change. Some houses have a single room measuring 5×8 m; others have two or more rooms in total length 10 to 12 m, but with width remaining the same or increasing to 6 to 9 m. Interhouse spacing ranged between 0.6 and 4 m, somewhat less than previously, and with clear concentrations of houses and well-defined, small open spaces (Chapter 5).

Continuing earlier local tradition, social groups of central Hungary also possessed dispersed farmsteads, hamlets, and mainly small villages, indicated archaeologically by clusters of pits found along the main waterways, usually on the sandy-loess dunes. It is generally believed that large open settlements are missing from the archaeological record, indicating that a large portion of the population lived on tells, the centres of social and economic interaction through long-term community participation. Politically, tells might have functioned as parent communities to the dispersed farmsteads, hamlets, and small villages. With centralisation, the number of open settlements in general became fewer, probably an indication of a movement of population into tells, although the fact that most excavations have focused on this type of settlement may bias conclusions. Research on open

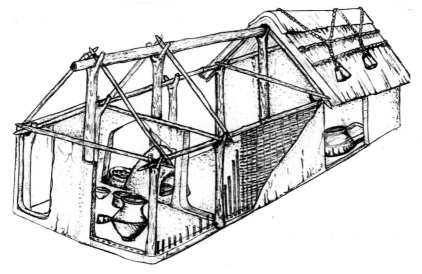

Figure 4.7.
Reconstruction of tell-house Százhalombatta-Földvár.

settlements is limited, with rescue excavations usually documenting only typical features, such as pits.

In the Benta valley and its uplands, research gives a reasonably good picture of the Vatya culture and its settlement structure, which developed directly out of Nagyrév antecedents. Importantly, results of our work appear to contradict, in terms of the importance of open settlements, the pattern just described. A dominant settlement of this period was indeed the tell, Százhalombatta-Földvár (27/2), first occupied in the Early Bronze Age and now grown in size to about 5.5 ha. SAX excavations here have exposed a 20 × 20 m area in the high, central core of the site, and documented in detail the house arrangements of the Vatya occupation (Chapter 5). Systematic coring of the site has dated to the Middle Bronze Age the defensive ditches that enclosed the central tell (Varga 2000). The fortified section was probably 2.5 ha in area and densely occupied. Based on the distribution of Middle Bronze Age ceramics, occupation had spread north across another 3.0 ha of land that was eventually to become enclosed by a major Iron Age rampart. The topography was defensive, located on a natural rise edged by the eroded bank of the Danube. Ceramic densities outside the core were low to medium, suggesting scattered houses. Although conclusions are preliminary, the central settlement appears to have had a dense and structured core arrangement of houses, surrounded by a secondary, less dense edge. Overall population was probably on the order of about fifty contemporaneous household units or three hundred occupants. Figure 4.7

illustrates a proposed reconstruction of what a house at the tell settlement of Százhalombatta-Földvár might have looked like in the Vatya period.

Elsewhere in the Benta valley, twelve additional Vatya residential settlements have been defined by ceramic distributions in the plough soil. These included both fortified and open sites distributed through the valley. Four fortified settlements appear to represent a spectrum in size and occupation density, suggesting a settlement hierarchy. Located on the Danube's cliff face north of the Benta's mouth was the main tell (27/2), dominant in size. Two second-order fortified tells were positioned on the periphery of the valley polity. A small tell (27/14), half the size of the main tell, was located above the Danube, flanking the Benta's floodplain to the south. It occupied 2 ha, much of it with very high-density ceramic finds suggestive of a proto-urban settlement. With an estimated twenty-four contemporaneous households, it would have had roughly 150 inhabitants. Then, the fairly large Bia hillfort (1/26) was located on a prominent hill above the lake at the top of the valley. As seen in aerial photographs, a double ditch complex enclosed the site, which contained a total residential area of 2.5 ha, much of it densely settled (Vicze et al 2005; figure 1). Size is estimated at seventeen houses with about one hundred inhabitants. The cultural layer (about 0.5 m) was shallower than typical for a tell. The fourth fortified settlement was the small Sóskút hillfort (26/11) high on a limestone ridge at mid-valley. This hillfort contained 1 ha of lower-density, shallow deposits, and we estimated it to have had nine houses with fifty-four inhabitants.

The importance of fortified settlements should not be overemphasised. In contrast to the conventional synthesis, much of the Middle Bronze Age population in the Benta appears to have lived in unfortified, open settlements, generally of lower density finds, but occasionally of considerable size. Based on plough soil investigations, nine nonfortified sites with Middle Bronze Age finds have been identified through the Benta valley. They ranged in size from the large Tárnok settlement to a scattering of smaller villages, hamlets, and isolated farms. Variable sizes suggest a settlement hierarchy, dominated by a single large village, mirroring the fortified settlement hierarchy. The Tárnok settlement (31/1) was dominant in size (12.75 ha), more than four times the size of the next largest open settlement. It was spread along the lower slope of a gradual slope above what was originally a small tributary of the Benta. Most of the site area (87 percent) had low to moderate densities of Middle Bronze Age ceramics, but a few locations had high or very high densities. Overall, the site was probably a broad scattering of houses with some dense concentrations. We estimate a total of ninety-one houses across this site that would have been a large village (five-hundred-plus inhabitants), actually larger than the central tell.

Second in the settlement hierarchy were five small villages of 2 to 3 ha (9/3, 2 ha; 9/4, 2.75 ha; 26/7, 3 ha; 26/4, 2.5 ha; 1/4, 3 ha) that, together, had a settlement area less than the dominant Tárnok settlement. These small villages were spread along the Benta and near productive loess soils for agriculture and animal herding. Most areas of these settlements (94 percent) had low to moderate density of Middle Bronze Age ceramics with only a few spots of high or very high densities. These settlements had fifteen to twenty houses each. Rescue excavations at 9/4 documented a scattering of Middle Bronze Age pits that probably were dug for clay and later filled with refuse. Because rescue procedures typically machine down to subsoil, the cultural layer (0.5–1 m) described by our test excavations may have contained preserved houses, and future rescue work on open Vatya settlements should consider alternative methods for research. Quite surprisingly, in the Middle Bronze Age refuse pits were the butchered remains of women and children, undoubtedly the victims of a massacre. Three additional small sites with less than 1 ha each (27/1, 0.75 ha; 31/3, 0.5 ha; 1/6, 0.25 ha) were defined in survey. These sites probably would have represented single farms or small hamlets scattered across more isolated pockets of good soils; the overall settlement area for these small sites was only 1.5 ha, a small fraction of the open settlement. Was the Benta pattern of open settlements exceptional for the Vatya culture? Other microregional studies are needed to assess the variation.

In Transdanubia, the period is represented by the Encrusted Ware culture. The settlements of this culture consist of hamlets and small villages (Honti 1996), often continuous with Kisapostag settlements. As in the earlier settlements, there is no clear evidence of houses or any other structures built on the surface, but this could be attributed to a different kind of architecture constituted by wooden buildings without dug-down features. The lack of buildings makes it hard to discuss the organisation and density of these settlements, but overall settlements appear to have been smaller and less dense than described for the Vatya settlements in the Benta valley and elsewhere,

where tells and other large settlements dominated the settlement pattern. However, a recently found large village, measuring more than 1 ha (Somogyi 2000, 2004), together with the already known large cemeteries of more than a hundred burials, imply a more complex social organisation than previously was envisaged.

Late Bronze Age (1500–800 BC)

Signalling the beginning of the Late Bronze Age, the appearance of the so-called Tumulus culture in Hungary brought on a significant change in settlement structure. From this point through the following Urnfield period, the settlement systems of the Carpathian Basin display a fairly uniform pattern. Settlements seem to get denser. The division between fortified and open settlements continued, but the proto-urban tell settlements were either abandoned or transformed into more dispersed settlements. Different types of houses can be found in the settlements, although the most common features recognized in rescue excavations are still scattered pits. Various ditch and rampart structures surround some sites and divide them internally. The function of these ditches may primarily be defence, but the internal partition of space may mark social divisions. On most settlements, the number of features and pit fill show long-term use.

In the Tumulus culture, a further separation is evident based on the size and organisation of settlements. They range from single farms to hamlets and small villages. The houses have different sizes and shapes, and smaller buildings with specialised functions may exist in some farmsteads (Horváth 1998). Dated by ceramics to the first half of the Late Bronze Age, the settlement at Dunakeszi, just north of Budapest, provides a good illustration of a small village (Horváth et al 2003). The settlement plan shows clusters of different building styles. Although sometimes interpreted as representing multifunctional buildings of contemporary farmsteads, based on comparison with southern Scandinavia we might consider that each cluster represented phases of rebuilding for a single farmstead. Regrettably, the chronological–typological model for houses from Bronze Age Hungary is not well established, and extensive use of radiometric dating of the individual buildings is needed.

Inside the excavated area at Dunakeszi, we believe there were 4 or 5 multiphased farmsteads within about 1 ha (Figure 4.8). Every

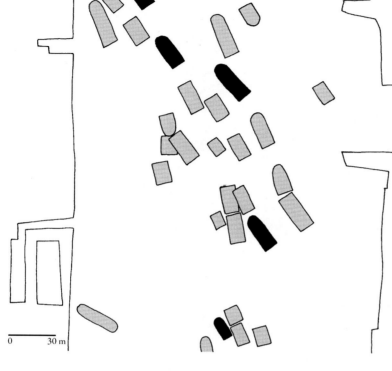

Figure 4.8.
Late Bronze Age settlement at Dunakeszi, north of Budapest, Hungary. Earlier phase houses are marked in black.

farmstead is represented by four or five houses, sometimes complemented by smaller buildings. All the buildings are orientated almost in the same direction, and the limited variation in spatial orientation, combined with the variation in the construction of the individual building, can be used to make a division into phases based on the chronological–typological model for houses in middle and northern Europe (Artursson 2005a). According to our proposed model, the different types of houses replace each other and the structure of the farmsteads changes over time. In the first two or three phases, the individual farmstead is represented by one two-aisled house. After that, the houses were replaced by a three-aisled type and, in some of the farmsteads, the house is complemented with a smaller building, probably used for storage and other specialised tasks. Although dating is not well established, a fence or palisade may have enclosed the settlement.

The next Late Bronze Age phase, the so-called Urnfield period, witnessed an overwhelming growth in the number of sites, a pattern that occurs uniformly in the entire Carpathian Basin (Kemenczei 1994a; V. Szabó 2003). The houses on open sites have an overall uniform size, shape, and construction. Their ground plan almost always is square and sunk into the subsoil. Their size varies between 4 × 4 m and 5.5 × 5 or 6 m, with two posts holding the roof structure. Recent rescue excavations, however, indicate that house remains may have been more variable in size and building techniques (Simon 2006; Domboróczki 2004). The most characteristic features of settlements are the large number, variation, and size of pits dominating the archaeological remains. Settlements vary from hamlets consisting of a few households to large, open or encircled villages to true hillforts. Substantial fortifications in unprecedented numbers and size were built at strategic high points all over the Carpathian Basin. This was a time when metallurgy was practiced on an equally unprecedented scale at larger sites, leading to the emergence of major production centres. With respect to richness, quality, and quantity, their products, both in ceramic and bronze, were never met before (Kemenczei 1994b, 2003). Networks of trade traversed all areas of Europe, preparing conditions for the development of the following complexity of the Early Iron Age.

In the Benta, research gives an intriguing picture of the settlement system of the Urnfield period of the Late Bronze Age. No Tumulus culture settlement was found. Despite unresolved chronological problems, perhaps resulting from little systematic radiocarbon dating, the overall picture of settlement continuity is quite striking. As discussed in Chapter 3, 85 percent of all Middle Bronze Age settlements were occupied in this phase of the Late Bronze Age. Although it has been broadly argued that tells were abandoned and that a gap exists prior to their reoccupation as hillforts, the possibility of continuous occupation should be considered. The dominant settlement of the Urnfield period was Százhalombatta-Földvár (27/2). It now occupied about 7.75 ha. SAX excavations documented many Late Bronze Age pits, but preserved houses were not recognized, perhaps because of later disturbance, but also because of the new wood-frame construction. Based on the density of remains, housing probably stood through the site area. Based on the distribution of Late Bronze Age ceramics, occupation spread to fill the area within the rampart and to include an additional hectare immediately outside the rampart. Ceramic density and associated household density across the site appears to have become substantially less. Now, 92 percent of the area shows low- or moderate-density ceramic remains, much lower than for the Middle Bronze Age occupation on the tell and equivalent to most open settlements. Although conclusions are preliminary and based on comparative artefact densities, this central settlement appears now to have had a density of perhaps four to eight structures per hectare. Overall population was on the order of about fifty-one contemporaneous household units with an estimated 306 inhabitants.

Elsewhere in the Benta valley, twelve additional Late Bronze Age settlements have been defined by ceramic distributions in the plough soil. These included both fortified and open sites. Among the fortified settlements, a settlement hierarchy is clear, now strongly dominated by the main tell. The secondary tell, located to the south of the valley's mouth, was abandoned, although the two smaller fortified settlements continued to be occupied. The Bia hillfort (1/26) habitation area decreased to 1.5 ha, with low-density ceramic remains. We estimate a scattered distribution of perhaps six households or thirty-six inhabitants. The Shóskút hillfort (26/11) now had an area reduced to 0.5 ha with low- and medium-density remains; we estimate that it held only three houses with perhaps eighteen inhabitants. Overall, population within the fortified sites was less dense and markedly concentrated at the central fort on the Danube.

As was the case in the previous period, much of the Late Bronze Age population lived in unfortified open settlements. Nine nonfortified sites have been recognized, and they continued to be distributed widely through the Benta valley. Overall, the range in settlement sizes appears to have been reduced, although it continues to suggest a settlement hierarchy. The Tárnok settlement (31/1) continued to dominate in size (7.75 ha), but it contracted in area and now was only twice the size of the next largest open settlement. All the site area had low to moderate densities of Late Bronze Age ceramics, without the evident concentrations of the previous period. Overall, the sites probably consisted of scatterings of houses with perhaps thirty-five houses and 210 inhabitants, a mid-sized village. Of about half the size each were five settlements (9/3, 2.0 ha; 9/4, 2.5 ha; 26/7, 3.75 ha; 26/4, 2.0 ha; 1/4, 2.25 ha). Occupation overlapped the earlier Vatya settlements on these sites, but they were typically somewhat smaller and lower in density. Most areas of these settlements (86 percent) had low to moderate density of Late Bronze Age ceramics with a few spots of high densities. These settlements were evidently small villages, with an estimate range in sizes from twelve to eighteen houses or 72 to 108 inhabitants. Rescue excavations at 9/4 documented a scattering of post-built houses that presumably date to this period. These results fit the expected picture for a small village of scattered houses. Four smaller (<1 ha of habitation) settlements (27/1, 0.5 ha; 31/3, 0.5 ha; 26/1, 0.25 ha; 1/25, 0.25 ha) had a combined area of 1.5 ha. With low or medium ceramic densities, these sites would have been single farms or small hamlets. Overall, the proportion of small settlements appears to have increased significantly during this period.

A number of trends appear in our analysis of the Benta valley evidence. Parallel hierarchies of fortified and open settlements were established in the Early Bronze Age, representing what appear to have been two small polities. In the Middle Bronze Age and through the Late Bronze Age, the valley was apparently united into a single polity with overlapping hierarchies of fortified and open settlements. Overall, settlement sizes increased substantially in the Middle Bronze Age, but seem to have hit some organisational limit, perhaps based on sustainable subsistence productivity (Chapter 2). The dense proto-urban, tell-settlement structure was established with the Nagyrév culture of the Early Bronze Age, when it structured the largest settlements, both fortified and open. A lower-density settlement structure of farm clusters (hamlets and villages) continued through the Bronze Age, and even came to characterise later fortified settlements. One of the clearest contrasts is between the Middle Bronze Age, with 15 percent high or very high ceramic densities, versus the Late Bronze Age, with only 8 percent high density and none very high. Through time, settlements appear to have become more dispersed, with a progressive loss of the dense household packing that characterised the proto-urban tell settlements. This shift was not an outcome of fortification or warfare as much as an apparent change in social structure.

SALEMI, SICILY

The knowledge concerning the settlement structure in Sicily during the Bronze and Iron Age is patchy, especially in the western part of the island, where our case study is located. The majority of known and excavated Bronze Age settlements are situated in the southeastern part of Sicily (Malone et al 1994:169ff), whereas just a few large

Table 4.6. Settlement structure and organisation in Sicily, Italy, from the Early Bronze Age to the Early Iron Age

	Early Bronze Age 2500–1500 BC	Middle Bronze Age 1500–1200 BC	Late and final Bronze Age 1200–900 BC	Early Iron Age 900–700 BC
Single farm	?	?	?	?
Clusters of farms	x	x	x	x
Hamlet	x	x	x	x
Small village	x	x	x	x
Village	x	x	x	x
Proto-urban center	?	x	x	x
Urban center		?	x	x

excavations have been conducted in the western area. This makes it difficult to give a general picture of the development in Sicily. The patterns described subsequently refer primarily to the results from excavations in the western region (Table 4.6).

In the Early Bronze Age (2500–1500 BC) in western Sicily, the general pattern shows increasing settlement numbers, their relative political complexity, and trade connections as portions of both Bell Beaker–influenced networks extended to the west and Aegean–Anatolian networks to the east involved trade in metals and other high-status goods. Although excavated areas are usually too small to discuss structure, settlements away from the coast appear to be small, probably single farms, hamlets, or, at most, small villages. No settlement has been documented from the Salemi region. On the coast and a little inland, however, larger villages are known, some apparently with what may have been a proto-urban layout. Then, during the Middle Bronze Age (1500–1200 BC), a significant transformation in social and economic organisation is seen in eastern Sicily as some proto-urban and urban-like centres were established on the coast with long-distance maritime trade links with the Mycenaean palace economies. In western Sicily, however, sites are less common, and most are caves or small, open-air sites. Settlements are still not recorded for this period in the Salemi region.

During the Late Bronze Age and Early Iron Age (1200–700 BC), settlements begin to be seen in our region associated with major social and economic transformations that characterised other indigenous Sicilian settlements. Sicily assumed a more prominent role as a bridge between the emerging trade states of the eastern Mediterranean and western indigenous populations, probably involving, at the beginning, the export of animal products (Chapter 6). Studies of more complex polities in western Sicily during this time have focused on Greek and Phoenician colonisation, especially along the coast, and we have studied the subsequent proto-urban, indigenous settlements inland (Kolb and Tusa 2001). These settlements may well have focused on animal husbandry and, increasingly, staple grain production for the new colonies that provided exotic luxury items in return.

Placed high on naturally fortified hilltop ridges was Mokarta (1300–900 BC), one of the best examples of an excavated Late Bronze Age site in the interior of western Sicily. It consists of four small village-sized clusters of houses. One of these clusters has been excavated (Figure 4.9), and three other nearby settlements have been located by field surveys (Cooney and Kolb 2007; Kolb 2007). Within the excavated 1 ha village were ten irregularly arranged, circular buildings, which were apparently contemporaneous. Overall, the settlement cluster was 6.5 ha with an estimated sixty-five household units. Thus, each small village probably contained one hundred or more residences with a total cluster size of perhaps 650. Two cemeteries are set into the cliffs below the hamlets, a typical pattern for cemeteries during this time (Leighton 1999:98). The location of the

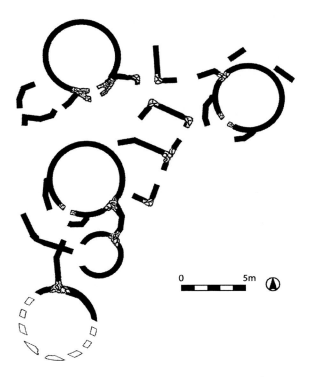

Figure 4.9.
Excavated structures at Mokarta, western Sicily (Cooney and Kolb 2007).

Figure 4.10.
Reconstruction of the merchant's house at Monte Polizzo.

settlement cluster appears isolated, controlling a large and productive territory and situated along the main lines of communication with the coast. A secondary pair of small village settlements was located at some distance.

Mokarta's settlement structure was firmly tied to Bronze Age Sicilian settlement elements. Traditional circular stone huts constituted the basic form of this relatively large settlement grouping. Additionally, innovative features include quadrangular stone structures (perhaps for animals) and multiple huts tied together to create multiroom buildings. Some of the stylistic elements of these constructions, such as a "herringbone" pattern for laying stones, may reference Aegean building traditions. Around 950 BC, the settlement was catastrophically destroyed. In all excavated structures, clear evidence existed of destruction and quick abandonment. Thanks to this destruction, traditional household activities such as cooking, milling, food storage, weaving, and so on are well documented in the circular buildings that were used for everyday life (Chapter 7).

In the Iron Age, the settlement pattern shifted dramatically to several fairly large proto-urban settlements. Primary documentation comes from our intensive, but fairly small-scale, excavations at Monte Polizzo that focused on a single house (Chapter 5). The site was first settled in the terminal phase of Mokarta and grew to perhaps 15 ha or more by its primary occupation during 575 to 475 BC, a time contemporaneous with coastal Greek colonies. At the end of this period, the settlement was abandoned suddenly.

Monte Polizzo has been mapped and partially sampled, but much of its settlement structure remains unclear. Settlement was evidently dense, as can be seen by the substantial architectural debris and dense spread of cultural material on the surface. Housing apparently spread out in a somewhat patchy fashion across the irregular hilltop that consisted of several lobes created by erosion. The settlement structure thus fits into that irregular topography, organised into at least three precincts, each laid out with its independent structure (Morris et al 2002; Cooney and Kolb 2007). These precincts undoubtedly were areas of intense interaction and some common activities within separate neighborhoods, and we believe that some level of social differentiation and craft specialisation was highly likely. House 1, for example, was probably an elite house with materials showing association with foreign cultural patterns of consumption. Other households were probably substantially less international. Apparently the houses were often of multiple rooms and perhaps multiple families (Chapter 5); they were laid out along what was probably an irregular network of streets. Public spaces undoubtedly existed in all precincts, including areas for common ceremonies, work, and refuse disposal. A central ceremonial acropolis was surrounded by dispersed houses or house clusters, without an apparent standardized urban geometry (c.f. Leighton 2000:29). Monte Polizzo was a large primate, proto-urban center around which most of the other sites of the region served auxiliary or logistical roles. Figure 4.10 illustrates what the settlement may have looked like in its heyday.

On the nearby hilltop of Salemi was a second major Iron Age settlement (Kolb et al 2007). Its earliest occupation overlapped with Monte Polizzo, but, after Monte Polizzo was abandoned, it grew to 4 ha during the fourth century BC and became predominant in the area. The distribution of architectural and artefact debris suggests a dense, urban settlement with perhaps twenty houses or two hundred people per hectare. Its size would thus have been about eight hundred people, probably organised as a dense settlement interconnected by a network of streets and public spaces, as described for Monte Polizzo. The artefactual assemblage included Greek imitation ceramics, Punic coins, tile, loom weights, and metal fragments, suggesting a prosperous settlement incorporated into a broader political orbit, perhaps as an independent center allied within a confederation of indigenous central places or as a conquered local population within a Punic or Greek territory.

COMPARATIVE ANALYSIS OF THE CASES

Emerging in the three areas of Europe that we studied, the political economies show a general gradient from south to north in terms of complexity based on the control of agricultural labour and staple production (Chapter 3). A similar gradient can be seen in the size and structure of settlements (Table 4.7). In southern Scandinavia, the range of settlement types is fairly small. In Thy and Tanum, single farms or small clusters consisting of two or three farms dominated the picture. In some regions of southern Scandinavia, however, the range of settlement types is wider. Already by the first half of the Late Neolithic, hamlets of four or more farms constitute the largest settlement type, and the size range of longhouses in these central regions is also quite large. This leads us to conclude that, by the beginning of the Late Neolithic, a modest settlement hierarchy was

Table 4.7. Comparison of the settlement structure and organisation from three regions in Europe

	Single farm	Cluster of farms	Hamlet	Small village	Village	Hillfort	Tell	Proto-urban centre	Urban centre
Tanum									
LN I–BAI	x	?							
BA II–III	x	x							
BA IV–VI	x	x							
Thy									
LN I–BAI	x	x	?						
BA II–III	x	x							
BA IV–VI	x	x							
Southern Scandinavia									
LN I–BAI	x	x	x	x		x			
BA II–III	x	x	x						
BA IV–VI	x	x	x						
Hungary									
Early BA	x	x	x	x	x	x	x		
Middle BA	x	x	x	x	x	x	x		
Late BA	x	x	x	x	x	x			
Sicily									
Early BA	?	x	x	x	x	?		?	x
Middle BA	?	x	x	x	x	?		x	x
Late BA	?	x	x	x	x	?		x	
Early IA	?	x	x	x	x	?		x	

LN = Late Neolithic; BA = Bronze Age; IA = Iron Age.

established in certain areas and that this organisation became more evident over time.

In Hungary, the settlement hierarchy was more pronounced through the Bronze Age. The largest settlements of Scandinavia would have been classified among Hungary's smaller sites. At the same time, the range in house sizes was not as great, and the largest Hungarian houses would be among the smallest in the north (Chapter 5). By the Early Bronze Nagyrév Age culture, settlement structures included relatively large and dense tells, and these continued to expand in size into the Middle Bronze Age Vatya culture, especially along the major rivers, where they undoubtedly benefitted from expanding trade. Tell excavations show an organised plan of house lots with rebuilding, streets, and open areas; enclosing fortifications defined these settlements. Fortified settlements varied greatly in size, suggesting a pronounced hierarchy. At the same time, in the Benta Valley at least, a parallel hierarchy existed in open settlements that had a less dense structure but could be quite large in area and estimated populations. In the Late Bronze Age Urnfield culture, the settlement hierarchy continued, or was reestablished, and became pronounced, especially in the fortified settlements. All settlements had less dense housing, suggesting large versions of the irregular aggregations of farmstead found in Scandinavia.

In Sicily, the regional pattern of settlements appears to respond quite dramatically to the particular patterns of association with external relationships involving trade and political relationships. Through the Bronze Age, settlements in Sicily were highly variable according to placement with respect to external trade. For example, in the Salemi region, no settlement was described until the Late Bronze Age, when a couple of small clusters of fortified villages were founded. Perhaps equivalent to the Nagyrév tells, these would have had several hundred inhabitants, and the polities they dominated would have been small in size for chiefdoms. However, the presence of luxury items of metal and complex internal site arrangements suggest a complexity that must reflect external relationships. In the Iron Age, trade conditions changed dramatically and apparently created the opportunities to create large fortified settlements. Monte Polizzo, for example, contained elements of elite housing, a central acropolis, and connecting streets that document a large proto-urban centre that dominated the local region. These settlements were larger than the Hungarian tells, but the same relationship of complexity to external trade relationships was evident.

The overall size of average and largest settlements appears to increase from north to south, and the internal organisation becomes increasingly complex as settlement size increases. The amount of fortification also increases, suggesting perhaps more warfare or perhaps just a more clearly defined local corporate group. The most important factor linked to changing settlement form within regions, through both time and space, appears to have been the localities' relationship to long-distance trade.

NOTE

1. To understand the relative density of residential activities, small test units (1 × 1 × 0.12 m) were excavated into plough soil on a 50 m grid here and at all Bronze Age sites. Ceramics from each test unit (representing 0.25 ha) were dated to phase, and those with Bronze Age ceramics were described by density: low (7–14 sherds), moderate (15–49), high (50–99), and very high (>100). Core areas of tells typically have high and very high ceramic densities.

5

Households

Marie Louise Stig Sørensen
With contributions by Jens-Henrik Bech, Brigitta Kulcsarne-Berzsenyi,
Kristian Kristiansen, Christian Mühlenbock, Christopher Prescott,
and Magdolna Vicze

This chapter discusses the similarities and differences in the household across the three regions. The household is approached as a significant basic element of these societies, and the chapter will use the data provided by the case studies to explore and characterise this in detail. Excavations have traditionally revealed scant evidence about the 'workings' and character of the household, but the systematic approach to sampling employed in these case studies makes it possible to begin outlining such characteristics. The aims are to consider variations in how the later prehistoric households, as a nexus of social and economic activities, functioned and to identify spatial characteristics. Particular attention is paid to architectural elaboration of the house as, for example, internal divisions and furnishings provide clues about the organisation of activities within and around the house. The spatial distribution of different classes of artefacts and of food remains at different stages of their processing are also considered to understand how the household operated.

Substantial variation existed in the settlement organisations in different parts of Europe during later prehistory, as discussed in Chapter 4. We may, therefore, expect differences in the characters of the households as settlement organisation provides some of the social framework within which households functioned. As a background to the analysis of the household, therefore, differences between the three areas must be compared. In Scandinavia, the Early Bronze Age household is part of a system of dispersed open settlements, which were usually composed of one or a few single farmsteads with some evidence for additional buildings. Using ideas formulated by Gerritsen (1999:291) categorised such organisation as 'house-based societies.' In contrast, the Hungarian case study had densely occupied settlements, which appear to have little evidence of differentiation among dwellings and apparently little internal hierarchical organisation. In Sicily, on the other hand, the household is set within a densely occupied, semi-urban settlement with differentiation between individual households. These later prehistoric households, irrespective of other similarities or differences, have to be understood as integrated within different social and political structures.

THE CONCEPT OF THE HOUSEHOLD AND ITS APPLICATION TO STUDIES OF BRONZE AGE SOCIETIES

Although presentations of later prehistoric settlement data are deeply affected by assumptions about the nature of the household, such assumptions are rarely clearly articulated or based on detailed data analysis, although the household is often equated with the extended family. Good studies of the north European household include Fokkens (2003), Gerritsen (1999, 2003), and Streiffert (2004), who analyse the household as a farm, composed of one or more buildings, and argue that it was the ontological centre of that social and economic world. Discussions of later prehistoric households on Sicily, in contrast, focus on their roles in the political spheres, involving urbanization and Greek interaction (e.g., Streiffert Eikeland 2006). Explicit considerations of Bronze Age households in Hungary are lacking. Although much literature has aimed to provide universal definitions of household, no such general definition seems possible (Sanjek 1996). In this chapter, we use 'household' to refer to a constellation of people who live together most of the time and who, between them, share the activities needed to sustain themselves as a group in terms of sustenance and social needs, or, in other words, 'the domestic environment' (Streiffert Eikeland 2006), and we assume a close correlation between this unit and domestic architecture and arrangements. Organisationally, it is the next step up from the individual, but it does not necessarily correspond with 'family,' as these may be organised in a number of ways. The task is to sift through the evidence to see whether we can characterise household relations across the three areas.

Table 5.1. Outline of analytical elements of households

The composition and size of the household	The materialisation of the household	The workings of the household
House size	Architectural forms	Social and economic activities
House duration	Divisions and elaborations	Spatial distribution of activities
Life expectancy	Furnishing	
Residence pattern	Use of materials	Types of objects
Biography of the house		

Analyses of the household depend on high-quality information about what and where activities were carried out within different structures on settlements. The systematic approach to data retrieval developed by the Emergence of European Societies project makes this comparison possible and also allows us to utilise existing data in new ways. The similarities of methodology means that the material from excavations can be used to discuss how different types of architecture, furnishings, and spaces may be interpreted in terms of the politics of space and the character of the household. The extensive and systematic sampling furthermore allows us to initiate mapping of where and what activities took place within individual rooms and distinct spaces, such as passages and open spaces. The comparable databases also allow investigation of how particular features, such as ovens or hearths, are located within the spectra of public–private, and whether their integration within the site changes through time. In other words, through the 'forensic' investigation of mundane material found through systematic recovery, including sieving and flotation, we can explore how specific households were constituted.

The household is a social, an economic, and a material unit, and by investigating the dynamics between its form and function we may find evidence for its structure and work. Moreover, although different aspects of the household are intertwined, they leave contrasting signatures in the archaeological record, making the investigation of components of the households intricate but possible. Its analysis does, however, necessitate a breakdown of observations into specific features and data, and the consideration of the household in each microregion is structured around three clusters of components and their physical correlates, as outlined in Table 5.1.

The composition and size of the household can be proposed based on several assumptions and an assessment of archaeological data. Household size appears dependent on various demographic factors. 'Household size can vary substantially and depending on family structure (e.g., conjugal versus extended families), completed family size, age at marriage of offspring, and other factors such as population density and subsistence practice, a range of estimates of number of persons per households are possible' (Chamberlain 2006:52). Although these variables are not directly accessible with archaeological data, we can still estimate them. Historical studies of rural censuses in Norway, England, and Roman Egypt come up with an average number of five individuals per household (ibid. 52). Another method is to calculate the household based on an assumed correlation between the number of people and either house size or floor area; this method has been used for periods lacking such census data. The numbers reached range widely, although many studies suggest 5 to 10 m^2 of roofed area per person (Chamberlain 2006:126). This method, however, universalises the social relationship between people and space, and therefore is somewhat problematic. For example, roofed area could cover different functions, such as the stalling of animals, such that equating roofed area with number of people must be qualified.

Other physical factors may have a direct bearing on the size of households as they functioned as a social and economic unit. In effect, threshold factors may determine the size required for the household's viability. With regard to the cases considered here, the spatial distance between households (houses) and the consequential impact on collaborations, such as needed for harvesting or ploughing, may have been important influences on the composition and size of households as these were integrated in different settlement systems. Moreover, for households located within a dispersed settlement pattern such as that in Scandinavia, it may have been desirable to appear physically as well as politically dominant, and that may have been a significant factor in household composition, while the presence of apprentices and workers within specialised households is another potential influence. Similarly, cultural ideas about the duration of the 'life cycle' of the inhabitants, the households, or the houses may have influenced the size of the household. Furthermore, in some cultural systems, the composition of households may be fluid; social mechanisms created pathways for movement among households, as individuals move by marriage and a wide range of roles, including apprentices, dependent people, seasonal workers, and visitors.

Estimates and discussions of the size and composition of the European household in later prehistory are rare in the literature, and even fewer are based on data from the three case study regions. An explicit argument about the household of the Dutch longhouses from the Bronze and Iron Age has been made by Fokkens (2003), and because this cultural landscape is similar to south Scandinavia, it may have relevance to that case study. Fokkens argues that the large longhouses were the home of an extended family of about twenty people (ibid. 15), basing his estimate on the size of the Bronze Age longhouse, with its large living compartment, similar to that found in south Scandinavia, as well as the much smaller houses of the Iron Age, which are seen to match more closely the spatial need of a core family. As another example, in the Early Iron Age enclosure settlement at Haddenham in southern England, composed of two round houses with auxiliary structures, Zubrow proposes that households contained ten to thirty people: 'At any given time, one might expect two infants, two children, two teenagers, six adults, and three elderly people' (Zubrow in Evans and Hodder 2006:311) and 'By the time one [a person living on the site] was 11, all four grandparents would be dead and most likely both parents. The living adult world would be represented by uncles and aunts' (ibid. 311).

Despite the complex factors affecting household size, as well as the many unknown aspects of their composition, working household models for the three case studies can be proposed. Although alternative methods produce different estimates of household sizes, models allow us to reach proposed numbers based on explicit assumptions and adjustments rooted in appreciation of the characteristics of particular settlements (Table 5.2).

Such differences in the likely size of the households suggest that the nature of these households may differ. In particular, whereas the small size of the Hungarian Bronze Age household makes it likely that there was substantial overlap between the family and the household, this is much less likely in the case of Sicily where the size and composition of households may have varied considerably between different building complexes. In Scandinavia, it is likely that the household was shaped around members of the extended family rather than just a core group. The differences in size also have implications for how gender, age, and other social structures were formulated, as the larger households with more members in each age–gender set could more easily result in complex differentiation of its members.

Description of the later prehistoric household: Three case studies

Evidence from each of the three areas enables comparison and further reflections on the nature of the European household. Although the data are methodologically comparable, they derive from three widely different areas, and so analytical cohesion is sought by comparing specific house forms and assemblage characteristics. For example, we identify the presence or absence of internal division or spatial separation of activities for each case.

THE BRONZE AGE HOUSEHOLD IN SOUTHERN SCANDINAVIA

For southern Scandinavia, considerable knowledge exists about the later prehistoric house *per se*, with an explicit focus on construction

Table 5.2. Various estimates of the size of the average household in the three study areas

Method of calculation	The south Scandinavian household	The Hungarian tell household	The Sicilian proto-urban household
Historical analogy	**Five persons** per household	**Five persons** per household	**Five persons** per household
House size × 5–10 m² per person	Early Bronze Age house Avg. 150–175 m² = **30/15–35/17.5 persons** per household Late Bronze Age Avg. 100–120 m² = **20/10–25/12.5 persons** per household	Large house Avg. 50–55 m² = **10/11–5/5.5 persons** per household Small house Avg. 40–45 m² **8/9–4/4.5 persons** per household	House 1, 175 m² = **35/17.5 persons** per household
Qualifying factor	Distance between households = Increased household size	No distance between households = No effect on household size Long duration = Possibly increase in household size during its life cycle	Little distance, specialisation of households = slight increase in household size
Adjustment based on relevant comparisons	Aim at around **20 people**	None	
Proposal	**10–15 persons** per household	**5–7 persons** per household, Possible increase to 7–9 at the end of the life cycle	**5–15 persons** per household

details and differences in size of longhouses (see Boas 1991; Ethelberg 2000; Mikkelsen 1986). There are fewer works studying the nature of the household, and concepts of settlement and household often blend together. As an exception, Webley (2007) recently investigated domestic arrangements inside Early Iron Age houses from western Denmark, using an approach that sees the house as a social and semantic 'stage' as well as an arena of routine practices – the household as *habitus*, so to speak. Detailed spatial data provided by the Thy project and by recent excavations in Jutland and Scania have begun to fill significant gaps in our understandings of the household.

In southern Scandinavia, the household of later prehistory generally took the form of single farmsteads composed of a large three-aisled longhouse (more rarely two or more buildings). Although the houses have different wall-construction techniques (Ethelberg 2000:186), they are structurally quite similar. In the marginal areas of the classic Nordic Bronze Age, the household may, however, take different forms. At Tanum, Sweden, small structures seem, for instance, to have been used, perhaps because of differences in the subsistence economy (Chapter 6). The following discussion focuses on the Bronze Age household from western Denmark, with evidence from other areas used to complement and supplement the picture that emerges.

As the dominant feature within any Scandinavian Bronze Age settlement and as the focus of many activities, including food preparation, the longhouse is likely to have provided the physical and symbolic frame for the household. As mentioned in Chapter 4, this household did not use fences to enclose its spaces. The house physically and symbolically accommodated the household, and the space outside the building merged with other spaces (Sørensen 2007). First during the later part of the first millennium BC, did fences and other physical borders became common, suggesting an emerging need to demarcate the household from the larger community.

Apart from differences in house size and evidence from burial monuments (Chapters 3 and 4), little evidence shows household differentiation; they were either largely self-sufficient or their dependencies involved activities that were not directly reflected in the physical organisation of the household.

The biography of Scandinavian houses is relatively simple. Longhouses seem to have had a limited use life, corresponding to one or two generations, some 30 to 60 years. This life span has increasingly been confirmed by ^{14}C-dating (Ethelberg 2000:206), although it may have been twice that long for the largest houses (ibid. 208). Although extensions and alterations have been documented (e.g., Bech and Olsen forthcoming) these are usually limited, and the form of the house was largely determined when the house was built and usually remained the same until it was given up. Whereas there can be evidence of repair or extension at one end, little evidence documents change in building use – for instance, the in-filling of hearths or change in room function.

The Materialisation of the Southern Scandinavian Bronze Age Household. The specific architectural form of the longhouse influenced how the household was organised. Two elements stand out. One is the variation in the size of the individual houses, and the other is the use of internal divisions and other architectural elements. Whereas the form of the houses, their 'blueprint' or morphology, varies little, considerable variation existed in size within clusters of houses, among regions, and over time (Chapter 4). For example, investigating the size of Bronze Age houses from southern Jutland, Ethelberg (2000:187) divides them into four size groups: short houses (floor area between 90–100 m²), medium sized (floor area between 150–175 m²), long (floor area 220–275 m²), and extremely long (floor area of 400–500 m²), with the medium-sized house being most common. As discussed in Chapters 3 and 4, the very large houses so far seem specific to southern Jutland, and they are, for example, not found in Thy, where the main part of the Early Bronze Age houses belong to the two first of Ethelberg's size groups with only a small number being longer, about 200 to 275 m² (Bech and Olsen forthcoming). These differences are apparently primarily attributable to function and status, with chronology having some influence as the houses become bigger during the Early Bronze Age, and then appear to become smaller again in the Late Bronze Age (Ethelberg 2000:215; Arthursson 2009).

The house usually has two entrances opposite each other in the long side of the house, although there may be more (see for example Bjerre 2 and 6, Bech 1997:6f; Mikkelsen 1996b:34ff). There are apparently some regional differences in wall construction technique with timber wall used more commonly in southwestern Denmark but only wattle-and-daub walls documented in Thy. This is most likely due to differences in locally available raw materials as documented by pollen analyses (e.g., Andersen 1993; Bech 2003:45f).

In addition to the predictable inside–outside distinction, the architecture also provides obvious potentials for differentiation between the front and the back of the house as well as between the two ends of the house (Sørensen 2007). The length of the longhouse is often divided through one or two internal walls (commonly of a lighter construction than the load-bearing outer walls), into two, three or more parts or rooms. Despite attempts at grouping the three-aisled longhouse on the basis of these internal divisions (Rasmussen 1999), houses vary considerably in this regard and no clear correlation exists between, for instance, the size of the house and the number of partition walls (Ethelberg 2000:181), suggesting that within the overarching shared norm there was a degree of flexibility regarding the interior organisation of houses according to the wishes and needs of individual households. In the details of the interior organisations, we glimpse a reality of different ways to structure household activities and the possibility that individual households functioned in different ways (see also Streiffert 2004) albeit within set shared norms and expectations.

Alternative ways to structure a household are seen in the pattern of activity areas within essentially the same architectural space. Hearths or clusters of cooking pits were usually restricted to one room, usually in the most western end (Ethelberg 2000:185), suggesting that the different parts of the house had specific functions (Figure 5.1). Some houses, however, had alternative arrangements, such as Legård, Thy, which was divided into three rooms, with both the eastern and western end of the house used for habitation (Mikkelsen and Kristiansen forthcoming). Some house elements, such as entrances or work spaces, may have been embellished. Examples include the paved entrances to the house at Bjerre 6 and 7 (Bech 2003:56; Olsen forthcoming a and b), and the Late Bronze Age houses at Fragtrup, where the floors at the two ends of the houses were made of different materials, corresponding to functional differences that are documented by the distribution of fine- and coarse-ware pottery (Figure 5.2).

The Workings of the Household. A question about these houses has been whether they included stalling for animals, which is important to understand how daily life was linked to animal management and their primary and secondary products. An example among the still very few Danish Bronze Age houses with indisputable stable is house III from Legård, Thy. The 33.5 m long and 7.5 to 8.0 m wide

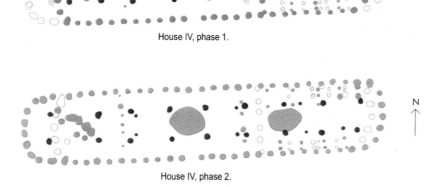

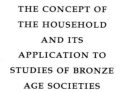

Figure 5.1.
Plan of Early Bronze Age longhouses from western Denmark (after Ethelberg 2000).

house was divided into three sections of almost equal size, where the middle part consisted of a stable with space for 12 to 16 animals – most likely cattle. Both the western and the eastern end of the house were used for habitation according to the layout of the rooms. Ceramics from the eastern end of the house indicate storage function (Mikkelsen and Kristiansen forthcoming, Kristensen forthcoming). Based on observations such as the presence of stalling, the location of

Figure 5.2.
Reconstruction of large Early Bronze Age house (House IV) (Drawing by Jørgen Andersen).

cooking pits, and different construction techniques used for divisions and walls, the norm for the Early Bronze Age house seems to be that the west end was used as the 'living quarter,' and the east end used as barn and stable.

Activities associated with the households were both clustered within the houses and more widely distributed, with general domestic debris and features such as cooking pits, hearths, and flint knapping located up to several hundred meters away from the house.

Evidence of metalworking is first found regularly on settlements in the Late Bronze Age with a few examples dating already to the Early Bronze Age including the site Brd Gram in southern Jutland (Ethelberg 2000:180). In general, there is little to suggest that specialised crafts were linked to particular households; even when evidence of metalworking becomes more regular it seems likely that most households were at times engaged with modest bronze working. For most households, metalworking and other crafts were probably supplementary activities, spread over the seasons and responding to opportunities, rather than playing a substantial part in the household economy. Metallurgy may have taken place at other, as yet unknown, locations, being the product of particular groups, such as particular age or gender sets, rather than being household activities.

Data from Thy suggest that some households in that area were involved with procurement, primary preparation, and production of specialised flint objects, often at some distance from the house and at a scale beyond household economy (see Chapter 7). At Vilhøj, in eastern Thy (Mikkelsen 1996a:113; Steinberg 1997) large-scale production of hundreds if not thousands of asymmetrical sickles has been documented for the Early Bronze Age in areas away from the house, whereas small-scale production of smaller tools took place inside and outside longhouses (Draiby 1985:134; Earle et al 1998). There is no evidence of similar scale of flint production during the Late Bronze Age in the area, although specialist production of preforms for sickle manufacturing might have been taking place. Substantial evidence for flint working (cores and blades) were found on the clay floors inside the Late Bronze Age houses at Fragtrup (Draiby 1984:134). The varied evidence of flint working raises an important question about the relationship between households and craft production and whether some production was organised outside the households, with possible scenarios being common rights, 'work gangs,' and specialised seasonal work. The specialised production of flint objects in Thy was probably attributable to the high quality of local flint sources, and may have taken place outside the sphere of the household rather than being a characteristic of the Danish Early Bronze Age household. In Thy collecting amber is witnessed during the Bronze Age from a number of sites close to the North Sea. The activity no doubt took place by members of the individual households when opportunity was presented. The amber was seldom processed but collected for further exchange. At Bjerre 7 dug-down storage vessels contained many hundreds of small unworked pieces of amber (Earle in press).

In the Bronze Age, with the exceptions of stone tool production and minor metallurgy, scant evidence exists for productive activities associated with the households beyond the production and preparation of food. An exceptional glimpse of what else may have been taking place is provided by macrofossil evidence from the Late Bronze Age site of Bjerre 7. It showed that gold of pleasure (*Camelina sativa*) was being cultivated. Processing (very likely extraction of oil from the oil-containing seeds) took place outside the house in an area with finds of large storage vessels but with no evidence of food processing (Henriksen et al. forthcoming, Kristensen forthcoming b).

Little evidence exists, for ceramic production and weaving and textile production especially considering the substantial number of pottery pieces recovered from households and textile pieces recovered from graves. Fragments of loam weights were found in the unusual cellar pit at Brd Gram (Ethelberg 2000:232), suggesting that such activities took place in particular working areas or structures. The abundance of scrapers at the Bjerre Enge households may suggest the production of hides. The evidence, however, remains partial, and more work is needed.

The pottery recovered from settlements, with its relatively limited functional variation and decoration, suggests that the household assemblage was used for storage and cooking, but that separate 'tableware' was not in use (Chapter 7). This is especially the case for the Early Bronze Age, but even the fine-ware pottery appearing during the Late Bronze Age is relatively limited in its range of forms and generally lacks decoration (Figure 5.3). Food was probably spooned directly from the cooking pot as the household ate together, making food and eating central to household socialisation including the performance of gender (Sørensen 2000:103). Compared with the other two regions discussed here, the range and usually also the amount of pottery recovered from and around houses is limited, although

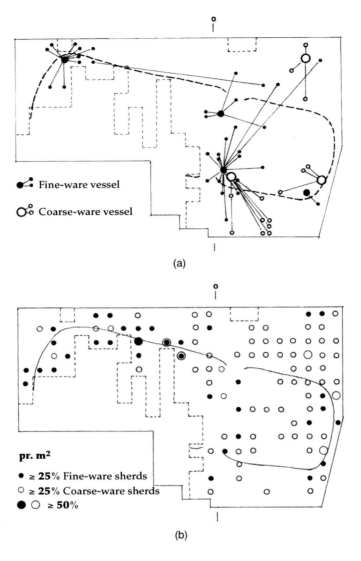

Figure 5.3.
Distribution of fine and coarse ware at House II Fragtrup, Denmark (after Draiby 1984).

substantial amounts of pottery were recovered from the Late Bronze Age site of Fragtrup (20,952 sherds, (Draiby 1984:175), and from Bjerre 7 (46,000 sherds). Where was the pottery made? The low firing conditions of the pottery suggest that it was made within the household for household use (Chapter 7), but evidence for ceramic production is lacking. This perhaps further supports the proposal that cooking and eating were not elaborated materially, although it is highly likely that eating helped integrate the household.

Generally, household and nonhousehold activities spread seamlessly into the wider surroundings. Such lack of rigid activity boundaries may well characterise the Scandinavian Bronze Age household, a feature that disappeared with the Iron Age and the emergence of the fenced, demarcated house. These households were not isolated, however, and some were clearly partners to long-distance exchange and trade as well as local bartering. It is nonetheless important to appreciate that many of the stable elements of life, such as domestic arrangements, craft production, and subsistence practices remained deeply rooted in the immediate local environment, processed as well as used within the household.

HOUSEHOLD AT THE BRONZE AGE TELL IN HUNGARY

The diversity of settlement forms and thus, presumably, households during the Hungarian Bronze Age must have been great, as some people lived on dense tells while others lived in open-field settlements (Chapter 4). Despite the diversity of settlements, the houses had many similarities as well as some regional differences, and, as one would expect, houses changed through time. During the Middle Bronze Age, houses were rectangular buildings composed typically of one or two rooms, with at least one hearth. Little is known about the number and location of entrances, although only one is commonly assumed. Evidence of household characteristics, rather than merely of the houses, is scant, and this chapter therefore discusses only tell sites of the Middle Bronze Age Vatya culture.

The size of the houses varies considerably in length but less in width, and the houses can sometimes be placed within distinct size groups. On some sites, the longest houses were typically twice as long as the smallest ones (Bóna 1975), which may be interpreted as an extension of the house to accommodate several generations living together. At the site of Füzesabony, there were apparently both small 'family' houses of 4 × 5 to 4 × 6 m and bigger houses of 5 × 12 to 5 × 14 m (Szathmári 1992:136). When a house was divided internally into two rooms (more rooms are rare), it has been shown to be caused by changes in the house 'life cycle.' As the furnishings of different rooms tend to suggest different uses, it is unlikely that two-roomed houses were merely reflections of an extended family, as the division into two rooms segregated activities taking place within the house. At the site of Tiszaug-Kéménytető, for example, one house was divided into two rooms by a 10 to 12 cm thick clay wall (Csányi and Stanczik 1992:118). The bigger room was probably the 'kitchen,' with a domed baking oven, a clay-rimmed hearth, a small clay bench built into the wall, and numerous fragments of large cooking vessels. In contrast, the smaller room, entered from the larger room through a threshold door, was empty, possibly for sleeping or storage. The houses usually have hearths inside the rooms and ovens both inside and outside. Hearths and ovens were often of sophisticated design and built of clay. Hearths are usually placed centrally in the house or, alternatively, close to the wall or even attached to it if several hearths are present within a house. An interesting type is the so-called portable hearth, which suggests a desire to cook or use heat away from the permanent fireplaces and ovens. An interest in pyrotechnology within the context of the household spaces was distinctive. Another distinctive feature of these Vatya tell sites are large pits located inside the houses, presumably for private storage.

The Households on the Tell at Százhalombatta-Földvár.[1] The households being discussed for the Bronze Age tells are the products of several hundred years of sedentary life on densely occupied places, displaying some of the resulting economic, social, and cultural constrains. The nature of the household within such social space is, however, a neglected topic. Several excavations of Bronze Age tells in Hungary have revealed how the sites were occupied by uniformly laid-out houses with narrow paths between them. One of the core questions about the tell household accordingly is how the separation between public/communal and private activities was made and how the single household was organised and managed within such settlements. Because of the size and complex stratigraphy of Bronze Age tells, their excavations have all been only 'keyholes' to the overall settlement (Chapter 4). Nonetheless, excavations suggest that the household was formed around the single house, most of which appear as self-sufficient units with hearth, cooking and storage pottery, some craft, and internal division of activities. Further characteristics of these households can be considered here through our excavation at Százhalombatta-Földvár. The limited extent of the excavations, however, must be stressed. How representative this settlement's households may be for Bronze Age tell communities is also, of course, unclear.

The evidence from explorations at Százhalombatta-Földvár suggests that the lower levels represent, together with larger communal areas, long unbroken sequences of 'house lots' laid out along narrow streets (Plate 5.1), and that this pattern changed during the last occupation period, when the communal area was built over. This change in use and layout has also been demonstrated at a more nuanced level

Plate 1.1. a, b. The tell site seen from the south with the steep sides due to recent clay-taking for a brick factory (photo from Claes Uhner).

Plate 1.2.
The landscape of Monte Polizzo (photo from Christian Mühlenbock).

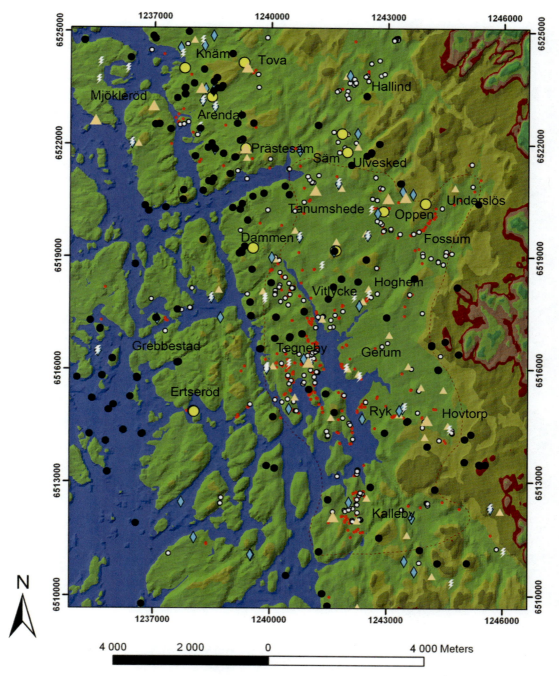

Plate 2.1. The Bronze Age shoreline in Tanum, Sweden, and the distribution of cairns (black dots), rock art sites (red dots), cupmark sites (white dots), settlement sites (large triangles), settlement indicators (small triangles), metal finds (yellow dots), flint daggers (blue rhombs), and flint sickles (white flashes). It shows the strong maritime orientation of cairns and rock art, the rock art sites defining places for gathering and harbors.

Plate 2.2. View of the Benta stream and floodplain north of Sóskút, Hungary, today (C. French).

Plate 2.3. The soil profile at Erd site 4 in Benta valley, Hungary, with Bronze Age features defined at the base and Roman features at the top of the profile just below the modern plough soil (C. French).

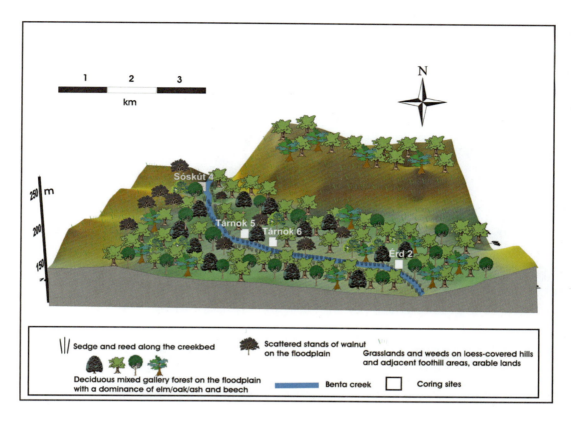

Plate 2.4.
Inferred view of the Benta valley for the early-middle Bronze Age in the lower Benta valley, Hungary (P. Sumegi/S. Guylas).

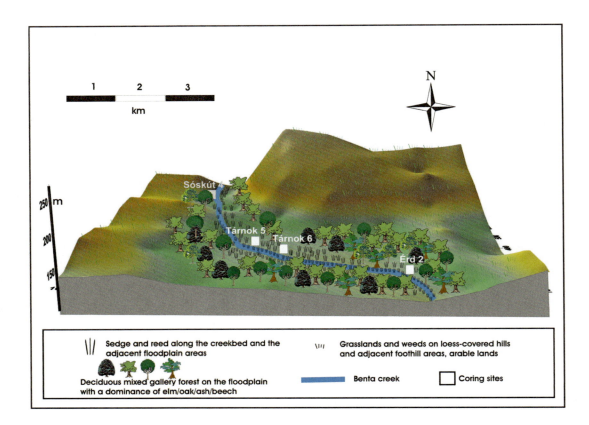

Plate 2.5.
Inferred view of the Benta valley for the late Bronze Age in the lower Benta valley, Hungary (P. Sumegi/S. Guylas).

Plate 5.1.
Distribution of activities across a middle Bronze Age house from Százhalombatta-Földvár.

Plate 5.2.
Typical oven feature located in most houses from Százhalombatta-Földvár.

Plate 5.3.
Adjacent specialised oven from Százhalombatta-Földvár.

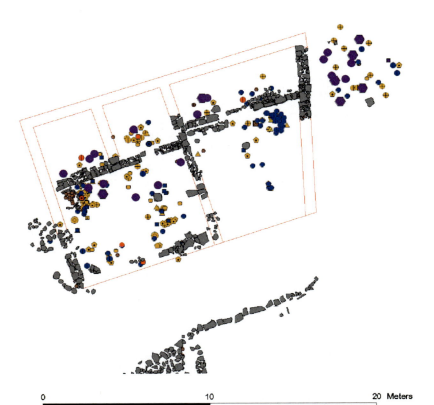
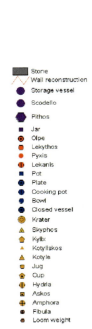

Plate 5.4.
Plan of the terminal phase of House 1 at Monte Polizzo. House was destroyed by fire.

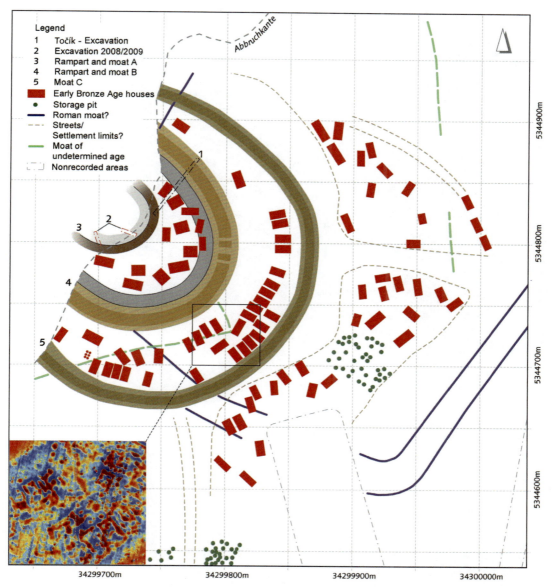

Plate 8.1. Fortified tell site at Fidvár, Slovakia. Ground plan of house clusters and fortifications based on magnetic prospection, shown in section (from: www.vfg.uni-wuerzburg.de/forschung/projekte/fidvar).

Plate 8.2. Reconstruction drawing of the tell site at Százhalombatta at its height (Drawing by Brigitta Kürtösi).

Plate 8.3. Reconstruction of the merchant's house at Monte Polizzo.

through an analysis of the 'open area' that existed within the later Middle Bronze Age layers (Sørensen and Vicze, forthcoming). Such evidence tantalisingly suggests changes that would have affected the relationship between households, but further studies must await the next phase of excavation. It does, however, remind us that the tell communities, despite their long-term continuities, were dynamic societies, and the role and definition of households (including ownership rights) could change.

In the following discussion of recent excavations, we assume that each house, with its access to and use of adjacent paths and communal areas, represented a household.[2] Five houses were from the same level (the eighth cultural layer from the top) and were contemporary neighbours for some time. This layer can be considered the latest densely occupied phase revealed by our excavations. A sixth house belongs to a different layer (the tenth layer) within the same cultural horizon. Although its excavation is ongoing, it will be used as a reference point because of its exceptional preservation. Of the five contemporary houses, four are only partly exposed by our trench, but they provide important information on construction details and the range and characteristics of activities (Plate 5.1).

Plate 5.1.
Example of narrow strait between Middle Bronze Age house is from Százhalombatta-Földvár with demarcated house walls and storage pits.

The question of whether the artefacts found on the floor of houses represent *in situ* use of the house or *in situ* abandonment or post-abandonment activities is important, but it often seems reasonable to presume that the material related to abandoned households. It can, however, be argued that even if the absolute number of artefacts cannot be interpreted as a direct indicator of activities, their proportions are likely to bear the imprint of the original life within the house. Moreover, at least for one house (the sixth house, ID 4340), which was apparently accidentally burned, we may reconstruct a full, in-use household assemblage.

Over time, patterns of activities were being accumulated that document routine divisions and tasks that took place within and around the houses. An important assumption, confirmed by excavations, is that within particular cultural horizons, new households were almost always erected immediately on top of the old ones; families and/or households did not move away and leave their 'plot.' These rebuilding activities for all houses that we have excavated are based on debris that does not extend more than 10 to 20 cm outside the outline of the wall-stump of the house it was part of. This suggests a controlled demolition of houses to avoid the spread of debris outside the house plot and onto communal paths and alleys. This pattern of spread probably reflects the dense nature of the settlement and the fact that in most cases house plots were not left abandoned, as the next house was soon raised on top of the debris. Potentially, aspects of this practice may be both symbolic and functional. The control of the debris may not just physically but also symbolically demarcate and delineate the extension of the household or the area of authority over the people's lot. The sense of authority and ownership might have been further strengthened by the knowledge that the house is resting on that of predecessors, endowing the current builders and the new building with the ancestors' economic and social status. The functional utility of building on the debris of a previous house may also provide a slight elevation for the new house, and the relatively thick (burnt or unburnt) clay created a kind of insulation, as seems to be supported by some micromorphological analyses.

The Materialisation of the Households at Százhalombatta-Földvár. So far, two house types can be defined on the basis of size and inner partition. One type is a large (5 × 10–11 m) two-room house, in which the smaller room (5 × 2–3 m) has no hearth and the larger room (5 × 8 m) contains at least one hearth. The smaller room is consistently found at the northern end of the two-room house. The other type is a smaller one-room house (5 × 8–9 m) with one or more hearths. Details provided by the wall remains show that, in most cases, first construction was of a one-roomed house (5 × 8 m) with the hearths, and then the second room could be added on. Excavations document one clear exception; House 3076 was built from the start with an inner partition. Here the difference between the two rooms was preplanned, as the two rooms, despite being built simultaneously, had different floors, with the northern having an earth floor and the southern, bigger room having a yellow plastered-clay floor. Several floor and wall-plastering incidents are documented in this house, including a major change when the floor of the entire house (both rooms) was covered by a new extra thick, yellow plaster floor. This was a major act within the life of the household; even the hearth was rebuilt; finds from the house's first phase were limited, indicating a planned and well-prepared rebuilding action following a clean-out of living surfaces. Looking at the neighbouring households, in two cases the houses have a second phase during which they were enlarged through the addition of a small room in the north end. In the case of House 3181, the extension consisted of a 2 m wide room (with clay plastering). The postabandonment activities on this part of the site were such that more detailed observation was not possible. House 3497 also had a northern extension added. This case is the first example noted where the general, mixed, greyish clayey matrix of the site was used for both repair and construction. The north extension of this house was built from this indistinguishable material, and the floor was stomped rather than, as in the other two houses, consisting of clean yellow clay (Kovács 2007). The full extent of the added room could not be identified because of later pit disturbances. Although it had two well-documented phases, the fourth house (House 3147) was not extended by an extra room, and it remained the same size (5 × 8.5 m) during both phases. The remains of the fifth house (3136), in the southeast corner, were too limited to document its size or inner division. House 4043, from layer 10, was 5.5 × 11 m with two rooms, the smaller (2.5 m wide) situated to the north. In addition to such major construction work, we find within all houses evidence of other remodelling, such as annual or seasonal plastering of the walls and floors and other repairs and maintenance.

To summarise, the average household was organised around a one-roomed house that could be extended with an extra room during its life cycle. In the larger room, the hearths and other structures as well as many household items and utensils are found, whereas the smaller room, which appears to be added during the life cycle of the house, had no inbuilt features. There seems to have been only one entrance, presumably placed in the southern end-wall. The tendency for houses to start as a large one-roomed house and then be extended is worth emphasis. As part of the life cycle of the house, its biography so to speak, an extension probably reveals changing needs and/or capacities of the household rather than reflecting social differentiation *per se* between households within the settlement. Such needs or capacities would typically be caused by an increase in the size of the household or changing social and/or economic abilities.

This proposal is important insofar as the life cycles of later prehistoric households in different parts of Europe seem to show varying characteristics in this regard, as discussed later. The hypothesis needs further investigation, but it seems to be warranted by the details recovered from the apparently complete household remains of House 4043. The small room of this house mainly contained remains of large, coarse vessels, a substantial amount of burnt organic remains, and a complete skeleton of a mouse burnt together with the house, suggesting this area was for storage or stocking. Many of these remains may not have survived less favourable preservation conditions, making the small rooms appear clean on other sites, or alternatively, the use of the extension may have had regional characteristics, meaning that in some areas it was used in a manner that makes it appear empty. The importance of the life cycle of the household as a way of understanding the building, maintenance, and final abandonment (and at times, burning) of the house has also been recognized by others (Chapman 1999; Stevanović 2002; Tringham 2005).

The degree of social differences displayed among households within a tell, as well as the differences in households from different contemporary sites, is complex but important. In particular, the lack of good contextual data from sites other than tells and the limited areas excavated on tells restrict our insights into horizontal differentiation of households both within and among sites. Surface collections suggest substantial variation through both time and space in terms of the apparent density of houses on open settlements and possibly also within a tell (Chapter 4), suggesting important differences in house arrangement and thus the character of households. Alas, although excavated materials exist from many tells and some open-air sites, it is not yet possible to identify distinct differences among households. However, although little concrete evidence supports the suggestion of social differences between the individual households (Chapter 4), some of the observations from Százhalombatta-Földvár do suggest that household access to material goods varied. In particular, variation in the material used in the construction of the floors, ranging from clean yellow clay to the general soil from the site, may suggest that not all households had equal access to all resources.

A very close link appears to have existed between the house (including its immediate surroundings) and the household, and our evidence also suggests generational change or alterations in household composition, and economic and political abilities factor in its life cycle. The excavations reveal the repeated rejuvenations and reparations of floors and even walls, and houses were used for some time as well as changing through time in the way they functioned. It is thus likely that the end of the house (rather than its phases) may relate to a major shift in the household such as that caused by death. Similar arguments have been employed to explain, for instance, the short-lived duration of English Bronze Age houses (Brück 1999) or the dispersed single farms of northern Europe (Gerritsen 1999). Distinctive to the Hungarian case, however, death and rebuilding did not require setting up a household at a new location, but rather rebuilding or remaking the house on the site of the previous one. We can see this as a 'recycling' of the previous household in the construction of the new one. The shifts in orientation and alignment of houses, which can be observed between the different cultural horizons, may thus indicate major reorganisation of the individual household and its rights and claims within the overall settlement organisation.

As mentioned earlier, more than one hearth or fireplace was typically found in each house. Most were situated close to the northern wall of the largest room. Usually one big (1–1.2 m diameter), simply constructed, round domed bread oven that had space for fire and cooking was built on a layer of stones (Plate 5.2). Ovens were renewed several times, most probably staying in use throughout the time the house was in use. This confirms the central 'household-making' quality of the hearth/oven. In addition to the universal qualities of hearth, these hearths contain the very matrix of the household's life cycle; they were probably symbolically infused with a sense of household history; and they often had individual designs distinctive to a particular house.

Next to the oven is a much smaller (0.4–0.5 m diameter) oven with a grill, in some cases attached to the big one or otherwise situated close to it (Plate 5.3). This oven could be used for cooking, as the grill (made of daub) would separate the fire from the place of cooking and create an artificial surface for the cooking pot. These features suggest highly specific food preparation with different steps of cooking (i.e., baking, boiling, frying) separated each from the other. The archaeobotanical remains indicate that household members did the final food processing stage in this part of each house, so both the spatial and the archaeobotanical analyses suggest that this is the general cooking area (Kulcsarne-Berzsenyi 2008). In this arrangement, the cooking area is situated farthest from the presumed entrance to the house. In houses 3181, 3497, and 4043 additional fireplaces were situated in the central area of the main room. In House 3497, a simple small (0.6 m in diameter) and open fireplace was used in both phases of the house. The fireplace in House 4043 is similar, with the exception that a small, elevated, rectangular, clean platform-like feature (not unlike a present-day kitchen working surface) made of clay was attached to

Plate 5.2.
Typical oven feature located in most houses from Százhalombatta-Földvár.

it. House 3181 was slightly different; the location of the fireplace was similar, but here there were two hearths, one an open fireplace and the other, a small grated cooker. The function and role of these hearths are intriguing in houses where there are already at least two possible places for cooking and baking. The desire for additional heating or for special cooking seems a plausible explanation, providing further suggestions of the distinctiveness of individual households.

Whereas tells of this period have substantial pits, their role within the settlement has been unclear. During the excavation, it has become evident that pits are only found inside the house, and they must have been important integrated parts of household activities. It is, however, difficult to definitively link pits to household floors, although more than one pit probably was in use by each household. The pits seem to have served various storage functions, as suggested by the straw lining of a central pit in House 3497 and by observations that they may have had moveable lids.

The Workings of the Household. The archaeological material from excavation throws light on the presence and importance of various

Plate 5.3. Adjacent specialised oven from Százhalombatta-Földvár.

economic activities within and around the houses. Although pottery is found in great quantity, so far there is no suggestion that particular types or amounts of pottery were specifically associated with one household rather than another. No evidence exists for pottery production, although local manufacture seems high likely (Chapter 7). Pottery types include storage vessels, cooking pots, and tableware (Chapter 7), suggesting fairly elaborate food preparation. Several types, such as serving bowls and cups, would have been central to the social activities of the household as they were used for presenting and eating food. These, included, possibly, items, such as cups, that were personalised and belonged to particular members within the household. The size of the cooking vessels is relatively small, supporting the suggestion that the size of the household was on the order of five to seven people.

Bone and antler were worked into tools, and a cache of horn we found was probably a store of raw material. Surprisingly, considering the fauna evidence for wool production (Chapter 6), little evidence exists for textile production, nor is there much evidence for other manufacturing activities, including flint working or bronze production, within the houses, although there is evidence in other parts of the site (Chapter 7). Again, the functions of tools need to be further investigated to establish production activities. Clear evidence exists for the secondary preparation of grain inside and around the houses. Moreover, the analysis of macrofossils shows that the different stages of food processing were commonly divided between the southern and northern end of the house (Chapter 6). Dehusking, selecting, and cleaning of cereals took place in the southern part of the house, and after this was done, the cleaned cereals were moved to the northern end with its oven and cooking area for grinding and further food preparing. This spatial pattern was the same in both phases of the houses, suggesting that activities were organised similarly throughout the life cycle of the household (Kulcsarne-Berzsenyi 2008).

At least during the warmer months, a probable scenario is primary processing of food and some craft activities in communal areas outside the houses, while secondary preparation of food, cooking, and eating took place within each household. It is also likely that each house stored its own resources, including processed grain, in its pits and ceramic vessels.

Some narrow paths between the houses have considerable accumulation of large and dirty rubbish, including what must have been smelly, large animal butchering debris. These narrow passages may thus not have been pathways as such, but rather functioned as an informal refuse zone for the households. We can propose that household life was largely framed by the houses themselves, and each of these social units had use-right over some of the pathways around it. In addition, each household used other spaces, which might have been considered public or communal, such as the broader paths and open area, and some primary food processing and craft activities took place there.

THE EARLY IRON AGE HOUSEHOLD IN SICILY, ITALY

The household on Sicily changed substantially during the later half of the second millennium BC (the Middle Bronze Age). The period witnessed increased variation in the size and function of settlement, as evidenced by Leighton's division of settlement data into seven different categories (Leighton 1999:150). As part of these changes, substantial transformation and variation in the architectural arrangements of individual households took place. Architecture changed from round or subcircular huts within compounds to complexes of rectangular buildings, with the two types coexisting or even being combined in some settlements during the Middle and Late Bronze Age (ibid. 152, 154).

The early Middle Bronze Age round huts are exemplified by buildings found in the urbanized coastal settlement of Thapsos, where more than twelve such buildings have been found in an orderly layout within compounds (Leighton 1999:150, 153). They are considered to be a local building type and appear to have been small (diameter 6–8 m), with an interval wall and floor plaster, and made of roughly shaped stones. Low benches may have flanked the inside wall, and a hearth and cooking platform were sometimes located centrally in the room (ibid. 152). Similar structures are found on other sites. Such a structure 'shows an indigenous urban phenomenon in which plots and enclosures had an important defining role' (ibid. 153). A range of cooking and serving vessels and utensils was used for food preparation in these buildings, and two houses may have held potters' kilns (ibid. 155). Rectangular building complexes are known from the slightly later phase 2 of the same site as well as from other contemporary sites, and such buildings gradually became dominant, raising questions about whether eastern Mediterranean contacts resulted in a new 'art of living.' Such complexes consist of various versions of rectangular rooms (7.5–10 m long) arranged in a U-shape around a central court (ibid. 152–54). At Thapsos, the courtyard building type was replaced during the Early Iron Age by quadrangular structures, the designs of which suggest a different spatial logic (ibid. 191).

The type of hilltop settlements represented by the case study of Monte Polizzo characterised developments during the Late Bronze Age into Early Iron Age in the interior of western Sicily. At the Late Bronze Age site of Morkarta, traditional Bronze Age round huts were still in use, although they were often combined with quadrangle structures or used together to create multiroomed buildings, indicating new ways of organising the activities of the household. The destroyed buildings at Mokarta held a wide range of food preparing, cooking, and serving utensils as well as tools used for weaving. In the subsequent period, building complexes composed of rectangular rooms became the norm in most areas of Sicily.

The Households on Monte Polizzo. The household considered here is the complex of buildings known as House 1 in the large protourban settlement of Monte Polizzo that includes buildings of different architectural types and functions (Johansson and Prescott 2004; Mühlenbock and Prescott 2004). House 1 raises the important issue of the very nature of the later prehistoric household as it became imbedded within semi-urban social constructions through this part of the Mediterranean world.

Despite relatively good preservation, some ambiguities remain about the relationships among the different building elements of House 1. In particular, the chronological phasing of the complex's parts remains somewhat in doubt, and whether it contained one or two households has not been absolutely determined (Streiffert Eikeland 2006). Despite these unresolved issues, the material from House 1 provides valuable insights into the Early Iron Age household of this area.

House 1's position within the settlement, the architectural layout, and the assemblage of the finds suggest a range of practices resulting from routine performances shaped around the household's interpretation of cultural norms. In contrast to the other two regions discussed, the household in Monte Polizzo appears specialised and its particular constructions seem to be affected by its political and economic position within the settlement, in addition to representing the idea of household shared throughout the settlement.

The Materialisation of the Households at Monte Polizzo. House 1 is located on the northern outskirt of the settlement, on a relatively level strip of a rocky shoulder that runs east–west along the northern slope. It was a single-level, multiroom structure, built on a lot created by artificial filling along the rock's slope. The siting of House 1 was thus not simply adapted to topographic features, but had a high degree of intentionality. Through comparison with other buildings sampled within the settlement, it can be observed that House 1 is not located in the most prestigious part of the settlement, and its layout is not typical for the settlement, being the result of intentional architectural planning (Mühlenbock 2008; Mühlenbock, Påhlsson, and Hauge 2004; Mühlenbock and Prescott 2004).

The layout of House 1, as excavated, gives an expression of the final stage of the house's use – the layout on the day it was destroyed by fire (Plate 5.4). Some features, however, show an entangled relative chronology that provides glimpses of its biography. Bronze Age sherds came from the fill used to level the plot (Prescott 2004),

Plate 5.4.
Plan of the terminal phase of House 1 at Monte Polizzo. House was destroyed by fire.

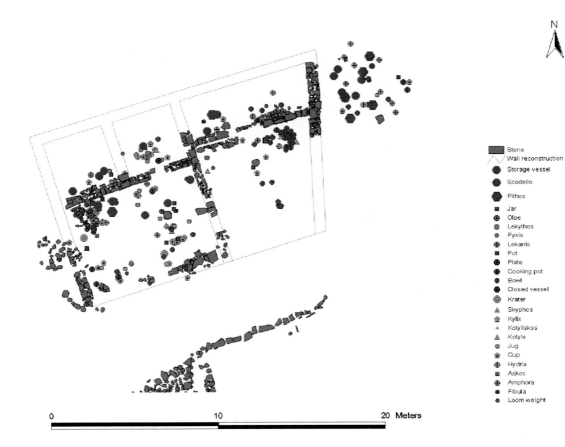

suggesting an earlier structure located in the vicinity. In terms of the complex itself, various relationships indicate that the structural complex developed and was elaborated over time, although differences in opinion remain about interpretation. The excavators propose, for example, that the connecting walls between rooms I and II, as well as between II and V, were added later because they were not bonded to the wall construction and were formed differently. This conclusion suggests that rooms III and IV were the first constructed, with room I taken in use slightly later and conceivably used as a more open activity area (Mühlenbock, Påhlsson, and Hauge 2004). Because of such complex architectural relationships, the question arises whether this was a single household with an expanding composite structure, or whether it was a joining of two households, one slightly older than the other. We shall return to this issue later, but, regarding our concerns here, the significant point is that the construction shows rooms with different functions and that the complex had a life cycle that seems to have allowed expansion and transformation.

Based on architectural features and artefact distributions, the excavators propose that the two smaller rooms III and IV in the northeast corner had doorways from each leading into the larger room, I, which may have opened towards the south. East of rooms I and IV were two more rooms – II and V – which were delimited to the east by a wall. On the other side of their wall was room VI, which may have been only an activity area containing dense refuse. All in all, they propose at least six rooms.

The floor area of House 1 is large, estimated to some 134 m^2 (Streiffert Eikeland 2006:266), and the sizes of the individual rooms vary from 15 m^2 to 46 m^2 (ibid. 266). The size of this complex is generous considering many contemporary houses (ibid.). There were at least two large doorways (1.25 m wide); the probable entrance was paved, and two limestone column bases stood nearby (Streiffert Eikeland 2006:266–67). Doorways, which indicate points of passage and movement, suggest that the entrance to the house was into room I, through which access to other rooms (apart from room VI) was gained. Room II was functionally tied to room V, as the latter could be accessed through room II.

There were only few inbuilt furnishings (Mühlenbock 2008): in the southwest corner of room I, an oven/hearth with a raised platform (1 m diameter, 15–20 cm high) lined with rounded cobbles; in the same room, a cobblestone foundation covered with pebbles along the wall; hearths in rooms II and IV; and a pit dug close to the wall in room VI.

The Workings of the Household. From the distribution of artefacts within the various rooms, we can propose the rooms' functions, with particular attention towards the social constitution of space (private vs. public, the symposium, and rituality). Generally, the house was kept clean, with little trash deposition (perhaps excepting the pit in room VI). The ceramics demonstrate storage, cooking, and consumption, and other finds project a similar set of functions across the rooms. Further analysis, however, reveal variations within the general finds categories, and these suggest some key differences among the rooms.

Room I is associated with weaving, with more than twenty terracotta loom weights found on top of a raised platform; it also had a hearth/oven. Various vessels linked to consumption were also found in the room: cooking vessels in the southwest corner, and plates and bowls to the north and east in the room – in total, a minimum of 290 different plates and vessels (Mühlenbock 2008; Mühlenbock and Prescott 2004). Most interesting, however, there were substantial numbers of objects linked to drinking, including amphoras, kraters, and cups; this room exhibited the largest and most comprehensive collection of drinking wares within House 1. This room, therefore, can be linked to food preparation and consumption, probably divided into two separate activity loci. The use of imported items and the focus on drinking and service utensils suggest that high-status foods were served here, and the room might have been an area for banquets or feasts (Mühlenbock, Påhlsson, and Hauge 2004). The presence of weaving equipment confirms the distinctive importance of the room, as weaving was an activity of major symbolic importance. Room III and IV may have had the same functions, and were subsidiary to room I.

Room V contained some storage vessels, mostly local grey wares, as well as elements associated with consumption. Room II contained a large amount of tableware, and may have functioned as a dining room (Mühlenbock, Påhlsson, and Hauge 2004:51). The entrance door to room V from room II suggest these two rooms were connected. Together they contain a significant number of cooking vessels, plates, and some drinking cups, and were probably linked to storage, preparation, and consumption of food. Despite the cooking ware, no oven or hearth was found here and, indeed, there is no significant trace of fire. Although the ceramics suggest that the rooms were related to food consumption, no imported wares were amongst the recovered sherds. These rooms may have served daily routine household consumption needs.

Room VI, which is to the east, suggests the remains of an older structure (Streiffert Eikeland 2006:264), although the excavators have proposed it was erected during the second building phase (Mühlenbock, Påhlsson, and Hauge 2004:50). It contains a large number of storage vessels (amphora, pithoi), but also elements perhaps of a more ritual character, including a pit with bones (Mühlenbock and Prescott 2004:181), an Attic cup, possibly a bronze cauldron, and an anthromorphic *capeduncola*. Such vessels are arguably related to the fertility goddess or idol, which had spread from Mesopotamia via the Eastern Mediterranean. The area may have had a mixed function of storage and ritual.

The previous observations allow for interesting comparisons among rooms. The crux of the argument put forward has rotated around rooms I, II, and IV versus II and V versus VI, and concerns the number and nature of households in House 1, and, indeed, whether House 1 represents a single household. The excavators have considered the option that House 1 does not represent a household at all; that the structure was a ritual or political compound. Supporting this idea would be the large numbers of pots, the emphasis on drinking, and the unusual architecture. To this might be added potential ritual features such as weaving, sacrifice (faunal material in pits), and cult (*capeduncola*) and feasting (symposium) equipment. However, all these elements may be explained in terms of household rituality and functionality. For example, the analysis of faunal remains from the ritual acropolis shows substantial differences from those from House 1, which had remains like those found in a common trash deposit (Chapter 6). They concluded that House 1 was a household(s).

If this premise is accepted, two interpretative avenues lay open. Both accentuate that this is a house, a dwelling place for households, containing different spaces – a semipublic stage and additional private spaces (Allison 1999). In the first interpretation, House 1 represents the development of two households, one being older and more affluent (rooms I, III, and IV), the other later and less socially prominent (V and II). This could indicate social differences between two independent households, or it could represent a hierarchical relationship of dependence, or generational links. The extreme version would be that one part represents a dominant family, the other subservient.

In the second interpretation, the complex represents a single unified household, where the variations in space represent distinct use of rooms. The spatial variations probably represent some age, gender, and activity distinction, but a prominent characteristic would seem to have been public social display versus more secluded private use. The public display area is of a high, virtually ritual status, with public weaving, drinking, and feasting. Here, consumption of wine took place with the ritualistic pouring from the amphora via the mixer into cups using referential Greek wares. We thus see an indigenous variant of the Greek symposium. Other parts of the building, not immediately accessible from the banquet area, were perhaps more private. This might suggest a degree of segregation of men and women, or perhaps a degree of seclusion of the women of the household from the outside world (Nevett 1999:30f). If weaving and drinking may be termed social rituals, further ritual indicators of household cult are the anthropomorphic drinking vessel, the *capeduncula* (which might have been related to a cult), and the pit with bones. This second interpretation seems the most likely, and although its details can be discussed, House 1 was in use as one building sometime during its life cycle (Streiffert Eikeland 2006:279).

COMPARATIVE ANALYSIS OF THE LATER PREHISTORIC HOUSEHOLD FROM THREE REGIONS

In all three regions, the household is assumed to have been closely connected with the house, with spaces for food preparation and consumption and some crafts. This framework, however, takes widely different forms across our cases. These differences are not merely physical variations in terms of different kinds of buildings; they seem to involve radically different ways of organising domestic life.

Architectural and organisational differences are found in the principal elements involved in the construction of the household as an economic, social, and material matrix, and pursuing these we can begin to outline some of the main differences among the areas. Although a number of features could be highlighted, we found the ones summarised in Table 5.3 particularly interesting and shall elaborate on some of these comparisons.

The life cycles of the household in the three areas have different characteristics, although in Scandinavia and Hungary, households show a relationship between household change and generational change. In Scandinavia, most houses last for a generation, some 30 to 60 years, with modest repair and little alteration in appearance or the way activities were organised. At the end of a house's 'life,' the roof-supporting posts of the house may have been pulled up (rather than left to decay), and the household either rebuilt near the former house or moved to another location, probably within the same farming area. Long-term continuity rested with the resource base rather than with the house plot.

On the tells of Hungary, we propose there was an ideal model for a two-roomed house. Some households were able to build like that from the beginning, but most extended or divided the house into two rooms. The life cycle of the houses would be shaped by two temporal cycles: One was regular replastering of walls and floors and the other, major building phases in response to changing needs or abilities. Despite this ability to change and adapt, the household would cease to exist after one or two generations; houses were abandoned, maybe deliberately burnt, but the location was not abandoned, and

Table 5.3. Some salient differences in household characteristics across the three areas

Theme	Scandinavia	Inner Carpathian	Sicily
House size	Variation in length	Two size groups	Individualised
Division	Variation in degree of division	Two categories (one roomed or two-roomed)	Several and ongoing divisions
Interior arrangements	Some variation in interior arrangements	Substantial variation in interior arrangement (number of hearths, size of pits)	Individualised but responding to an ideal
Biography	Usually one phase	Two or more phases	Several phases?
Location of productive activities	At informally defined places, mainly outside and at a distance from the house	At communal places, and specialised activities at particular places within the house	In purposeful rooms (for example weaving or cooking)
Characteristics of food preparation and consumption	Little elaboration, probably communal eating, no vessels for individual servicing	Elaborate food preparation, specialised objects used for servicing and consumption	Specialised and strongly ritualised food consumption practices and utensils
Private: public	No clear delimitation	Clear categories	Clear categories – with prohibitions attached?

the debris of the destroyed house was used as the foundation for the next. The previous house was literally recycled as the foundation for the next house, providing long-term continuity.

The situation in Sicily is still unclear, but the building complex seems to have the ability for expansion and change, and the relationships among buildings, place, and households may have been influenced by a range of social and economic factors through which the life cycle of the household was entangled within the range of other buildings on the site.

The life cycle of the Danish Bronze Age house brought uniformity to the sense of household, its duration, and relationship to space; but within the longhouses, individual households could constitute themselves in different ways, and it is only at a general level that houses were organised according to well-defined norms. In contrast, both in Hungary and Sicily, strong cultural norms dictated the arrangement of household spaces. Different households, within their social and economic means, might have been striving towards the same ideal arrangement of the household.

A further interesting difference is how the various spaces of the house were reached; in other words, how permeable the household was. The Scandinavian longhouse provides easy and uncontrolled access to all its parts – and it seems possible that the number of doorways relate to the number of rooms (Ethelberg 2000). There is no 'deep space' in these constructions and, together with the location of productive activities widely around the house, this may suggest that there was not a distinction between private and public space. The houses on the tell were clearly private spaces, and activities associated with the final preparation of food took place inside the houses. In the two-roomed houses, a room was created that could only be accessed through the larger room, thus demarcating a more private area. In Monte Polizzo, the complex structure, similar to ancient Greek households (Nevett 1999), had a strictly controlled access route so that some rooms, used for storage as well as consumption, were private and had elements of segregation.

We still have limited knowledge about what activities took place within the households and the degree of differences among households within a particular region. It is, however, interesting that weaving, despite taking place in all three areas and possibly being a central economic concern in Hungary, is only clearly documented in the Sicilian case, a cultural milieu in which weaving had gained high status.

Another interesting observation is the increasing materialisation of food consumption. In Scandinavia, food preparation is documented but little suggests any elaboration. In Hungary, strong indicators exist for elaborate procedures used to prepare food in different ways, as well as the use of fine tableware for its consumption. In the case of Sicily, some aspects of food consumption had become part of the political arena and strongly ritualised through external connections to an international world. The household evidence also raises seminal questions about where craft activities were located and how they were organised.

The new data from the three areas helped make it possible to place the 'household' under the microscope. There are a myriad of further questions and concerns and the task of discussing the household has only been initiated here – not completed. The comparative perspective has, however, proven itself to be a helpful way of coming to terms with some of the most fundamental differences among the three case studies.

NOTES
1. The excavation of the tell at Százhalombatta, Hungary, is still ongoing and although much analysis has been carried out, not all analyses were finished at the time of completing this chapter.
2. The relationship between houses and households is not always simple. For instance, L. Horne's ethnoarchaeological study of a contemporary village in Bakhestan showed that "rooms owned by a single household may be spatially dispersed within the village, contiguous rooms sometimes being owned by people who are not immediate kin.... it relates to local patterns of marriage and inherence" (David and Kramer 2001:294).

6

Subsistence Strategies

Maria Vretemark

With contributions by Hans-Peter Stika (archaeobotanical case study, Southern Scandinavia, Sicily, and Hungary), Brigitta Berzsényi (archaeobotanical case study, Hungary), and Peter Steen Henriksen (archaeobotanical case study, Southern Scandinavia)

INTRODUCTION

Food resources from animals and plants provided the necessities of life for any population, whatever period in history or geographical position. Raw material for clothes and tools had also to be gained from animals and plants. Activities of procurement, farming, and husbandry were necessarily imbedded within particular social organisations (Chapter 5). Different natural geographic, environmental and climatologically prerequisites have resulted in a variety of subsistence strategies and organisation outcomes. By comparing the results of archaeozoological and macro-botanical case study analysis from settlements in three contrasting regions of Europe, we can propose general tendencies for agrarian economy, and subsistence patterns can be suggested. The comparative analyses focus on production, consumption, and trade by studying the development of animal and plant exploitation as reflected in bone material and botanical remains. Consumption versus production and the balance between supply and demand are discussed as well as signs of surplus production and exchange.

Archaeozoological and archaeobotanical macro-botanical analyses carried out as part of our broad study (Chapter 1) have generated rich raw data and information. Together with information from other major studies, results document developments during the period ca 2400 to 1400 BC in Hungary, 1500 to 500 BC in Scandinavia, and 600 to 300 BC in Sicily. The main goal here is to describe subsistence strategies in three different kinds of societies in geographically widely separate parts of Europe. The majority of the animal bones and plant remains found within the settlements can be considered normal everyday household waste, reflecting animal and plant exploitation, mainly connected to agricultural and subsistence strategies. In all areas, procurement mixed both animal husbandry and cereal production; wild resources, although of little importance as a food, were used for tools and ritual. Of particular importance, the mixes of crops and animals varied from one locale to the next, reflecting local adaptation within the general mix of European domesticates, and the mix varied from period to period, reflecting intensification in land use. A key conclusion is that animal husbandry dominated the subsistence strategies in Southern Scandinavia and Hungary, and that the animal mixes and patterns of culling document trade in animal products locally and perhaps at a distance.

SOUTHERN SCANDINAVIA – ARCHAEOZOOLOGICAL CASE STUDY

Although many Bronze Age settlements have been excavated in Scandinavia, faunal remains are poorly preserved in most sites of that period, and conclusions about animal exploitation must be tentative. On most sites, only a small number of burnt bones are left to investigate and, in those cases, the composition of the animal remains are heavily biased and not fit to be used in this comparative survey. Fortunately, however, a handful of excavations provide large assemblages of unburnt faunal remains to help glimpse subsistence patterns.

In Denmark, the Bjerre Enge Thy assemblage from northern Jutland is the largest from the Early Bronze Age (1500–1000 BC) (Nyegaard 1996). From Late Bronze Age (1000–500 BC), in addition to Bjerre Enge, substantial collections exist for Kirkebjerg, Bulbjerg, Voldtofte, Hasmark, and Kolby in Denmark (Nyegaard 1996) and Ängdala in southern and Apalle in central Sweden (Nyegaard 1983; Lepiksaar 1969; Ericson et al 2003). At the west coast of Sweden, Tanum represents different subsistence strategies, so it brings forth an understanding of the complexity of subsistence patterns in Bronze Age Scandinavia. However, only a poor sample of bone was preserved here, because soil conditions are unsuitable for preservation.

Species distribution

Among the livestock, cattle are more or less dominant throughout southern Scandinavia. A general trend in bone material is that the

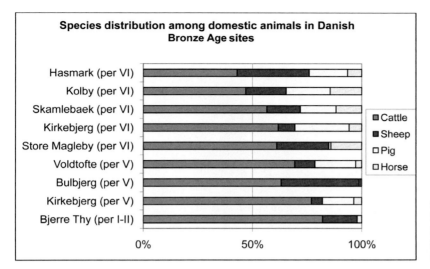

Figure 6.1.
Decrease in cattle from Early Bronze Age to Late Bronze Age settlements in south Scandinavia.

amount of cattle decreases from the older to later phases of the Bronze Age. On the contrary, sheep and sometimes pig increase to become more frequent in the assemblages (Figure 6.1). These changes occur sometime during 1000 to 500 BC in southern Scandinavia. In middle Scandinavia, the same changes take place, but with some time delay (Vretemark 2008; Petersson 2006). Simultaneously, cropping strategies change notably. The age distribution of cattle shows that a majority of the cattle now were kept until older age and that slaughtering of calves and juveniles became rarer. Among adult cattle, about 30 percent were male. This age distribution suggests an increasing value of the cattle as milking cows and working oxen, as meat supply came increasingly from expanded stocks of sheep and pig. Cattle were the most valuable animals among the domestic stock, and also the most expensive to breed and bring to adult age. A substantial value was invested in a draught ox.

The changes in species distribution reflect an attempt to increase and maximise the outcome of meat, perhaps to meet population growth. This intensification obviously put more pressure on the pastures, and consequently increased the importance of sheep and goat, which are better suited to poor pasturage (Figure 6.1).

The age distribution of sheep shows that a high proportion were kept as adults. The percentage of adult male sheep, however, seems to be rather low, suggesting that wool production during the Bronze Age was not a main objective in sheep farming. Adult ewes were kept as breeding animals, giving lambs to slaughter, milk, and wool for household needs, but not for trade. Pigs were kept solely for meat, probably for the household. This is clear by the age distribution.

Nearly all of the pigs were slaughtered by 2 years of age, leaving only a few breeding animals.

Dogs could be found on every settlement, illustrating their importance for herding, hunting, and guarding. Size differentiation among dogs suggests that breeds for different roles already existed in the Bronze Age. Cut marks are recorded on some dog bones at Kirkebjerg, Ängdala, and Apalle; the dogs appear to have been defleshed and their meat may have been eaten. The percentage of horse bones varies exceedingly among the settlements, making up between 1 and 30 percent of the domestic animals. A general trend is that the amount of horses increases towards the end of the Bronze Age period (800–500 BC), and horses became even more plentiful by the Early Iron Age (500 BC – 0).

In the Bronze Age, the fact that domestic animals were the prime source of animal products is confirmed in most of the cases, but the species distribution apparently varied considerably from one settlement to another. At some, fish and molluscs obviously made up a substantial part of the animal food; on others, there are no fish bones. In Tanum, evidence of fishing includes deep-water fishing equipment for codfish as well as bones of large pollack and cod (Ling 2008). This indicates a well-organised society, a developed specialisation of subsistence strategies, and an ability to adapt to natural prerequisites. Away from the coast, in the pastoral landscape of central Sweden, animal husbandry totally dominated the animal economy (Vretemark 2005); however, one cannot rule out the possibility of seasonal movement from inland agrarian sites to coastal fishing camps. At some inland sites in Denmark and in Sweden, fish and molluscs are found. These finds either indicate some exchanges between settlements, or support seasonal movement between summer coastal and winter inland settlements during the Bronze Age.

Bones from wild game are often very limited but, again, significant percentages (5–15 percent) exist in the assemblages at some sites. The single most frequent wild species in the south Scandinavian settlements is red deer (*Cervus elaphus*). In addition are a small number of fragments from roe deer (*Capreolus capreolus*), fox (*Vulpes vulpes*), wild cat (*Felis silvestris*), hare (*Lepus timidus*), bear (*Ursus arctos*), beaver (*Castor fiber*), otter (*Lutra lutra*) and wolf (*Canis lupus*). Bird bones are seldom found here. The largest numbers of wild game have been recorded at Apalle in middle Sweden, where twelve separate species were identified. In addition to those already mentioned, elk (*Alces alces*), badger (*Meles meles*), polecat (*Mustela putoris*), and marten (*Martes martes*) were found, in addition to many wild birds (Ericson et al 2003). Hunting wild game and birds as well as fishing complemented domesticated meat sources, for which husbandry was marginal.

Surplus production and exchange systems

Evidence of substantial cattle breeding at some settlements suggests that a surplus of calves could be traded or gifted. On the Kirkebjerg settlement, a low percentage (15 percent) of cattle were juveniles (Figure 6.2), well below what might be expected. Female calves probably were kept to replace old milking cows, but juvenile males may have been traded out as part of an exchange system in valuables.

SOUTHERN SCANDINAVIA – ARCHAEOBOTANICAL CASE STUDY

Archaeobotanical analysis of remains from the Danish sites at Bjerre Enge and Legård on Jutland and the Swedish site at Tanum on the west coast are used as examples to describe plant exploitation in Bronze Age Scandinavia. Although the ranges of crops are quite similar, the different sites represent different assemblages that represented local choices based on efficiency, desirability, and methods of cultivation.

Bjerre Enge and Legård

Substantial evidence of plant use during the Bronze Age is available from recent research in Thy, northwestern Jutland. The most

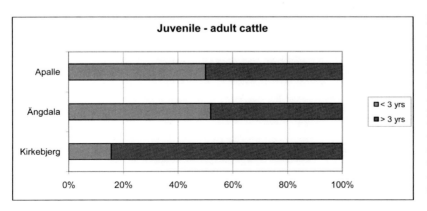

Figure 6.2. At most Scandinavian sites, the amount of young calves among the slaughtered animals is quite high, similar to Apalle or Ängdala. The pattern at Kirkebjerg, on the other hand, where the calves are missing, suggests a continuous disposal of juvenile cattle away from the settlement in an exchange system.

Table 6.1. Bronze Age crops in Thy, Denmark

	Thy in Early Bronze Age	Thy in Late Bronze Age
Dominant crops	naked barley emmer	naked barley bread wheat
Subdominant crops	einkorn	emmer spelt broomcorn millet gold of pleasure
Additional crops	hulled barley	hulled barley

extensive recovery of macro-botanical remains was carried out at Bjerre Enge, where rescue excavations revealed several Bronze Age houses and a large Late Bronze Age field system. The site had been inhabited for 700 years from 1500 to 800 BC until most of the area was covered by aeolian sand, protecting the deposits. A systematic sampling strategy was instituted. Macrofossil analysis has been carried out on material from five sites at Bjerre Enge (Henriksen et al in press). At site 6 (1500–1000 BC) and site 7 (1000–800 BC), excavated by Thy Archaeological Project (TAP), systematic samples were taken from pits and from the culture layers in a 2 × 2 m grid covering the houses and surrounding areas. At the settlement sites 2 and 3 (1500–1000 BC), samples were taken from postholes. At site 4 (1500–800 BC), a field area, samples were taken from the prehistoric plough soil of small fields and between the fields. The concentration of macro-botanicals from sites 2, 3, 4, and 6 was low, primarily consisting of cereal grains and field-weed seeds. Most of the samples from site 7 contained many cereal grains, spikelets, seeds from field weeds, and seeds from plants deriving from meadows and heathland.

Throughout the Bronze Age, the main crop at the Bjerre settlements was naked six-rowed barley (*Hordeum vulgare* var. *nudum*) (Table 6.1). In the Early Bronze Age, emmer (*Triticum dicoccum*) was also common, whereas spelt (*Triticum spelta*) was less common. In the Late Bronze Age, the importance of emmer and spelt shifted and other crops gained in importance. Many grains and rachis segments from bread wheat (*Triticum aestivum*) were found in two samples from the house at site 7, but the importance of this species is difficult to establish from only two samples. Gold of pleasure (*Camelina sativa*) was also introduced in the Late Bronze Age, and this is the oldest known find of this plant in Denmark.

At site 7, because of the good recovery and broad-scale sampling, the distribution of macrofossils reveals information about the localisation of different plant-processing activities. In the culture layer outside the house, spikelets from emmer and spelt were widespread; inside the house, the spikelets were concentrated in two fire pits in its western end, indicating that the dehusking of hulled wheats took place there. Concentrations of seeds from field weeds such as fat hen (*Chenopodium album*), field brome (*Bromus arvensis*), and persicarias (*Persicaria* spp.) in a pit in the eastern end of the house indicate that the fine cleaning of cereal crops took place there. Most of the seeds from gold of pleasure were found outside the house in "the activity area" as identified by excavators. This could indicate that processing of this plant took place outside the house and the seeds therefore may not be for food.

The field-weed flora suggest intensified use of fields at Bjerre Enge. From the Early Bronze Age, when the weed flora consist of a few ruderal species, it became more diverse in the Late Bronze Age, indicating a shift towards permanent fields. The diversification of weed flora is indirect evidence for manuring as it is not possible to grow crops permanently on pure sand without manure. The manuring is also indicated by household refuse such as potsherds and charcoal found broadly spread through the plough soil of the Late Bronze Age fields at site 4. Because many cattle bones are known here, the placement of the farms on sandy soils with good grazing options further suggests that the Bronze Age economy in Thy heavily focused on animal husbandry. Access to manure from the animals would then have been used for the fields.

The charcoal from Bjerre Enge supports the palaeo pollen evidence (Chapter 2) that forest in Thy had been largely cleared. The house at site 6 was build of poor timber, including willow (*Salix* sp.) and poplars (*Populus* sp.) (Malmros, in press). Remains that form the fire pits, especially at site 7 (Late Bronze Age), also demonstrate that fuel no longer relied on wood, having shifted primarily to peat from bog and heath. In the macrofossil analysis, seeds from *Carex* and twigs and flowers from heather (*Caluna vulgaris* and *Erica tetralix*) were amongst the most abundant. Even branches from hawthorn (*Hippophae rhamnoides*) (Malmros in press) and animal dung were used for fuel.

At the Bronze Age farm of Legård in central Thy, soil conditions were better than at Bjerre Enge because of rather fertile moraine landscape of Sønderhå parish with sand-mixed clayey sediments, and its crop mix was correspondingly richer. Multi-rowed naked barley (*Hordeum vulgare* var. *nudum*) was dominant, with only few remains of hulled barley (*Hordeum vulgare* var. *vulgare*). The subdominant cereal was emmer (*Triticum dicoccum*). Club wheat (*T. compactum*) and bread wheat (*T. aestivum*), spelt (*T. spelta*), einkorn (*T. monococcum*), and common millet (*Panicum milliaceum*) were of minor importance, appearing at the Legård site during Late Bronze Age (1000–500 BC). Rye brome (*Bromus* cf. *secalinus*) and oats (*Avena* sp.) casually occurred in the cereal fields from this period, and they might also have been used for consumption, as might wild beetroot (*Beta vulgaris*) collected at wild habitats close to the shoreline. Hazel (*Corylus avellana*) was available. As documented by some arable weeds and grassland species of rich soils that were found at Legård site but missing at Bjerre Enge, environmental conditions for agriculture at Legård were better. Like Bjerre Enge, a scarcity of firewood at Legård apparently required use of peat and dung as fuels. Among the macro-fossils were many remains of sedges (*Carex* spp.) and other wetland vegetation.

In Thy, farming activities were apparently heavily based on stockbreeding. In addition, crops were raised most for household consumption but probably not for surplus. In the Early Bronze Age, naked barley and emmer were the main crops. Into the Late Bronze Age, naked barley and emmer persisted as the main crops, but the crop spectrum was enlarged to include free-threshing wheat (*Triticum aestivum* s.l.), common millet (*Panicum miliaceum*), and gold of pleasure (*Camelina sativa*), among others. No shift from free-threshing to hulled barley as a main crop was visible from the Early to the Late Bronze Age. In northern Jutland, the shift from naked to hulled barley happened in the Roman Iron Age around 100 AD. In eastern Denmark and southern Sweden, the shift happened almost 1,000 years earlier, somewhere around 1000 to 800 BC.

Tanum

The landscape of Tanum is dominated by rocky coasts, forests, and meadows; arable land is very limited (Bertilsson 1987). Taking into account changes in sea level (Chapter 2), even less arable land was available during the Bronze Age than today. Although only a few samples with archaebotanical remains exist for Tanum,

Table 6.2. Bronze Age crops in southern Sweden and Iron Age crops in Tanum

	Sweden in Early Bronze Age	Sweden in Late Bronze Age	Tanum in Early Iron Age
Dominant crops	naked barley emmer spelt einkorn	hulled barley bread wheat	hulled barley
Subdominant crops	hulled barley bread wheat broomcorn millet gold of pleasure	naked barley emmer spelt broomcorn millet gold of pleasure linseed	bread wheat emmer oat gold of pleasure linseed pulses

dating 500 to 250 BC, multi-rowed hulled barley (*Hordeum vulgare*) was the dominating crop. Oat (*Avena* sp.) grains are rare, and even less common are emmer (*Triticum dicoccum*) and free-threshing wheat (*T. aestivum/T. durum*). Seeds of gold of pleasure (*Camelina sativa*) were present, as well as hazelnuts (*Corylus avellana*). The weed flora (*Chenopodium album, Persicaria lapathifolium, Solanum nigrum, Stellaria media, Thlaspi arvense*) suggest some good soil conditions, while other weeds (*Rumex acetosella, Scleranthus annuus, Spergula arvensis*) derived from poor, acidic, sandy soils.

In his review, Gustafsson (1998) summarises palaeo-botanical finds from six Early and nine Late Bronze Age sites in central and southern Sweden, more fertile landscapes than in northern Bohuslän. In the Early Bronze Age, agriculture was based on emmer, spelt, einkorn, and naked barley, with limited cultivation of hulled barley and a little bread wheat. Millet (*Panicum milliaceum*) and gold of pleasure (*Camelina sativa*) were introduced in the Early Bronze Age. In the Late Bronze Age, hulled barley became the dominating crop and the hulled wheat species and free-threshing barley decreased (Table 6.2). There are more finds of oat, gold of pleasure, millet, and rye brome. Flax (*Linum usitatissimum*) was also introduced during this period. Gustafsson suggests an interpretation of the finds of weeds as follows: During the Early Bronze Age, a shifting agriculture on nonpermanent fields was practised, and the systems switched to systematic manuring of permanent fields in the Late Bronze Age. The switch to hulled barley cultivation can be related to manuring. As experiments proved, in comparison to free-threshing barley and hulled wheat species, hulled barley reacts more positively to manuring (Viklund 1998). In the northern Bohuslän region, the Bronze Age spectrum of crops seems to be reduced in comparison to more fertile regions of Sweden.

HUNGARY – ARCHAEOZOOLOGICAL CASE STUDY

Animal husbandry appears to have been an extremely important part of the Hungarian subsistence economy during the Bronze Age in the Benta valley. The bone assemblages, collected during excavations in 1989–91 and 1999–2005 at Százhalombatta-Földvár, make up one of the largest faunal collections from Hungary. All together, about 800 kg or 150,000 fragments of bones were retrieved (Vretemark and Sten, in press.). Thanks to the fact that Százhalombatta Archaeological Expedition (SAX) systematically screened the cultural layers, this material comprises a fairly solid ground for speculations about subsistence strategies and animal husbandry during the period ca 2400 to 1400 BC. The systematic collection methods used also made it possible to find bones from fish, bird and rodents, conditions that are rare among Hungarian faunal assemblages. We can conclude that the primary source of animal products was domesticates, especially cattle, sheep, and pig, and that horses and dogs were also quite common, probably used as work animals and pets. Hunting and fishing were of only minor significance. Perhaps most importantly, the raising of animals appears to have shifted through the Bronze Age to emphasise increasingly special products that could be traded.

Species distribution

Animal husbandry was the main source for animal products of different kinds. Among the domestic animals, the relative abundance is surprisingly constant throughout the period 2000 to 1400 BC, with very small changes, if any (Vretemark and Sten 2005:158). Numerically, sheep represent the dominant species, followed by cattle. Pig is least common. If we look into the oldest settlement phases of the tell, some changes in the relative frequencies among domestic animals did take place. The percentage of cattle bones was significantly larger in the layers from 2400 to 2000 BC compared with the later ones (Figure 6.3). The decrease in the transition from Early Bronze

Age into Middle Bronze Age, around 2000 BC, marks a change in animal exploitation strategies. During the early phase, most of the slaughtered cattle were young, reflecting a system in which meat was the main objective and cattle provided most of it. In a more developed agricultural system, adult cattle of both sexes became valuable and slaughtering of young calves would be limited. An increase in pig and sheep in meat consumption, to fill in the loss of meat from juvenile cattle, is documented in the faunal remains after 2000 BC.

The cattle bones from the Middle Bronze Age (2000–1400 BC) reflect a cropping strategy in which most of the individuals were kept until old age or at least until they were fully-grown at about 3 years of age. Only 30 percent (mostly young males) were slaughtered as juveniles. Among the adult cattle, a third were male, probably used as draught animals. The need for animal traction power in cultivation and transportation must have been substantial. Even some female cattle show draught-related pathologies in the pelvic region. The dominating category of cattle, adult females, was important for milk production and for breeding.

The increased sheep exploitation around 2000 BC reveals the growing general importance of this domestic animal to the inhabitants of the tell. A major change of sheep husbandry strategy also took place at this time. The age distribution of the population in the Early Bronze Age layers of the tell reveals an exploitation pattern in which the majority of the stock was harvested young (Figure 6.4). Meat production was the main reason for keeping sheep during the period 2400–2000 BC. As the relative importance of sheep increased around 2000 BC, the kill-off patterns became totally different and age distribution altered towards predominance for older sheep. This is

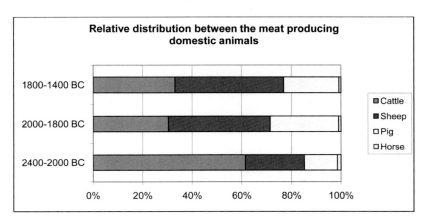

Figure 6.3.
Percentage of cattle at Százhalombatta was higher during the Early Bronze Age, before 2000 BC.

probably a sign of more intensive sheep exploitation and a growing emphasis on wool production. During the centuries after 2000 BC, about 60 percent of the sheep were kept as adults. Among these, the stock was heavily female, but about a third was, in fact, male. This supports the probable importance of wool production, because, after growth has stopped, the only reason to keep an adult male sheep would be for its wool.

The pigs were kept for meat production. Most individuals were slaughtered as juveniles and the distribution between males and females was even. No changes in pig exploitation could be revealed during the Bronze Age.

Horse bones make up about 4 percent throughout the different layers of the tell. Most of the horses were older animals and some horse bones reveal pathologies attributable to traction or other kind of work. Cut marks suggest that horse bodies were butchered and their skins were taken. The horse meat was probably eaten, but this was only a tiny part of the meat consumption. Horses were kept mainly for traction and riding, perhaps by warriors.

The frequency of dog bones makes up nearly 5 percent of the identified fragments from domestic species. Many of the dogs were kept until very old. In life, the dogs were used for hunting, herding, protection, and guarding. These functions were of vital importance in a culture in which identity and wealth focused on domestic animal stocks and where the productive yield from husbandry represented survival. Dogs may have had a special position in the society (Choyke and Vretemark 2004). The surprising observation about the dog bones is the large number of thin cut marks. Butchering followed a specific pattern: After death, bones were defleshed to minimise damage. It is possible that dog meat was eaten, perhaps as a part of a ritual behaviour (Vretemark and Sten 2008).

Only a limited part of the bone remains represented wild species. Hunting was probably socially significant, but not primarily for food. Obtaining furs, hides, and other special materials, such as red deer antler or bear claws, was probably important. The percentage of fragments from wild animal bones during Middle Bronze Age (2000–1400 BC) is only about 2 percent of the total material. During the Early Bronze Age (2400–2000 BC), the amount is somewhat larger though, around 8 percent. The species hunted were mainly hare and red deer, although another ten species are identified in the assemblage. Bird hunting was practised, as was some fishing. Bones from cyprinid,

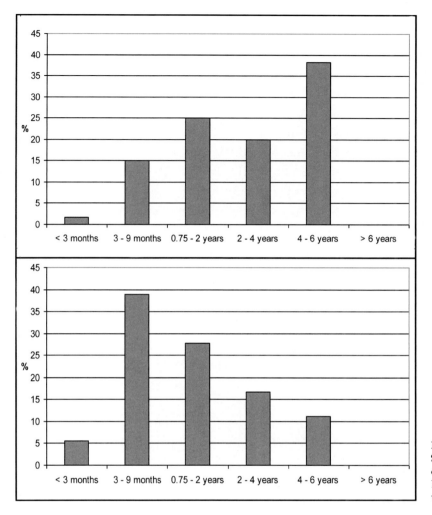

Figure 6.4.
Sheep kill-off patterns changed around 2000 BC, indicating increased wool production.

sturgeon, and pike were identified, but their importance as food resources is difficult to assess because the fish bones probably are underrepresented.

Surplus production and exchange systems

Was animal husbandry at the tell sufficient for the inhabitants' uses or were some animal raised elsewhere? Could the tell have been self-sufficient in animal production? To supply a population of let's say, 600 persons with the desired range of animal products, large quantities had to be obtained; for instance, a yearly supply of at least about 2 to 3 kg of wool and 50 kg of meat per person would have been needed. Of course, they could have used other kind of fibres for textiles and they could have eaten more vegetables and fish than we assume, but still the calculated amount corresponds with what we know from written sources about rations in the Roman Empire (White 1970:364) or in Medieval societies (Morell 1989). Based on these assumptions, the calculation experiment shows that a yearly supply of 1,200 kg of wool or more was used for clothing and other textile needs, along with a minimum of 30 tons of meat. To get this amount of wool, a flock of about 2,500 wool sheep would be needed if every sheep produced 0.5 kg each per year (Halstead 1981:328). This could be possible if large grazing areas were available for the sheep. The number of animals needed to cover 30 tons of meat supply could be estimated from the relative distribution of species in the faunal remains (cattle 30%, sheep 40%, pig 30%) and the slaughtering weight per species (cattle 100 kg, sheep 20 kg, pig 40 kg) (Vretemark 1995:116). Because of the different amount of meat gained from a cattle compared to a sheep or a pig, about 60 percent of the consumed meat would have been cattle meat, ca 15 percent came from sheep and ca 25 percent from pig. If we go further with this theoretical calculation it appears that at least 180 cattle, 320 sheep, and 180 pigs must be slaughtered every year to support 600 persons at the Middle Bronze Age tell settlement with 30,000 kg of meat. If the population size where larger, consequently even more animals were needed. This requires large-scale animal husbandry and a living stock of several thousands of animals.

Considering the size of the tell settlement, consumption needs probably exceeded production from the site's catchment area, which was truncated by placement at the river (Chapter 3). Food supply and other goods must have been brought in from other sites. Furthermore, the macro-botanical evidence gives no proof of large-scale animal husbandry and handling of fodder within the excavated part of the tell site. This supports the conclusion that most of the animals were kept outside the main settlement, probably in settlements through the Benta. If the tell settlement were the centre of a larger settlement system, animals may have been mobilised as tribute from outlying settlements. Probably some kind of fixed exchange system was established in order to maintain animal consumption at the central settlement. The unchanging relative abundance of species throughout several centuries of occupation strongly supports this assumption as it seems to mirror a stable system of long-term subsistence strategy. Smaller sites at some distance away from the tell could have been like satellites, making it possible to establish a

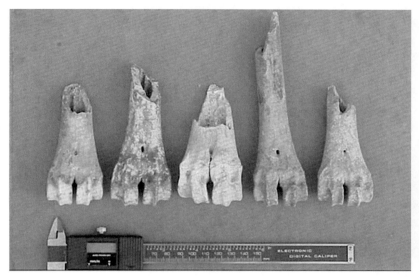

Figure 6.5.
Red deer was the prime wild animal hunted in Bronze Age and Early Iron Age Europe. Antlers and distal parts of metapodials, cut off like the ones in the picture, dominate the assemblages.

system with large-scale pastoralism. In such a system, animals ready for slaughter or other uses could be brought to the tell.

Regional exchange is also documented by wild animal utilisation. Bones of red deer (*Cervus elaphus*), roe deer (*Capreolus capreolus*), aurochs (*Bos primigenius*), hare (*Lepus europaeus*), wild boar (*Sus scrofa*), fox (*Vulpes vulpes*), bear (*Ursus arctos*), ermine (*Mustela erminea*), polecat (*Mustela putoris*), wolf (*Canis lupus*), beaver (*Castor fiber*), wild cat (*Felis silvestris*), and birds speak to hunting, but this hunting may have taken place elsewhere. Red deer antler was a valuable raw material for tools or other objects (Chapter 7; Choyke 1984, 2000). The fragments from red deer consist mainly of antler and lower extremities. This pattern suggests that red deer skins, with attached toe bones and cranium, and shed antlers were brought to the settlement from elsewhere. The same goes for bear claws, wild boar tusks, wolf paws, and other specialty items. Wild animals arrived at the tell "in pieces" (Figure 6.5). Only certain parts, such as teeth, claws, antler, and hide are found, and they could have circulated as special gifts in the social economy.

In contrast, the majority of the bones, coming from domestic animals, represent slaughter and kitchen waste from the daily handling and preparation of food utilised by the site's households (Chapter 5). Refuse was thrown away within the settlement, not far from the buildings. The anatomical representation of bones from different body parts reveals that the domestic animals were slaughtered, butchered, and consumed within the area.

HUNGARY – ARCHAEOBOTANICAL CASE STUDY

Site methodology

Recovery of samples for flotation followed procedures originally developed by Thy Archaeological Project in Denmark. The excavated area at Százhalombatta-Földvár was gridded by 2 m × 2 m units, and soil samples of 10 litres were collected from the general matrix of each unit. Special features, such as hearths, ovens, working areas, house floors, burnt spots, pits, postholes, stake-holes, and surrounding of the grinding stones, were sampled additionally. Flotation was used to separate light from heavy fractions and both fractions were sampled separately. Three hundred to 600 samples were collected annually.

Identified plant remains

The archaeobotanical part of the excavation has focused on Middle Bronze Age (2000–1400 BC). Plant remains investigation resulted in a variety of cultivated cereals and pulses as the main crops. From the pits, einkorn (*Triticum monococcum*) and hulled barley *(Hordeum vulgare)* were dominating regarding the number of grain finds and frequency of appearance (1571 einkorn grain finds in 91 percent of analysed samples, hulled barley with 1,227 grain finds in 77.5 percent samples). Emmer (*T. dicoccum*), spelt (*T. spelta*), bread/hard wheat (*T. aestivum/durum*), and broomcorn millet (*Panicum milliaceum*) were subdominant, with considerably less importance both in number of finds and in frequency of appearance. Naked barley *(H. vulgare* var. *nudum)* and rye (*Secale cereale*) are represented only by single finds (Table 6.3).

The different crop processing activities were localised inside the Százhalombatta-Földvár settlement and apparently associated with everyday householding activities (Chapter 5). The frequency of chaff finds, which are removed in dehusking, is often used to locate areas of cereal production as opposed to consumption, and the ratio between chaff finds of hulled wheat species and barley was completely different. From hulled wheats (mainly einkorn) 9210 finds of chaff were counted, while barley contributed only 137 chaff remains. This is due to the fact that, most likely, daily dehusking activities of hulled wheats for everyday consumption produced lots

Table 6.3. Bronze Age crops at Százhalombatta

	Százhalombatta-Földvar Middle Bronze Age	Százhalombatta-Földvar Late Bronze Age/Early Iron Age
Dominant crops	einkorn hulled barley lentil pea	No substantial changes
Subdominant crops	"new type glume wheat" emmer bitter vetch	No substantial changes
Additional crops	spelt bread wheat broomcorn millet (free-threshing barley) (rye) faba bean gold of pleasure linseed poppy safflower	

of carbonised remains in and outside the houses and those remains were discarded into pits. The crop processing of barley appears to have been different, producing less charred chaff found in the settlement. Chaff finds cannot, therefore, be used to calculate the importance of cereal processing. Pit samples rich in cereal finds more often were dominated by chaff remains (30 samples) than by grains finds (10 samples) and represent dehusking activities versus storage finds in the case of pure grain assemblages. The taphonomy of other samples is of mixed nature (46 samples). Some less rich cereal samples are representing final crop processing such as fine sieving and hand sorting.

Cereal grain fragments can be distinguished regarding whether charring happened before or after fragmentation. Some fragmented grains mainly from einkorn, prior to carbonisation were recognized in many samples. These fragments show a puffed out, smooth surface (Willcox 2002), and they may be associated with coarse grinding, as in bulgur production (Valamoti 2002).

Within the hulled wheat species chaff finds, the dominant einkorn is followed in abundance by "new type glume wheat" (Jones et al 2000; Kohler-Schneider 2001; Jacomet 2006), characterised by spikelet fork morphology found at Százhalombatta-Földvár. Partly this new type glume wheat is interpreted as Timopheev's wheat (*Triticum timopheevi* Zhuk; for a modern classification of wheat species see Zohary and Hopf 2000). New type glume wheat is found in Neolithic and Bronze Age sites of the Near East, the Balkans, and southeastern central Europe, although missing elsewhere in Europe. It was probably an important cultivated crop in the Százhalombatta-Földvár tell site, but hard proof – that is, DNA – is still lacking. Much less frequently identified in our samples, emmer and spelt are subdominant.

At Százhalombatta-Földvár, pulses were of considerable importance, and other noncereals were also important. More than 85 percent of the Middle Bronze Age pit samples contained pulses (938 remains). In three-fourths of the rich cereal samples, seeds of pulses are more than 10 percent of the total sum of all crop seeds. The dominant pulse is lentil (*Lens culinaris*), followed by pea (*Pisum sativum*) and bitter vetch (*Vicia ervilia*). Finds of faba bean (*V. faba*) are rare. In one storage pit, pulses were dominated by pea and were mixed with lots of hulled wheat chaff. Finds of oil plants are rare: Some seed of gold of pleasure (*Camelina sativa*) were found, and single finds of linseed (*Linum usitatissimum*), opium poppy (*Papaver somniferum*), and safflower (*Carthamus tinctoria*), which is the oldest find from Hungary so far. Finds of wild fruits are quite rare in Százhalombatta-Földvár: cornelian cherry (*Cornus mas*) is the most common, followed by elderberry (*Sambucus nigra* and *S. ebulus*), wild strawberry (*Fragaria vesca*), wild apple (*Malus sylvestris*), and blackberry (*Rubus fruticosus* agg.).

After 1400 BC, in the Late Bronze Age and Early Iron Age samples, the spectrum of crops did not change substantially, and there appears to have been no structural change in the agricultural system in comparison to the Middle Bronze Age. The archaeobotanical results from the later periods are much less representative than those from Middle Bronze Age contexts.

At Százhalombatta-Földvár during the Middle Bronze Age, the weed species suggest a productive pattern of two-season cropping on fertile soils. Some of the weeds are classified as summer, and others as winter annuals, representing in today's agricultural systems weeds of summer and winter cereals crops. Most common weeds were white goosefoot (*Chenopodium album*), with 1445 finds in 86.5 percent of pit samples, followed by black bindweed (*Polygonum convolvulus*), with 241 finds in 62.9 percent of samples. The ten next most frequent wild plants, in descending, order were: wall germander (*Teucrium* cf. *chamaedrys*), black medic (*Medicago lupulina*), hooked/green bristlegrass (*Setaria verticillata/viridis*), clover species (*Trifolium* sp.), field brome (*Bromus* cf. *arvensis*), prostrate knotweed (*Polygonum aviculare* agg.), bedstraw species (*Galium* sp.), corn gromwell (*Lithospermum arvense*), little hodgeweed (*Portulaca oleracea*), and corn cockle (*Agrostemma githago*). Hulled wheat species are typical winter crops (sown in late autumn); barley and broomcorn millet are typical summer crops (sown in early spring). A long list of forty different weed taxa display a weed flora typical of fertile soils, while fewer, less numerous taxa indicate cultivation on poor sandy soils.

The low frequency of weed finds typically associated with fodder or animal dung suggests that stockbreeding was done outside the settlement. Persistant ruderals (nine taxa) might have been growing within the settlement as well as other plants from ruderal grassland (nine taxa). Dry grassland (eleven taxa) and grassland on productive stands (seven taxa) are only represented by few remains. This evidence therefore reinforces the suggestion made earlier that the source of animals was probably off-tell, perhaps received as tribute or gift from other settlements.

Vegetation from wetlands, located downhill from the settlement at the floodplains of the Danube, was apparently used in construction. Charred remains include common reed (*Phragmites australis*), bulrush (*Schoenoplectus* cf. *lacustris*), sawgrass (*Cladium mariscus*), and bur-reed (*Sparganium* sp.). Materials from these species can be used for roofing, wickerwork, or coarse tempering for house wall constructions. Analysis of plant imprints points to the addition of common reed to daub. Aside from plant material from wetland vegetation, mainly dehusking byproducts from glume wheat crop processing were used for tempering daub.

SICILY – ARCHAEOZOOLOGICAL CASE STUDY

The analysed bone material, collected during the excavation campaigns of 1998–2004 at Monte Polizzo, comes from house structures (Houses 1–3) and a midden, the "Profile" (Vretemark 2003). Altogether, about 28 kg, or 12,000 fragments of animal bones, from the Iron Age (600–500 BC) were retrieved (Chapter 1). Additionally, excavations recovered a faunal assemblage from the layers around the acropolis, where about 8,500 fragments were identified (Hnatiuk

2004). The possibility of comparing three different areas within the same settlement is at hand, which could enlighten us regarding some of the internal structure of this Early Iron Age community. The layers from the houses and from the acropolis were screened, but the Profile regrettably was not. Fragmentation of bones is severe, with an average fragment weight of only 1.5 g in the houses and 3.7 g in the Profile. The preservation of the material also is quite poor, with heavily eroded surfaces. The material from the houses and from the Profile is mainly unburnt, but a great deal of the fragments from the acropolis has been exposed to fire, perhaps in connection with ritual activities at the temple.

Species distribution

A general similarity in species distribution exists among the different areas of the settlement. Animal husbandry was the main source for the different animal products. Only a limited, but apparently significant, contribution came from wild species. Sheep, with a small element of goat, was dominant, whereas cattle and pig were similar in abundance (Figure 6.6). A few fragments of dog, cat, horse, and donkey were also found.

The age at slaughter and the gender distribution reveal the major aim of production concerning domestic animal stock. The majority of the cattle were slaughtered young, with about 40 percent kept until old age. Cropping of young, mostly male, individuals was carried out before the age of 2 years, sometimes even as newborn calves. Little evidence, such as draught-related pathologies, exists for ox traction, and other labour animals, presumably donkey, were perhaps used instead. The percentage of adult male cattle were revealed to be only about 20 percent, and we can conclude that adult cattle were used for milking and breeding, which is confirmed by the gender identification of the pelvic bones. Age and gender distribution of sheep reveals that 40 percent were kept until older age and many fully grown adult sheep were male, indicating the importance of wool production. The pigs were kept for meat production, as most were slaughtered young, with an even distribution between males and females.

Hunting was probably socially significant, but not aimed primarily for food. Red deer (*Cervus elaphus*) is the most common of the wild animals; in fact, the *most common* species of all in the assemblage from

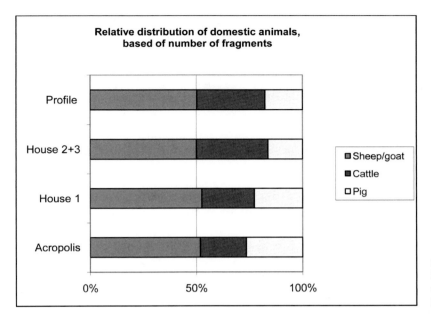

Figure 6.6.
Distribution among domestic animals across Monte Polizzo.

the acropolis. The percentage of wild animals in household waste does not exceed 4 to 5 percent, but in the acropolis, fragments of red deer alone make up about 85 percent of the identified specimens (Figure 6.7). In household waste from the Houses 1 through 3 and from the midden, red deer is more limited, but still an element of importance. Other remains of the wild fauna speak of hunting wolf (*Canis lupus*), hare (*Lepus europaeus*), and birds. In addition, some fish, squid, and turtle were consumed by the inhabitants.

Among the red deer, about 30 percent were juvenile individuals. Most of red deer fragments from Houses 1 through 3 and the Profile derive from the lower extremities, such as metapodials and toe bones.

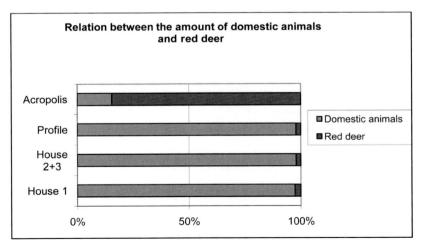

Figure 6.7.
Red deer fragments differ between the acropolis and waste from the households at Monte Polizzo.

This may indicate that the bodies of deer were butchered outside the settlement. Perhaps parts of meat were distributed to separate households, together with raw hides for preparation. Maybe the killed red deer were taken to the temple, where they were butchered and ritually distributed to inhabitants. Pieces of unworked antler seldom reached the household given that they are quite uncommon in the household waste. In the acropolis, on the contrary, red deer antler was handled, stored, and used in substantial quantities, probably for religious purpose.

The bone material from Houses 1 through 3 and the Profile represent butchering and kitchen waste from the daily handling and preparation of food utilised from the domestic animal stock. Because of the similarities in distribution of species and elements, the impression is that the Profile mirrors the household economy – in other words, waste from the settlement was gathered and thrown into commonly used heaps of refuse. Some effort was evidently made to tidy up and keep the house clean of kitchen waste.

Surplus production and exchange systems

Because of the size of the settlement, a supplement of food and other necessities may have been brought in from other sites. Fish, along with squid and other marine resources, may be signs of developed trade, in which coastal colonies could have traded marine produce in exchange for wool, textiles, hides, and grains.

SICILY – ARCHAEOBOTANICAL CASE STUDY

Site methodology

At the Iron Age site (seventh to fourth centuries BC) of Monte Polizzo, archaeobotanical investigations were carried out on a large scale to yield data comparable to the other microregional studies (Morris et al 2004, 2005; Mühlenbock and Prescott 2004a; Mühlenbock and Prescott 2004b). Various structures from different parts of the wide-stretched excavations were systematically sampled for botanical macro-remains. Sediment samples ranging from 5 to 10 litres in volume were taken inside and outside of houses, from pits, fireplaces, ashy layers, ritual places, the bottom of a reservoir, and from a huge

Table 6.4. Early Iron Age crops in Western Sicily

	Elymian Monte Polizzo	Greek Selinunte
Dominant crops	hulled barley	bread/hard wheat
Subdominant crops	emmer bread/hard wheat (oat) faba bean linseed fig grape-vine	hulled barley lentil bitter vetch olive fig grape-vine

midden layer (Stika 2005; Stika and Heiss in prep. a, in prep. b; Stika et al 2008.).

Identified plant remains

In general, the find density is very low. The frequency of appearance of crop remains displays the importance of the different cultivated species (Table 6.4). Three cereals were the main crops: hulled multi-rowed barley (*Hordeum vulgare*), the hulled wheat species emmer (*Triticum dicoccum*), and free-threshing wheat (*T. aestivum / T. durum*). Only few remains of the hulled wheat einkorn (*T. monococcum*) were found. Oats (*Avena* sp.) are regarded as being from wild *Avena* species. Another important food crop was the faba bean/field bean (*Vicia faba*); so far, other pulses are missing from the site. Oilseed flax (*Linum usitatissimum*) and poppy (*Papaver somniferum*) were found, as well as the fruits of fig (*Ficus carica*), grapevine (*Vitis vinifera*), and nuts (*Amygdalus communis*). Coriander (*Coriandrum sativum*) is a typical horticultural plant but another find, the narrow-fruited corn salad (*Valerianella dentata*), might also have been gathered wild.

Based on the pattern of cereal chaff and weed flora, crop processing took place inside the town. The types of weeds and the ratios among chaff, weeds, and grains indicate different stages of crop processing and storage in different locales. Capsule fragments of linseed/flax show that this crop was processed for seeds and/or fibres within the town. Large-scale archaeological surveys in the fertile valleys around Monte Polizzo (Chapter 3) did not detect small rural settlements from the Early Iron Age, probably because of security concerns at that time.

Charcoal analyses (Stika and Heiss in prep. a, in prep. b) document the use of massive beams of evergreen oaks (*Quercus* subgen. *Sclerophyllodrys*) and deciduous oaks (*Quercus* subgen. *Quercus* and *Q.* subgen. *Cerris*) to roof houses. Tall trees from an undisturbed climax vegetation must have been felled for timberwork. Because local deciduous oaks are restricted to higher elevations, we can expect that this undisturbed forest was probably growing on the northern slopes of Monte Polizzo. It seems likely that these forests were carefully managed for timber, as anthropogenic disturbances would have resulted in a succession to pine, which is missing from the charcoal analyses of timberwork here.

Trade and exchange with vegetable products

Archaeobotanical results from Monte Polizzo can be compared with the macro-botanical remains from the contemporaneous Greek town of Selinunte, which is situated at the southern coast of western Sicily, 35 km south of the Monte Polizzo site. The excavated area around the *agora* (latest Mertens 2003) yielded structures (rows of shops were arranged with living areas in their rear buildings) from the late seventh until the third century BC. In the Greek town of Selinunte, free-threshing wheat was the dominant cereal and hulled barley was subdominant. Emmer was represented by single finds only. The pulses lentil (*Lens culinaris*) and bitter vetch (*Vicia ervilia*) are listed for Selinunte, but faba bean is missing. Not much is known about the rural hinterland of Selinunte, but we can expect more information from an archaeological survey. Local forests were cleared by the Greek colonists and replaced by pasture, but cereals apparently were rare for the first millennium BC (Chapter 2). In the area surrounding Selinunte today, the fields are less fertile than those around Monte Polizzo. Concerning the fertility, the cultivation of free-threshing wheat is more demanding than the growing of emmer and barley. For the local production of free-threshing wheats, the surroundings of Monte Polizzo can be regarded as suitable. The Greek town of Selinunte may well have imported free-threshing wheats from the indigenous Elymians, who may have based their own nutrition on barley and emmer. Cultural distinctions in the use of pulses still have to be discussed. The archaeobotanical finds from two sites suggest that whereas the Greeks exclusively used lentil and bitter vetch, the Elymians preferred faba bean. Another cultural difference can be seen in the use of oil and fat. Whereas Selinunte samples provided many olive pits (*Olea europaea*), they were missing from Monte Polizzo – even though charcoal analyses detected the use of olive tree wood for timberwork there (Figure 6.8). Chemical analysis of an amphora from Monte Polizzo resulted in animal fat as a content of the vessels (Agozzino 2004). These results suggest a major difference of the diets: Greek olive oil versus Elymian animal fat as well as the use of different cereals and pulses.

SUBSISTENCE – CONCLUSIONS

The trends in animal exploitation systems are general, but the timing is quite different if we compare central and peripheral parts of Europe. The animal bones no doubt are a rich source of information about animal husbandry. The gender and age distributions reveal the kill-off pattern and thus the major aim of production. This gives a key to the subsistence strategy concerning animal products. Bones from wild game, birds, and fish tell us about the importance of other animal resources. For example, one common factor in Bronze Age–Early Iron Age faunal remains all over Europe is the occurrence of red deer. Bones and antler of red deer are often found in certain find contexts, indicating that this animal held a special position in society, shared among people in widely different parts of Europe.

In the case of Scandinavia, a general conclusion is that a substantial variation in economy and food supply is reflected in the faunal assemblages. Even though there are overall similarities in the microregion concerning material culture, buildings, and grave customs, a clear diversity existed in subsistence strategies and preferences. This could be explained by a variety in natural preconditions, giving different opportunities for animal production, political development, and social interactions.

A general trend in the Scandinavian bone material from larger settlements is the decrease in cattle bone proportions from the Early to the Late Bronze Age. This happened sometime during the Late Bronze Age (1000–500 BC) in the southern parts and somewhat later during the Iron Age farther north. It would be misleading to interpret these changes as a diminishing importance of cattle breeding in the Bronze Age economy; rather, the record of age and gender distribution of the slaughtered animals reveals a growing importance of milking cows and draught oxen in cattle husbandry. Calves became too valuable to be harvested young only to gain meat. The amount of sheep, and sometimes also pig, increased instead and became more frequent as meat supply.

During the Bronze Age, the animal husbandry in Scandinavia seems to have reached some level of specialisation. Large-scale cattle breeding may have existed on some of the high-rank settlements, and a surplus of calves or hides could be used in exchange or as valuable gifts. Wool production, however, was still not a main objective in sheep farming above the household's needs. At this time, the use of manure to fertilise the fields was established and more intensified farming was possible. The access to oxen draught power was crucial to intensify farming. Cultivation and animal breeding were linked together and had to be balanced within the agricultural system.

The macro-botanical evidence gives us a good idea of farming activities concerning vegetable production and consumption. In northern Bohuslän, the Bronze Age spectrum of crops seems to be reduced in comparison to more fertile regions of Sweden. This indicates the subordinate position of agriculture compared with herding, fishing, and other activities.

In Thy, hulled barley and emmer were the main crops from 1500 to 1000 BC. Growing of crops was for household consumption only and not for surplus. Toward the Late Bronze Age, the crop spectrum was enlarged, with free-threshing wheat, common millet, and gold of pleasure. No shift from free-threshing towards hulled barley as a

Figure 6.8a.
Macro-botanical remains from Monte Polizzo. Carbonised plant remains from the Elymian (E) and Medieval (M) settlements at Monte Polizzo. **a, b.** Triticum dicoccum (emmer, E), **a.** caryopsis, **b.** spikelet, **c.** Triticum aestivum-type (bread wheat, M) rachis, **d.** Hordeum vulgare (barley, E) caryopsis, **e.** Vicia faba (faba bean, E) seed, **f.** Vitis vinifera (grape, E) seed, **g.** Prunus spinosa (sloe, E) stone.

main crop was visible from Early Bronze Age to Late Bronze Age; this happened later, at around AD 100. In eastern Denmark and southern Sweden, on the contrary, the shift happened almost 1,500 years earlier, somewhere around 1000 to 800 BC. The switch to hulled barley cultivation could be related to manuring. The change around 1000 BC from two-aisled to three-aisled houses, with the possibility of having byres inside the houses for keeping the cattle during wintertime, made large quantities of manure available.

In the Hungarian case study of Százhalombatta, alterations in animal economy occurred around 2000 BC. The same changes that took place in Scandinavian around 1000 BC took place about 1,000 years earlier in central Europe. A massive intensifying in husbandry and animal economy was associated with population growth. The major

Figure 6.8b.
Charcoal remains from Iron Age Monte Polizzo. **a, b, c.** Olea europaea (olive tree), **d, e, f.** Ulmus sp. (elm), **g, h, i.** Quercus sp. (deciduous oak), **j, k, l.** Quercus sp. (evergreen oak).

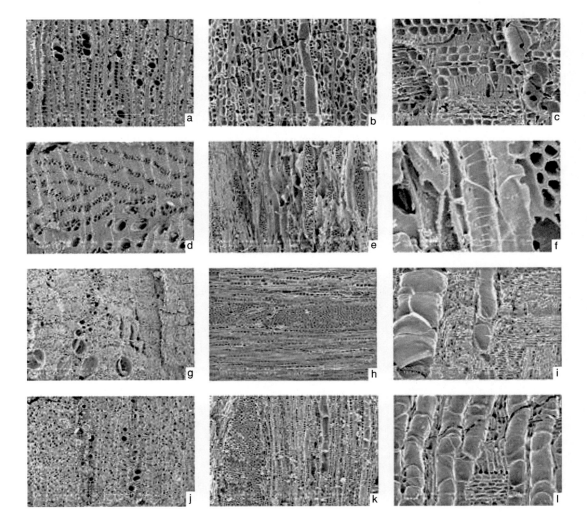

differences were a decrease proportionally in cattle and significant changes in age distribution (fewer young cattle among slaughtered animals). Sheep exploitation increased proportionately, and a greater proportion of older sheep were in the stock, indicating a surplus production of wool after 2000 BC.

After the changing process around 2000 BC, the relative abundance among the domestic animals was surprisingly constant through the period 2000 to 1400 BC, with very small changes, if any. Sheep was the dominant species, followed by cattle, and pig was least common. Such unchanging relative abundance seems to mirror a stable subsistence strategy system during a long period of time. The palaeo-environmental factors (Chapter 2), the settlement pattern continuity (Chapter 3), and the macro-botanical remains all support this impression of continuity without substantial changes in the environment, economy, and society. This is a result of an ability to manage environmental resources and restrict population growth. An exchange system, perhaps involving political mobilisation, was established to support the central settlement. Large quantities of animals ready for slaughter were brought in from surrounding areas. This conclusion is strongly supported also by the botanical evidence showing a low amount of grassland remains within the site, suggesting that the majorities of the animal stock were kept elsewhere.

Plant remains investigation from Százhalombatta resulted in the main crops einkorn and hulled barley, as well as lentil and pea. "New type glume wheat" (probably Timopheev's wheat) was cultivated there in the Bronze Age, as well as in the Early Iron Age. The list of cultivated crops is quite long, additionally including emmer, spelt, bread/hard wheat, broomcorn millet, naked barley, rye, gold of pleasure, linseed, poppy, and safflower. The Hungarian agriculture pattern, based on a highly diversified species mix, was totally different from that of Scandinavia, where only few crops were grown, and displays a Balkan or Near East tradition. The hints for bulgur production point to the same conclusion. No plant remains suggest distance trade, emphasising local production, much for household use. The comparatively low amount of grassland remains within the Százhalombatta-Földvár tell site points to stockbreeding outside the settlement and differs from Scandinavian case studies (byres inside the houses). For Százhalombatta, neither plant remains nor architecture of the Bronze Age houses suggest byres at the tell.

The high importance of pulses in Bronze Age Százhalombatta also contrasts with Scandinavia. In Early Iron Age Sicily, again, pulses were used as main crops. Pulses are an important protein source when human consumption consists mainly of vegetable food or if the available amount of meat is insufficient as a protein source for a large population. Another important factor is that growing pulses improves soil fertility. Both in Hungarian Bronze Age and Early Iron Age western Sicily, dung seems to have been less well available close to the fields because of different economic arrangements within settlements. In Scandinavia, dung was readily available from the byres and badly needed because of poor soil quality compared with the richer soils of Hungary and Sicily.

In the Mediterranean case study of Monte Polizzo, the faunal assemblage was small, but still informative. The possibility to compare four different areas within the settlement revealed some aspects of its internal structure. A general agreement in species distribution indicates a general subsistence strategy for the society, and the distribution of bone finds suggests that waste from the settlement was gathered and thrown into common refuse heaps, an adjustment to large and dense settlements.

The adult cattle population consisted mainly of milking and breeding cows. Among sheep, a great proportion of fully grown adults were males. This emphasises the importance of wool production. Fish, along with squid, speak of developed exchange systems with coastal settlements involving trade for wool, textile, hides, and other agricultural products.

The presence of cereal chaff as well as weeds in the macro-botanical remains of Monte Polizzo indicate that different stages of crop processing and storage took place inside the town. Capsule fragments of linseed/flax show that this crop also was processed for the use of seeds and/or fibres within the town. Finds of charcoal reveal the use of different trees. The ongoing deforestation was not complete, as some undisturbed forest must have been maintained for building material.

Cultural differences in food supply and diet apparently existed between the local settlements and the Greek colonies. The Greeks used olive oil and the locals, animal fat, as well as different uses of cereals and pulses. Trade in crops appears to have existed between these settlements.

When evidence from macro-botanical and archaeozoological remains are combined, the animal economy generally was the main base of subsistence in Bronze Age Europe, at least in the microregions we studied. The relative importance of domestic animals varies, but cattle were apparently the most valuable. The level of specialisation differs substantially among regions. Improvements in cultivation and animal husbandry, in connection with an ability and ambition to control larger areas, created possibilities to produce surplus. In the Scandinavian case studies and in Hungary, the surplus products could have been linked to cattle breeding and, in Hungary, also to wool. In the more developed urban society of Monte Polizzo in Sicily, the crops also seem to have been a part of the surplus production used in exchange economy.

7

Technology and Craft

Joanna Sofaer

With contributions by Jens-Henrik Bech, Sandy Budden, Alice Choyke, Berit Valentin Eriksen, Tünde Horváth, Gabriella Kovács, Attila Kreiter, Christian Mühlenbock, and Hans-Peter Stika

Investigations of technology and crafts have resulted in well-understood technological trajectories, particularly for the development of prehistoric metalworking (Tylecote 1987; Craddock 1995; Ottaway 1994). The frequent emphasis on metalworking, however, has often been to the detriment of other crafts. The bringing together of different materials specialists, and the comparative approach taken by the Emergence of European Communities Project, allow us to explore contrasting, regionally distinct attitudes to a range of crafts at specific historical moments. Although craftspeople's technical decisions are affected by differential access to resources, their choices are not solely confined to the environment, raw materials, and tools; decisions are also socially and culturally defined (Lemonnier 1992; van der Leeuw 1993; Dobres 2000) and the investigation of such choices informs on regional social relations.

The most significant craft activities at our sites provided the material culture to support daily life: ceramic production, the manufacture of chipped and ground stone objects, and the construction of houses – the latter involving woodworking, stonemasonry, and clay manipulation. In addition, Százhalombatta had a substantial corpus of worked bone.[1] Detailed excavation, recording, and use of modern scientific techniques, including petrology, micromorphology, archaeobotany, and use–wear analysis, along with experimental archaeology, illuminate these crafts. Interestingly, despite the frequent emphasis on metal technology in Bronze Age social models, at Thy and Monte Polizzo, our work has revealed little direct evidence for metalworking. At Százhalombatta, fragments of bronze, moulds, and slag attest to metalworking from the Early Bronze Age

(Horváth et al 2000; Poroszlai 2000; Sørensen and Vicze in press), but are relatively few. With little substantial to add to knowledge about metal technology, we do not consider it here.

We begin by describing how crafts were differently articulated within each of our case study areas, focusing on object forms, materials selection, and production processes. We compare craft activities in relation to scale of production, the range of objects, and the social value of finished items. We then explore the archaeological evidence for contrasting strategies for the organisation of craft production and the involvement of specialists and nonspecialists. Finally, this chapter looks at relationships between craft activities, and the implications of differing links between crafts for the construction of social relations between craftspeople.

OBJECT FORMS, MATERIALS, AND PRODUCTION PROCESSES

Case study 1: Thy, Denmark (Figure 7.1)

CERAMICS

In settlements from Thy, the quantity of pottery increased considerably from the Early to the Late Bronze Age. Early Bronze Age ceramics are highly fragmented and relatively scarce, while more complete vessels and many more sherds are found in the Late Bronze Age; there are, for example, more than 46,000 sherds from Bjerre 7 alone. This contrast probably reflects differential preservation and contrasting disposal patterns. The coarsely tempered ceramics from the Early Bronze Age are not as well preserved as the more finely tempered and better-fired ceramics of the Late Bronze Age. Furthermore, in the Late Bronze Age, pottery is frequently found in refuse pits within settlements, whereas refuse disposal seems to have taken place elsewhere during the Early Bronze Age. Large storage vessels placed in hollows dug down into the ground also seem to occur more frequently in the Late Bronze Age.

Despite this variability in abundance, the range of vessel types was rather narrow and relatively consistent from the Early to Late Bronze Age, although vessel shape categories became more distinct in the Late Bronze Age. Forms include biconical or cylinder-necked urns of various sizes and different kinds of domestic vessels, including storage and cooking vessels, with a few strainers and pot lids added late in the Bronze Age. There are also some small bowls and drinking cups, although these are found more frequently in burials. There

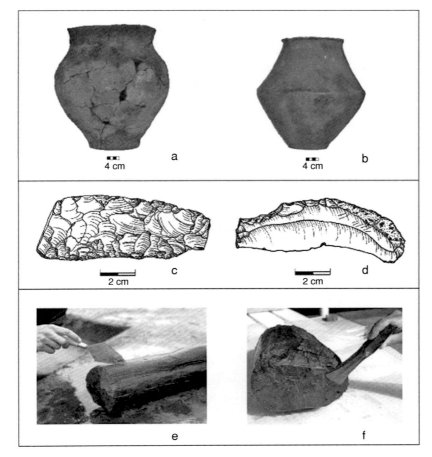

Figure 7.1. Material culture indicating craft activities from Thy, Denmark: **a.** Early Bronze Age vessel from Egshvile, V. Vandet parish, **b.** Late Bronze Age vessel from Højbjerggård, Vesløs parish, **c.** Early Bronze Age bifacial sickle from Bjerre 6, **d.** Late Bronze Age heavy blade knife from Bjerre 1, **e.** oak timber from Bjerre 6, **f.** roof support from Bjerre 6 showing cut marks from a bronze axe similar to that shown.

are no plates, although large open forms sometimes occur in the Late Bronze Age. In addition to ceramic vessels, there is at least one fragment of a clay mould and some fragments of clay crucibles from Late Bronze Age Bjerre 7. There were no ceramic weaving tools from Bjerre sites.

Pottery was locally made. Except for very close-lying sites, each of the Thy settlements exploited a different clay source (Rasmussen and Bech in press), and no clear evidence exists for imported wares (Rasmussen and Bech in press). A limited range of resources was used for tempers, although within these, potters were capable of exercising choices (Kristensen in press). Early Bronze Age vessels frequently have a coarse temper made of crushed granite, likely derived from reusing heating stones from fire pits. Finer ware tempered with sand occurs occasionally, mainly for small vessels such as cups. Late Bronze Age ceramics are made with similar materials but are more frequently tempered with sand.

Pots were handmade, probably by coiling. Overall, the quality of the pottery is relatively poor, although, as in other regions of southern Scandinavia, from the Early to the Late Bronze Age, pottery quality shifted to finer ware and better craftsmanship (cf. Draiby 1984). In the Early Bronze Age, simple, coarse wares were the norm (Rasmussen 1993; Kristensen in press). Seventy percent of all sherds from the Early Bronze Age sites of Bjerre had a wall thickness more than 1 cm (Kristensen in press). Although most of the pottery from the Late Bronze Age was still relatively simple, it had thinner walls, possibly resulting from use of a paddle technique. Ninety-three percent of all Late Bronze Age sherds from Bjerre had walls less than 1 cm thick; 50 percent had wall thicknesses of 6 mm or less (Kristensen in press).

In the Early Bronze Age Bjerre sites, a characteristic trait is the treatment of the outside of vessels with a form of rustication known as *beklasket*, for which clay was deliberately roughly applied to the outside to make an uneven surface, often with fingerprints and nail marks from the potter's hand (Kristensen in press). Vessel interiors are smoother. Technically the Early Bronze Age pottery from Jutland shares traits with the Middle Bronze Age ceramics of the Netherlands (Bakker et al 1977:208). Only 1.4 percent of all Early Bronze Age sherds were decorated (Kristensen in press). Where decoration was applied, it was rather simple, with irregular incised lines, crisscross lines, and occasional horizontal cordons. In the Late Bronze Age, vessels from Thy were still rarely decorated and were no longer *beklasket*. At Bjerre 7, only 0.7 percent of the Late Bronze Age sherds were ornamented. Decoration consisted mainly of narrow bands of horizontal lines at the shoulder, sometimes with a hatched border or bundles of alternating hatched and plain parallel stripes, and infrequent application of cordons, small ornamental handles, or bosses. The finer ware was normally burnished. When combined with use of a paddle technique, this resulted in a smooth surface so that the temper does not stick out from the surface as in earlier vessels (Kristensen in press).

In the Early and Late Bronze Age, the pots have a brown or red-brown surface colour, indicating an oxidising atmosphere during firing, most likely in a low-temperature bonfire. However, the atmosphere was not necessarily consistent throughout the firing process. In cross section, many of the sherds display colour variation; only about 50 percent of the rim sherds from the Early Bronze Age have a homogeneous firing core. This figure rises to 77 percent in Late Bronze Age Bjerre (Kristensen in press), suggesting that production became more controlled.

CHIPPED AND GROUND STONE

Consistent screening of all soils by the Thy Archaeological Project means that the size and completeness of the stone assemblage is unusual, and the study of stoneworking represents one of the largest and most thorough analyses of lithic material from settlement sites of the Danish Bronze Age (Eriksen in press). Contemporary assemblages from Klostergaard[2], an Early Bronze Age (Montelius period I-III) settlement 16 km south of Bjerre, and Krogstrup[3], a Late Bronze Age (Montelius Period V) settlement from central Jutland 125 km south of Bjerre, provide additional lithic inventories. Together, the material from these sites amounts to some 30,000 pieces of flint. Ground stone objects are relatively poorly represented, although fragments of grinding stones are found on all Bjerre sites. At Bjerre 7, a couple were likely re-used as whetstones. Stone implements used for metalworking include fragments of a probable mould preform and a hammer also found at Bjerre 7.

The lithic inventories from these Bronze Age sites were typologically quite simple. In the Early Bronze Age assemblage, bifacially worked, asymmetrical sickles were most prominent. Microwear analyses confirm that these tools were used exclusively to harvest cereals (Aperlo and Juel Jensen in press). Other formal tools include well-made scrapers, knives, perforators, and a few strike-a-lights. Scrapers and strike-a-lights were sometimes made out of modified sickles. Often, as much as one-third or even half of the total number of tools at each site were crude, *ad hoc* tools, flakes or blades with irregular retouch. In the Late Bronze Age, the well-made asymmetrical, bifacial sickles were replaced by heavy blade knives. In contrast to the unifunctional tools of the Early Bronze Age, these were multifunctional objects. Use–wear analysis reveals that blade knives were used predominantly for cutting plants, including cereals and reeds, but additionally some exhibit macro-chipping along the edges resulting from use against fairly hard substances such as wood (Juel Jensen in press). They may sometimes have been used as pollarding knives to cut leaf fodder for livestock. The remaining tool inventory remains largely unchanged.

The Early Bronze Age flint knappers of Bjerre and Klostergaard exploited nodules from primary outcrops as well as erratic flints, and some tools were made from debris from a nearby Neolithic quarry (Eriksen 2007). With respect to formal tools, especially the bifacial sickles, direct procurement with consistent selection of the best raw material is apparent. Procurement involved a regional-scale strategy as some of the preferred raw material nodules were brought from at least 5 km from the knapping location. The *ad hoc* tools, however, were made from any available raw material lying around, including frost flakes and other erratic pieces. The Late Bronze Age inventory from Bjerre 7 indicates a simple and rather uniform exploitation pattern. There is little to suggest direct procurement or the exploitation of flint from primary outcrops. Most tools used locally available erratic flint. The raw material procurement strategy was likely imbedded in other activities performed within the locality.

From Early Bronze Age Bjerre, there is evidence of on-site production of asymmetrical sickles, some scrapers, and numerous crude *ad hoc* tools. At Bjerre 1 and 3, analyses of debitage and broken preforms, supplemented with refitting, confirm that bifacially worked asymmetrical sickles were produced fairly extensively (Eriksen 2008). However, most of the sickles found there are worn-out, broken, discarded pieces, sometimes reworked into scrapers or strike-a-lights, that were originally made outside the excavated areas at Bjerre. A similar pattern is visible at Klostergaard. The sickles produced at Bjerre and Klostergaard were therefore used and left somewhere else; well-made sickles would have been used for harvesting outside the settlement area (Eriksen 2008). Despite the large quantity of lithics found at Early Bronze Age settlements at Thy, production at domestic sites was relatively small scale. Evidence of debitage and sickles broken during production document large specialised production locations elsewhere in Thy, where asymmetrical sickles were made in the thousands, and certainly not just for home consumption (Steinberg 1997).

The manufacture of bifacial sickles was generally characterised by a high degree of precision, control, and anticipation of explicit intentions. The preferred blank was usually a flat nodule or core. The sickle preform was shaped by initial hard direct percussion, and the manufacture was completed by increasingly delicate soft direct percussion, probably using an antler billet. Pressure flaking was used exclusively for the final trimming of lateral edges. The selection of the best raw material for the sickles was matched by a generally high quality of the flint knapping. Most of these tools were obviously made by very skilled flint knappers. Similarly, we find that among the flake tools, some scrapers and knives were particularly well made and regular, suggesting that they demonstrated technological capability similar to that used in making the sickles, perhaps produced by the same knappers. The crude *ad hoc* tools were usually manufactured by rather careless direct percussion, without skilled knapping.

In the Late Bronze Age, bifacial technology ceased, and heavy flint blades were made by hard direct percussion to large blade cores. At Bjerre, this technology was rather *ad hoc*. The platform was hardly prepared. Evidence for bipolar knapping, a simple technique often associated with beginners, is also present at Late Bronze Age settlement sites, but not those from the Early Bronze Age.

Over the course of the Bronze Age at Thy, changes in lithic technology argue for a general loss of knowledge concerning flint technology, which bears the marks of a dying craft (Eriksen 2010). That is not to say, however, that it was obsolete. On the contrary, flint tools were vital to daily life and remained so well into the Iron Age. The simplified technology, however, could now have been fairly easily performed within each household.

THE CONSTRUCTION OF HOUSES

Architecture and building techniques at Thy remained relatively stable throughout the Bronze Age. Indeed, the technology of architecture at Thy is quite uniform, indicating a widespread understanding of the correct way to build a house. Rectangular, single-story, three-aisled longhouses were the main form of domestic architecture (Chapter 5).

Building materials were local, and builders combined them simply without prepared foundations or ritual deposits. Vertical timbers were placed in postholes to support timbers running across the house's width and rafters for a gabled roof. This meant that the width of the house was restricted by the length of the crossbeams, resulting in consistent house widths of 5.5 to 7.5 m (a very few houses being up to 8 m wide), but the length of houses was flexible, depending largely on the number of vertical posts added to the structure. Thus, while most houses from Thy were small to medium-sized, ranging from 8 to 20 m in length, some exceed 20 m. The house at Legård was 32 m long (Chapters 3, 4, 5).

Thanks to the excellent wetland preservation conditions at Bjerre Enge, especially Bjerre 2 and 6, the sites reveal the variety of woods used as building materials, along with woodworking techniques (Bech 2003). Oak was the most common timber used in house construction, but the occasional use of willow, aspen, alder, birch, elm, and larch (a driftwood) for various architectural elements suggests a scarcity of desired woods (Malmros et al in press). Timber for roof supports was squared off at the ends; cut marks on the end of the beams were made by small bronze axes. External walls were most commonly made of wattle and daub, but some Early Bronze Age houses had walls made of wood planking, using a bole technique with horizontal split planks or trunks between vertical posts. The percentage of houses with this construction technique is smaller in Thy than in southern Jutland, probably reflecting poor wood availability in Thy. Decorative materials may have existed on walls, such as the painted daub from the Late Bronze Age site of Voldtofte in southwestern Fünen (Thrane 1979), but they are rarely preserved in southern Scandinavia. Although evidence is also lacking, roofs were probably thatched using straw or reeds.

Within about a third of the houses in Thy, pairs of close-lying postholes near the centre line of the house suggest doors passing through internal subdividing walls. Floors were most likely bare earth, although areas of stone paving have been found elsewhere in Jutland (Draiby 1984). No evidence exists for clay floors, contrasting with the Early Iron Age. Very few formal hearths have been preserved, but those that have feature a stone foundation made of natural rocks. Ovens were dug into the floor close to hearths with fire-heated rocks used for cooking (Chapter 5).

Case study 2: Százhalombatta, Hungary (Figure 7.2)

CERAMICS

The site of Százhalombatta has a rich assemblage of ceramic vessels. The range of vessel types is wide and varied, representing the work of accomplished potters capable of producing an array of technically complex forms (Budden and Sofaer 2009). Basic types include cups, bowls, jugs, and storage vessels as the core of the assemblage, but the elaboration of vessel forms changed substantially over time, resulting in considerable typological development (Vicze 2001; Budden 2007). As the Vatya cultural tradition emerged at the transition from the Early to Middle Bronze Age, the range of vessel forms increased and new types were introduced (Bóna 1975, 1992; Poroszlai 2000, 2003; Vicze 2001). Vatya vessel forms include small cups, sieves, fish dishes, deep domestic bowls, small domestic bowls, cooking jars, storage vessels, fine-ware bowls, jugs, globular and biconical urns, ember covers, and miniatures that replicate the assemblage as a whole. In the

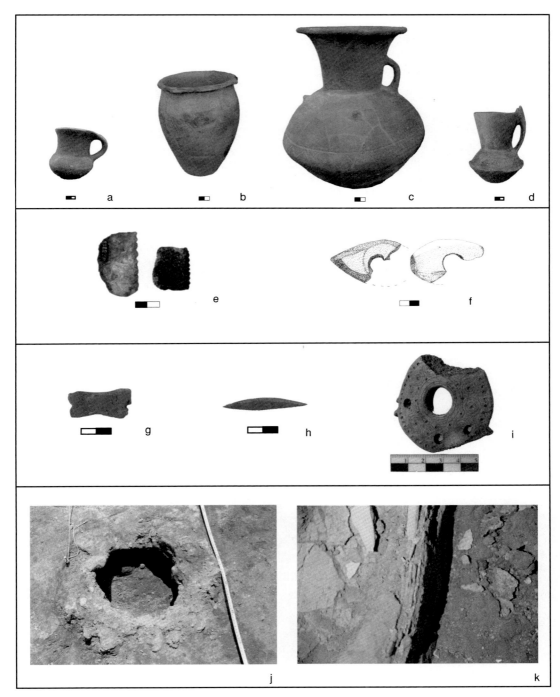

Figure 7.2. Material culture indicating craft activities at Százhalombatta, Hungary: **a.** cup, **b.** cooking vessel, **c.** urn, **d.** jug, **e.** sickle blades, **f.** shaft-hole axe, **g.** cattle phalange 'burnisher,' **h.** double point, **i.** ornamented horse harness, **j.** posthole packed with debris, **k.** layers of plaster on a house wall.

later Vatya-Koszider phase, the range of vessel forms decreased but with noticeable elaboration and exaggeration of existing forms (Vicze 2001; Sofaer 2006; Budden 2007). The typological development at Százhalombatta was not, however, matched by changes in resources used for tempers or vessel-forming techniques, suggesting continuity of craft traditions on the tell (Kreiter 2007a).

Most vessels at the site were locally made (Kreiter 2007a), although there are some imports, notably from the neighbouring Encrusted Pottery culture (Poroszlai 1996; Poroszlai and Vicze 2004). Many fine wares were lightly tempered with grog or fine sand. Storage vessels, globular urns, and biconical urns have a restricted range of fabrics characterised by the addition of small amounts of grog temper, with or without other tempers such as limestone or quartz, in concentrations that were functionally redundant; 82 percent of storage vessels and urns were made with fabrics containing 1 to 7 percent grog (Kreiter 2007a). The grog exhibits remarkably similar composition (type, size, and mineralogy) to the surrounding clay matrix, strongly suggesting that potters used their own broken vessels as temper in 'potting recipes' (Kreiter 2007a). The fabrics of storage vessels and urns from Százhalombatta indicate that potters may have been working to culturally defined practices rather than functionality when adding grog temper (Kreiter 2006, 2007a, 2007b).

All Százhalombatta pots were hand built, as potters engaged a diverse suite of technological options that included pinching, coiling, and slab building. Additionally, a paddle and anvil technique was used occasionally to secondarily refine walls of large vessels, although this was a more common practice at contemporary Gyulavarsand sites (Kreiter et al 2006). Press moulding or rotary methods were not used. Forming techniques were drawn upon either singly, or in combination, depending on the form being produced and the exigencies placed on the technology. The bodies of Vatya urns were made by slab building, whereas the trumpet-shaped flared neck and rim were coiled. The steady move towards increased exaggeration and embellishment of pottery forms over the course of the Middle Bronze Age required a fluid attitude towards the practical actions that made up technological know-how. Thus, development of the tripartite shape and everted rims of Koszider cups meant that the pinching method alone ceased to be appropriate to form these vessels, and a new combination of pinching and coiling was adopted (Budden 2007). Nonetheless, technological practice did not always fully exploit the plasticity of clay. Cup and jug handles were attached using a method redolent of pegs in woodworking or rivets in metalworking (Sofaer 2006). Potters were, therefore, borrowing techniques from other crafts, but their adoption may also reflect a reluctance to step outside technical solutions that had already been established in other media.

Although vessel forming was played out fluidly, the relationship between vessel form and surface treatment was quite proscribed. Entire ranges of surface treatments and decorative schemes were identified with specific vessel forms. For instance, while applied and finger-impressed cordons appeared on urns, storage vessels, and large domestic bowls, their placement and treatment were specific to each vessel type. The same holds true for the various forms of rusticated surface treatments. Cups, small bowls, and fine wares were finished by smoothing, burnishing, and impressed and incised decoration specific to those vessel forms. Some Nagyrév fine wares, in particular small bowls and pedestal vessels, had distinctive incised textile-like decoration (Horváth and Marton 2002). On Vatya fine wares, a high burnish combined with complex and ordered decorative motifs suggest the deliberate combination of technical strategies in order to produce objects with exceptionally striking visual characteristics.

Pottery from Százhalombatta conforms to the characteristics associated with bonfire or nonkiln-fired pottery, although the use of simple updraft kilns cannot be ruled out. Experimental replicas of the daub ovens from Százhalombatta performed satisfactorily as kilns (Budden 2002), although they would not have been large enough to fire many vessels in the assemblage, and we have not found substantial deposits of wasters in or near the ovens. Many domestic vessels are fire-clouded, suggesting an irregular atmosphere. Vatya and Koszider fine wares, however, were overwhelmingly reduction fired to a rich black that extends through the firing core, indicating the deliberate use of a reduction atmosphere rather than simple smudging. Reduction firing, in combination with highly burnished surfaces and angular forms, resulted in vessels that evoked associations with metal objects (Sofaer 2006). The firing temperatures achieved (600–825°C) and exceptional rarity of underfired or overfired vessels in the archaeological record (Budden 2007) suggest knowledgeable and deliberate manipulation of fuel resources with control of fire settings (Rye 1981; Pool 2000; Sillar 2000). Nagyrév vessels were higher fired than those of the later phases. This may reflect altered fuel availability that required potters to become more expedient in the selection and quantity of fuel used (Budden 2002).

An additional use of clay tools was for weaving. Sun-dried circular and perforated pyramid clay objects were loom weights, but their rarity suggests only limited weaving. This contrasts with the faunal evidence for a shift towards wool production by the Middle Bronze Age (Chapter 6).

CHIPPED AND GROUND STONE

The quantity of stone material used at Százhalombatta was much less than that used in Bronze Age Scandinavia, but stone objects were perhaps surprisingly more common than has been previously assumed. The chipped and ground stone from Százhalombatta provides the first detailed assemblage available for the Hungarian Bronze Age and provides critical insights into the technological range of local craftspeople (Horváth 2004a).

Chipped stone tools are the most abundant stone objects at the site, representing regular, although never common finds. More than 90 percent of these finds are lunate or trapezoid flakes with bifacial flat retouch. So far, several hundred such flakes have been recovered and analysed. The largest are 50 mm in length but they are frequently broken and abraded. Larger pieces were probably simple handheld or hafted cutting tools, whereas smaller abraded flakes were apparently re-used as small blades in composite sickles or in larger threshing boards (Anderson 2006). Multiple retouching on the blade edge after breakage or exhaustion can be observed on many tools and the flakes have bifacial sickle gloss from cutting cereal stalks (Horváth 2005). An unusual group of eight slim, barbed arrowheads with a concave base may have served as weapons of war or for hunting, although wild animal bone was rare at the settlement (Chapter 6).

Ground stone objects include polished stone hammers and axes, the latter used for woodworking. Long, slim shoe-last axes functioned as chisels, small axes with a trapezoid cutting edge were suitable for working on smaller trunks and branches, whereas larger shaft-hole axes were used for chopping bigger timbers. There are also several grinding stones. The standard grinding kit includes a hemispherical grinding stone with elliptic grinding surface and a disc-shaped hand stone. The grain size of the grinding stones varies from fine-grained to rather coarse, suggesting that they were used to grind flour of various qualities.

As at other Vatya tell sites, there is a small and fragmentary assemblage of stone moulds for bronze ornaments, tools, and weapons. Some hammers and polishing stones with distinctive use wear were probably also used for metalworking (Horváth 2004b). In addition, there are several *ad hoc* implements including pebbles that may have served to polish or burnish ceramics.

Most stone used at Százhalombatta was not locally available but needed to be procured from some distance, probably involving regional and long-distance exchange. Specific stone sources were used for particular implements, indicating both expediency and considerable choice in the exploitation of materials used from local, regional, and distant sources (Horváth 2005). Flakes and arrowheads were most frequently made from Buda chert, a poor-quality, quickly wearing material that is not well suited for chipping, but readily available 10 to 30 km north from Százhalombatta. Occasionally, materials were brought from greater distances (Horváth 2005). Grinding stones were made from Hárshegy sandstone from the Buda hills, as well as granite from the Velence hills 30 km away, and granite and crystallised sandstone from the Visegrád hills 75 km upstream along the Danube. In addition, there are some imported limey-micaceous sandstones from the northeast of the Transdanubian Mountains. The hand stones were made of more durable and harder stones such as Buda hornstone or quartzite, probably from local Danube gravels. Axes were made from a range of different rock types, including andesites from the Visegrád hills and metabasite and serpentine ultrabasite found in the Eastern Alps. Hárshegy sandstone was used for the production of moulds. Pebble-clay washed ashore from the Danube bed was used for making *ad hoc* tools.

Stone production techniques of different kinds of flaking and grinding were quite straightforward and apparently took place at the site of Százhalombatta. Preforms for sickles and arrowheads and considerable waste flakes were found. Chipped stone tools were made using a simple knapping technique widespread among the earlier Eneolithic and Early Bronze Age cultures of the Carpathians (Kopacz 2001), and similar to the splinter technique used in Middle Bronze Age Poland (Lech 1981). A hard hammer was used to remove flakes from a core (Horváth 2005), and quartzite pebbles from Százhalombatta display use wear from hammering (Horváth 2005). The chipped stone material from the site contains a high proportion of waste flakes to useable tools; almost half the finds are waste (Horváth 2005). Extensive waste may have resulted from the low quality of the dominant Buda chert, a conclusion supported by experimental work (Antoni and Horváth 2003). Retouching was done in at least two stages. After the thick flakes were removed with a hard hammer and thinned crosswise or along the cutting edge, a bifacial form with serrated edge was created, probably using a bone tool such as a rib; retouching was uneven when the stone did not afford careful flaking (Horváth 2005). Arrowheads were quite carefully knapped to create strong ventral and dorsal ridges, and resins may have been used to fasten their concave bases to arrow shafts (Bátora 1994; Junkmanns 2001). Ground stone implements were manufactured by repeated grinding with abrasive stone, using water as the lubricant. Polishing the surface improved the mechanical strength and cutting effectiveness of axes when used to chop wood. A large flake created during manufacture and traces of reshaping of axe bodies after damage and breakage document local axe working.

The lithic material from Százhalombatta represents the end of a long tradition of stoneworking in the Carpathian Basin. At the end of the Middle Bronze Age, there was a drastic decline in the quality and number of stone tools. Many objects previously made of stone began to be made of metal. Thus, for example, bronze sickles and arrowheads eventually replaced their stone counterparts.

WORKED BONE, ANTLER, AND TEETH
In Hungary, as in much of central Europe, systematic studies of assemblages of objects made from animal bone, antler, and teeth are quite rare. The careful recovery of all bone from Százhalombatta makes the analysis of its bone tools an important contribution (Choyke and Schibler 2007). The tools include common types found on sites associated with other contemporary cultural groups in the Carpathian Basin, such as long-bone awls possibly used as beaters in weaving or in coiled basketry and 'burnishers' made from phalanges and astragalii. Tools specific to Vatya sites include cattle-rib scrapers, probably used for hide scraping (Choyke 1984; Choyke and Bartosiewicz 2000). Objects unique to Százhalombatta include small double-pointed tools made from both rib and long-bone diaphysis splinters, some with heavy polish and use wear suggesting use in composite tools. Some of the finer ones may have been used for body tattooing or scarification.

Several cattle radii had worked longitudinal facets on their dorsal surfaces, a type that first appeared earlier at Bell Beaker sites. These objects have been described as ice skates (Choyke and Bartosiewicz 2005:318; Furmánek et al 1999), although examination of similar artefacts from Middle Bronze Age sites in Slovakia has revealed considerable variation in wear and species that questions this function. They may have been used to work hides after curing (Drzewicz 2004).

Unusual objects include decorated horse harness pieces and a pair of extremely worn, polished antler handles with holes for leather straps, such as might be used for reins. The extensive wear on these handles suggests long-term use, perhaps by multiple generations. Other items include three examples of token-like bone discs and a variety of carved antler objects that formed part of more complex composite objects, including stopper-like items with antler inlay. Such objects are more common from the Middle Bronze Age onwards. A further example of a composite object made from antler is a unique and elaborate hammer haft. The antler beam spongiosa was cut away and filled with two concentric antler inlays fixed in place with bone pins, the ends of which were carefully shaved down.

The people of Százhalombatta used bone and teeth items as ornaments. As at other Vatya sites, dog canines and, more unusually, drilled and polished dog molars and metapodia, were used to make pendants, suggesting the symbolic importance of dogs (Chapter 6; Choyke et al 2004). Drilled metapodia from hare were also used for ornaments, as were split wild boar tusks, beaver bone, and drilled teeth of sheep and horse. An unusual miniature axe blade was made of cattle bone.

Depending on the objects being made, the craftspeople of Százhalombatta selected particular species and skeletal elements. Consistent with the dominance of domestic animals in the faunal assemblage (Chapter 6), 98 percent of the worked bone derived from domestic animals, with only 2 percent made of deer antler. Cattle provided most of the bone for tools, augmented by bone from other domestic animals. A wider variety of species, including wild animals, was used for other items, including ornaments and amulets. The overall balance may have reflected the availability of raw materials at the site. Within dwellings, boxes stored antler rough-outs for future use, a practice observed elsewhere (Szilas pers. comm.). Such local curation probably suggests manufacture at the site.

At Százhalombatta, bone working techniques using stone tools were part of a tradition continuous from the Middle Neolithic until the Late Bronze Age, when metal tools began to be more widely used.

In the Middle Bronze Age, metal tools were used rarely; the smooth, 'V-shaped' walls of incised decoration on horse equipment suggest the use of a fine metal tool, and metal axes were occasionally used to plane or chop antler. Most of the bone tools were made using flaked stone tools for cutting and scraping, and rough abrasive stone for grinding. Bone tools may also have been used to manufacture antler objects after the antler had been softened by soaking in cold water (Osipowicz 2007). Antler was never ground into shape, nor is there evidence that flaking or cutting with twine was used. Several bone, antler, and tooth objects at Százhalombatta were carefully repaired when they broke or became worn. Even the edge of a simple tool, such as rib scrapers, could be resharpened several times. Drilled holes on teeth or antler hammer/adze tools often broke, requiring modification of the object proportions and relocation of the holes for suspension or hafting.

THE CONSTRUCTION OF HOUSES

Burnt houses document well the architectural technology at Százhalombatta. The houses are rectangular with rounded corners, approximately 8 m by 15 m in size (Poroszlai 2003), with a single entrance off a trampled earth street and a south-facing porch. They are frequently divided into at least two rooms (one larger and one smaller) (Poroszlai 2000), with a series of out-buildings or smaller structures linked to the main building added over the life of the house (Chapter 5).

The domestic architecture used local materials, including wood, clay, reeds, and other vegetation. These materials were combined in specific ways to create architectural elements. Walls were made of wattle and daub, floors of beaten earth that were sometimes layered with clay, and roofs of straw thatch. This general description, however, disguises a complex and sophisticated use of building supplies.

The start of the Bronze Age saw increased use of wood in architecture (Máthé 1988). At Százhalombatta, oak provided major structural load-bearing elements and timber-framed doorways. Rafters for pitched roofs were made from long-lasting oak heartwood. Between rafters were batons of elm. Outside the houses, facing the street, wooden planks protected the walls from erosion caused by passers-by. Much of the timber probably originated from the floodplain across the Danube; the tree rings suggest good growing conditions as found there, and oak is too heavy for long-distance flotation down the river.

Over the course of the Bronze Age, the external walls of houses were built thicker and more massive (Poroszlai 2000). Construction techniques, however, varied even within the same house, resulting from the need to tailor building solutions to individual, slightly unpredictable, situations arising from the inconsistency found on a tell surface. For example, there were several different methods for fixing posts in postholes. In some cases, posts were inserted into pre-cut holes and then packed with domestic refuse or with clay around the post; in others, postholes that were cut into cultural layers were left unpacked, perhaps because they were sufficiently stable as a result of existing material.

Between the upright posts, thick wall foundations were sometimes constructed from compacted refuse from the settlement (Kovács 2008). The walls themselves were made of clayey daub with large amounts of organic temper applied on a wattle frame (Kovács 2008). Most commonly, the temper consisted of byproducts of barley and einkorn processing, with some emmer and 'new type' glume wheat, as well as reeds and grasses. The temper not only loosened up the heavy clay but also reduced unwanted cracking resulting from shrinking and swelling (Courty et al 1989; Goldberg and Whitbread 1993). The high frequency of pore spaces in the daub indicates that it was well mixed (Kovács 2008). Given the need for the clay to dry, construction of houses was probably a summer activity, when rain is less common. In some cases, wattle and daub walls were covered inside and out with 5 to 10 cm of clay to create an insulating 'sandwich' wall. Sometimes deliberate deposits of grinding stones or pots were placed into walls and postholes as foundation deposits, suggesting that ritual was part of house construction.

Interior finishes for house walls included variously daub, clay, and plaster. Daub walls show evidence of smoothing: Randomly orientated pores exist inside the daub as a result of mixing, but its surfaces show parallel orientation of these pores. Ten percent of daub was wiped with grasses or other vegetation, sometimes using a technique similar to the surface treatment found on some domestic vessels (Sofaer 2006). The wiped surfaces were chaff tempered to obtain a fine quality surface. Plaster could be applied to all walls but was frequently applied to those incorporating compacted domestic refuse, perhaps as an attempt to separate the 'clean' area of the house from the 'dirty' material (Kovács 2008). Plaster does not seem to have been applied externally. Walls were plastered immediately following their construction, leaving no time for the accumulation of material between layers (Kovács 2008). The plaster was fine and compact, made mainly of mineral materials with occasional phytoliths and almost no anthropogenic inclusions (Kovács 2008). The low frequency of faecal spherulites in the plaster suggests that dung was rarely used (Kovács 2008). The parallel orientation of voids in the plaster indicates that it was applied using a smoothing technique (Kovács 2008). The initial layer of plaster was relatively thick, although over the life of the houses, walls were carefully replastered up to seven times with fine layers only a couple of millimetres thick. Different mixes of materials indicate separate plastering events (Kovács 2008). Some posts were plastered, giving the appearance of a column sticking out from the wall, and some internal walls were decorated with applied plaster decorations. The exterior surfaces of walls were sometimes whitewashed using a lime mixture. Although we have not yet found evidence for external decoration, this may have existed. At the Nagyrév tell at Tiszaug-Kéménytető, house walls were covered with geometric designs (Csányi 2003).

Within the houses, unbaked clay storage vessels similar in shape to ceramic globular and biconical urns were built into the floor. Hearths were constructed using clean clay abundantly tempered with organic matter and frequently renovated (Kovács 2008). Ovens were made from clay tempered with grog, perhaps referring back to its nonutilitarian use in pots, and a possible symbolic relationship to heat and fire. Floors were made of beaten earth, which was sometimes covered with a layer of yellow clay 3 to 5 cm thick to create a new floor (Kovács 2008); houses could have different floor surfaces in different rooms simultaneously. The floors exhibit a low frequency of pore spaces, high compaction, and no tempering. The moderate mixing of the raw materials prevented weakening of the floor resulting from too much air being captured (Kovács 2008). In some parts of the houses, layers of ash were spread deliberately over the floor (Kovács 2008), possibly to disinfect the surface (Hakbijl 2002) or to absorb moisture and thus reduce dampness (Milek 2006). Phytoliths on the floors show that they were sometimes laid with reed mats.

Case study 3: Monte Polizzo, Sicily (Figure 7.3)

CERAMICS
From Monte Polizzo, the ceramic assemblage included a wide range of forms used in everyday domestic contexts and for special events

(Chapter 5). Indigenous Sicilian vessels dominated the assemblage, which also included imported Attic, Corinthian, and Ionian wares. In comparison with other indigenous sites in Sicily, relatively few Greek ceramics were used by 550 BC at the settlement, suggesting that local pottery production was unusually strong.

The local pottery belongs to the west Sicilian incised–impressed grey wares, the distinctive material from the site giving rise to its designation as 'Monte Polizzo ware.' Locally produced vessels are dominated by carinated bowls but also include pithoi (large storage vessels), small to medium size storage vessels, cups, other bowls, amphorae, and cooking pots (Mühlenbock 2008). The range of vessels produced was particularly wide and innovative, with considerable variation within each type. New forms were frequently added. Although many vessel forms continued old traditional shapes from the Middle and Late Bronze Age, some copied directly seventh- to sixth-century imports and others were inspired by foreign shapes but given an indigenous twist (Mühlenbock 2008). The interplay between traditional forms and new elements inspired craftspeople, most visibly in experimentation with 'odd' forms and shapes (Mühlenbock 2008).

Petrographic examination of thin sections indicates that Greek-imported fine wares were made of distinctive untempered clays or, occasionally, tempered with grog (Brorsson and Sköld forthcoming).

Figure 7.3. Material culture indicating craft activities at Monte Polizzo, Sicily: **a.** carinated cup, **b.** dente de lupo bowl, **c.** jug, **d.** capeduncola, **e.** hewn limestone walls from House 1.

Local wares were made of readily available coarse clays and were also often untempered, but, when temper was added, as in the case of local imitations of the B1 cup, this was in greater proportions than in the Greek originals. Local domestic vessels were tempered using sand or grog to enhance the thermodynamic function of vessels, for example through the sand tempering of cooking vessels produced to withstand repeated heating (Brorsson and Sköld forthcoming). Vessel function affected the choice of temper, and perhaps the choice of clay. Tests reveal a range of different sintering and melting points for ceramic forms, indicating that different sources of raw materials were exploited (Brorsson and Sköld forthcoming). Neutron activation analyses of indigenous household grey tablewares demonstrates that, for this group of vessels, the potters of Monte Polizzo shared a common clay source with other settlements in the west of Sicily. The spatial distribution of vessels made from this clay also corresponds with epigraphic data regarding the presence of an Elymian ethnic identity in the fifth century BC (Kolb and Speakman 2005).

Locally produced ceramics were made using different techniques for different vessel types: Pithoi were built of large slabs, and cooking pots (pentole) were coiled. The local pottery production at Monte Polizzo did not fully incorporate foreign vessel manufacturing technology, although there were other indigenous settlements on the island that began to use this technology during the course of the sixth and fifth centuries BC (Antonaccio 2004). Greek imported vessels were thrown on the fast wheel, although local imitations of Greek vessels were made on the slow wheel. Furthermore, whereas imported vessels were fired in kilns at temperatures between 900° and 1000°C, the majority of locally produced material was bonfire or pit fired at temperatures between 500 and 600°C. As raw clay becomes ceramic at 450°C, pottery at Monte Polizzo was fired to as low a temperature as possible, perhaps indicating a need to conserve fuel resources (Brorsson and Sköld forthcoming). The black surface colour and light grey to charcoal grey core that characterise Monte Polizzo tableware (Dixon 2004) suggests deliberate manipulation of the fire setting to create a reduction atmosphere. The semi-lustrous surface, combined with the sharp carinated form of Monte Polizzo bowls, may have been inspired by bronze vessels or have been designed to evoke associations with metal technology (Dixon 2004). Potters were therefore selective and creative in their decisions concerning pottery production in the context of indigenous identity formation in a period of multicultural contact and trade (De Angelis 2003).

The potters of western Sicily worked within a common tradition but with strong local variations (Gargini 1995; Di Noto 1995; De Vido 1997). The grey wares at Monte Polizzo display a range of decorative elements that distinguished them from other contemporary indigenous sites, which produced matte-painted Sant' Angelo Muxaro pottery with meander patterns inspired by the geometric repertoire found in the Aegean during the ninth and eighth centuries BC. At Monte Polizzo, the most common element is two or three straight lines incised along the body of the vessel. These were used on all forms of grey-ware vessels, but are most common on type 1 bowls, jugs, and table amphorae. Triangles are another common motif, known as *dente di lupo*. They are drawn in different ways, from intricate filling of the triangles to schematic representation of the triangles as simple lines, similar to designs on Sicilian bronzes. The style has local antecendents (Spatafora 1996:98), and regional affinities with Protovillanovan and Villanova ceramic traditions in mainland Italy (Giardino 1987). This style, however, survived considerably longer in the hills of Monte Polizzo than in other places, indicating a local conservatism (Tusa 2000) that does not match the experimentation with vessel form. Whereas the incised/impressed style generally gave way to matte-painted styles after 600 BC at other indigenous sites on Sicily (Nenci 1995; Palermo 1996), the incised/impressed style remained dominant at Monte Polizzo into the fifth century BC (Morris et al 2001; Cooper 2007), perhaps to stamp a local identity and cultural autonomy onto the pots (Cooper 2007:175).

In addition to pottery vessels, clay tools also served for spinning and weaving. In House 1, two spindle whorls and several perforated clay loom weights were recovered in excavations (Prescott and Mühlenbock 2004a).

CHIPPED AND GROUND STONE

Stone tools were almost absent from Monte Polizzo. No chipped stone was found. Used for food preparation, two or three simple hemispherical grinding stones of local sandstone were found in each house, as were elliptical grinding surfaces, together with hand stones. A granite axe was also found in House 1. Perhaps an heirloom piece, this axe was probably originally imported from northern Italy (Prescott and Mühlenbock 2004a).

THE CONSTRUCTION OF HOUSES

The settlement was established on flat ground on the hill's crest, but, as its population expanded, houses were built down the hill slopes. Techniques were developed to level building sites, sometimes with terraces and artificial fill among rock outcrops (Prescott 2004). Preparation of the building site involved considerable work and planning.

The houses at Monte Polizzo varied in design, size, and orientation (Chapter 5). They were single-level, frequently multiroomed and differing in internal layout. Building complexity appears to have varied with location in the settlement, probably indicative of social status. More complex structures were built towards the top of the hill, while less complex ones were built on the slopes.

Despite variability in house plans, the same basic building materials and architectural solutions were deployed over large parts of the site. Materials included stone, wood, and clay. The visual effect of different structures on the site would thus have been modulated by a similar look. In particular, the common use of local limestone would have given the impression that the settlement almost grew out of the hill.

Principles of building at Monte Polizzo were much in line with those in other indigenous settlements of western Sicily, and a special Elymian style is not apparent (Streiffert Eikeland 2006; Spatafora 1997; Leighton 1999, 2000). Hewn limestones quarried from the slope of the hill approximately 1 km from the settlement and rounded boulders, probably from the conglomerate on the site, were used to build both walls and footings that supported wattle and daub walls, techniques which could be used in the same house. Solid limestone was primarily used for external load-bearing walls, whereas wattle and daub was used for nonsupporting internal divisions. Even today, the upstanding limestone walls may be up to 1.85 m high (Mühlenbock 2008). Limestone drums were used to support timber pillars, which, in turn, may have supported roof beams (Prescott and Mühlenbock 2004a), a common building technique at other contemporary sites (Streiffert Eikeland 2006:267).

As elsewhere on the island, the interior walls were plastered with a smooth clay plaster coating, sometimes covered with a red slip (Leighton 1993). Floors were cut into the bare rock and some were stone paved. The sunken floors helped insulate the building during winter, as well as maintaining a cooler temperature in the summer (Leighton 1993:141). The roofs were constructed primarily from locally available deciduous oak beams (Stika et al 2008). Evergreen oak, olive, and elm were also used in building but much less frequently (Stika et al 2008). Analysis of charcoal fragments shows the presence of heartwood, indicating that the beams were stripped of sapwood that is susceptible to insect and fungal attack (Stika et al 2008). A few high-status buildings on the top of the hill had roof tiles, but they appear to be exceptional. Roof tiles were introduced in Etruria by in the mid seventh century BC, but were not particularly common in Sicily until the end of the sixth century (Vassallo 1999; Di Vita 1990). In most cases, the house roofs were probably thatched, although the use of wooden shingles has been suggested for some Sicilian settlements (Leighton 1999).

INVESTMENT IN MATERIAL CULTURE

The material culture at each of the sites demonstrates variable investment linked to the social importance of finished objects in the three regions. The inhabitants of Thy, Százhalombatta, and Monte Polizzo employed different technologies for the production of ceramics, lithics, and architecture, which were, in part, a response to the contrasting resources available and to varying operational needs. However, the specific technologies also reflect attitudes towards creativity and choices regarding differential investment in crafts that need to be understood in cultural terms (Table 7.1).

Thy. During the Early Bronze Age in Thy, the ceramic assemblage suggests little investment in pottery with few vessel types and a lack of fine wares or complex decoration. Greater emphasis was placed on lithics. Flint working formed part of a long-standing tradition of investment in this material dating back to the Neolithic, with objects made in large numbers. The Late Bronze Age saw some shift in emphasis. Lithics remained common but declined in production quality, while the quantity and quality of ceramics increased. With regard to houses, although they share very similar simple building techniques, differences in size indicate considerable contrasts in the initial investment in architecture in the Early Bronze Age, which lessens in the Late Bronze Age. The dominance of lithics probably reflects their use in everyday activities, but the low emphasis on ceramics is striking. In the Early Bronze Age, houses, rather than domestic artefacts, appear to have been used to express hierarchy in the Thy settlements.

Százhalombatta. At Százhalombatta, ceramics were an important and highly visible arena of investment. Typological and decorative developments reflect the work of confident, creative craftspeople pushing the boundaries of their technology (Sofaer 2006). However, investment in the production of ceramics was not evenly distributed throughout the assemblage. Particular attention was paid to the decoration and surface treatment of urns and fine wares, suggesting that these were central to the visual ordering of society (Budden 2007). In the Koszider phase, some vessels were specifically designed to be hung on walls as decorative pieces (Sofaer 2006). Stone and bone tools are not as visible as ceramics, but the range of objects made in both materials is striking. Using objects of imported stone and crafted from valued animals may have demonstrated prestige. Little apparent differentiation among houses existed for their initial construction, as they followed similar plans and construction details. Repeated house maintenance, such as replastering, reflects a continued investment in architecture. Although maintaining the external appearance of houses was important, what mattered most to people were the objects of everyday use and decorations within the house, rather than the houses themselves. A suggestion of intimacy of performance may link to the density of domestic life of the tell settlement (Chapter 5).

Table 7.1. Investment levels in different crafts at Thy, Százhalombatta, and Monte Polizzo

	Thy	**Százhalombatta**	**Monte Polizzo**
Ceramics	Small scale in the Early Bronze Age; Medium scale in the Late Bronze Age Restricted range Low investment	Large scale Wide range High investment	Medium scale Wide range Moderate investment
Chipped and ground stone	Large scale Restricted range High investment in the Early Bronze Age	Small scale Wide range Moderate investment	Few contemporary stone objects Low investment
Bone		Medium scale Wide range Moderate investment	
Architecture	Moderate range Primary investment in wood	Restricted range Primary investment in clay and wood	Wide range Primary investment in stone and wood

Monte Polizzo. The ceramics at Monte Polizzo are very visible in household contexts. The incorporation of external style elements into local ceramics indicates a creative attitude towards the production of pottery used within domestic settings. Nonetheless, although individuals evidently used foreign vessels to demonstrate prestige (Chapter 5), traditional indigenous ceramics and manufacturing techniques were also carefully guarded. The retention of local traditions suggests that, unlike other parts of the island, in West Sicily, the Greek and Phoenician coastal colonies may not have dominated the hinterland (Tusa 2000). The political independence of Monte Polizzo meant that the tension between indigenous people and Greek colonists was not felt at the site (Tusa 2000) and so potters were freer to play with forms as they chose. The main investment in material culture at Monte Polizzo, however, was in architecture. Considerable time and effort were put into house construction. The variety in house plans suggests the personalisation of buildings; at the same time, the hierarchy in house sizes (with the largest positioned visibly on the hilltop), indicates the use of architecture as a status marker (Mühlenbock 2008).

THE ORGANISATION OF PRODUCTION

The organisation of production for individual crafts varies among the sites, with different arenas of specialisation and strategies at play in each (Table 7.2).

Thy. In Thy, the limited range of vessel types and forming techniques suggests little specialisation in ceramic production (Kristensen in press; Rasmussen and Bech in press), although in a few cases some of the Late Bronze Age ceramics were higher quality, indicating skilled production. As elsewhere in Southern Scandinavia, ceramics were mostly produced for local use in the domestic domain.

The lithics, however, tell a different story. In the Early Bronze Age, different tools were produced by flint knappers with quite different skills, abilities, and goals. Three different *chaînes opératoires* can be observed: (1) a systematic production of bifacial sickles by highly skilled flint-knapping specialists; (2) a systematic production of flake tools by competent flint knappers; and (3) *ad hoc* production of informal tools by nonspecialists. Formal tools were carefully curated, often resharpened or recycled. The bifacial sickles were not resharpened by the same person who originally made them. Perhaps 'journeymen' knappers visited different farmsteads as handymen through the year (Eriksen 2007).

A few hundred years later, things changed significantly. Bronze tools were now becoming increasingly important and widespread, and flint knapping went into decline. In particular, the quantity of crude *ad hoc* tools in the inventories from Bjerre 7 and Krogstrup points to an expedient production strategy. Although the inventory displays ample technological variation, there is no evidence for

Table 7.2. The organisation of production for different crafts at Thy, Százhalombatta and Monte Polizzo

	Thy	Százhalombatta	Monte Polizzo
Ceramics	Nonspecialists (possibly some in the Late Bronze Age) Low quality (Early Bronze Age) to mixed quality (Late Bronze Age) Technically simple Domestic production Local materials	Specialists High quality Technically complex Workshop production Local materials and some imported vessels	Specialists Mixed quality Technically complex Workshop and domestic production Local and regional materials and imported vessels
Chipped and ground stone	Specialists and nonspecialists Mainly high quality but also some low-quality objects. In the Late Bronze Age low-quality objects dominate. Technically complex and simple Journeymen and domestic production Regional (Early Bronze Age) and local (Late Bronze Age) materials	Specialists and nonspecialists Mainly low quality but also some higher-quality objects Technically complex and simple Domestic production Local, regional, and long-distance materials	
Bone		Specialists and nonspecialists Continuum of quality Technically simple Domestic production Local materials	
Architecture	Specialist foremen overseeing local nonspecialist working teams? Simple combination of materials Local materials	Contributions from specialist woodworkers and clayworkers? Complex combination of materials Local materials	Specialist stonemasons Complex combination of materials Local materials

different skill levels or specialists. The blade knives found at these sites are usually rather small and irregular and, with a few exceptions, correspond well with the *ad hoc* character of the rest of the assemblage. Some flint-knapping specialists apparently continued to exist elsewhere; for example, well-made heavy blade knives were available elsewhere in Jutland (Olesen and Eriksen 2007), and in eastern Denmark and Scania, specialists made heavy blade knives from carefully prepared cores (Högberg 2004).

With regard to the architecture, the question of possible specialist builders is intriguing. Some houses display very standardized common traits, which could indicate that foremen from outside single farmsteads took part in construction. The scale of the largest houses in Thy, and elsewhere in Demark, probably required communal construction.

Százhalombatta. At least some of the pottery manufactured at Százhalombatta was produced by specialised craftspeople, as indicated by the interesting pattern of variation in technical error observed in vessels (Budden and Sofaer 2009). The most technically complex vessels (fine wares and urns) show the least technical error, those that are moderately difficult to make (domestic vessels) show modest error, and those that are technically easiest (cups) show the most faults (Budden 2007). In a system of casual household production where potters are not specialists, one might expect more complex vessels to be most error prone and simplest forms to suffer least. The pattern at Százhalombatta, however, indicates a range in potting proficiency associated with a structure of apprenticeship, where less skilled potters learned on easier pieces before progressing to more complex forms (Budden 2007, 2008; Budden and Sofaer 2009). Given that fine wares were desirable objects implicated in display and prestige (Sofaer 2006; Vicze 2001), highly skilled potters may have held distinctive positions within the social hierarchy (Sofaer 2006).

The stone tools from Százhalombatta offer tantalising glimpses into specialisation at the site. Many of the locally produced flakes made from low-quality materials are relatively poorly executed and may be identified as domestic products. Objects made from better imported materials display higher quality manufacture and may have been kept for more experienced or talented knappers.

The worked bone, antler, and teeth objects from Százhalombatta also fall along a continuum of manufacturing quality (Choyke 1997, 2001). At one end are a few carefully planned and executed objects including elaborate horse gear made from highly selected raw materials. Their formal shape and decoration were widely spread across Middle and Late Bronze Age settlements, suggesting that horse gear may have been made by specialists located at production centres and then broadly traded as special objects, or perhaps produced by itinerant craftspeople. At the other of the scale are highly variable, *ad hoc* tools made with little modification. Most bone tools, including rib scrapers, 'burnishers,' and cattle radii, lie between these two extremes, with carefully selected raw materials but only modified in technically straightforward ways. Most bone, antler, and tooth objects at Százhalombatta were certainly products of household production, using readily available domestic refuse as the basic materials.

The size and complexity of the architecture at Százhalombatta indicates that the construction of houses was almost certainly communal. Whether there were specialist woodworkers or plasterers is difficult to tell, but contributions from such specialists are possible (cf. Waterson 1997; Leggett and Nussbaum 2001). Relatively few bronze tools exist from Hungary compared with surrounding countries (Mozsolics 1967), but the two Százhalombatta hoards contained tools that may have been used for woodworking (Poroszlai 1998, 2000; Kemenczei 2003). Furthermore, the polished stone axes used for woodworking were made from imported materials. If some metal and stone tools were high-status objects with restricted ownership, skilled specialist woodworkers may have worked at the settlement (Sofaer 2006).

Monte Polizzo. The skill needed to produce the more complicated and large vessels, such as *pithoi*, argues for specialized manufacture of some ceramic forms used at Monte Polizzo. The use of a single clay source for indigenous household grey tableware points to regional organisation of production and strong economic ties between settlements, either via a single ceramic producer, or the sharing of a single clay source by multiple producers (Kolb and Speakman 2005).

The masonry work at Monte Polizzo is complex, with the use of stones of different shapes and sizes (Streiffert Eikeland 2006: 273), displaying a degree of craftsmanship that suggests specialist stonemasons. In this proto-urban society, other specialist builders might include woodworkers, particularly for high-status buildings. When roof tiles were used, they were probably manufactured in a workshop.

RELATIONSHIPS BETWEEN CRAFTS

Objects are rarely made or used in isolation, and relationships appear to have existed between different craft activities. The first and perhaps most straightforward relationship is the use of an object made in one craft tradition as a tool in another, as, for example, the use of stone knives to cut the plants for roofing in Thy. Such a relationship implies either exchange between craftspeople or craftspeople with many skills who are able to competently produce objects in more than one area. A second link between crafts arises from the implementation of shared technical solutions, as when materials have similar decorative, plastic, or transformative potentials (Sofaer 2006). At Százhalombatta, the peg joint to attach handles to ceramic vessels echoes rivets in metal, as do the bone pins used to fix antler inlay. Such a relationship requires sharing of knowledge and transfer of know-how among practitioners, which in turn suggest social networks (Bromberger and Chevallier 1999; Sofaer 2006). A third relationship plays on the formal qualities of objects, moving between different media in order to deliberately evoke an object made in another material (Knappett 2002, 2005; Vickers and Gill 1994). Thus, at Monte Polizzo the semi-lustrous surface and sharply carinated form of bowls evoke metal objects (Dixon 2004), implying a transfer of prestige from a highly valued medium to another material. Observed in the architecture in all three regions, the fourth relationship is seen in composite objects made from multiple materials involving different craft skills (Hurcombe 2007). This implies cooperation among craftspeople and/or multiskilled craftspeople moving between different technologies.

These four intercraft relationships exist to differing degrees in our three case studies (Table 7.3). Their analysis can be used to explore contrasting configurations of contextually specific social relations at the sites. They also shed light on other crafts such as leatherworking, textile production, and metalworking, for which little direct evidence exists in our cases.

Thy. In Thy, use of stone tools was a key axis for relationships between crafts. Whereas some tools were *ad hoc*, the specialist production of others implies exchanges through which craftspeople acquired tools. The widespread use of lithics did not, therefore, reflect a pooling of knowledge and resources among craftspeople, and the exchange of technical knowledge between crafts was apparently restricted and rather general, as in pyrotechnology. The social organisation of craftspeople appears to have been rather decentralized as webs of relationships.

The lack of communication between potters, knappers, and builders at Thy suggests distinct roles in craft production for individuals, whether specialised or not. Nonetheless, this separation of roles may not have been the case for all craft activities. In a discussion of gender and metalworkers in northwest Europe, Sørensen (1996) points out that, in these contexts, as in southern Scandinavia, moulds for bronze casting are often made of clay. Applying different gender scenarios has contrasting consequences for how we understand both pottery and metalworking. Thus, a traditional gender association between women and clay technologies might, in fact, suggest that women shaped the appearance of bronze objects. On the other hand, suggesting that men made the moulds would imply that they may have been active in pottery production. A third permutation – that clay technologies and therefore metalworking are not necessarily gender-exclusive – makes for a richer and more complex model. In northwest Europe, especially later in the Bronze Age, metalworking is documented by moulds and crucibles from general settlement and midden contexts, rather than other spatially distinct locations. Being a local and regular activity, this means that metalworking would impinge on everyone in the settlement (Sørensen 1996:49). Members of different gender groups may, therefore, have been involved in different stages of the production process or in negotiations surrounding it, particularly in its planning and scheduling (Sørensen 1996).

Százhalombatta. At Százhalombatta, ceramic, lithic, and bone tool manufacture and building activities were intimately connected to each other, as well as to other crafts, including metalwork. Given the evidence for craft specialisation at the site, the number, variety, and specificity of technical links between crafts is revealing. For the transfer of technical knowledge to take place, the transmission of know-how must have existed among craftspeople (cf. Layton 1989). These social networks allowed pooling of resources, knowledge, techniques, and human potential (Faure-Rouesnel 2001; Bromberger and Chevallier 1999). Transfer of knowledge and resources is quicker and more easily assimilated when the social relations are closer. In a hierarchical society such as the European Bronze Age, one form of network in which this can take place is a caste-like system (Sofaer 2006). Based around kin networks, in such a system it is to

Table 7.3. Cross-craft relationships at Thy, Százhalombatta, and Monte Polizzo

Thy

Tool use	Stone → Architecture: knives and sickles for cutting of vegetation for roofs; knives for pollarding of trees for wattle
	Stone → Metalworking: fire-setting; hammers; moulds
	Stone → Ceramics: fire-setting; burnishing pebbles
	Stone → Leatherworking: scrapers and borers
	Stone → Agriculture
	Antler → Lithics: Antler hammers for knapping
	Metal → Architecture: axes and chisels for woodworking in houses
Formal links	None
Technical links	Ceramics ↔ Houses: manipulation and tempering of clay
	Ceramics ↔ Metalworking: pyrotechnology; prospection and preparation of raw materials
Composite objects	Houses: clay working, woodworking
	Sickles and knives: stone object with wood haft

Százhalombatta

Tool use	Ceramics → Textiles: loom weights
	Stone → Architecture: knives and sickles for cutting of vegetation for roofs; knives for pollarding of trees for wattle; threshing boards with by-products of threshing used for daub
	Stone → Ceramics: burnishing pebbles
	Stone → Architecture: stone axes for woodworking
	Stone → Metalworking: polished stone tools; stone moulds
	Stone → Agriculture
	Stone → Bone working
	Bone → Ceramics: scrapers and perforators as decorating tools
	Bone → Leatherworking: scrapers and borers/points
	Metal → Architecture: axes and chisels for woodworking in houses
	Metal → Antler working
Formal links	Ceramics + Metalwork: ceramic vessels echo metal forms and metallic sheen
	Ceramics + Textiles: decorative motifs echo textiles
	Stone + Metalwork: polished stone tools echo metal forms
Technical links	Ceramics ↔ Architecture: manipulation and tempering of clay; use of woodworking techniques to attach handles to ceramic vessels; pottery forming techniques used for specific architectural elements (e.g., coiling for built-in pots and clay storage bins); use of grog temper in pots and ovens; scraping and smoothing of clay and wood
	Ceramics ↔ Metalworking: pyrotechnology; prospection and preparation of raw materials; use of metalwoking techniques to attach handles to ceramic vessels; punched dot and incised decorative techniques; hammering and beating techniques
Composite objects	Houses: clay working, woodworking, basketry (reed mats)
	Sickles and knives: stone objects with wood or bone haft

Monte Polizzo

Tool use	Ceramics → Textiles: loom weights
Formal links	Ceramics + Metalwork: ceramic vessels echo metal forms and metallic sheen
Technical links	Ceramics ↔ Architecture: manipulation and tempering of clay
	Ceramics ↔ Metalworking: pyrotechnology; prospection and preparation of raw materials; punched dot and incised decorative techniques
Composite objects	Houses: clay working, woodworking, stonemasonry, ceramics (tiles)

everyone's advantage to work together and exchange knowledge and services. The potential exists for specialists at many stages in the commodity chain, from prospection of raw materials to production of the finished articles.

Such a model also has implications for the gendered division of labour. Based on ethnographic observations, a widespread assumption is that later prehistoric potters were female. The manufacture of bone tools is viewed as gender neutral or female because of its association with hide working and sewing, whereas flint knappers and house builders are thought to be male. Costumes and pots decorated with male and female characteristics (Kovács 1973; Poroszlai 2000) suggest that gender distinctions were important in the Hungarian Bronze Age. The exchange of knowledge between crafts, however, suggests that social boundaries were rather fluid. If one accepts a gendered model of craft production, this would, in turn, imply that although aspects of craft production activities may have been gendered, they also involved cooperation between the genders (Sørensen 1996; Sofaer and Sørensen 2002, 2005). Even where craft production is, on the whole, strongly gendered, local traditions may permit men and women to participate in different steps of the production process, suggesting that the social dynamics of craft production may be quite complex (David 1990; Brown 1995; Nicholson and Wendrich 1994).

Monte Polizzo. At Monte Polizzo, relationships between crafts show in the clay imitation of metal forms and surface finish, reflecting the use of pottery in status display. Evidence for practical links among crafts is rather limited. We know little of tool uses at the site other than for loom weights. Furthermore, the technical links between crafts are restricted and rather general in nature, suggesting a lack of communication among craftspeople. Perhaps, given that the evidence for craft production and specialisation is strongest for pottery production and stonemasonry at the site, the transfer of knowledge between crafts may simply have been of little use. There is no evidence that specialists had close social or kin relationships with each other, perhaps suggesting a rather open 'job market.' Nonetheless, craft activities within the home were probably organised along gendered lines. As in other indigenous settlements on Sicily, the division of internal space within the houses suggests the segmentation of activities, which related not only to public and private domains but also to gendered space (Rundin 1996:190; Spatafora 2003:75–82).

CONCLUSION

The crafts discussed in this chapter represent the material culture most involved in everyday life at Thy, Százhalombatta, and Monte Polizzo. Each community articulated specific technological choices at historical moments. These choices were affected by the accessibility of local resouces, as seen, for example, in the contrasting building materials for houses in the three regions. Technological choices cannot, however, be understood in isolation from the wider cultural milieu in which they were situated. Rather, they mediate between what is materially possible and aspects of social organisation (van der Leeuw 1993:240).

The three communities placed quite different emphasis on individual crafts. Regardless of environmental differences, craftspeople engaged creatively with materials, producing both simple and complex forms used in everyday subsistence and identity display. Each community chose to invest distinctly in objects, deploying different kinds of knowledge and skills, with contrasting strategies and technical demands; this variation in crafts involved people with quite different degrees of specialisation. Each community also reveals different linkages among crafts, with distinct technical and social relationships between crafts and craftspeople. Taking a comparative perspective allows us to articulate the notion of contextual difference in specific ways. Yet much remains to explore, and our understanding of the technology and craft of later prehistory is only beginning.

NOTES

1. There are relatively few bone objects at Thy and Monte Polizzo. In the case of the former, this is the consequence of poor bone preservation. At the latter, the production of bone tools does not appear to have been important.
2. Excavated by Thisted Museum.
3. Excavated by Herning Museum.

8

Organising Bronze Age Societies: Concluding Thoughts

Timothy Earle and Kristian Kristiansen

Organising Bronze Age societies involved prehistoric European groups in dynamic and contested material processes. With varying outcomes, forces of top-down domination balanced with bottom-up household and community self-organising independence. We draw together here evidence from the thematic chapters into a set of new conclusions and research questions about European Bronze Age societies. We examine how consumption and production interacted locally, and later we consider how foreign connections affected local societies. We look especially to how social groups used material culture to forge institutions with different roles and identities. Finally we draw up the larger picture of Bronze Age political economies and social development. Fundamental to our synthesis has been our confederacy of microregional studies, organised with common interests and methods, to consider contrasting trajectories of long-term social change within the common themes of European late prehistory.

LOCAL PRODUCTION AND PATTERNS OF CONSUMPTION

To begin with, technology sets absolute barriers to economic expansion. Degrees of specialisation and division of labour, however, allowed for a more elaborate production that can be expanded beyond the needs of immediate consumers. In short, a more complex economic system arose in the Bronze Age in which demand and consumption patterns were widely shared but could not be fully satisfied locally. This led to the formation of a complex interplay among local, regional, and international economies. We begin by delineating local technologies and their economies, which created the basic conditions.

As with an ability to adjust subsistence to local conditions, the technology of everyday life was, by and large, technically quite simple, made mostly from local materials with skilled human labour that households could have provided for themselves within a gendered division of labour or, alternatively, was available from small-scale specialists trading locally (Chapter 7). Thus, the stone tools in Scandinavia or the bone tools in Hungary, used by all households, were made primarily from local materials and apparently manufactured by the household for its own uses or by specialists living at no great distance. In Thy, flint was locally available to households as field pieces and as the extensive debris from nearby Neolithic flint mines. Some specialised production, however, did exist. Formal tools appear to exhibit more care in knapping, suggesting some specialisation, and the manufacture of the fine flint daggers and asymmetrical sickles certainly was specialised. The sickles, for example, were produced at a few settlements where mounds of waste and unused tools document specialised production by flint-knapping households. In Hungary, lithics were quite rare, but were from materials that needed to be traded in from some distance, and small-scale specialist flint workers probably made a few tools.

Specialisation is also observed in ceramic production (Chapter 7). Pottery, unlike most stone tools, has an intrinsic economy of scale in manufacture, such that it is only marginally more costly to make multiple pots than a single pot, and production for exchange outside of a potting family is inherently efficient. Despite this, the impression is that most ceramics used by households in our microregional studies were technically quite simple and involved hand forming and low-temperature firing, tasks that would have been mastered by local potters. In Scandinavia, where people lived on separate farms, ceramics were so low fired that they probably travelled only short distances; pottery was thus likely produced on the farm where it was used or on a closely neighbouring farm. However, elaborately decorated wooden bowls and spoons, along with simpler birch bark containers that served as drinking service, go some way to explain the lack of fine pottery. Although locally produced, they emulated foreign forms and their decorative patterns were lined with tin nails to demonstrate their exclusive character (Jensen 1998:pages 108, 135; Kristiansen and Larsson 2005:figure 138). In Hungary, where most people lived in villages, households appear to have been less self-sufficient. Ceramics were more varied and show higher technical skill, suggesting more specialisation linked to the role of pottery in households. Several potters living at a tell, or in other nearby settlements probably produced pottery for their neighbours and neighbouring settlements. Preliminary results of chemical characterisation of ceramics suggest quite local production, without extensive exchange and specialisation (Kreiter 2007). One of the features still in need of better archaeological documentation is the relationship between the households at the acropolis and the lower town, a feature also evidenced at Feudvar (Hänsel 2003:abb. 11) and probably many other tell settlements. Did a division of labour exist between them? The households at the central tell in Százhalombatta and elsewhere often had several ovens and big storage pits for grain. Was this an exclusive feature of the acropolis, and did they produce bread for other households? In Sicily, some pottery, especially the Greek forms, evidently was produced by ceramic specialists and traded quite broadly into local settlements such as Monte Polizzo, where it was part of new patterns of consumption and drinking (wine). Other technically simpler pottery for everyday household use was produced by small-scale, local specialists (Mühlenbock 2008).

How independent were households in each of the microregions that we studied? The bulk of household waste was involved in everyday food production, preparation, and serving (Chapter 5). In these activities, each household in all areas appears to have operated largely independently. The classic example would have been the farmstead in Scandinavia, for which virtually all household activities were performed on household land, and few items came from the outside. In Hungary and Sicily, the households lived clustered together, often in dense settlements, and we can presume that much activity, including farming, grazing, working, and the like, took place outside the house in more common areas, but the household here appears, too, to have retained substantial independence in subsistence activities, although some households were larger than others. Certainly, part-time specialists made some stone tools and most ceramics used by households. A relatively simple network of exchanges probably linked neighbours in most of the necessities of everyday life, and, as community structures became more complex, local specialisation probably increased. The economic and social relations behind such apparent small-scale divisions of labour among households could,

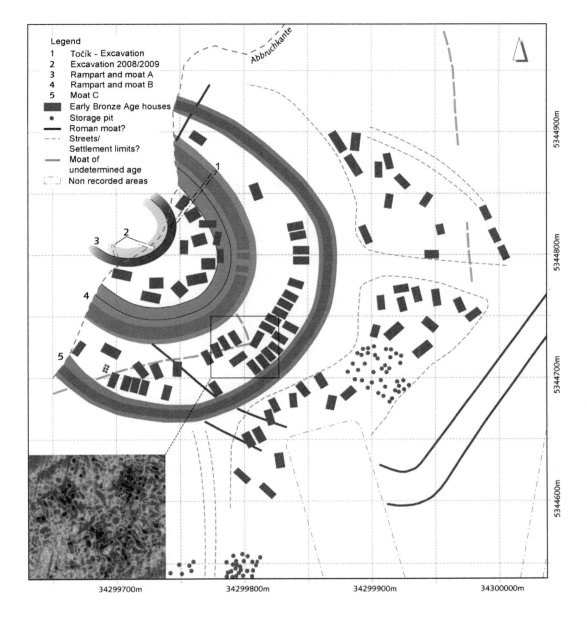

Plate 8.1.
Fortified tell site at Fidvár, Slovakia. Ground plan of house clusters and fortifications based on magnetic prospection, shown in section (from: www.vfg.uni-wuerzburg.de/forschung/projekte/fidvar).

however, have been complex. Dependent producers or even slave labour may have been part of the local economy among the larger households. In Scandinavia, they may have lived in some of the very small houses that existed throughout the Bronze Age; in the tell societies, they could have been herders and farm labourers living outside the tell. Some big tells probably housed many different social groups and, as documented by penetrating radar at the tell-settlement Fidvár in Slovakia (Plate 8.1), houses could cluster, probably as social groupings. With gradual population growth, groups moved into the tell site and left their local settlements, a process that, in the final stage, was reversed as the tell depopulated.

As a basic social and economic unit, the household existed through European late prehistory and apparently kept substantial self-sufficiency and autonomy. The household can be thought of as a modular, co-residential group organised to provide for its members' wants (Chapter 5). In Scandinavia, farmhouses were quite large, allowing for storage capacity and winter fodder and allowing for big households that could organise the needed diversity of farmwork. Associated with chieftains, the largest houses and their organisation within chiefly hamlets may have allowed for a more complex division of labour with a range of attached specialists supported by tributary farms. In Hungary, in contrast, the house sizes and probable number of their members were smaller. Clustered quite densely within villages, households were probably less self-sufficient, obtaining a larger range of goods and services from partially specialised neighbouring families. Provisions of meat at the central tell settlements came as ready cut-out pieces, testifying to a rather developed economic system. In Sicily, these two patterns appear to have combined. Many households were apparently fairly small and therefore would not have had a complex internal division of labour. Part-time specialist exchanges in goods and services were probably common in this proto-urban world. Larger households such as House 1 may well have had servants and attached specialists to support the more complex activities associated with an elevated lifestyle. Certainly these households also obtained substantial status goods from outside.

The central questions then become the extent to which households actually became imbedded within larger community settlements and political organisations. Why do groups organise with larger and more centralised structures? Based on an analysis of settlement structure and settlement patterns, we posit that, in later prehistory, alternative super-household organisations were formed across Europe and obtained greater or lesser amounts of sway over households. In sharply contrasting patterns, households were organised into settlements of varying sizes and internal structures, including separate households, hamlet and village groupings of households, and proto-urban large villages or towns (Chapter 4). The tell-settlement tradition, with its numerous and yet fairly small households, belongs with a similar tradition in the Balkans (Hänsel 2003) and, as reflected in cooking stands and cuisine (Horejs 2005), connections existed among these areas and the Aegean (Bolohan 2005). In Scandinavia, farmsteads were scattered across the landscape, often quite separate one from the next. Sometimes a few farms clustered together, especially associated with chiefly farms, but the relative separation and independence of households were maintained. This tradition encompassed most of northern and middle Europe, from Holland to Scandinavia, and from south Germany to Jutland (Arnoldussen and Fontijn 2006). Also here a network of connections goes a long way to explain the shared tradition (Kristiansen and Larsson 2005:figure 107). At the opposite end of the spectrum were the proto-urban settlements of Sicily, in which nearly 800 houses were packed within large settlements, organised with streets and public areas. Intermediate between these extremes were the settlements of Hungary, where some were dense, central tells and others were scattered households in villages and hamlet.

To understand the causes of this variation, we imagine a new tension between local interests and regional politics, households and local groups pushing to retaining local autonomy and identity versus chieftains attempting to assert regional power through control over local resources and international relationships. These tensions were driven by the emergence of new elite lifestyles and corresponding novel patterns of consumption. Therefore, we now approach local production from the perspective of consumption, which provides much of the motivation for the acquisition of status goods (discussion in Manning and Hulin 2004).

Consumption in the Bronze Age was linked to the establishment of novel value systems with corresponding new demands, which boosted production to provide for those needs. Throughout Europe, the metal-based economy emerged with a regional division of labour from mining to finished product linked by relatively high-volume international trade, probably couched in long-distance political alliances. Once the systems were in place, new needs and new patterns of consumption could be spread along these very same lines and new products could enter the system. Thus, we can demonstrate the onset of a wool-producing economy after 2000 BC in Hungary (Chapter 6), when elaborate textiles and clothing became vital ingredients in the new Bronze Age culture, as demonstrated, for example, by the rich Danish oak coffin burials from the middle of the second millennium BC (Broholm and Hald 1940). Wool corresponds to the role played by fine textiles and their trade in the Near East and Greece (Larsen 1987; Killen 2007; Barber 1991:chapter 15). Similarly, the herding economy developed new control over cattle as a means of prestige, meat, traction, and hides, and animals could be moved long distances as well. The new body culture of textile clothing was, in all probability, accompanied by a new cuisine, which led to patterns of consumption and production for elite food and drinking (mead and, later, wine), such as evidenced by the elaborate ovens in Hungary and Sicily, whereas in northern Europe outdoor earth ovens and the use of heated stones in cooking were common. Finally, new needs for maritime and land transport had already led to innovations in ship building and to the introduction of the two-wheeled chariot, which placed new demands on the chiefly court to maintain well-trained horses, skilled craftsmen, warriors, and paddlers for the maritime and overland trade expeditions. All in all, a new system of craft specialisations, lifestyles, and corresponding novel patterns of consumption accompanied the onset of the Bronze Age proper after 2000 BC. Some of these new needs unfolded early in Hungary and adjacent areas, whereas they reached Scandinavia a few hundred years later. In Sicily, they probably were restricted to areas in contact with Mycenaean traders (Vianello 2008; Marazzi and Tusa 2005; Miliktello 2005), unfolding fully only with the beginning of Iron Age urbanisation.

What are the implications of these new patterns of consumption? Part-time specialists, perhaps even full-time specialists, for casting of bronze were attached to the largest chiefly houses. The manufacture of weaponry and wealth thus came under the control of chiefs. This specialisation is demonstrated in the exclusive use of unmixed copper from a single source and a high tin content of 10 to 15 percent in the production of full-hilted swords in south Scandinavia and northern Europe (Riederer 2004). Feeding additional household members on the chiefly farms, however, also demanded surpluses produced by yet more workers for cereal and animal raising. The large farmhouses that housed these larger households took its toll on forest resources, as evidenced in Thy in Denmark, where building timber became scarce after 1400 BC and fuel for fireplaces was provided not by wood but by dried bog turfs. Craftspeople were evidently travelling locally to build new and enlarged farmhouses, evidenced in identical layout for farms across regions (Gröhn 2004:figure 61).

Textiles for more elaborate clothing represented a new domain of consumption and prestige display, as seen in well-preserved Danish oak coffin burials from the late fifteenth and the early fourteenth centuries BC, in which pieces of textiles were simply added for the sake of display and use in the otherworld. The various garments, from belts and caps to huge capes with added pile, demonstrate a fully developed textile tradition. It displays a variety of both simple and complex textile technologies and of quality ranging from ordinary to high. Exceptional weavers, perhaps living in centres of textile production, evidently produced fine high-quality textiles. Cut lengths of several meters of cloth woven by two or three weavers working simultaneously demonstrate substantial scales in production, and such long pieces would have demanded special weaves with two beams, as no loom weights are found (Barber 1991:176 ff.); their manufacture suggests some bulk trade in textiles. However, highly elaborate fine pieces also were produced, such as caps with pile. The widespread importance of textiles among local Bronze Age elites suggests an economy geared to wool production, perhaps for a market, as suggested by the case of Hungary. In Scandinavia, sheep rise to dominance only during the Late Bronze Age. With reference to the economic importance of contemporary textile trade in the Near East, huge profits were achieved by selling fine textiles from Assur in the city states of Anatolia and beyond (Barber 1994:chapter 7; Larsen 2007); as suggested by the Hungarian and Sicilian evidence, similar systems, although on a smaller scale, could well have operated in Europe.

Could wool from Hungary have been traded to a textile-producing centre, from which it travelled to Denmark with new bronze weapons in exchange for amber, and probably beeswax for casting, and hides? Trade carried Carpathian metal and weapons to Scandinavia during the same period (1750–1500 BC) (Liversage 1994), and it would have been profitable to add other marketable products to the trade as well. Among them we can list the chariot, images of which appear in rock-art of south Scandinavia, just as antler cheek pieces occur on Hungarian Bronze Age tells and in Scandinavia (Thrane 1999). In Monte Polizzo, every house and room displayed weaving weights of different size, for different qualities. Weaving was linked to the female sphere and to high status for finer textiles. Thus, by the Early Iron Age, the upright weave with loom weights was standard, employed in every household. No doubt textile manufacturing and trade were widespread and important to the emerging European Bronze Age economy.

In terms of meat, hides, and traction animals, cattle were most important. In Scandinavia, cattle production peaked in the Early Bronze Age and its management was evidently in the hands of the chiefly farms, where cattle apparently were raised on owned pastures and stalled within the large houses. In the Late Bronze Age, the chiefly settlement at Voldtofte outsourced calves to dependent settlements. By now, horses were a common source of both traction/riding and meat consumption, and by this time their breeding may well have become a specialised, export industry in Hungary.

Drinking and feasting played an important role in the new society, as evidenced by drinking sets found from the Mediterranean to Scandinavia (Kristiansen and Larsson 2005:figure 60), and mead has been documented in bark containers of Scandinavia (Kock 2003). Inhabitants of Monte Polizzo adopted the practices of the Greek symposium, as evidenced by imported Corinthian ware, and transport amphorae from a variety of places in the Mediterranean and Italy testify to trade in wine and olive oil. By the Iron Age, a commercial economy in staples prevailed, and Monte Polizzo provided grain to the Greek colony of Selinunte in exchange for the trappings of a 'civilised' lifestyle (Mühlenbock 2008).

By turning the perspective from production to consumption, we can understand the desires and motivations behind the widespread changes in local economies during the Bronze Age, some of which are documented in detail for the first time in our case studies. These economic activities became part of a larger world of trade and alliances that tied European societies together, supported by new regional weight standards (Primas 2008:160 ff.; Vandkilde 2005), which had been in use since the Early Bronze Age in the Aegean and the Near East (Rahmstorf 2006).

TRADE AND ALLIANCE NETWORKS

The role of wealth exchange, always part of the chiefly strategies of political expansion, changed dramatically with the Bronze Age. With a developing boat technology, metal moved broadly across the land and along the rivers and open seas of Europe. Emergent chiefs could use the new metal for display, to reward supporters, and to arm warriors, and a chief's ability to access metal helped extend networks of support and alliance. To access metal, chieftains needed to channel metal flows, and this was feasible in a number of ways determined by placement in and developments of the networks of flows. In Jutland, a network analysis of several thousand barrows, coupled to an analysis of burial wealth during the Early Bronze Age, demonstrated that the nodal points in the network accumulated the most wealth in gold and full-hilted swords (Johansen, Laursen, and Holst 2004). In this situation, the chiefs of Thy rose to power, primarily by asserting ownership over productive pasturelands and the export of animal products, and secondarily by attempting to monopolize amber exports. Our proposition is that many, if not most, areas of Europe participated in broad networks of export production and exchange in valuables that ranged from cattle hides to woollen textiles to specialty stones and amber to furs, antlers, and probably slaves as well.

Late prehistory in Europe emphasised trade, warriors to protect and control that trade, and dynastic marriages to forge the necessary political alliances (Bergerbrant 2005). Although overland exchange of many goods existed in the Neolithic, with the emergence of Bronze Age chiefdoms, the movement increasingly by boat of very special objects, often of specialist manufacture and of local availability, made possible targeted control over expansive exchange networks (Needham 2009).

Trade in luxury objects became increasingly politically significant. As most weapons and objects of personal display became made of metal and other rare materials, households and communities became dependent on trade with the outside (Earle 2002). The significance of these special materials, both for defence and status, effectively broke down a household and community's self-sufficiency. The movement of metals decisively changed society in the Bronze Age, establishing networks of dominance as emerging chieftains could control their procurement and distribution. Trade in the Bronze Age appears to have followed established routes, especially along rivers, where it could have been relatively easily extorted by local warrior elites. Elsewhere, wealth could be accumulated by controlling export production, as in Thy, or by becoming raider/traders, as for the maritime specialists of Tanum (Figures 8.1 and 8.2). What is striking is how the movement of wealth through Europe created diverse opportunities for distinction through action at bottlenecks in the production and distribution systems. An entrepreneurial spirit must have pervaded the networks of chieftains and their supporters that spread as an expansive web, linking an elite warrior sector into broad regional systems of beliefs and status and making something of a single cultural and economic system across Europe.

Ultimately, the rise and fall of chiefly power was tied to specific logistics of participation in international trade. Thus, the changing nature of the trade through the Bronze Age would have created or denied opportunities to local leaders. In the Early Bronze Age, for example, Jutland witnessed the emergence of quite strong local chiefs in the south, as seen by their exceptional large halls (Chapter 5). We believe that this local development can be explained by its position in the regional exchange system. An early land-based trade in animals would have created especially rich opportunities to these chiefs of the south; they could control the drove roads that connected the rich pastures for animals in northern Jutland with the markets for these animals southward across the continent, the source for the metal. The more discrete hierarchy that we describe for Thy would

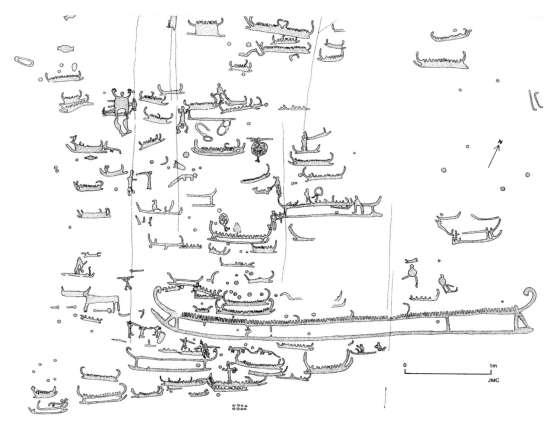

Figure 8.1.
Maritime rock-art scene from Torsbo, Kville in western Sweden showing a fleet of ships setting out on a sea journey. The number of paddlers was typically around 20 (after Coles 2005:figure 226).

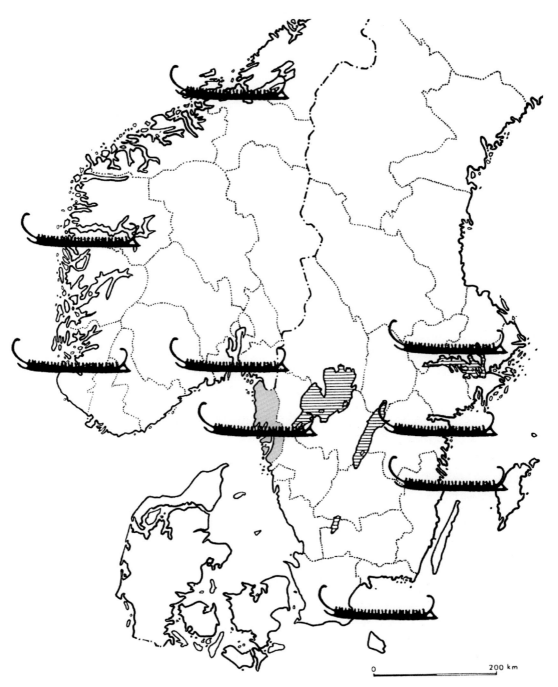

Figure 8.2. Map showing the appearance of identical rock-art ships from the Early Bronze Age along the Scandinavian coastline, testifying to the importance of long-distance maritime trade and sea journeys along the Scandinavian coastline. Similar networks must have connected other maritime regions, such as the Atlantic seaboard.

have been based on controlling the production of those animals that would have been channelled through the territories of the southern chiefdoms. Into the Late Bronze Age, the locations of primary chiefly development in Scandinavia shifted to the central islands and coastal areas, and we propose that a new emphasis on maritime, ships-based trade shifted opportunities more towards the east and social stratification in Jutland declined. This may also have been caused by the decline in productive potential in western and northern Jutland, as we saw in the case of Thy (Kristiansen 1978). For Hungary, a major route for the trade in metal was undoubtedly the Danube River, and, as metal trade increased and became more concentrated on the main arteries of the river systems, the construction of Vatya tell settlements along the Danube would have given trading opportunities for local production of animal products at the same time that it offered chances to extract wealth paid for safe passage along the river thoroughfare.

In Sicily, through the Bronze Age, the region was apparently quite marginal to developing exchange systems until relatively late, when a new boat technology for trade and a warrior organisation to protect the trade emerged. Then local chieftains participated in international trade largely by developing herding and exchanging their products, probably including slaves, with Mycenaean traders (Marazzi and Tusa 2005; Miliktello 2005; Vianello 2008). In the Iron Age, however, as Greek and Phoenician colonies were established in Sicily, the settlement of Monte Polizzo grew, rapidly receiving the material trappings of civilisation in exchange for local products. The expanding colonial systems of the Phoenicians and Greeks, each based on a new trade-based colonial economy, created a radical change in the opportunities for local leaders and entrepreneurs (Hodos 2006:chapter 3). The colonists' need for cereal grain (Chapter 6) would have created significant opportunities for local leaders, who could demand surpluses from the town's fields, and for local traders, who would handle the actual negotiations. Distinction then was gained by a new set of economic opportunities to obtain and display wealth representing the international world of civilised people.

In the Bronze and Iron Ages, any position through Europe offered different opportunities for export production in special products, salt, grains, and the like, but at the same time, varying relationships to the actual location of markets and trade routes presented locales with better chances for accumulation. Chiefs no doubt emerged or lost power depending on changing circumstances in the political economies on which their power depended. We present an interpretative narrative based upon three select households from our project where specific objects and household biographies allow an admittedly rather free interpretation relevant to our trade theme.

The warrior's house

In southern Scandinavia, at the raised seabed in Bjerre, Thy, a deserted farm was covered at the end of the Early Bronze Age by wind-blown sand from the nearby North Sea coast. This house was excavated by TAP as site 6, described in previous chapters. Within Bjerre, the house was its largest (24 m long), having been expanded once to create more space for its occupants. The well-preserved floor deposit contained numerous flint scrapers with distinctive use ware from hide working, and the bone remains recovered from its garbage contained an absolute dominance of cattle with more than 80 percent (Bech 2003). We believe that the occupants of the house raised cattle and prepared their hides for international trade. In addition, the most prominent find from the house was a small cache of raw amber, originally stored in a small bag and buried beneath the floor. At this time, amber was not used locally, but was exported through much of the continent, where it served as prestige material. In return for these exports, the members of the house must have received important imports, including metal (Hughes-Brock 2005). Two small personal bronze objects, a double stud and a fibula, reinforced the rather special status of this household. Both belonged to a male warrior dress, in which the double stud would have been employed to keep together the leather belt, from which the sword hung in its scabbard. These were the objects of an elite person, probably a warrior supporting his local ritual chief. We imagine that he travelled abroad to trade his personal amber and animals and those of his chief. In return, he brought home the precious objects of foreign origin for his chief and himself. His role as warrior on this journey would have been essential to protect the wealth he carried. He would have travelled south along well-connected routes, eventually taking him to south-central Germany, where similar warrior graves were linked to larger farmsteads (Sperber 1999).

On Figure 8.3b, we show a reconstruction of a large period 2 chiefly farm from Legård in Thy, with two living sections and a stall in the middle for cattle. It demonstrates the essential role of

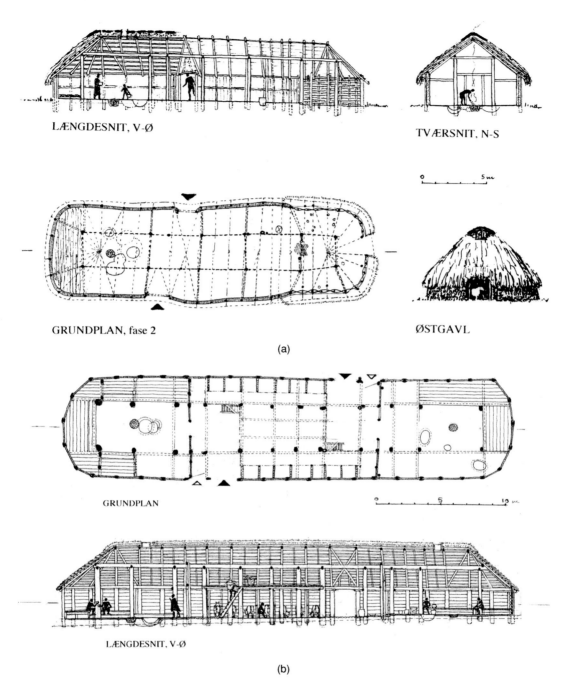

Figure 8.3. a. A reconstruction of traditional farmhouse at Bjerre, Thy, b. The twin chiefs' farm at Legård, Thy. They demonstrate the differential access to and control over resources, from timber to cattle. Reconstruction carried out by Bente Draiby.

cattle as an indicator of prestige and value. Such a large farmhouse, 8 meters wide and 34 meters long, with solid wooden walls, was a manifestation of grandeur, but it also depleted the remaining high forest in Thy, leading to an economic recession during the following periods. Compared to the ordinary farm in Thy, normally 6 meters wide and some 16 to 20 meters long reconstructed in Figure 8.3a it demonstrates the differential access to wealth and resources within the Thy region.

The charioteer's house

In Hungary, within the defended core of the tell settlement Százhalombatta, sat a cluster of houses overlooking the Danube (Plate 8.2). In the largest excavated house there, a huge pot contained two pairs of decorated antler cheek pieces covered with a fat brownish substance. We interpret these to have been part of a full-horse harness of leather, with only the antler cheek pieces for the bits fully preserved (Figure 8.4a). Such gear is special, the type used to harness the horse, which perhaps drew a chariot. The use of antler is

Plate 8.2.
Reconstruction drawing of the tell site at Százhalombatta at its height (Drawing by Brigitta Kürtösi).

also specific for the Carpathians (Kristiansen and Larsson 2005:figure 79), but with some also reaching Scandinavia (Thrane 1999). In Figure 8.4b we show a reconstruction of its use, based on pieces found in Bronze Age tells. We imagine this house as that of either a warrior or charioteer, members of a new warrior elite in the Middle Bronze Age cultures of Hungary. These were a class of new military specialists, undoubtedly charged with protecting their people and overseeing an emergent trade economy along the Danube that stretched out on the river below. Chariots and charioteers brought new skills in horse dressage as well as new construction techniques for the chariots. Also, simple roads had to be maintained between settlements. In Denmark, the linear distribution of barrows suggests the existence of trackways between local polities over land, where ships could not be used.

The new elite warriors employed the long-sword and shared with the early Mycenaean culture not only chariots, but also the characteristic boar-tusk helmets. The early helmet form consisted of separate leather bands onto which rectangular pieces of carved out boar tusks were sewn. This early form is well described in the Iliad (*Illiad* Book 9:260–72), and is preserved in a shaft grave from Aegina from the eighteenth century BC (Kilian-Dirlmeier 1997). Identical pieces were found in a grave from Nizna Mysl'a in the Carpathians (Hughes-Brock 2005:figure 5), but they are also well known from tell sites in both Hungary and Rumania (*Bronzezeit in Ungarn* 1992:abbildung 88; Kasco 2004:plate XLI:1). From here, well-bred horses may have been exported south, where horse breeding was difficult, and these horses appear in the graves of Mycenae. Warrior elites created long-distance connections that channelled not only amber from Scandinavia and horses from the Carpathians to the south, but ideas and institutions of warrior elites and weapons were carried back north. Because much of this was immaterial or of organic material (textiles, chariots, boar-tusk helmets), it is not easily discerned today, and swords and other warrior equipment were soon manufactured to local standards. However, we may detect such institutions in the appearance of a package of objects, for example, for weaving (Barber 1991:303–10); in the use of specific ritual paraphernalia, such as clay figurines (Biehl 2008) or in the material indications for the chariot and its derived institutional support, from rock-art pictures in Scandinavia to cheek pieces in the Carpathians and the east Mediterranean (David 2007; Harding 2007).

The merchant's house

In Sicily, high on the hilltop of Monte Polizzo, House 1 (Plate 8.3) stands overlooking the agricultural valley below. It is among the largest households excavated here, and its spatial layout defines several discrete rooms, apparently with special activities (Chapter 5). A rather large room was filled with tableware for many persons to eat special cuisine and drink wine. A good deal of the tableware was of Greek manufacture (Figure 8.5), and the owners of this house must have traded for these exotic items in order to host Greek-inspired symposia parties. Wine amphorae from all over the Mediterranean testify to its import (Mühlenbock 2008: Figure 37 and 38). Additionally, members of the house wove textiles of different quality, and these were likely items for trade. We propose that House 1 was a merchant's house, and the status of its owner was clothed in international Greek manners and customs that mark foreign connections.

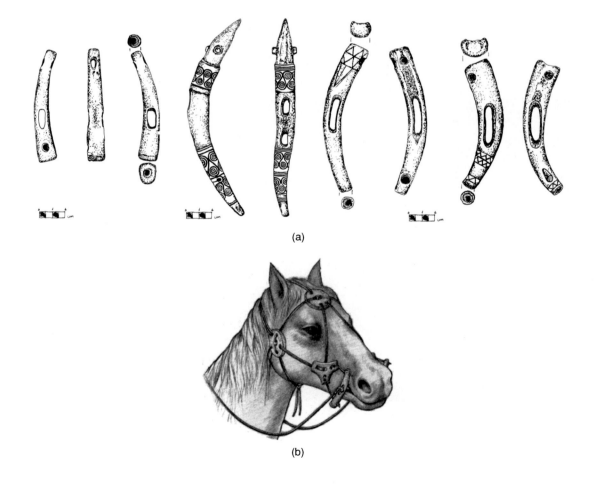

Figure 8.4.
a. Two pairs of decorated antler cheek pieces found in a pot in the largest house at the tell site of Százhalombatta.
b. Reconstruction of the use of horse harness from Danubian tell sites (after *Bronzezeit in Ungarn*, figure 36).

We may further suppose that they traded grain with Selinunte and, in return, received wine and Greek tableware (Chapter 6).

From farmsteads to a regional settlement system to international patterns of trade and travel, the world of chiefs and their communities created a patchwork of material connections that served diverse purposes in local, regional, and interregional flows of goods and people. Reproduction of this European world of chiefs and commoners built on the political economy, but it also created different material identities, to which we now turn.

FORGING IDENTITIES: INSTITUTIONS AND MATERIAL CULTURE

How was household consumption linked to the wider local and regional patterns of settlements and social relationships? We have suggested that some persons and their accompanying groups travelled longer distances for trade and political gain. Although most flows of goods and people were local, we expect that households and their members crafted identity and affiliation by creatively combining local and foreign material culture practices involving weapons of war and objects of local and regional identity.

Plate 8.3.
Reconstruction of the merchant's house at Monte Polizzo (Drawing by Andreas Åhman).

In south Scandinavia, metalwork defined the identity of Nordic society. Two recurring packages of objects in graves of males distinguished ritual chiefs and warrior chiefs (Kristiansen 1984). The ritual chief had special objects, such as camp stools and drinking vessels with sun symbols at the bottom, so that the sun would rise when lifting their cups of mead. Also, razor and tweezer were linked to this group, which shared the exclusive use of spiral decoration, a symbol of sun cult in the Nordic identity. The sword often was full-hilted and used for parade rather than combat, rarely sharp, and rarely damaged.

The warrior chief had an undecorated, flange-hilted sword, an international type distributed from south-central Europe to Scandinavia. It was the sword of the professional warrior, always sharp edged and often resharpened following damage in combat. They did not display the symbols of Nordic identity. Both groups shared burial under a barrow, dressed with a cape and round cap, distinctive of the free man of chiefly lineage. With a distribution similar to that of the flange-hilted sword, another international sword type was octagonal-hilted. Could these be foreign warrior chiefs and traders from south Germany, who travelled to and settled in Denmark? Material culture is meaningfully constituted; different sword types in the Bronze Age were linked to distinct social identities imbedded within social and ritual institutions.

FORGING IDENTITIES: INSTITUTIONS AND MATERIAL CULTURE

Figure 8.5.
Greek Ionian, Corinthian, and colonial tableware from the merchant's house.

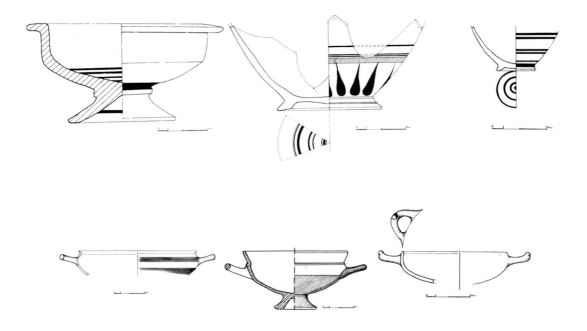

Although archaeologists have long recognized the social complexity of prehistoric societies, the derived complexity of culture is understudied (but see Bürmeister and Müller-Schessel 2007). Archaeologists delimit social institutions by analysing the symbolic and cultural field of meaning for objects – as for example, associated with ritual chiefs and warrior chiefs; the next step is to move from identifying social groups to understanding the identities that they represent. Did the symbolic fields of meaning that constituted the institutions of ritual chiefs and warrior chiefs also carry a wider collective identity? We encounter here the formation of the self through a dialectical relationship with collective identities from social groups/classes to polities/ethnicity. Although ethnicity undoubtedly played a central role in human societies, its material expressions have not been well studied. We propose that it is possible to delimit social and, ultimately, ethnic identity from the geographical distribution of social institutions and their symbolic meaning.

Thus, the two institutions of ritual chiefs and warrior chiefs have radically different distributions (Figure 8.6a and 8.6b), and this informs us about their different roles in the reproduction of a complex set of regional and interregional identities, some of which formed a collective ethnicity and some of which formed a political identity. The ritual chiefs maintained the cosmological order of society, defined by a symbolic package of objects and decoration, which signalled Nordic identity and a shared religious cosmology. In charge of rituals, they probably controlled the religious and legal knowledge vital to the correct performance of rituals and the maintenance of order. Therefore, Nordic ritual chiefs did not move outside the cultural boundaries of their symbolic worlds, and their distinctive objects had a geographically circumscribed use (Figure 8.6b). They provided an ethnic identity rooted in a shared cosmology, which corresponds to one of the most commonly used definitions of ethnic identity (Jones 1997). This group of male ritual chiefs was paralleled by a group of female priests with richly spiral-decorated ornaments, central among them the sun disc carried in a belt on the stomach (Kristiansen and Larsson 2005:figures 135–37).

The warrior chiefs, on the contrary, were culturally defined as 'foreign,' which allowed them to travel and maintain political connections of trade and alliance outside the symbolically defined world of Nordic culture (Figure 8.6a). They most probably maintained and carried the relationships and material objects that constituted the interregional networks of bronze flows. Less ideological, these persons were involved in more elemental or universal power of force.

Ethno-historical evidence of warrior cultures supports an interpretation of warriors and traders on the move. Warriors often formed special group identities (sodalities) that linked them in a spatial network defined by rules of special behaviour and etiquette. This could be employed both for recruiting war bands and for travelling to more distant chiefs to earn fame and foreign prestige goods, as documented among the Japanese samurai and as a recurring theme in the literature on warriors and warfare.

In this way, institutions took care of separate needs that were vital to Bronze Age societies: the internal maintenance of a shared religious world and the external maintenance of political and commercial relations. Their relationship could become strained and competitive if foreign relations collapsed, and in periods of warfare the war chiefs would be particularly powerful; from 1300 to 1100 BC, for example, flange-hilted swords become especially numerous. The dual institution of ritual and war chief represented a clever division of power found in many societies in anthropological literature and in early European history. In Mycenaean texts, the ritual political leader is named Wanax and the war leader Lavagetas.

In Hungary, full-hilted decorated swords formed a category of their own, often deposited with decorated ritual axes (Hansen 2005). The decoration was likewise charged with symbolic and cosmological meaning (Jockenhövel 2005). A related decoration is found on horse bits and antler cheek pieces for horses, which define an even larger elite horizon stretching from the Urals to the Carpathians. Rich hoards of elaborate female ornaments testify to the important role of women in ritual functions, as in Scandinavia. The warrior sword was the rapier and early forms of flange-hilted swords. Also, in Hungary and in the wider region of the Carpathians, we find a linkage between a ruling warrior elite and a specific decoration loaded with ritual and cosmological significance, and during the Middle Bronze Age they probably defined an overriding ethnic elite identity in the Carpathians.

At Százhalombatta, chiefly and community identities combined ambiguously and also included a local and regional mix. No obvious differences existed in household sizes, and a community ethos expressed shared involvement in production and consumption. Most evident in large urnfield cemeteries, all burials were of a single kind,

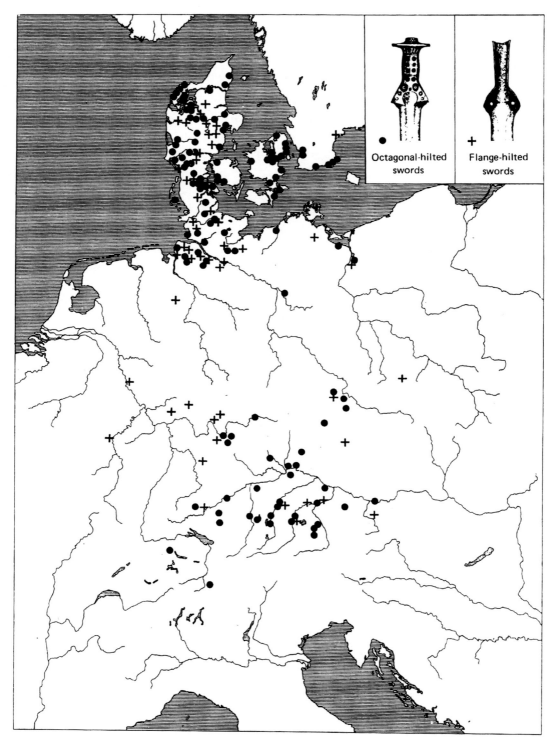

Figure 8.6a. Distribution of foreign swords connecting south Germany and Denmark.

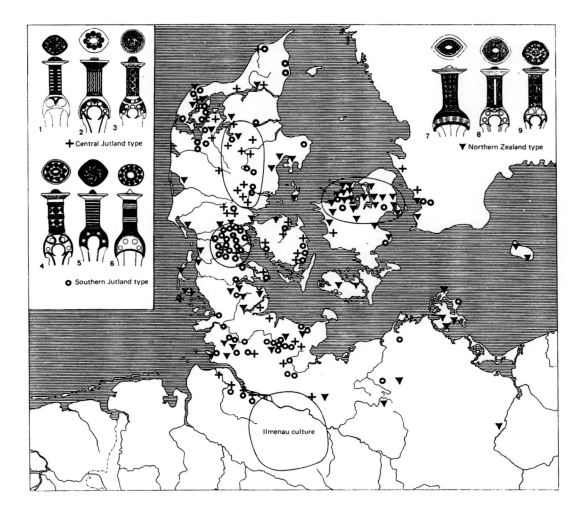

Figure 8.6b. Distribution of Nordic full-hilted swords (after Kristiansen 1987: Figure 4.6 and 4.8).

although distinctions in metal wealth were evident (Sørensen and Rebay-Salisbury 2009). Metalwork and elaborate hoards suggest a leadership class of warriors and wealthy women that dominated the sameness in cultural practice. The special female role probably involved ritual significance, as suggested from clay figurines. Along a similar vein, most pottery, although finely crafted, was of local manufacture and broadly distributed across households. A small number of encrusted-ware pots, however, documented trade or relations with the west. Although no detailed analysis has been undertaken of pottery assemblage differences among households, at the well-excavated tell site of Feudvar at the junction of the river Tizsa and the Danube, differences in pottery among households suggest patterned contact with other regional groups (Hänsel 2003). The formation of the tell community perhaps drew people in from a wide region, bringing with them different pottery traditions and cultural associations.

The Vatya culture comprises a line of tell settlements along the Danube with their local hinterlands. The local interaction among them created similarities in pottery forms that define the ethnic culture, despite the fact that metal forms were shared more widely in the Carpathian and beyond. There was less frequent local interaction towards the west, where we find a distinctive pottery tradition of incrusted ware. Thus, pottery, used in everyday life and ritual, served as an arena for the playing out of local cultural affinities that most likely represented a certain form of more specific local ethnic identity shared by the tell societies along the Danube and its hinterlands.

In Sicily, the Bronze Age societies shared a tradition of roundhouses, often forming small hamlets (McConnell 1992). It is difficult to delineate ethnic identities except in general terms. We have to move down into the urbanised world of the Iron Age to find an indigenous Elymian identity. Ethnic boundaries were apparently created to form a distinctive identity in opposition to the Greek and Phoenician colonists with whom Elymians traded. Local groups often interacted peacefully, but, according to literary sources, hostilities sometimes broke out. The urbanised lifestyle and the use of Corinthian pottery for elite consumption in the symposium suggest that the wealthy families of local groups adopted foreign Greek culture. They were leading a process of cultural hybridization (Mühlenbock 2008:chapter 7) that was both more intense and had far deeper consequences than during the Bronze Age, when Mycenaean presence was more sporadic and selective (Vianello 2005, 2008). However, the Elymians retained their cosmological links with the past, expressed in the capaduncola pots for ritual use and the hearths in the houses. (Figure 8.7).

From this comparative survey we show that, in the Bronze Age, symbolic fields corresponded to institutions with different roles and geographical distributions. It illustrates how societies were highly complex, with a capacity to maintain parallel, coexisting forms of identity, some linked to a larger 'foreign' political world and some linked to a more ethnic and ritual world of 'national' identity. In this, the Bronze Age is not vastly different from what we know from slightly later periods, such as Archaic Greece, which exhibited similarly hybrid identities and ethnicities, described in written sources

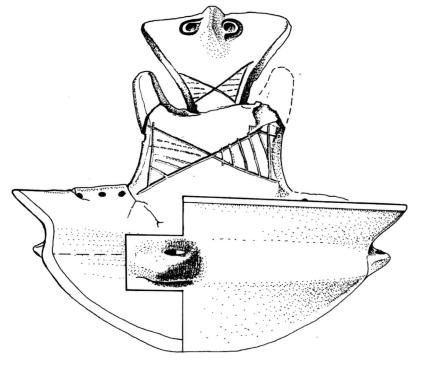

Figure 8.7.
Capaduncola pot from the merchant's house.

(Finkelberg 2005; Hall 1997, 2002; Renfrew 1998). Although the jury is still out as to the existence of larger, shared ethnic identities in the past, our projects suggest that, by the Bronze Age, new forms of more bounded ethnic commonalities had emerged. They were based upon shared cosmology and shared institutions, which would, in all probability, also imply some measure of a shared language. Thus, prehistoric material culture holds the potential to unfold social institutions and political and ethnic identities, if unlocked with proper historical and anthropological insights and interpretative strategies.

BRONZE AGE POLITICAL ECONOMIES

The political economy is basic to all chiefdom-like political formations; the flow of goods through a central chiefly node supports the chief and the elaboration of his political ambitions. The political economy appears usually to have been based on the control over specific economic bottlenecks (Earle 1997), most commonly involving surplus mobilisation of food used to support labour (staple finance) and prestige goods (wealth finance) such as swords used to develop relationships of power (D'Altroy and Earle 1985). In staple finance, control is exercised through ownership over the productive landscapes, divided up and marked. Describing the Bronze Age landscapes of the Netherlands, Arnoldussen and Fontijn talk of a 'humanly ordered landscape:' 'from c. 1500 cal BC onwards the landscape was organized and structured by specific ideological concepts of regularity and categorization' (2005:289). The construction of such an ordered landscape throughout much of Europe, starting, in fact, in the Neolithic, involved the assertion of property rights through which emergent chiefs could claim rights to surpluses.

In wealth finance, control over bottlenecks in the production and trade of special goods could alternatively be used to direct the distribution of symbolic items as a means to build networks of power. As trade in wealth developed along the rivers and open waters of Europe, local chieftains with their warriors and ships could dominate the accumulation of metal wealth. The manufacture and bestowal of metal weapons and display objects by chiefs then established networks of support and alliance.

Through the Bronze Age and into the Iron Age, the construction of farmsteads and settlements, barrows and cemeteries, and increasingly defined agrarian landscapes created the humanly ordered landscape that surely involved overlapping and contested property rights used by emergent chiefs to mobilise agricultural surpluses and community labour. It defines the economic foundation of emerging social divisions, which had to be based on some form of control over productive resources (staple finance).

The alternative ability to create a wealth-financed political economy depended on control over the movement of special goods. Exchange in wealth goes back to the Neolithic, involving, for example, exchange in axes and other special goods, but stone for axes or daggers and other natural objects could not be controlled easily. They tended to have many sources and to move along land-based networks of down-the-line exchange. With the increasing use of metal, things changed. First, the metal had fewer sources, and those sources were at greater distances. Second, the early movement, most probably largely by land, became increasingly replaced by movement over water. Water transportation had major routes along the larger rivers and seacoasts that made metal more easily controlled by would-be chiefs. As metal moved great distances and was transformed with complicated pyrotechnical techniques, the use of metal wealth in weaponry, gift exchange, and prestige display created various conditions in which control by expansive leaders became feasible. The creation of a warrior elite, armed with new bronze weapons, could then have asserted a more exclusive control over the land, and the gifting of weapons and objects of bodily display created opportunities to build elaborate networks of dependency and alliance. These new conditions allowed for active involvement in long-distance trade, highly gifted craft production, the accumulation of wealth, and the creation of what Renfrew called individualising chiefdoms. Generally, the systems of staple and wealth finance were joined, creating a highly dynamic and creative political strategy for chieftains. Renfrew's ideal chiefdoms types (group-oriented and individualising) are what Blanton et al (1996) refer to as corporate (based on land ownership) and networked (based on wealth exchanges) political strategies. Any individual chiefdom can be fashioned by resourcefully developing an ever-changing mixture of strategies based on changing conditions. Changing conditions and changing chiefly strategies thus created much of the variation that we observe across Europe.

By the end of the Neolithic, we imagine the formation of a world of chiefdoms through Europe, based on rights in productive land for farming, but especially for herding of animals broadly exchanged by chiefs and other would-be leaders. In Thy, the barrow landscape was one of those 'humanly ordered landscapes,' in which ownership of pasture lands probably rested in the hands of chiefs (Earle 1991); cattle dominated the animal assemblage (Chapter 6), and the chiefly halls had stalls for the moveable wealth cattle represented (Chapter 5). In the Benta, the economy was apparently heavily focused on animal raising as well, and the tell settlements received cattle, presumably as tribute, from surrounding communities. The cattle and sheep became managed for milk and wool, both as exchange commodities (Chapter 6). In Salemi, the Late Bronze Age environment was also largely open, and we presume that animal herding dominated the economy here as well (Chapter 6). The fortified settlements suggest territorial control over the surrounding region, with the animals and their products, and perhaps slaves, being exchanged externally with Mycenaean traders (Chapter 3). In these circumstances, the more productive the land, the more animals could be raised, and the more complex the chiefly hierarchy could become.

The chiefdom matrix was composed locally of polities significantly different in organisational character across the north–south spectrum described in Chapter 3. Although the local chiefdoms increased in number of people organised, the spatial extent of their organisation actually declined: Scandinavia numbered perhaps 1000 people in 80 square kilometres; Hungary, 2000 in 50 square kilometres; and Sicily, 4000 in 36 square kilometres. Why? Chiefdoms appear to have characterised late prehistory in Europe because of their extraordinary adaptability. They must mobilise surplus to finance central power, and, across Europe in late prehistory, diverse economic bottlenecks were created as permutations of property rights, trade, and warrior might changed. Which was most important? The important conclusion is that for chiefdoms generally, no one factor was ultimately most important, but all represented a changing set of options that any would-be chieftains could creatively fashion for power (Earle 1997). On a regional basis, individual chiefs constantly rose and fell from power as specific regional configurations changed. Chiefdoms in Thy, the Benta, or Salemi rose and fell based on the opportunities for control and probably on the creativity of individual chiefs.

Politics and warfare go together (Otto, Thrane, and Vandkilde 2006) – leaders justify their positions through defence of the groups and the building of defences defines social groups as corporate units (recent summaries of Bronze Age warfare in Harding 2007; Jockenhövel 2004/2005). The character of settlements across Europe probably was largely an outcome of the emergent political systems that organised the households into broader social institutions. The concentration of population documents real threats of conflict, but it also materialises quite dramatic changes in social and political organisation, involving varying degrees of political centrality.

Figure 8.8.
Model of a decentralised Bronze Age chiefdom of northern Europe, at times also expanding into central Europe.

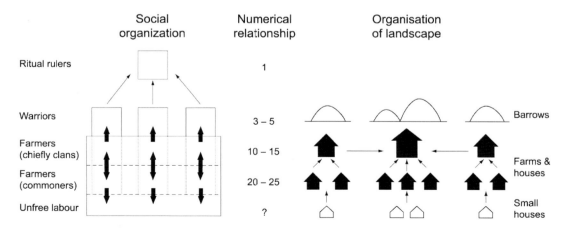

We shift now to an explanation of social evolution as recognized in our case studies. Probably all of the cases we studied could be considered chiefdoms, but this simple classification seems inadequate to explain the varying character and dynamics of the political developments. As materialists, we turn to a general model of the political economy that may help in our attempts to unravel the divergent trajectories of change.

Two different traditions of organisation were the central and northwest European tradition of decentralised chiefdoms and the southeast European tradition of more centralised chiefdoms. These traditions represent alternative, structurally recurring principles of late European prehistory and, at times, one or the other principle would become dominant (Kristiansen 1998:figures 224 and 225). However, once a more centralised social organisation based upon the agglomeration of people in larger fortified settlements dominated, it sowed the seeds for its later demise. There existed a number of constraints, in part ecological, as discussed subsequently, and in part social and ideological, and these constraints hindered state formation. We have localised the power of these constraints in semi-autonomous households, which represented a deeply rooted European tradition. The widespread dispersal of productive resources and the households involved in their exploitation tended to constraint centralised political control, however. In Figures 8.8 and 8.9, we summarise the two organisational principles in later European prehistory, which also involved different ideological perceptions of

Figure 8.9.
Model of a centralised Bronze Age chiefdom of southeast-central Europe, at times also expanding into west-central Europe.

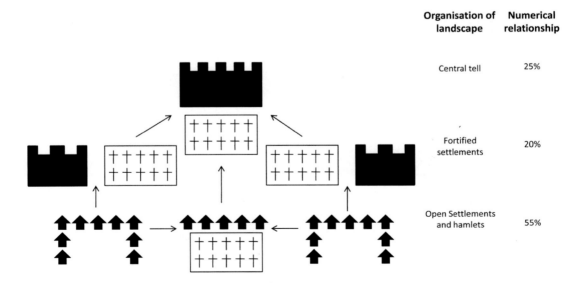

the individual versus the community, as reflected in burial rituals. The ritual ethos of an egalitarian community, as it manifests itself in the large urnfield cemeteries of centralised settlements, as documented in Hungary, is contrasted by the more aristocratic tumulus or barrow rituals of individual farms and hamlets, defining the free farmer of chiefly lineage.

Yet, we have to think of these burial rituals as being the reserve for a certain segment of society, the free farmers/herders of the tumulus tradition versus the free peasants, probably with shared ownership of land and animals, of the large urnfield and inhumation cemeteries. Although the urnfield cemetery promotes a more egalitarian ethos, this could also reflect the beginning of a class-divided society in which producers (peasants and craftspeople) had their own burial rituals, whereas the elite had a more exclusive burial ritual, as found during the Late Bronze Age and Early Iron Age. The warrior elites of the tell tradition mainly deposited their weapons in hoards, although few warrior burials exist. We therefore assume a leadership above the level of ordinary household producers.

Similar organisational principles were at work in the way chiefdoms were organised in western Europe, along the Atlantic façade from Iberia to England and Ireland (Henderson 2007). Also, throughout Eurasia, from the Pontic steppe to east of the Urals, the same principles of decentralised versus centralised chiefdoms competed for dominance, although decentralised chiefdoms dominated (Kohl 2007; Koryakova and Epimakhov 2007). Chiefly power strategies were highly adaptable and therefore persistent. With many and diverse bottlenecks, small and ever-changing political economies emerged across Europe through the Bronze and Iron Ages. The sizes of these individual polities were characteristically in the low thousands, but their area extent and density of control were highly variable. It was impossible for the decentralised character of staple production and the web-like character of wealth exchanges to dominate beyond a fairly restricted region, so state-like powers were the exception in Europe. They were probably the goal of many local chieftains, but the resistance to expansion and expropriation exhibited by independent households and communities made such expansion always problematic. Individual chiefdoms cycled up and down with changing circumstances, but the overall system of highly dispersed and small chiefdoms was remarkably stable. From time to time, outstanding burials suggest that a successful local chief rose to power over a larger region, but such successes were probably short-lived and institutionally unstable. Exceptional were the trading empires that emerged across the Mediterranean during the end of the second millennium and again in the first millennium BC, which, in turn, created zones of chiefdoms arching around their edges and deep into the European peripheries. However, ecological constraints forced societies to rethink and eventually reorganise their political economies. In conclusion, we look more closely into the concrete processes that operated to expand and constrain power, and their long-term outcome.

LONG-TERM TRENDS: BRONZE AGE POWER STRUCTURES AND EMERGING SOCIAL DIVISIONS

We set out to analyse how power could have been transmitted from independent producers to ruling chiefs, until the bond was broken between farmer and farm, and the farmer became a peasant labouring for the chief or king, as we assume happened with the formation of large villages and proto-urban settlements in Sicily and perhaps Hungary.

In his famous work, *Outline of a Theory of Practice*, Pierre Bourdieu describes the processes operating in establishing symbolic power (Bourdieu 1977:chapter 4). He is concerned with the conversion of symbolic capital back into economic capital.

Symbolic capital, which in the form of prestige and renown attached to a family and a name is readily convertible back into economic capital, is perhaps the most valuable form of accumulation in a society in which the severity of the climate (the major work – ploughing and harvesting – having to be done in a very short space of time) and the limited technical resources (harvesting is done with the sickle) demand collective labour.

(Bourdieu 1977:179)

This system contains only two ways [by which a local chief can mobilise labour] (and they prove in the end to be just one way) of getting and keeping lasting hold over someone: gifts or debts, the overtly economic obligations of debt, or the 'moral,' 'affective' obligations created and maintained by exchange.

(Bourdieu 1977:191)

The endless reconversion of economic capital into symbolic capital, at the cost of a wastage of social energy, which is the condition for the permanence of domination, cannot succeed without the complicity of the whole group.... As Mauss put it, the whole society pays itself in the false coin of its dream.

(Bourdieu 1977:195)

To these forms of legitimate accumulation, through which the dominant groups or classes secure a capital of 'credit' which seems to owe nothing to the logic of exploitation, must be added another form of accumulation of symbolic capital, the collection of luxury goods attesting to the taste and distinction of their owner.

(Bourdieu 1977:197)

Bourdieu's description of the mechanisms of power in a peasant society corresponds well to what we know of Bronze Age society, and in Figure 8.10 we summarise his argument as a dynamic model that, over time, may transform gift obligations into tribute and slavery.

An active network of wealth exchange interconnected the European mosaic of regional polities based on differing agrarian systems. An original patchwork based on local productivities thus would have been reformulated continually as the routes and technologies of transport changed opportunities for trade and wealth accumulations. The Bronze Age imbedded a matrix of local chiefdoms within international systems that could result in rapid and radical transformations of peoples and populations in cycles of political centralisation and dissolution across the face of Europe. This variety of cyclical changes, however, produced long-term effects.

First, we need to recognize the long-term impact of human exploitation of the environment and its social consequences (Chapter 2). Most European Bronze Age societies had established economies dominated by herding in open landscapes, intersected with fields (Falkenstein 2009). These landscapes were not absolutely stable, however; without a system of crop rotation, grazing exhausts the soil, just as it halts secondary forest regeneration. With the introduction of new patterns of consumption, the Bronze Age economies became highly dynamic and, in many regions, tended to operate close to carrying capacities in terms of animals and people. Increasing populations, therefore, threatened the economy that could only partially compensate through increased productivity. Instead, increased exploitation gradually transformed free famers into dependent peasants, while population in the large tells of central Europe continued to expand. This had visible effects on the exploitation of both humans and landscapes. Ideology often had to be sustained by brute force, showing that, when necessary, the warrior regimes of Bronze Age Europe served to keep dependent groups in check.

Both in Scandinavia and in Hungary, increased exploitation of the environment led to visible changes in the economy towards agrarian intensification of crops from the Late Bronze Age onwards (Chapter 6). Thus, the termination of the classic tell settlements and the decline of the large farmhouses in Scandinavia occur more or less simultaneously, after 1300 BC, whereas the tell settlements in their classic form apparently terminated during the fifteenth century and were replaced by a new agrarian economy from the thirteenth century onwards. In Sicily, we see changes in settlements with the advent of the Iron Age. Whereas the Scandinavian settlement system and basic economy remained intact, in Hungary, as in most of central Europe, new economic regimes were introduced based upon more intensive cropping and manuring, leading to the formation of brown soils, but also leading to soil erosion on valley slopes (Chapter 2). Thus, agrarian intensification on a grand scale replaced the centuries-old tell economies with their reliance on large herds, and whether that happened peacefully or was the result of a social revolution is hard to determine on archaeological grounds alone.

The accumulation of short-term decisions of individual households created long-term consequences beyond the intended horizon of individual communities. Societies paved the way for adjustments and changes in households to maintain their traditions. In the short term, from one generation to the next, slight adjustment can be made to maintain prestige and convention. At Legård in Thy, for example, the first massive chiefly farm of period 2, from around 1400 BC, was replaced by one of exactly similar construction and size – except that timber used for wall posts and central posts was less massive. Changes testify to an increasing shortage of building timber from mature forest, which, over the next generations, led to a downsizing of the houses and the use of wattle and daub instead of timber for the walls (Bech 2003:figure 9). At the transition to the Late Bronze Age, the houses of Legård, along with all other houses in Thy, became more unified in size and construction, defining the close family as the household unit. Whereas chiefs retained more power

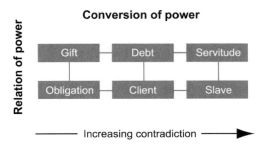

Figure 8.10. Dynamic historical model of the potential transformation of gift obligations into tribute and slavery.

in some regions, apparently based on control over maritime trading and raiding, they lost out in other regions such as Thy. A direct line existed from decisions and adjustments made on a year-to-year basis to their impact upon long-term changes in the size and integration of households. Compromises had to be made as populations faced ecological overexploitation, yet the overall social and economic framework remained intact, as far as we can judge. Here, a mixture of contradictory factors and forces were at work. Tradition in the form of ritual places, ancestor barrows, must have had a strong impact on decisions to stay rather than move when economic conditions worsened. Worsening conditions caused the use of smaller, poor-quality timber for house construction and bog turf for heating, and placed constraints on export production as grazing pressure increased (Bech and Mikkelsen 1999; Kristiansen 1998b).

Known to exist in Thy by the Early Bronze Age (period 3), these conditions became widespread throughout Scandinavia in the course of the Late Bronze Age. Generally speaking, the old inhabited areas of the Bronze Age remained unaltered until some fundamental thresholds were passed. Factors at work were a combination of population expansion and economic intensification that reached an initial threshold around 1300 BC in Thy, somewhat later in the rest of south Scandinavia (Thrane 2003:figure 8). Subsequently, in period 3, primary barrows were still erected in new locations, but supplies of metal from central Europe came to a temporary halt because of revolutionary social and religious changes associated with the expansion of the Urnfield culture. Over the next one or two generations throughout northern Europe, chiefly swords were kept in circulation until their metal hilts were worn through and the clay core was laid bare. Towards the end of period 3, new supplies of metal became available and worn-out swords were placed into graves on a massive scale, as tradition proscribed, but for the last time. From now on, barrow building ceased, having taken its toll of good grazing land; metal was ritually economised as urn burials took over; and ritual hoarding was practised. We should not underestimate the religious meaning of these changes, but, on the whole, the changing rituals at the beginning of the Late Bronze Age were part of a social and economic consolidation of ruling elite and conserved valued resources.

Through the Late Bronze Age, adjustments intensified the economy with the introduction of the composite, efficient ard plough and new, more resistant crops. Manuring was practised, and the more tolerant, wool-producing sheep became dominant. The reduction of farm size was part of these adjustments; more and smaller households replaced the earlier larger farmsteads. The house became increasingly the domain of a single, multigenerational family with its animals. Chiefly households seem to have become bigger and fewer, whereas the ordinary farming family household became the norm. Evidence from southwestern Fünen shows a more hierarchical political structure, and regional chiefs evidently controlled much larger territory than in the Early Bronze Age (Thrane 1994). New ritual meeting places now held groups that used several hundred cooking pits (Gustafson, Heibreen, and Martens 2005).

During the Late Bronze Age, households reduced in size; to conform to single-family households, a new ritual cycle integrated regions formally under the sway of local chiefs; and a few rich chiefs, probably controlling long-distance maritime movements of metal,

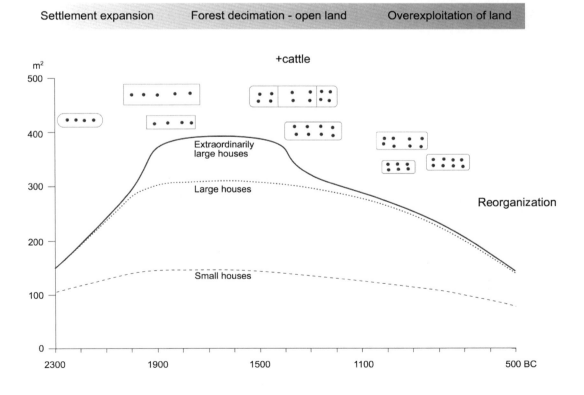

Figure 8.11. Long-term model of the rise and decline of the Bronze Age farm, compared with changes in metal supplies and ecology.

exerted broad, but likely limited, control. This paved the way for the reorganisation taking place at the beginning of the Iron Age, when, suddenly, separate farmsteads were abandoned for the first time in more than a thousand years, and everyone moved together into small villages in some regions, such as Jutland. The break of a continuous settlement pattern undoubtedly also ruptured the established cosmology engraved on the landscape of barrows, Urnfield cemeteries, and ritual sites and deliberately broke with traditions to create a new social and economic order. Was it a rebellion of numerous ordinary farmers against an outdated chiefly culture, economically undermined and lacking legitimacy? Perhaps the spreading use of iron created a new equalising access to weapons that levelled the fighting field of political and social action. Or was it the result of the chiefly elite's capacity to reinvent dominance under a banner of collective village life? We do not now know, but scarce evidence suggests a new social order of collective farmers, materialised in the much larger, collective cemeteries of the Iron Age. In other regions in Scandinavia, the break in settlement structure was less drastic, and some Bronze Age traditions continued.

Similar long-term sequences and revolutionary transformation unfolded in Hungary and the Mediterranean, but within different time frames. The social pattern in Hungary parallels that of Scandinavia (Chapter 3). On the tells, new houses were constructed right on the levelled remains and preserved social traditions of old houses. The accretion of houses over centuries served as a house genealogy in much the same way barrows and farmsteads did in northern Europe. It reinforced the continuity of the people living inside the tell's strong fortifications, which stressed corporate defence and military power. The large cemeteries with sparse grave goods underscored an ideology of equality in death, and no rich or monumental burials monumentalised distinction. Wealth placed in hoards, as illustrated at Százhalombatta, was impressive, and apparently personal in reference, although with persistent regional and temporal variation (Hansen 2005). The group stood together, but some appear to have stood out.

Late in the third millennium BC, the first fortified tells were built along the Danube and subsequently expanded greatly in size and number (Gogaltan 2005). The settlement history around Százhalombatta documents the formation of a Bronze Age chiefdom dominating the Benta valley with a hierarchy of forts, probably mirroring a warrior hierarchy. An increase in fortification through the Bronze Age may reflect an increase in the intensity of warfare, but it certainly documents a settlement pattern of political control. At the same time, however, most people lived in open-field settlements; the single largest village contained 50 percent or more of the undefended population, a measure of political significance perhaps in opposition to the fortified settlements. What remains to be explained are the rather dramatic transformations at the transition between the Middle and Late Bronze Ages, changes probably interconnected to those throughout central Europe. Long-term continuity was punctuated by rather abrupt social revolutions that need to be understood as broadly felt historical events. The overall trend, though, was one towards agrarian intensification.

In Sicily, abrupt changes of settlements and population marked the transition from the Bronze Age into the Iron Age. Small and rather scattered populations were replaced by new proto-urban settlements of a remarkably different character. More than other regions in Europe, throughout its history, Sicily seems to have been subject to changes affected by outside relations. We propose a model for the development of urban societies because of increasing articulation with coastal colonies. During the Late Bronze Age, a fairly small chiefdom apparently emerged with a dominant cluster of fortified hamlets dominating the region. The fairly low population density suggests that herding was important to the economy, both for subsistence and for trade in secondary products exchanged for metal riches. By the Early Iron Age, a single polity of substantially larger size had formed, most probably broken into multiple communities dependent on agriculture and trading. Monte Polizzo evidently served as a primate centre around which other sites served logistical roles. Most settlements were placed defensively at high elevations, well away from the valley's agricultural areas. This region evidently became the indigenous supply zone for farm produce for coastal colonies. The settlement evidence corresponds with the paleo-botanical evidence, indicating an increasingly cleared landscape during the Late Bronze Age, and soil erosion and intensification during the first millennium BC, at which time we also see the agglomeration of people in proto-urban settlements.

The observed long-term trends are comparable across our three areas of European study, but the time frames and population densities differed substantially. A general development moved from forests to open grassland regimes of animal herding in the Early and Middle Bronze Ages towards agrarian intensification and soil erosion during the Late Bronze Age in Hungary and the Iron Age in Sicily. Adjustments to these changes apparently implied some major social and political upheavals at the transition between herding and agrarian economies, which probably also occurred in south Scandinavia. In this, the character of late prehistoric societies in central and northern Europe was to include local regional polities organised against state formation. Our study elucidated local long-term conditions in the interactions among environment, settlements, and household economies, which we believe highlight processes at work in the numerous polities, settlements, and independent households. We hope that our comparative approach inspires colleagues to pursue similar microregional field projects, because only by increasing systematically studied regions can we hope to understand the unity and diversity of historical forces across Europe in late prehistory.

Appendix 1

Participating Institutions

The following universities participated as partners in the projects: University College London, Cambridge University, University of Southampton, University of Oslo, University of Gothenburg, Northern Illinois University, Northwestern University, Stanford University, the University and later the Spanish Academy in Santiago de Compostela. Other institutions: the National Heritage Boards from Denmark and Sweden, the Matrica Müzeum in Szazhalombatta, Magyar Nemzeti Müzeum, the Superintendenze in Trapani, the museum in Salemi, the Thy Archaeological Museum, the rock-art museum in Vitlycke.

Appendix 2

Doctoral Dissertations Based on the Projects

Budden, S. 2007 *Renewal and Reinvention: the role of learning strategies in the Early to Late Bronze Age of the Carpathian Basin*. PhD: University of Southampton.

Kelertas, Kristina 1997 Changing political economy of Thy, Denmark. *The paleobotanical evidence*. PhD, Department of Archaeology, University of California – Los Angeles.

Kovács, Gabrielle 2007 Geological investigations of Szazhalombatta-Foldvar Bronze Age tell settlement in Hungary. PhD, University of Cambridge.

Kreiter, Attila 2007 *Technological choices and material meanings in early and middle Bronze Age Hungary. Understanding the active role of material culture through ceramic analysis*. Oxford: BAR International Series 1604.

Kulcsarne-Berzsenyi, Brigitta n.d. Household activities within a Bronze Age tell settlement in Hungary. Different crop-processing stages and storing activities at Százhalombatta-Földvár. PhD to be submitted, University of Cambridge.

Ling, Johan 2008 *Elevated rock art. Towards a maritime understanding of Bronze Age rock art in northern Bohuslän, Sweden*. GOTARC Serie B. Gothenburg Archaeological Theses 49.

Mühlenbock, Christian 2008 *Fragments from a Mountain Society. Tradition, innovation and interaction at Archaic Monte Polizzo, Sicily*. GOTARC Serie B. Gothenburg Archaeological Theses 50.

Oma, Kerstin Armstron 2007 Human-animal relationships. Mutual becoming in Scandinavian and Sicilian households 900–500 BC. *Oslo Archaeological Series* 9.

Sabatini, Serena 2007 *House Urns. A European Late Bronze Age Trans-cultural Phenomenon*. GOTARC Serie B. Gothenburg Archaeological Theses 47.

Steinberg, John 1997 Changing patterns of economic organization in the production, distribution and use of flint in Thy, Denmark. Analysis of flints from the plowzone. PhD, University of California – Los Angeles.

Streiffert, Katarina Eikeland 2006 *Indigenous households. Transculturation of Sicily and southern Italy in the Archaic period*. GOTARC series B 44. Gothenburg Archaeological Theses.

Uhner, Claes 2010 *Makt och samhälle: politisk ekonomi under bronzåldern i Karpaterbäcknet*. GOTARC Series B. Gothenburg.

Appendix 3

Selected Publications Related to the Four Projects

MONTE POLIZZO

Aspeborg, H. and K. Lund 2004 *Outline of a Project. A Preliminary Description of the Sub Project on the infrastructure of Monte Polizzo*. Riksantikvarieämbetet UV Syd.

Brorson, T. 2007 Analyses of pottery from area A, B and C at Monte Polizzo, Sicily. Pottery from the 6th century BC. Ware analyses and chemical analyses. *Ceramic Studies, KKS Report* **14**.

Holtorf, C. 2006 Studying archaeological fieldwork in the field: Views from Monte Polizzo. In M. Edgeworth (ed.) *Ethnographies of Archaeological Practice*. Lanham: Altamira Press, pp. 81–94.

Kolb, M. J. and S. Tusa 2001 The late Bronze Age and early Iron Age landscape of interior western Sicily. *Antiquity* **75**: 503–04.

Kolb, M. J. and R. Speakerman 2005 Elymian regional interaction in Iron Age western Sicily: A preliminary neutron activation study of incised/impressed tablewares. *Journal of Archaeological Science* **32**: 795–804.

Morris, I. 2003 Mediterraneanization. *Mediterranean Historical Review* **18** (2): 30–55.

Morris, I. et al 2001 Stanford University excavations on the Acropolis of Monte Polizzo I: Preliminary report on the 2000 season. *Memoirs of the American Academy in Rome* **46**.

Morris, I. et al 2002. Stanford University excavations on the Acropolis of Monte Polizzo II: Preliminary report on the 2001 season. *Memoirs of the American Academy in Rome* **47**.

Morris, I. et al 2003. Stanford University excavations on the Acropolis of Monte Polizzo III: Preliminary report on the 2002 season. *Memoirs of the American Academy in Rome* **48**.

Morris, I. et al 2004 Stanford University excavations on the Acropolis of Monte Polizzo, Sicily, IV: Preliminary report on the 2003 season. *Memoirs of the American Academy in Rome* **49**.

Morris, I. and S. Tusa 2004 Scavi sull'acropoli di Monte Polizzo, 2000–2003. *Sicilia-Archeologica* **37**: 35–84.

Mühlenbock, C. and C. Prescott (eds.) 2004a *The Scandinavian Sicilian Archaeological Project Archaeological Excavations at Monte Polizzo Sicily. Reports 1998–2001*. GOTARC Serie C nr. 56. Göteborg: University of Gothenburg.

Mühlenbock, C. 2004. (ed.) *The Scandinavian Sicilian Archaeological Project. Excavations at Monte Polizzo Sicily. Reports 2002–2003*. GOTARC Serie C nr 57. Göteborg: University of Gothenburg.

Mühlenbock, C. 2008 *Fragments from a Mountain Society: Tradition, Innovation and Interaction at Archaic Monte Polizzo, Sicily*. Gotarc Series B, 50. Gothenburg Archaeological Thesis. Göteborg: University of Gothenburg.

Mühlenbock, C., N.O. Sunden, and K. Kristiansen (eds.) in press *Scandinavian-Sicilian Archaeological Project. Excavations 2004–2008*. University of Rothenberg.

Prescott, C and C. Mühlenbock 2003 Mt. Polizzo, Sicily: Preliminary views on Elymians and ethnicity, landscape and identity. The Nordic TAG Conference, *Scandinavian Archaeological Practice – in Theory: Proceedings from the 6th Nordic TAG, Oslo 2001*. Oslo: Institutt for arkeologi, kunsthistorie og konservering, Universitetet i Oslo, pp. 26–37.

Stika, H.-P., A. G. Heiss, and B. Zach 2008 Plant remains from early Iron Age in western Sicily – differences in subsistence strategies of Greek and Elymian sites. *Vegetation History and Archaeobotany*.

Tusa, S. 2005 Fenici, Indigeni ed Elimi alla luce delle nuove scoperte, *Atti del V Congresso Internazionale di Studi Fenici e Punici*, Palermo, pp. 533–49.

Tusa, V. 1972 Monte Polizzo-Scavi 1970. *Sicilia Archeologica* **5**: 119–21.

SZÁZHALOMBATTA

Budden, S. and J. Sofaer 2009 Non-discursive knowledge and the construction of identity. Potters, potting and performance at the Bronze Age Tell of Százhalombatta, Hungary. *Cambridge Archaeological Journal*.

Poroszlai, I. and M. Vicze (eds.) 1998 *Százhalombatta Archaeological Expedition (SAX). Emergence of European Communities Archaeological Research Report 1*. Százhalombatta: Matrica Museum.

Poroszlai, I. and M. Vicze (eds.) 2005 *Százhalombatta Archaeological Expedition (SAX). Emergence of European Archaeological Communities Research Report 2*. Százhalombatta: Matrica Museum.

Sofaer, J. R. 2006 Pots, houses and metal: Technological relations at the Bronze Age tell at Százhalombatta, Hungary. *Oxford Journal of Archaeology* **25** (2): 127–47.

TANUM

Aulin, A. and A. Gustavsson 1997–1998 *Tanumprojektet. Arkeologiska undersökningar vid lilla Oppen år 1999*. GOTARC Serie D. Arkeologiska rapporter No. 46. Göteborg: University of Gothenburg.

Aulin, A. and A. Gustavsson 2002 *Tanumprojektet. Arkeologiska undersökningar vid lilla Oppen år 1999*. En teknisk rapport GOTARC Serie D. Arkeologiska rapporter No. 47. Göteborg: University of Gothenburg.

Aulin, A. and A. Gustavsson 2002 *Tanumprojektet. Arkeologiska undersökningar vid lilla Oppen år 2000*. GOTARC Serie D. Arkeologiska rapporter No. 48. Göteborg: University of Gothenburg.

Bengtsson, L. Att gräva ut bilder. In J. Goldhahn (ed.) bilder av bronsålder. *Acta Archaeologica Lundensia*. Series in **8**: (37).

Bengtsson, L. 2004 *Bilder vid vatten. Kring hällristningar I Askum sn, Bohuslän*. GOTARC Serie C. Arkeologiska Skrifter No 51. Göteborg: University of Gothenburg.

Bengtsson, L. 2010 To excavate images. Some results from the Tanum rock art project 1997–2004. In Å. Fredell, F. Criado, and K. Kristiansen (eds.) *Representations and Communications in Bronze Age Rock Art*. Oxford: Oxbow Monographs.

Bengtsson, L., A. Gustafsson, and L. Strid (eds.) *Tanum projecktet*. Arkeologiska Undersökningar 1998–2004. GOTARC Serie D, no. 57. Göteborg.

Bengtsson, L, and J. Ling 2008 Scandinavia's most finds associated rock art sites. *Adoranten* 2007: 40–50.

Bengtsson, L, and J. Ling 2008 Utgrävningar vid hällristningar i Tossene. *Fynd* **08**: 21–27.

Fredell, Å., F. B. Criado, and K. Kristiansen (eds.) 2010 *Representations and Communications in Bronze Age Rock Art*. Oxford: Oxbow Monographs.

Ling, J. 2004 Beyond transgressive lands and forgotten seas. Towards a maritime understanding of rock art in Bohuslän. *Current Swedish Archaeology* **12**: 121–40.

Ling, J. 2008. *Elevated rock art – Towards a Maritime Understanding of Bronze Age Rock Art in Northern Bohuslän, Sweden*. GOTARC Serie B. Gothenburg Archaeological Thesis 49. Göteborg: University of Gothenburg.

Ling, J. and U. Ragnesten (eds.) *Tanum projecktet*. Arkeologiska Undersökningar vid Hällristningar 2005–2008. GOTARC Serie D, no. 72. Göteborg.

THY

Andersen, S. T. 1990 Pollen spectra from the Bronze Age barrow at Egshvile, Thy, Denmark. *Journal of Danish Archaeology* **9**: 153–56.

Andersen, S. Th. 1995 History of vegetation and agriculture at Hassing Huse Mose, Thy, Northwest Denmark, since the Ice Age. *Journal of Danish Archaeology* **11** (1992–93): 57–79.

Bech, J.-H. 1997 Bronze Age Settlements on raised sea-beds at Bjerre, Thy, NW-Jutland. In J. J. Assendorp (ed.) *Forschungen zur bronzezeitlichen Besiedlung Mittel – und Nordeuropas*. Internationales Symposium vom 9–11 Mai 1996 in Hitzacker. Internationale Archäeologie 38, Espelkamp, 3–15.

Bech, J.-H. 2003 The Thy Archaeological Project – Results and reflections from a multinational archaeological project. In H. Thrane (ed.) *Diachronic Settlement Studies in the Metal Ages. Report on the ESF Workshop Moesgård, Denmark, 14–18 October 2000*. Højbjerg: Jutland Archaeological Society, pp. 45–60.

Bech, J.-H. and M. Mikkelsen 1999 Landscapes, settlement and subsistence in Bronze Age Thy, NW Denmark. In C. Fabech and J. Ringtved (eds.)

Settlement and Landscape. Proceedings of a Conference in Århus, Denmark May 4–7 1998. Århus: 69–77. Jutland Archaeological Society.

Earle, T. 1997 *How Chiefs Come to Power. The Political Economy in Prehistory.* Palo Alto, CA: Stanford University Press.

Earle, T. 2002 *Bronze Age Economics. The Beginnings of Political Economies.* Boulder, CO: Westview Press.

Earle, T., et al 1998 The political economy of late Neolithic and early Bronze Age society: The Thy Archaeological Project. *Norwegian Archaeological Review* **31** (1): 1–28.

Eriksen, B. V. 2007 Travelling craftsmen in early Bronze Age Denmark. Addressing the evidence of leftover lithics. In B. Hårdh, K. Jennbert, and D. Olausson (eds.) On the Road. Studies in Honour of Lars Larsson. *Acta Archaeologica Lundensia* **4** (26): 253–58.

Kristiansen, K. 1998 The construction of a Bronze Age landscape. Cosmology, economy and social organisation in Thy, Northwestern Jutland. In B. Hänsel (ed.) *Man and Environment in European Bronze Age*, Kiel: pp. 281–92.

Martinéz, M. P. P. 2008 Bell Beaker communities in Thy: The first Bronze Age society in Denmark. *Norwegian Archaeological Review* **41**(2): 71–100.

Steinberg, J. M. 1996 : Ploughzone sampling in Denmark: Isolating and interpreting site signatures from disturbed contexts. *Antiquity* **70** (268): 368–92.

Thorpe, I. J. N. 2001 Bare but bountiful: The later Neolithic social and physical landscape of Thy, Jutland. In A. Ritchie (ed.) *Neolithic Orkney in Its European Context.* Cambridge: University of Cambridge, pp. 72–78.

Bibliography

Adamsen, C. and M. Rasmussen 1993 Settlement. In S. Hvass and B. Storgaard (eds.) *Digging into the Past. 25 Years of Archaeology in Denmark*. Copenhagen: Højbjerg, pp. 136–41.

Agozzino, P. 2004 Preliminary report on gas chromatography analysis of residues in storage vessels. Appendix 1 (244–46). In I. Morris, et al, Stanford University Excavations on the Acropolis of Monte Polizzo, Sicily, IV: Preliminary Report on the 2003 Season. *Memoirs American Academy Rome* **49**: 197–279.

Alcock, S. and J. Cherry 2004 *Side-by-side Survey: Comparative Regional Studies in the Mediterranean World*. Oxford: Oxbow Books.

Algotsson, Å. and S. Swedberg 1997 *Bronsålderns bosättningsmönster, Värdsarvsprojektet*. Udevalla, Bohuslän Museum.

Allison, P. M. (ed.) 1999 *Archaeology of Household Activities*. London: Routledge.

Andersen, S. T. 1989 Natural and cultural landscapes since the Ice Age shown by pollen analyses from small hollows in a forested area in Denmark. *Journal of Danish Archaeology* **8**: 188–99.

Andersen, S. T. 1990 Pollen spectra from the Bronze Age barrow at Egshvile, Thy, Denmark. *Journal of Danish Archaeology* **9**: 153–56.

Andersen, S. T. 1992 Early and Middle-Neolithic agriculture in Denmark: Pollen spectra from soils in burial mounds of the Funnel Beaker Culture. *Journal of European Archaeology* **1**: 153–80.

Andersen, S. T. 1992–93 History of vegetation and agriculture at Hassing Huse Mose, Thy, northwest Denmark, since the Ice Age. *Journal of Danish Archaeology* **11**: 57–79.

Andersen, S. T. 1994–95 Pollen analytical investigations of barrows from the Funnel Beaker and Single Grave Cultures in the Vroue area, west Jutland, Denmark. *Journal of Danish Archaeology* **12**: 107–32.

Andersen, S. T. 1995a History of vegetation and agriculture at Hassing Huse Mose, Thy, northwest Denmark, since the Ice Age. *Journal of Danish Archaeology* **11**(1992–93): 57–79.

Andersen, S. T. 1995b Pollenanalyser fra Ove Sø, Thy. In S. Th Andersen and P. Rasmussen. *Geobotaniske undersøgelser af kulturlandskabets historie*.

Pollenanalyser fra gravhøje og søer 1994. Copenhagen: Danmarks Geologiske Undersøgelser.

Andersen, S. T. 1996–97 Pollen analyses from Early Bronze Age barrows in Thy. *Journal of Danish Archaeology* **13**: 7–17.

Andersen, S. T. and P. Rasmussen 1996 Geobotaniske underogelser af kulturlandskabets historie. *Danmarks og Gronlands Geologiske Undersoglse, Rapport* 1996/8.

Anderson, P. C. 2006 Premiers tribulums, premières tractions animales au Proche-Orient vers 8000–7500 BP? In P. Pétrequin et al (eds.) *Premiers chariots, premiers araires. La diffusion de la traction animale en Europa pendant les IVe et IIIe ère*. Paris: Centre National de la Recherche Scientifique, Centre d'études Préhistoire, Antiquité, Moyen Âge, CRA 29 Monographies, pp. 299–317.

Antonaccio, C. 2004 Siculo-Geometric and the Sikels: Ceramics and identity in eastern Sicily. In K. Lomas (ed.) *Greek Identity in the Western Mediterranean. Papers in honour of Brian Shefton*. BRILL, pp. 55–81.

Antoni, J. and T. Horváth. 2003 *Bronzkori Kézműves-technikak. Kő-és csonteszközök* (Bronze Age handicraft techniques. Stone and bone tools). Kisérleti oktató CD és munkafüzet. Százhalombatta: Matrica Museum.

Apel, J. 2000 Flint daggers and technological knowledge. Production and consumption during LN I. In D. Olausson and H. Vandkilde (eds.) *Form, Function & Context. Material culture studies in Scandinavian archaeology*. Acta Archaeologica Lundensia. Series in 8°, No. 31. Lund: Institute of Archaeology, pp. 135–54.

Apel, J. 2001 *Daggers, Knowledge & Power. The Social Aspects of Flint-Dagger Technology in Scandinavia 2350–1500 cal BC. Coast to coast book 3*. Uppsala: Uppsala University.

Aperlo, P. and H. Juel Jensen in press. Household production based on microwear analysis of the flint tools. In J-H. Bech, B. V. Eriksen, and K. Kristiansen (eds.) *Bronze Age Settlement Structure and Land Use in Thy Northwest Denmark – primarily based on settlements from Bjerre Enge, Northern Thy*. Højbjerg: Jutland Archaeological Society.

Appadurai, A. 1986 Introduction: Commodities and the politics of value. In A. Appadurai (ed.) *The Social Life of Things: Commodities in Cultural Perspective*. Cambridge: Cambridge University Press.

Arnoldussen, S. and H. Fokkens (eds.) 2008 *Bronze Age Settlements in the Low Countries*. Oxford: Oxbow Books.

Arnoldussen, S. and D. Fontijn 2006 Towards familiar landscapes? On the nature and orgin of Middle Bronze Age landscapes in the Netherlands. *Proceedings of the Prehistoric Society* **72**: 289–317.

Artursson, M. 2000 Stångby stationssamhälle. Boplats- och bebyggelselämningar från sennolitikum till yngre järnålder. Skåne, Vallkärra sn, väg 930. Arkeologisk förundersökning och undersökning. *Riksantikvarieämbetet UV Syd Rapport*.

Artursson, M. 2005a Byggnadstradition. In P. Lagerås and B. Strömberg (eds.) *Bronsåldersbygd 2300–500 f. Kr. Skånska spår – arkeologi längs Västkustbanan*. Stockholm: Riksantikvarieämbetet, pp. 20–83.

Artursson, M. 2005b Gårds – och bebyggelsestruktur. In P. Lagerås and B. Strömberg (eds.) *Bronsåldersbygd 2300–500 f. Kr. Skånska spår – arkeologi längs Västkustbanan*. Stockholm: Riksantikvarieämbetet, pp. 84–159.

Artursson, M. 2009 *Bebyggelse och samhällsstruktur. Södra och mellersta Skandinavien under senneolitikum och bronsålder 2300–500 f. Kr.* Riksantikvarieämbetet. Arkeologiska undersökningar. Skrifter No 73 and GOTARC Serie B. Gothenburg Archaeological Thesis No 52. Stockholm and Gothenburg.

Artursson, M. and T. Björk 2007 Vætland – ett vattenrike. Tankar kring en bronsåldersbygd 2300–500 f. Kr. In M. Artursson (ed.) *Vägar till Vætland. En bronsåldersbygd i nordöstra Skåne 2300–500 f. Kr.* Riksantikvarieämbetet. Regionmuseet i Kristianstad & Landsantikvarien i Skåne. Stockholm, pp. 295–359.

Artursson, M., P. Karsten, and B. Strömberg 2005 Aspekter på samhällsutveckling. In P. Lagerås and B. Strömberg (eds.) *Bronsåldersbygd 2300–500 f. Kr. Skånska spår – arkeologi längs Västkustbanan*. Stockholm: Riksantikvarieämbetet, pp. 496–547.

Ashmore, W. 2002 Decisions and dispositions: Socializing spatial archaeology. *American Anthropologist* **104**: 1172–83.

Ayala, G. and C. French 2003 Holocene landscape dynamics in a Sicilian upland river valley. In M. G. Macklin, D. G. Passmore, and A. J. Howard (eds.): *Alluvial Archaeology in Europe*. Rotterdam: Balkema, pp. 229–35.

Ayala, G. and C. French 2005 Erosion modelling of past land-use practices in the Fiume di Sotto di Triona River valley, north-central Sicily. *Geoarchaeology* **20**: 149–68.

Bakker et al 1977 *Hoogkarspel-Watertoren: Towards a reconstruction of ecology and archaeology of an agrarian settlement of 1000 BC*. In Ex horreo (Festschrift W. A. Glasbergen, Cingula 4), Amsterdam, pp. 187–225.

Banning, E. B. 2002 *Archaeological Survey*. New York: Kluwer Press.

Barber, E. J. W. 1991 *Prehistoric Textiles. The Development of Cloth in the Neolithic and Bronze Ages*. Princeton, NJ: Princeton University Press.

Barber, E. W. W. 1994 *Women's Work: The First 20,000 Years*. New York: Norton.

Bátora, J. 1994 Hunting in the Early Bronze Age in Slovakia. In *Bronze Age in Slovakia*. Pamiatky Múzea, pp. 11–13.

Bech, J.-H. 1997 Bronze Age settlements on raised sea beds at Bjerre, Thy, NW-Jutland. In J. J. Assendorp (ed.) *Forschungen zur bronzezeitlichen Besiedlung in Nord – und Mitteleuropa. Internationales Symposium vom 1.-11. Mai 1996 in Hitzacker. Internationale Archeologie* **38**. Espelkamp: Leidorf.

Bech, J.-H. 2003 The Thy Archaeological Project – Results and reflections from a multinational archaeological project. In H. Thrane (ed.) *Diachronic Settlement Studies in the Metal Ages. Report on the ESF workshop, Moesgard, Denmark, 14–18 October 2000*. Højbjerg: Jutland Archaeological Society, pp. 45–60.

Bech, J.-H., B. V. Eriksen, and K. Kristiansen (eds.) in press. *Bronze Age Settlement Structure and Land Use in Thy, Northwest Denmark – Primarily Based on Settlements from Bjerre Enge, Northern Thy*.

Bech, J.-H. and A-L Haack Olsen in press. Bronze Age houses from Thy. In J-H. Bech, B. V. Eriksen, and K. Kristiansen (eds.) *Bronze Age Settlement Structure and Land Use in Thy Northwest Denmark – Primarily Based on Settlements from Bjerre Enge, Northern Thy*. Højbjerg: Jutland Archaeological Society.

Bech, J.-H. and M. Mikkelsen 1999 Landscapes, settlement and subsistence in Bronze Age Thy, NW Denmark. In C. Fabech and J. Ringtved (eds.)

Settlement and Landscape: 69–77. Proceedings of a Conference in Århus, Denmark, May 4–7 1998. Jutland Archaeological Society.

Becker, C.-J. 1980 Bebyggelseformer i Danmarks yngre bronsålder set i forhold till ældste jernalders landsbysamfund. In H. Thrane (ed.) *Broncealderbebyggelse i Norden. beretning fra det andet nordiske symosium for broncealderforskning.* Odense 9.-11 – april 1980. Odense: Skrifter fra historisk institut, Odense University **28**, pp. 127–41.

Becker, C. J. 1982 Siedlungen der Bronzezeit und der vorrömischen Eisenzeit in Dänemark. *Offa* **39**: 53–71.

Bengtsson, L. and L. Strid 2005 *Tanum Projektet. Arkeologiska undersökningar 1998–2004*. Göteborg: Institutionen för Arkeologi, Göteborgs Universitet.

Bergerbrant, S. 2005 Female interaction during the early and middle Bronze Age Europe, with special focus on bronze tubes. In T. Hjörungdal (ed.) *Gender Locales and Local Genders in Archaeology*. BAR International Series 1425. Oxford: Archaeopress, pp. 13–23.

Berglund, B., N. Malmer, and T. Persson 1991 Landscape-ecological aspects of long-term change in the Ystad area. In B. Berglund (ed.) The cultural landscape during 6000 years in southern Sweden. *Ecological Bulletin* **41**: 405–24.

Berntsson, A. 2005 *The Isolation of Lake Rafttötångstjärnet and its Implications of the Dating of Rock Art in Tanum, Bohuslän, Sweden*. Stockholm: Institutionen för Naturgeografi och Kvartärgeologi, Stockholms Universitet.

Bertemes, F. 2000 Zur Entstehung der danubischen Frühbronzezeit in Mitteleuropa. In Memoriam Jan Rulf. *Pamatky archeologické – Supplementum* **13**: 25–37.

Bertilsson, U. 1987 The rock carvings of Northern Bohuslän. Spatial structures and social symbols. *Stockholm Studies in Archaeology* **7**.

Bevan, A. and J. Conolly 2002 GIS, archaeological survey, and landscape archaeology on the island of Kythera, Greece. *Journal of Field Archaeology* **29**: 123–38.

Bevan, A. and J. Conolly 2006 Multiscalar approaches to settlement pattern analysis. In G. Lock and B. L. Molyneaux (eds.) *Confronting Scale in Archaeology. Issues of Theory and Practice*. Springer, pp. 217–34.

Biehl, P. F: 2008 'Import', 'Imitation' or 'Communication'? Figures from the lower Danube and Mycenae. In P. F. Biehl and Y. Rassamakin (eds.) *Import and Imitation in Archaeology*. Schriften des Centrums für Archäologie und Kulturgeschichte des Schwarzmeerraumes **11**: 105–24. Beier & Beran. Langeswissbach.

Bintliff, J. (ed.) 1991 *The Annales School and Archaeology*. Leicester: Leicester University Press.

Bintliff, J., M. Kuna, and V. Natalie 2000 *The Future of Surface Artefact Survey in Europe*. Sheffield: Sheffield Academic Press.

Biró, K. 2000 Kőeszközök a bronzkorban. *(Lithics in the Bronze Age). Komárom-Esztergom Megyei Múzeumok Közleményei* **7**: 237–52.

Björhem, N. and U. Säfvestad 1989 *Fosie IV. Byggnadstradition och bosättningsmönster under senneolitikum*. Malmöfynd 5. Malmö Museer. Malmö.

Björhem, N. and U. Säfvestad 1993 *Fosie IV. Bebyggelsen under brons- och järnålder*. Malmöfynd 6. Malmö Museer. Malmö.

Blake, E. Forthcoming. The ceramic material from House 1 at Monte Polizzo, Sicily. In C. Mühlenbock, C. Prescott, and K. Kristiansen (eds.) *Monte Polizzo Excavations, The Urban House Structures. Vol. 1. Scandinavian Excavations 1998–2001*. Göteborg: Göteborg University.

Blanton, R. E. et al 1996 A dual-processual theory for the evolution of Mesoamerican civilisation. *Current Anthropology* **37**: 1–14.

Boas, N. A. 1991 Bronze Age Houses at Hemmed Church, East Jutland. *Journal of Danish Archaeology* **10**: 119–35.

Bolohan, N. 2005 The Danube, Balkans, and Northern Aegean. Trade routes, influences and buffer zones in the late Bronze Age. In R. Laffineur and E. Greco (eds.) *EMPORIA. Aegeans in the Central and Eastern Mediterranean. Aegeum* **25**: 161–75.

Bóna, I. 1975 *Die mittlere Bronzezeit Ungarns und ihre südöstlichen Beziehungen. Archaeologia Hungarica* **49**. Budapest: Akadémiai Kiadó.

Bóna, I. 1991 A Nagyrév-kultúra településeiről, *A Tapolcai Városi Múzeum Közleményei* **2**: 73–82.

Bóna, I. 1992 Bronzezeitliche Tell-Kulturen in Ungarn. In W. Meier-Arendt (ed) *Bronzezeit in Ungarn. Forschungen in Tell-Siedlungen an Donau und Thiess*. Frankfurt am Main: Museum für Vor- und Frühgeschichte, Archaeologisches Museum. p. 9.

Borna-Ahlkvist, H. 2002 *Hällristarnas hem. Gårdsbebyggelse och struktur I Pryssgården under bronsålder*. Riksantikvarieämbetet. Arkeologiska undersökningar, Skrifter No 42. Stockholm.

Bourdieu, P. 1977 *Outline of a Theory of Practice*. Cambridge: Cambridge University Press.

Bridges, E. M. 1970 *World Soils* (2nd edition) Cambridge: Cambridge University Press.

Broholm, H.-C. and M. Hald 1940 *Costumes of the Bronze Age in Denmark*. Copenhagen.

Bromberger, C. and D. Chevallier (eds.) 1999 *Carrières d'Objets. Innovation et Relances*. Collection Ethnologie de la France Cahier 13. Paris: Éditions de la Maison des Sciences de L'Homme.

1992 *Bronzezeit in Ungarn: Forschungen in Tell Siedlungen an Donau und Theiss*. Frankfurt am Main: Ausstellungskatalog.

Brorsson, T. and P. Sköld Forthcoming. Technological analyses of pottery from House 1 at Monte Polizzo, Sicily. In C. Mühlenbock, C. Prescott, and K. Kristiansen (eds.) *Monte Polizzo Excavations, The Urban House Structures. Vol. 2. Scandinavian Excavations 2002–2006*. Göteborg: Göteborg University.

Brown, J. 1995 *Traditional Metalworking in Kenya* (Oxbow Monograph 44. Cambridge Monographs in African Archaeology 38). Oxford: Oxbow Books.

Brück, J. 1999 Houses, lifecycles and deposition on Middle Bronze Age settlements in southern England *Proceedings of the Prehistoric Society* **65**: 245–77.

Brück, J. 2006 Material metaphors. The relational construction of identity in Early Bronze Age burials in Ireland and Britain. *Journal of Social Archaeology* **4**(3): 307–33.

Brumfield, E. M. and T. K. Earle 1987 Specialization, exchange and complex societies: An introduction. In E. M. Brumfield and T. K. Earle (eds.) *Specialization, Exchange and Complex Societies*. Cambridge: Cambridge University Press, pp. 1–9.

Budden, S. 2002 *Black is Beautiful. The Technology and Social Practice of producing black burnished Koszider wares at Százhalombatta, Hungary*. Unpublished MA dissertation. University of Southampton.

Budden, S. 2007 *Renewal and Reinvention: The Role of learning Strategies in the Early to Late Middle Bronze Age of the Carpathian Basin*. Unpublished PhD dissertation. University of Southampton.

Budden, S. 2008 Skill amongst the sherds: Understanding the role of skill in the Early to Late Middle Bronze Age in Hungary. In I. Berg (ed.) *Breaking the Mould: Challenging the Past through Pottery, Manchester 2006*. Oxford: BAR.

Budden, S. and J. Sofaer 2009 Non-discursive knowledge and the construction of identity. Potters, potting and performance at the Bronze Age Tell of Sazhalombatta, Hungary. *Cambridge Archaeological Journal* **19**(2): 203–20.

Bürmeister, S. and N. Müller-Schessel (eds.) 2007 *Soziale Gruppen, Kulturelle Grenzen*. Die Interpretation sozialer Identitäten in der prähistorischen Archäologie. Tübinger Archäolgsiche Taschenbücher, Band 5. Waxman Verlag.

Castro, P. V. et al (eds.) 1998 *Aguas Project: Palaeoclimatic Reconstruction and the Dynamics of Human Settlement and Land Use in the Area of the Middle Aguas (Almeria), in the South-east of the Iberian Peninsula*. Luxembourg: European Commission.

Castro, P. V. et al 1999 Agricultural production and social change in the Bronze Age of southeast Spain: The Gatas Project. *Antiquity* **73**: 846–56.

Castro, P. V. et al 2000 Archaeology and desertification in the Vera Basin (Almeria, South-east Spain). *European Journal of Archaeology* **3**(2): 147–66.

Chamberlain, A. 2006 *Demography in Archaeology. Cambridge Manuals in Archaeology*. Cambridge: Cambridge University Press.

Chapman, J. C. 1991 The early Balkan Village. In O. Gron, E. Engelstad, and I. Lindblom (eds) *Social space. Human spatial behaviour in dwellings and settlements. Proceedings of an Interdisciplinary Conference*. Odense University Press, pp. 79–99.

Chapman, J. 1999 Burning the ancestors: Deliberate housefiring in Balkan prehistory. In A. Gustafsson and H. Karlsson (eds.) *Glyfer og Arkeologiska Rum – en vanbok till Jarl Nordbladh*. Göteborg: Gothenborg University, Department of Archaeology, pp. 113–26.

Choyke, A. M. 1984 An analysis of bone, antler and tooth tools from Bronze Age Hungary. *Mitteilungen des archäologischen Instituts der ungarischen Akademie der Wissenschaften* **12/13**: 13–57.

Choyke, A. M. 1997 The bone manufacturing continuum. *Anthropozoologica* **25–26**: 65–72.

Choyke, A. 2000 Refuse and modified bone from Százhalombatta-Földvar. Some preliminary observations. In *Százhalombatta Archaeological Expedition. Report 1*. Százhalombatta: Matrica Muzeum.

Choyke, A. M. 2001 A quantitative approach to the concept of quality in prehistoric bone manufacturing. In H. Buitenhuis and W. Prummel (eds.) *Animals and Man in the Past*. (ARC-Publicatie 41). Groningen: ARC, pp. 59–66.

Choyke, A. M. and L. Bartosiewicz 2000 Bronze Age animal exploitation in the central Great Hungarian Plain. *Acta Archaeologica Academiae Scientarum Hungaricae* **51**: 43–70.

Choyke, A. and L. Bartosiewicz 2005 Skating with horses: Continuity and parallelism in prehistoric Hungary. *Revue de Paléobiologie, Genève* (décembre 2005) Special vol. **10**: 317–26.

Choyke, A. and J. Schibler 2007 Prehistoric bone tools and the archaeozoological perspective: Research in central Europe. In C. Gates St-Pierre and R. B. Walker (eds.) *Bones as Tools: Current Methods and Interpretations in Worked Bone Studies.* BAR International Series 1622. Oxford: Archaeopress, pp. 51–65.

Choyke, A. M., M. Vretemark, and S. Sten 2004 Levels of social identity expressed in the refuse and worked bone from the Middle Bronze Age Százhalombatta – Földvár, Vatya Culture, Hungary. In S. J. O'Day, W. van Neer, and A. Ervynck (eds.) *Behaviour Behind Bones: The Zooarchaeology of Ritual, Religion, Status and Identity.* Oxford: Oxbow Books, pp. 177–89.

Chropovsky, B. and J. Herrmann (eds.) 1982 Beiträge zum bronzezeitlichen Burgenbau in Mitteleuropa. Zentralinstitut für alte Geschichte und Archaeologie. Berlin-Nitra.

Coles, J. 2005 *Shadows of a Northern Past.* Rock Carvings of Bohuslän and Østfold. Oxford: Oxbow Books.

Cooney, K. and M. Kolb 2007 Urbanisation in western Sicily. An indigenous perspective. In Matthew Fitzjohn (ed.) *Uplands of Ancient Sicily and Calabria: The Archaeology of Landscape Revisited.* London: Accordia Press, 209–21, 2007.

Cooper, J. M. 2007 *Traditions in Profile: A Chronological Sequence of Western Sicilian Ceramics (7th-6th centuries BC.).* Unpublished doctoral dissertation. State University of New York – Buffalo.

Courty, M. A., P. Goldberg, and R. I. Macphail 1989 *Soils and Micromorphology in Archaeology.* Cambridge: Cambridge University Press.

Courty, M-A. et al 1994 Environmental dynamics. In P. V. Castro, et al (eds.) *Temporalities and Desertification in the Vera Basin, South East Spain.* Archaeomedes Project, Vol. **2**, pp. 19–84.

Craddock, P. T. 1995 *Early Metal Mining and Production.* Edinburgh: Edinburgh University Press.

Csányi, M. 2003 Tiszaug-Kéménytető: A Bronze Age settlement in the Tiszazug. In Z. Visy (ed.) *Hungarian Archaeology at the Turn of the Millenium.* Budapest: Department of Monuments of the Ministry of Cultural Heritage, pp. 143–44.

Csányi, M., and I. Stanczik 1992 Tiszaug-Kéménytető. In W. Meier-Arend (ed.) *Bronzezeit in Ungarn. Forschungen in Tell-Siedlungen an Donau und Theiss.* Frankfurt: Pytheas, pp. 115–19.

D'Altroy, T. N. and T. K. Earle 1985 Staple finance, wealth finance and storage in the Inka political economy. *Current Anthropology* **26**(2).

David, N. 1990 *Vessels of the spirits: Pots and people in North Cameroon* (video). Calgary: University of Calgary.

David, N. and C. Kramer 2001 *Ethnoarchaeology in Action.* Cambridge: Cambridge University Press.

David, W. 2007 Gold and bone artefacts as evidence of mutual contacts between the Aegean, the Carpathian Basin and southern Germany in the second millennium BC. In I. Galanki et al (eds.) Between the Aegean and Baltic Seas. Prehistory across borders. *Aegaeum* **27**: 411–20.

De Angelis, S. F. 2003 Equations of Culture. The meeting of natives and Greeks in Sicily (ca. 750–450 BC). *Ancient West and East* **2**: 19–50.

DeMarrais, E., L. J. Castillo, and T. Earle 1996 Ideology, materialization, and power strategies. *Current Anthropology* **37**(1).

DeMarrais, E., C. Gosden, and C. Renfrew (eds.) 2005 *Rethinking magerialitythe engagement of mind with the material world*. McDonald Institute Monographs. Cambridge.

De Vido, S. 1997 *Gli Elimi: storie di contatti e de rappresentaziono*. Pisa.

Diaz-Andreu, M., S. Lucy, S. Babic, and D. N. Edwards (eds.) 2005 *The Archaeology of Identity. Approaches to Gender, Age, Status, Ethnicity and Religion*. London and New York: Routledge.

Dinnyés, I. et al 1986 *Magyarország Régészeti Topográfiája 7*. Budapest: Akadémiai Kiadó.

Di Noto, C. A. 1995 La Ceramica Indigena a decorazione geometrica incise ed impressa. In G. Nenci (ed.) *Entella I*, Pisa: Scuola Normale Superiore, pp. 77–110.

Di Vita, A. 1990 Town planning in Greek colonies of Sicily from the time of their foundations to the Punic wars. In J.-P. Descoeudres (ed.) *Greek Colonies and Native Populations. Proceedings of the First Australian Congress of Classical Archaeology held in Honour of Emeritus Professor A. D. Trendall. Sydney 9–14th July 1985*. Oxford: Clarendon Press, pp. 343–63.

Dixon, C. 2004 Notes on the Ceramic Assemblage. In C. Mühlenbock and C. Prescott (eds.) *The Scandinavian Sicilian Archaeological Project. Archaeological Excavation at Monte Polizzo. Field Reports 1998–2001*. GOTARC Serie C. No. 56. Göteborg: University of Göteborg, pp. 53–68.

Dobres, M. A. 2000 *Technology and Social Agency*, Oxford: Blackwell.

Dobres, M. A. and J. E. Robb (eds.) 2000 *Agency in Archaeology*. London: Routledge.

Domboróczki, L. 2004 Archaeological investigations at Ludas, Varjú-dűlő between 1998 and 2002, *Archaeological Investigations in Hungary 2002*. Budapest, pp. 5–24.

Draiby, B. 1984 Fragtrup – en boplads fra yngre bronzealder i Vesthimmerland. *Aarbøger for Nordisk Oldkyndighed og Historie 1984*: 157–216.

Drzewicz, A. 2004 *Wyroby z koœci poroża z osiedla obronnego ludnoœci kultury lużyckiej w Briskupinie* (Antler and Bone Artefacts from the Lusatian Culture Fortified Settlement at Biskupin). Warsaw: Wydawnictwo Naukiwe Semper.

Earle, T. 1991 Property rights and the evolution of chiefdoms. In T. Earle (ed.) *Chiefdoms: Power, Economy and Ideology*. Cambridge: School of American Research/Cambridge University Press, pp. 71–99.

Earle, T. 1997 *How Chiefs Come to Power. The Political Economy in Prehistory*. Stanford, CA: Stanford University Press.

Earle, T. 2002 *Bronze Age Economics. The Beginnings of Political Economies*. Boulder, CO: Westview Press.

Earle, T. 2004 Culture matters: The Neolithic transition and emergence of hierarchy in Thy, Denmark. *American Anthropologist*. **106**: 111–25.

Earle, T. 2005 Culture matters: Why symbolic objects change. In C. Renfrew, E. DeMarrais, and C. Gosden (eds.) *Rethinking Materiality, the Engagement of Mind with Material World*. Cambridge: Cambridge University Press, pp. 153–65.

Earle, T. forthcoming Amber collection at Bjerre. In J-H. Bech, B.V. Eriksen, and K. Kristiansen (eds.) *Bronze Age Settlement Structure and Land Use in Thy Northwest Denmark – primarily based on settlements from Bjerre Enge, Northern Thy*. Højbjerg: Jutland Archaeological Society.

Earle, T. et al 1998 The political economy of late Neolithic and Early Bronze Age society: The Thy Archaeological Project. *Norwegian Archaeological Review* 31(1): 1–29.

Ekman, S. 2004 Bohusländsk kulturmarksutveckling från stenålder till historisk tid. In *Materialanalys*. In P. Claesson and B. Munkenberg (eds.) *Metod – och*. Uddevalla: Bohusläns Museum, pp. 113–44.

Endrődi, A. and L. Reményi 2007 Kora bronzkori ház-és településrekonstrukció a Harangedény-Csepel csoport Budapest (XI. Kerület)-Albertfalva lelőhelyén/Reconstruction of an Early Bronze Age house and settlement at the Budapest-Albertfalva site of the Bell Beaker-Csepel group. *Ősrégészeti Levelek/Prehistoric Newsletter* 7 (2005), Budapest, 128–134.

Ericson, P. G. et al 2003 Osteologisk analys av djurbensmaterialet. In *Bronsåldersboplatsen vid Apalle i Uppland*. Riksantikvarieämbetet: UV Uppsala Rapport 1997: 64. Uppsala.

Eriksen, B. V. 2007 Travelling craftsmen in Early Bronze Age Denmark – addressing the evidence of leftover lithics. In B. Hårdh, K. Jennbert and D. Olausson (eds.) *On the Road. Studies in honour of Lars Larsson*. Acta Archaeologica Lundensia, Series in 4°, No. 26. Lund: University of Lund, pp. 253–58.

Eriksen, B. V. 2008 Dynamic technological analysis of Bronze Age lithics. A tribute to an unconventional archaeologist. In Z. Sulgostowska and A. J. Tomaszewski (eds.) *Man – Millennia – Environment. Studies in honour of Romuald Schild*. Warsaw: Institute of Archaeology and Ethnology, Polish Academy of Sciences, pp. 301–06.

Eriksen B. V. 2010 Flint working in the Danish Bronze Age – The decline and fall of a master craft. In B. V. Eriksen (ed.) *Lithic Technology in Metal Using Societies*. Højbjerg: Jutland Archaeological Society, pp. 81–93.

Eriksen, B. V. in press. The flintworking. In J-H. Bech, B. V. Eriksen, and K. Kristiansen (eds.) *Bronze Age Settlement Structure and Land Use in Thy, Northwest Denmark – primarily based on settlements from Bjerre Enge, Northern Thy*. Højbjerg: Jutland Archaeological Society.

Ethelberg, P. 2000 Bronzealderen. In P. Ethelberg, D. Meier, and D. Robinson (eds.) *Det Sønderjyske Landbrugs Historie. Sten – og Bronzealder* Haderslev: Haderslev Museum, pp. 135–280.

Evans, C. and I. Hodder 2006 *The Haddenham Project: Marshland Communities and Cultural Landscape. From the Bronze Age to the Present Day*. McDonald Institute Monographs. Cambridge: Cambridge McDonald Institute for Archaeological Research.

Falkenstein, F. 2009 Zur Subsistenzwirtschaft der Bronzezeit in Mittel- und Südosteuropa. In M. Bartelheim and H. Stäuble (eds.): *Die Wirtschaftlichen Grundlagen der Bronzezeit Europas/The Economic Foundations of the European Bronze Age*: 147–77. Rahden/Westf.:Verlag Marie Leidorf.

Faure-Rouesnel, L. 2001. French anthropology and material culture. *Journal of Material Culture* **6**(2): 237–47.

Fernández-Götz, M. A. 2008 *La construccion arqueologica de la etnicidad*. Prologo de Gonzalo Ruiz Zapatero. Editorial Toxosoutos. Serie Keltia 42. Coruna.

Finkelberg, M. 2005 *Greeks and Pre-Greeks. Aegean Prehistory and Greek Heroic Tradition*. Cambridge: Cambridge University Press.

Fish, S. K. and S. Kowalewski (eds.) 1990 *The Archaeology of Regions: A Case for Full-Coverage Survey*. Washington, DC: Smithsonian Institution Press.

Flannery, K. V. 1976 *The Early Mesoamerican Village*. New York: Academic Press.

Fletcher, R. 1986 Settlement archaeology: World-wide comparisons. *World Archaeology* **18**: 59–83.

Fokkens, H. 2003 The longhouse as a central element in Bronze Age daily life. In J. Bourgeois, I. Bourgeois, and B. Charetté, (eds.) *Bronze Age and Iron Age Communities in North-Western Europe*. Brussels: Vlaams Kennis en Kulturforum, pp. 9–38.

French, C. 2003 *Geoarchaeology in Action: Studies in Soil Micromorphology and Landscape Evolution*. London: Routledge.

French, C. 2007 Sustaining past and modern landscape systems in semi-arid lands. In L. Wilson, P. Dickinson, and J. Jeandrou (eds.) *Proceedings of the First Developing International Geoarchaeology Conference (2005)*. Newcastle-upon-Tyne: Cambridge Scholar Press.

French, C. and H. Lee 2006a 'A micromorphological assessment and analysis of house floor and occupation deposits in structure 4 at Mokarta, near Salemi, Sicily.' Unpublished report, Department of Archaeology, University of Cambridge.

French, C. and H. Lee 2006b 'A micromorphological assessment and analysis of floor deposits within hill-top structures at Monte Polizzo, near Salemi, Sicily.' Unpublished report, Department of Archaeology, University of Cambridge.

French, C., D. Passmore, and L. Schulte 1998 Geomorphology and edaphic factors. In P. V. Castro et al (eds.) *Aguas Project: Palaeoclimatic Reconstruction and the Dynamics of Human Settlement and Land Use in the Area of the Middle Aguas (Almeria), in the South-east of the Iberian Peninsula*. Luxembourg: European Commission, pp. 45–52.

Friedman, J. and M. Rowlands 1977. Notes towards an epigenetic model of the evolution of 'civilisation'. In. J. Friedman and M. Rowlands (eds.) *The Evolution of Social Systems*. Duckworth, pp. 201–76. London.

Fries, M. 1951 Pollenanalytiska vittnesbörd om senkvartär vegetationsutveckling. *Acta Phytogeographica Suecia* **29**: 24–83.

Fuhrholt, M. 2008 Pottery, cultures, people? The European Baden material re-examined. *Antiquity* **82**: 614–28.

Fuleky, Gy. 2001 Soils of the Bronze Age tell. In Gy. Fuleky (ed.) *Proceedings of the 1st International Conference on Soils and Archaeology, Százhalombatta Hungary*. Godollo: Kornyezetkimelo Agrokemiaert Alapitvany, pp. 149–52.

Fuleky, Gy. 2005. Soils of the Bronze Age tell in Százhalombatta. In I. Poroszlai and M. Vicze (eds.) *SAX, Százhalombatta Archaeological*

Expedition, Annual Report 2 – Field Season 2000–2003. Százhalombatta: 'Matrica' Museum, pp. 80–110.

Fuleky, Gy. and M. Vicze 2003 Soil and archaeological evidence of the periods of tell development of Százhalombatta-Földvár. In G. Boschian (ed.) *Second International Conference on Soils and Archaeology*. Pisa: Felici Editore, pp. 34–7.

Furmánek, V., L. Veliánek, and J. Vladár 1999 Die Bronzezeit in Slowakischen Raum. Die Arbeitung von Geweih und Knochen. *Prähistorische Archäologie in Südosteuropa* **15**: 143–45.

Galaty, M. 2005 European regional studies: A coming of age? *Journal of Archaeological Research* **13**: 291–363.

Gargini, M. 1995 La ceramica indigena a decorazione geometrica dipinta di Roca di Entella. *Entella I (Nenci, G)*. Pisa: Scuola Normale Superiore, pp. 111–61.

Gell, A. 1998 *Art and Agency. An Anthropological Theory*. Oxford: Oxford University Press.

Gerritsen, F. 1999a To build or to abandon. The cultural biography of late prehistoric houses and farmsteads in the southern Netherlands. *Archaeological Dialoques* **6**: 78–97.

Gerritsen, F. 1999b The cultural biography of Iron Age houses and the long-term transformation of settlement patterns in the southern Netherlands. In C. Fabech and J. Ringtved (eds.) *Settlement and Landscape*. Proceedings of a Conference in Århus, Denmark May 4–7, 1998. Århus: Jutland Archaeological Society, pp. 139–48.

Gerritsen, F. 2003 Local identities. Landscape and community in the late prehistoric Meuse-Demer-Scheldt region. *Amsterdam Archaelogical Studies* **9**.

Giardino, C. 1987 "Il ripostiglio di Polizzello." *Sicilia Archeologica* **65**.

Gidlöf, K. Hammarstrand Dehman, and T. Johansson. 2006 Almhov – delområde 1. *Rapport över arkeologisk slutundersökning*. Citytunnelprojektet. Rapport Nr. 39. Malmö Kulturmiljö.

Gilman, A. 1981 The development of social stratification in Bronze Age Europe. *Current Anthropology* **22**(1): 1–23.

Godelier, M. 1978 Infrastructures, Societies and History. *Current Anthropology*, **19**(4): 763–71.

Gogaltan, F. 2005 Der Beginn der bronzezeitlichen Tellsiedlungen im Karpartenbecken: Chronologische Probleme. In B. Horejs et al (eds.) *Interpretationsraum Bronzezeit. Berhard Hänsel von seinen Schüler gewiedmet*. Dr. Rudolf Habelt, Bonn, pp. 161–79.

Goldberg, P. and I. Whitbread 1993 Micromorphological study of a Bedouin tent floor. In P. Goldberg, D. T. Nash, and M. Petraglia (eds.) *Formation processes in archaeological context*. Monographs in World Archaeology, No. 17. Madison, WI: Prehistory Press, pp. 165–88.

Gosden, C. 2004 *Archaeology and Colonialism. Cultural Contact from 5000 BC to the Present*. Cambridge: Cambridge University Press.

Gröhn, A. 2004 Positioning the Bronze Age in social theory and research context. *Acta Archaeologica Lundensia Series* **8**(47). Stockholm.

Gustafson, L., T. Heibreen, and J. Martens (ed.) 2005 *De gåtefulle kokegroper*. Varia 58. Oslo: Kulturhistorisk Museum, Fornminnesektionen.

Gustafsson, S. 1998 The farming economy in south and central Sweden during the Bronze Age. A study based on carbonised botanical evidence. *Current Swedish Archaeology* 6: 63–71.

Hakbijl, T. 2002 The traditional, historical and prehistoric use of ashes as an insecticide, with an experimental study on the insecticidal efficacy of washed ash. *Environmental Archaeology* 7: 13–22.

Hall, J. 1997 *Ethnic Identity in Greek Antiquity*. Cambridge: Cambridge University Press.

Hall, J. 2002 *Hellenicity: Between Ethnicity and Culture*. Chicago: Chicago University Press.

Halstead, P. 1981 Counting sheep in Neolithic and Bronze Age Greece. In *Patterns of the past. Studies in honour of David Clarke*. Cambridge: Cambridge University Press.

Hänsel, B. 2003 Stationen der Bronzezeit zwischen Griechenland un Mitteleuropa. *Bericht der Römisch-Germanischen Kommission*, Band 83, 2002: 66–99. Mainz am Rhein.

Hansen, S. 2005 Über bronzezeitlichen Horte in Ungarn – Horte als sozialer Praxis. In B. Horejs et al (eds.) *Interpretationsraum Bronzezeit*. Bonn Berhard Hänsel von seinen Schüler gewiedmet. Dr. Rudolf Habelt, pp. 211–30.

Hansen, V. 1957 Sandflugten i Thy og dens indflydelse pa kulturlandskabet. *Geografisk Tidsskrift* 56: 69–88.

Harding, A. 2007a Interconnections between the Aegean and Continental Europe in the Bronze and early Iron Ages: Moving beyond scepticism. In I. Galanki et al (eds.) Between the Aegean and Baltic Seas. Prehistory across Borders. *Aegaeum* 27: 47–55.

Harding, A. 2007b *Warriors and Weapons in Bronze Age Europe*. Archaeolingua, Series Minor. Budapest.

Harrisson, R. and V. Heyd 2007 The transformation of Europe in the third millennium BC: The example of 'Le Petit-Chasseur I+III' (Sion, Valais, Switzerland). *Praehistorische Zeitschrift* 82. Band: 129–214.

Hauser, M. W. and D. Hicks 2007 Colonianism and landscape: Power, materiality and scales of analysis in Caribbean historical archaeology. In D. Hicks, L. McAtackney, and G. Fairclough (eds.) *Envisioning Landscape. Situations and Standpoints in Archaeology and Heritage. One World Archaeology*. Walnut Creek, CA: Left Coast Press, p. 52.

Heinzel, C. E. and M. Kolb in press. Late Holocene land use on the Island of Sicily: A geoarchaeological perspective. In P. Dickinson (ed.) *Human Interaction with the Geosphere: The Geoarchaeological Perspective*. Bath: GSL Books.

Heinzel, C. E., J. A. Stravers, and M. J. Kolb 2004 *'Geoarchaeology of the Chuddia valley, western Sicily.'* Paper given to the 32nd International Geologic Congress, Florence, Italy.

Henderson, J. C. 2007 *The Atlantic Iron Age: Settlement and Identity in the First Millennium BC*. Routledge.

Henriksen, P. S. and J. A. Harild in press. Iron Age agriculture and landuse in Thy. In B.-H. Nielsen (ed.) *Smedegård*.

Henriksen, P. S., D. E. Robinson, and K. Kelertas in press. Bronze Age agriculture, land use and vegetation in Bjerre Enge based on archaebotanical investigations. In J. H. Bech, B. V. Eriksen and K. Kristiansen (eds.) *Bronze Age Settlement Structure and Land Use in Thy, Northwest Denmark*.

Heyd, V. 2007 Families, prestige goods, warriors and complex societies: Beaker groups and the 3rd millennium cal BC. *Proceedings of the Prehistoric Society* **73**: 327–81.

Hicks, D. forthcoming The multiscalar debate in historical archaeology. *International Journal of Historical Archaeology*.

Hjelle, K. 2004a The Scandinavian Sicilian Archaeological Project (SSAP): Palynological investigations 1998. In C. Mühlenbock et al. *The Scandinavian Sicilian Archaeological Project. Archaeological Excavations at Monte Polizzo Sicily. Reports 1998–2001*. GOTARC Serie C, nr. **56**: 80–83. University of Gothenburg.

Hjelle, K. 2004b Pollen analytical investigations in the Scandinavian Sicilian Archaeological Project (SSAP) 1999–2000. In C. Mühlenbock et al. *The Scandinavian Sicilian Archaeological Project. Archaeological Excavations at Monte Polizzo Sicily. Reports 1998–2001*. GOTARC Serie C, nr. **56**: 123–39. University of Gothenburg.

Hnatiuk, T. 2004 Preliminary faunal report on the acropolis of Monte Polizzo, 2003. Appendix 2 (247–53). In I. Morris et al Stanford University Excavations on the Acropolis of Monte Polizzo, Sicily, IV: Preliminary Report on the 2003 Season. *Memoirs American Academy Rome* **49**: 197–279.

Hodder, I. 1982 *Symbols in Action*. Cambridge: Cambridge University Press.

Hodder, I. 1990 *The Domestication of Europe*. London: Blackwell Publishers.

Hodos, T. 2006 *Local Response to Colonization in the Iron Age Mediterranean*. Oxford: Routledge.

Högberg, A. 2004 The use of flint during the south Scandinavian Late Bronze Age: Two technologies, two traditions. In E. A. Walker, F. Wenban-Smith, and F. Healey (eds.) *Lithics in Action. Papers from the Conference Lithic Studies in the Year 2000*. Oxford: Oxbow Books, pp. 229–42.

Honti, Sz. 1996 A kisapostagi kultúra. A mészbetétes kerámia kultúrája. In *Évezredek üzenete a láp világából. Régészeti kutatások a Kis-Balaton területén 1979–1992*. Kaposvár-Zalaegerszeg, 47–56.

Horejs, B. 2005 Kochen am Schnittpunkt der Kulturen – zwischen Karpatenbecken und Ägäis. In B. Horejs et al (eds.) *Interpretationsraum Bronzezeit*. Bonn: Berhard Hänsel von seinen Schüler gewiedmet. Dr. Rudolf Habelt, pp. 71–94.

Horváth, L. A., G. Szilas, A. Endrödi, and A. M. Horváth 2003 Vorbericht über die Ausgrabung der urzeitlichen Siedlingen von Dunakeszi, Székes-dülö. In J. Kisfaludi (ed.) *Régészeti kutatások Magyarországon 2000. Archeaological Investigations in Hungary 2000*. Budapest: Magyar Nezeti Múseum, pp. 5–15.

Horváth, T. 2004a *A Vatya kultúra településeinek kőanyaga. Komplex régészeti és petrográfiai feldolgozás*. Unpublished PhD Thesis, Budapest.

Horváth, T. 2004b Néhány megjegyzés a vatyai kultúra fémművességéhez – Technológiai megfigyelések a kultúra kőeszközein (Die Metallkunst der Vatya-Kultur – Technologische Beobachtungen an ihren Steingeräten). *CommArchHung* 2004, 11–64.

Horváth, T. 2005 Stone finds from excavation seasons 1998, 1999 and 2000. Typological and technical analysis. In I. Poroszlai and M. Vicze (eds.) *Százhalombatta Archaeological Expedition (SAX). Report 2 – Field Seasons 2000–2003*. Százhalombatta: Matrica Museum, pp. 135–55.

Horváth, T., M. Kozák and A. Pető 2000 Complex analysis of stone industry on the Százhalombatta-Földvár (Early and Middle Bronze Age). In I. Poroszlai and M. Vicze (eds.) *SAX. Százhalombatta Archaeological Expedition. Annual Report 1 – Field Season 1998*. Százhalombatta: Archaeolingua and Matrica Museum, pp. 103–18.

Horváth, T., M. Kozák and A. Pető 2001 Adatok a bronzkori kőeszközök kutatásához. In J. Dani (eds.) *MΩMOΣ I. "Fiatal Őskoros Kutatók" I. Összejövetelének konferenciakötete. Debrecen, 1997 november 10–13*. Debrecen, pp. 199–215.

Horváth, T. and E. Marton 2002 The warp-weighted loom in the Carpathian Basin (Hungary). Experiment in the Archaeological Park Százhalombatta. In E. Jerem and K. T. Biró (eds.) *Archaeometry 98. Proceedings of the 31st International Symposium Budapest, 1998*. BAR International Series 1043. Oxford: Archaeopress, pp. 783–93.

Hughes-Brock, H. 2005 Amber and some other travelers in the Bronze Age Aegean and Europe. In A. Dakouri-Hild and S. Sherratt (eds.) *Autochthon. Papers Presented to O. T. P. K. Dickinson on the occasion of his retirement* Oxford: AR-International Series 1432, pp. 302–16.

Hurcombe, L. 2007 *Archaeological Artefacts as Material Culture*. Abingdon and New York: Routledge.

Hvass, S. 1985 *Hodde. Et vestjysk landsbysamfund fra ældre jernalder*. Arkæologiske Studier, Københavns Universitet VII.

Jacomet, S. 2006 *Identification of Cereal Remains from Archaeological Sites*. Institute for Prehistory and Archaeological Science IPAS Basel University.

Jensen, J. 1998 *Manden i kisten. Hvad bronzealderens gravhøje gemte*. Copenhagen: Gyldendal.

Jensen, J. 2002 *Danmarks Oldtid. Bronzealder 2000–500 f. Kr*. Köpenhamn.

Jockenhövel, A. 2004/2005 Zur Archäologie der Gewalt: Bemerkungen zur Agression und Krieg in der Bronzezeit Alteuropas. *Anados. Studies of the Ancient World* **4–5**: 101–32.

Jockenhövel, A. 2005 Bronzezeitliche Dolche under Schwerter als Bilder auf Objekten? Zur Ikonographie einer Waffengattung. In V. Spinei, C.-M. Lazarovici, and D. Monah (eds.) *Scripta praehistorica. Miscellanea in honorem nonagenarii magistri Mircea Petruscu-Dimbovita oblata*. Iasi: Trinitas, pp. 600–19.

Johansen, K. L., S. T. Laursen, and M. K. Holst 2004 Spatial patterns of social organization in the Early Bronze Age of south Scandinavia. *Journal of Anthropological Archaeology* **23**: 33–55.

Johansson, L. G., and C. Prescott 2004 Surveying and mapping the Monte Polizzo Site 1998. In C. Mühlenbock and C. Prescott (eds.) *The Scandinavian Sicilian Archaeological Project. Archaeological Excavations at Monte Polizzo Sicily. Reports 1998–2001*. GOTARC Serie C. No. 56. Göteborg: University of Gothenburg, pp. 27–32.

Johnson, A. and T. Earle 2000 *Evolution of Human Societies*, 2nd edition. Stanford, CA: Stanford University Press.

Jones, G. E. M., S. Valamoti, and M. Charles 2000 Early crop diversity: A "new" glume wheat from northern Greece. *Vegetation History and Archaeobotany* **9**, 133–46.

Jones, S. 1997 *The Archaeology of Ethnicity. Constructing Identities in the Past and the Present*. London and New York: Routledge.

Jonsson, L. 2005 Bilaga 11. Rapport över inledande osteologisk undersökning, Bo, Morlanda socken, RAÄ 89. In B. Nordqvist (ed.) *Husby klev: en kustboplats med bevarat organiskt material från äldsta mesoliticum till järnålder*. Avd: Riksantikvarieämbetet. UV Väst, pp. 96–104.

Juel Jensen, H. in press. The flint knives from Bjerre 7. In J.-H. Bech, B. V. Eriksen, and K. Kristiansen (eds.) *Bronze Age Settlement Structure and Land Use in Thy Northwest Denmark – Primarily based on Settlements from Bjerre Enge, Northern Thy*. Højbjerg: Jutland Archaeological Society.

Junkmanns, J. 2001 *Pfeil und Bogen. Herstellung und Gebrauch in der Jungsteinzeit*. Biel: Museum Schwab.

Kalicz-Schreiber, R. and N. Kalicz 2001 Were the Bell Beakers Social Indicators of the Early Bronze Age in Budapest? In F. Nicolis (ed.) *Bell Beakers today. Pottery, people, culture, symbols in prehistoric Europe*. Proceedings of the International Colloquium Riva del Garda (Trento, Italy) 11–16 May 1998. Volume II. pp. 439–58, Provincia Autonoma di Trento. Servizio Beni Culturali. Ufficio Benu Archeologici.

Kasco, C. 2004 *Maturii arheologice*. Editura Nereamia Napocae. Baia Mare.

Kemenczei, T. 2003 Bronze Age metallurgy. In Z. Visy (ed) *Hungarian Archaeology at the Turn of the Millenium*. Budapest: Department of Monuments of the Ministry of Cultural Heritage, pp. 167–74.

Kemenczei, T. 1994a The Final Centuries of the Late Bronze Age. In T. Kovács (ed.) *Treasures of the Hungarian Bronze Age. Catalogue to the Temporary Exhibition of the Hungarian National Museum, September 20–December 31, 1994*. Hungarian National Museum, 1994. Budapest, 29–36.

Kemenczei, T. 1994b Late Bronze Age Workshops: Centers of Metallurgy. In T. Kovács (ed.) *Treasures of the Hungarian Bronze Age. Catalogue to the Temporary Exhibition of the Hungarian National Museum, September 20–December 31, 1994*. Hungarian National Museum, 1994. Budapest, 52–62.

Kilian-Dirlmeier, I. 1997 *Das Mittelbronzezeitliche Schachtgrab von Ägina*. Römisch-Germanisches Zentralmuseum Forshcungsinstitutt für Vor- und Frühgeschichte. Kataloge Vor- und Frühgeschichtliche Altertümer, Banda 27/ Alt Ägina Band IV, 3. Mainz: Verlag Phillip von Zabern.

Killen, J. T. 2007 Cloth production in late Bronze Age Greece: The documentary evidence. In C. Gillis and M.-L. B. Nosch (eds.) *Ancient Textiles. Production, Craft and Society*. Oxford: Oxbow Books, pp. 50–59.

Klehm, C. 2006 Bowling for Budapest: Social structure and ceramics at the Hungarian Bronze Age site of Százhalombatta. Undergraduate Honors Thesis, Department of Anthropology, Northwestern University, Evanston.

Knappett, C. 2002 Photographs, skeuomorphs and marionettes. Some thoughts on mind, agency and object. *Journal of Material Culture* 7(1): 97–117.

Knappett, C. 2005 *Thinking Through Material Culture. An Interdisciplinary Perspective*. Philadelphia: Pennsylvania Press.

Kock, E. 2003 Mead, chiefs and feasts in later prehistoric Europe. In M. Parker Pearson (ed.) *Food, Culture and Identity in the Neolithic and Early Bronze Age*. BAR International Series 1117. Oxford: Archaeopress, pp. 125–43.

Kohl, P. 2007 *The Making of Bronze Age Eurasia*. Cambridge World Archaeology. Cambridge: Cambridge University Press.

Kohl, P. 2008 Shared Social Fields: Evolutionary Convergence in Prehistory and Contemporary Practice. *American Anthropologist* **110**(4): 495–506.

Kohler-Schneider, M. 2001 *Verkohlte Kultur- und Wildpflanzenreste aus Stillfried an der March als Spiegel spätbronzezeitlicher Landwirtschaft im Weinviertel, Niederösterreich*. Mitteilungen der Prähistorischen Kommission **37**, Wien.

Kolb, J. 2007 The Salemi Survey project: Long-term landscape change and political consolidation in interior western Sicily 3000 BC – AD 600. In M. Fitzjohn (ed.) *Uplands of Ancient Sicily and Calabria: The Archaeology of Landscape Revisited*. London: Accordia Press, pp. 171–85.

Kolb, M. J. 2004 1998 Regional survey report Monte Polizzo region. In Ch. Mühlenbock et al *The Scandinavian Archaeological Project – Archaeological excavations at Monte Polizzo, Sicily, Reports 1998–2001*. GOTARC Series C nr 56. Göteborg: University of Gothenburg, pp. 33–38.

Kolb, M. and J. Snead 1997 It's a small world after all: Comparative analyses of community organization in archaeology. *American Antiquity* **62**: 609–28.

Kolb, M. and R. Speakman. 2005 Elymian regional interaction in Iron Age western Sicily: A preliminary neutron activation study of incised/impressed tablewares. *Journal of Archaeological Science* **32**: 795–804.

Kolb, M. J. and S. Tusa 2001 The Late Bronze Age and Early Iron Age landscape of interior western Sicily. *Antiquity* **75**: 503–04.

Kolb, M. J., P. Vecchio, and C. Tyers 2007 The lost settlement of Halikyai and excavations at Cappasanta, Salemi, Sicily. In M. Fitzjohn (ed.) *Uplands of Ancient Sicily and Calabria: The Archaeology of Landscape Revisited*. London: Accordia Press, pp. 197–208.

Kopacz, J. 2001 *Początki epoki brązu w strefie karpackiej w świetle materiałów kammienych*. Kraków.

Kopytoff, I. 1986 The cultural biography of things. Commoditization as process. In A. Appadurai (ed.) *The Social Life of Things: Commodities in Cultural Perspective*. Cambridge: Cambridge University Press, pp. 64–91.

Koryakova, L. and A. Epimakhov 2007 *The Urals and Western Siberia in the Bronze and Iron Ages. Cambridge World Archaeology*. Cambridge: Cambridge University Press.

Kovács, G. 2005 Reconstruction of the former environment and investigation of human activity at Százhalombatta-Földvár Bronze Age tell settlement. In I. Poroszlai and M. Vicze (eds.) *SAX, Százhalombatta Archaeological Expedition, Annual Report 2 – Field Season 2000–2003*. Százhalombatta: 'Matrica' Museum, 125–34.

Kovács, G. 2008 Geoarchaeological investigation of Százhalombatta-Földvár Bronze Age tell settlement in Hungary. Unpublished PhD thesis, University of Cambridge.

Kovács T. 1973 Representations of Weapons on Bronze Age Pottery. *Folia Archaeologica* **XXIV**: 7–31

Kovács, T. 1982 Befestigungsanlagen um die Mitte des 2. Jahrtausends v.u.Z. in Mittelungarn. In B. Chropovsky and J. Herrmann (eds.) *Beiträge zum bronzezeitlichen Burgenbau in Mitteleuropa*. Zentralinstitut für alte Gesschichte und Archaeologie. Berlin-Nitra.

Kovács, T. 1988 Review of the Bronze Age settlement research during the past one and a half centuries in Hungary. In T. Kovács and I. Stanczik (eds.) *Bronze Age tell settlements on the great Hungarian plain*. Budapest: Inventaria Praehistorica Hvngariae, pp. 17–25.

Kővári, K. and R. Patay 2005 A settlement of the Makó culture at Üllő. New evidence for Early Bronze Age metalworking. *CommArchHung 2005*, 83–137.

Kowalewski, S. 2008 Regional settlement patterns studies. *Journal of Archaeological Research* **16**: 225–85.

Kreiter, A. 2006 Kerámia technológiai vizsgálatok a Halomsíros kultúra Esztergályhorváti – alsóbárándpusztai településéről: hagyomány és identitás – Technological examination of Tumulus culture pottery from Esztergályhorváti – Alsóbárándpuszta: Tradition and identity. *Zalai Múzeum* **15**: 149–70.

Kreiter, A. 2007a *Technological Choices and Material Meanings in Early and Middle Bronze Age Hungary: Understanding the Active Role of Material Culture Through Ceramic Analysis*. BAR International Series 1604. Oxford: Archaeopress.

Kreiter, A. 2007b Kerámia technológiai tradíció és az idő koncepciója a bronzkorban – Ceramic technological tradition and the concept of time in the Bronze Age. *Ősrégészeti Levelek (Prehistoric Newsletters)* **8–9**: 146–66.

Kreiter, A., J. Sofaer, and S. Budden 2006 Early and Middle Bronze Age storage vessel building techniques in Hungary. *Ősrégészeti Levelek (Prehistoric Newsletters)*, (2004) **6**: 85–91.

Kremenetski, K. 2003 Steppe and forest steppe belt of Eurasia: Holocene environmental history. In M. Levine, C. Renfrew, and K. Boyle (eds.) *Prehistoric Steppe Adaptations and the Horse*. Cambridge: McDonald Institute monographs, pp. 11–29.

Kristensen, I. K. in press. The ceramics. In J.-H. Bech, B. V. Eriksen, and K. Kristiansen (eds.) *Bronze Age Settlement Structure and Land Use in Thy Northwest Denmark – Primarily Based on Settlements from Bjerre Enge, Northern Thy*. Højbjerg: Jutland Archaeological Society.

Kristiansen, K. 1978. Bebyggelse, erhversstrategi og arealudnyttelse i Danmarks bronzealder. Fortid og Nutid 27.

Kristiansen, K. 1978 The consumption of wealth in Bronze Age Denmark. A study in the dynamics of economic processes in tribal societies. In K. Kristiansen and C. Paludan-Müller (eds.) *New Directions in Scandinavian Archaeology*. The Copenhagen: National Museum of Denmark, pp. 158–90.

Kristiansen, K. 1984a Krieger und Häuptling in der Bronzezeit Dänemarks. Ein Beitrag zur Geschichte des bronzezeitlichen Schwertes. *Jahrbuch des Römisch-Gremanische Zentralmuseums Mainz*, **31** pp. 187–208.

Kristiansen, K. 1984b Ideology and material culture: An archaeological perspective. In M. Spriggs (ed.) *Marxist Perspectives in Archaeology*. Cambridge: Cambridge University Press.

Kristiansen, K. 1987 From stone to bronze: The evolution of social complexity in Northern Europe, 2300-1200 BC. In E. M. Brumfiel and T. K. Earle (eds.) *Specialization, exchange, and complex societies:30–52*. Cambridge: Cambridge University Press.

Kristiansen, K. 1998a Construction of a Bronze Age landscape. Cosmology, Economy and Social Organisation in Thy, Nortwestern Jutland. In B. Hänsel (ed.) *Mensch und Umwelt in der Bronzezeit Europas. Die Bronzezeit. Das erste goldene Zeitalter Europas*. pp. 281–91.

Kristiansen, K. 1998b *Europe before History*. Cambridge: Cambridge University Press.

Kristiansen, K. 2002 The tale of the sword. Swords and swordfighters in Bronze Age Europe. *Oxford Journal of Archaeology* 21(4): 319–32.

Kristiansen, K. 2006a Cosmology, economy and long-term change in the Bronze Age of Northern Europe. In K.-G. Sjögren (ed.) *Ecology and Economy in Stone Age and Bronze Age Scania*. Skånska spor – arkeologi längs Västkustnanan. Stockholm: Riksantikvarieämbetet, pp. 171–218.

Kristiansen, K. 2006b Eurasian transformations: Mobility, ecological change, and the transmission of social institutions in the third and early second millennium BCE. In A. Hornborg and C. L. Crumley (eds.) *The World System and the Earth System. Global Socio-Environmental Change and Sustainability Since the Neolithic*. Walnut Creek, CA: Left Coast Press.

Kristiansen, K. 2007 The Rules of the Game. Decentralised Complexity and Power Structures. In S. Kohring and S. Wynne-Jones (eds.): *Socialising Complexity. Structure, Interaction and Power in Archaeological Discourse*, Oxford: Oxbow Books, 60–76.

Kristiansen, K. 2008 From memory to monument: The construction of time in the Bronze Age. In A. Lehöerff (ed.) *Construire le temps*. Histoire et méthodes des chronologies et calendriers des derniers millénaires avant notre ère en Europe occidentale. Actes du XXXe colloque international de Halma-Ipel, UMR 8164 (CNRS, Lille 3, MCC), 7–9 Décembre 2006, Lille. Glux-en-Glenne : Bibracte, 2008, p. 41–50 (Bibracte).

Kristiansen, K. and T. B. Larsson 2005 *The rise of Bronze Age society. Travels, Transmissions and Transformations*. Cambridge University Press. Cambridge.

Kulcsarne-Berzsenyi, B. 2008 *Crop Processing and Social Relations in Middle Bronze Age Hungary*. Cambridge: University of Cambridge.

Kuna, M. and D. Dreslerova 2007 Landscape archaeology and 'community areas' in the archaeology of central Europe. In D. Hicks, L. McAtackney, and G. Fairclough (eds.). *Envisioning Landscape. Situations and Standpoints in Archaeology and Heritage*. One World Archaeology, 52. Walnut Creek, CA: Left Coast Press.

Larsen. M. T. 1987 Commercial networks in the ancient Near East. In M. Rowlands, M. Larsen, and K. Kristiansen (eds.) *Centre and Periphery in the Ancient World*. Cambridge: Cambridge University Press, pp. 47–57.

Larsen, M. T. 2007 Individual and family in Old Assyrian society. *Journal of Cuneiform Studies* 59: 93–106.

Layton, R. 1989 Pellaport. In S. E. van der Leeuw and R. Torrence *What's New? A Closer Look at The Process of Innovation*. One World Archaeology 14. London: Unwin Hyman, pp. 33–53.

Lech, J. 1981 Flint mining among the early farming communities of Central Europe. *Przeglad Archeologiczny* 28: 5–57.

Leggett, E. and S. Nussbaum 2001 Raising the roof – a time-honored tradition. *Amish Heartland*, August 2001.

Leighton, R. 1993 *The Protohistoric Settlement on the Cittadella*. Morgantina Studies vol. IV. Princeton, NJ: Princeton University Press.

Leighton, R. 1999 *Sicily before History: An Archaeological Survey from the Palaeolithic to the Iron Age*. Ithaca, NY: Cornell University Press.

Leighton, R. 2000 Indigenous society between the ninth and sixth centuries BC: Territorial, urban and social evolution. In C. Smith and J. Serrati (eds.) *Sicily from Aeneas to Augustus*. Edinburgh: Edinburgh University Press, pp. 15–40.

Leighton, R. 2005 Later prehistoric settlement patterns in Sicily. Old paradigms and new surveys. *European Journal of Archaeology* **8**(3): 261–87.

Lekberg, P. 2002 *Yxors liv. Människors landskap. En studie av kulturlandskap och samhälle I Mellansveriges senneolitikum*. Coast to coast books-no.5. Uppsala.

Lemonnier, P. 1992 *Elements for an Anthropology of Technology*. Anthropological Papers No. 88. Ann Arbor: Museum of Anthropology, University of Michigan.

Lepiksaar, J. 1969 Knochenfunde aus den bronzezeitlichen Siedlungen von Hötofta. In *Acta Archaeologica Lundensia Series nr* **8**.

Lindahl, A. 1986 *Information through Sherds. A case study of the early glazed earthenware from Dalby, Scania*. Lund Studies in Medieval Archaeology 3. Lund: University of Lund.

Lindman, G. 1997. Forntid i Bua. Arkeologiska undersökningar av fornlämningarna 345. 383 och 483. Morlanda sn, Orust, Bohuslän. *Riksantikvarieämbetet UV Väst Rapport* 1997:31.

Ling, J. 2004 Beyond transgressive lands and forgotten seas. Towards a maritime understanding of rock art in Bohuslän. *Current Swedish Archaeology* **12**: 121–40.

Ling, J. 2005 The fluidity of rock art. In J. Goldhahn (ed.) *Mellan sten och järn. Rapport från det 9:e nordiska bronsålderssymposiet, Göteborg 2003-10-09/12*. Del 2. GOTARC Serie C. Arkeologiska Skrifter No. 59. Göteborg: University of Gothenburg, pp. 437–60.

Ling, J. 2006 Elevated rock art. *Maritime images and situations*. Adoranten 2005, pp. 5–32.

Ling, J. 2008 *Elevated Rock Art. Towards a Maritime Understanding of Rock Art in Northern Bohuslän, Sweden*. GOTARC Serie B. Gothenburg Archaeological Thesis 49. Göteborg: University of Gothenburg.

Liversage, D. 1987 Mortens Sande 2 – A single grave camp site in Northwest Jutland. *Journal of Danish Archaeology* **6**: 101–24.

Liversage, D. 1994 Interpreting composition patterns in ancient bronze: The Carpathian basin. *Acta Archaeologica* **65**: 57–134.

Lock, G. and B. L. Molyneaux (eds.) 2007 *Confronting Scale in Archaeology. Issues of Theory and Practice*. Springer.

Malmros, C. in press. Exploitation of wood resources illuminated by wood and charcoal analysis. In: J.-H. Bech, B. V. Eriksen, and K. Kristiansen (eds.) *Bronze Age Settlement Structure and Land Use in Thy, Northwest Denmark*.

Malmros, C., J. Huston, and K. Christensen in press. The wood resources. Wood anatomical investigations of wood from Bjerre site 2, 6 and 7. In J.-H. Bech, B. V. Eriksen, and K. Kristiansen (eds.) *Bronze Age Settlement Structure and Land Use in Thy Northwest Denmark – Primarily Based on Settlements from Bjerre Enge, Northern Thy*. Højbjerg: Jutland Archaeological Society.

Malone, C., S. Stoddart and R. Whitehouse 1994 The Bronze Age of Southern Italy, Sicily and Malta c. 2000–800 BC. In C. Mathers and S. Stoddart (eds.) *Development and Decline in the Mediterranean Bronze Age*. Sheffield Archaeological Monographs **8**: 167–94, Sheffield: J. R. Collis Publications.

Manning, S. W. and L. Hulin 2004 Maritime commerce and geographies of mobility in the late Bronze Age of the eastern Mediterranean: Problematizations. In E. Blake and A. B. Knapp (eds.) *The Archaeology of Mediterranean Prehistory*. Oxford: Blackwell Publishing, pp. 270–303.

Mannino, G. and F. Spatafora 1995 *Mokarta. La Necropoli di Cresta di Gallo*. Palermo: Quaderni del Meseo Archaeolgico Regionale 'Antonio Salinas' 1. Palermo, Italy: Museo Archeologico Regionale Antonio Salinas.

Marazzi, M. and S. Tusa 2005 Egei in Occidente. Le pi antiche vie maritime alla luce dei n uovi scavi sulli'isola di Pantalleria. In R. Laffineur and E. Greco (eds.) *EMPORIA. Aegeans in the Central and Eastern Mediterranean. Aegeum* **25**: 599–611.

Marx, K. 1973 *Grundrisse*. Introduction to the Critique of Political Economy. London: Penguin.

Marx, K. 1975 *Marx's Capital*. London: MacMillan Publishing Company.

Máthé, M. 1988 Bronze Age tells in the Berettyó valley. In T. Kovács and I. Stanczik, *Bronze Age Tell Settlements of the Great Hungarian Plain I* (Inventaria Praehistorica Hungariae). Budapest: Magyar Nemzeti Múzeum, pp. 27–122.

McConnell, B. E. 1992 The early Bronze Age Village of La Muculufa and prehistoric hut architecture in Sicily. *American Journal of Archaeology* **96**(1): 23–44.

Mertens, D. 2003 Die Agora von Selinunt. Neue Grabungsergebnisse zur Frühzeit der griechischen Kolonialstadt. Ein Vorbericht. *Mitteilungen des Deutschen Archäologischen Instituts, Römische Abteilung*, **110**: 389–446.

Meskell, L. and R. A. Joyce 2003 *Embodied Lives. Figuring Ancient Maya and Egyptian Experience*. London: Routledge.

Mikkelsen, M. 1996 Bronzealderbosættelserne på Ås-højderyggen i Thy. In J. Bertelsen et al (eds.) *Bronzealderens bopladser i Midt – og Nordvestjylland*. Skive: Arkæologiske Museer i Viborg Amt, pp. 110–23.

Mikkelsen, M. 2003 *Bebyggelsen i bronzealder og tidlig ældre jernalder i Østthy*. Unpublished PhD dissertation, University of Århus.

Mikkelsen, M. in press. The Bronze Age Settlement at Aas, Østthy, Denmark. In J-H. Bech, B. V. Eriksen, and K. Kristiansen (eds) *Bronze Age Settlement Structure and Land Use in Thy Northwest Denmark – Primarily Based on Settlements from Bjerre Enge, Northern Thy*. Højbjerg: Jutland Archaeological Society.

Mikkelsen, M. and K. Kristiansen in press. Bronze Age sites in Sønderhå, Central Thy 2. Legård. In J.-H. Bech, B. V. Eriksen, and K. Kristiansen (eds.) *Bronze Age Settlement Structure and Land Use in Thy Northwest Denmark – Primarily Based on Settlements from Bjerre Enge, Northern Thy*. Højbjerg: Jutland Archaeological Society.

Milek, K. 2006 *Houses and Households in Early Icelandic Society: Geoarchaeology and the Interpretation of Social Space*. Unpublished PhD thesis. University of Cambridge.

Miliktello, P. 2005 Mycenaean palaces and western trade: A problematic relationship. In R. Laffineur and E. Greco (eds.) *EMPORIA. Aegeans in the Central and Eastern Mediterranean. Aegeum* **25**: 611–23.

Miller, U. and A.-M. Robertsson 1988 Late Weichselian and Holocene environmental changes in Bohuslän, south-western Sweden. *Geographia Polonica* **55**: 103–13.

Molloy, B. P. C. 2007 What's the bloody point? Bronze Age swordsmanship in Ireland and Britain. In B. Molloy (ed.) *The Cutting Edge*. Gloucestershire: Tempus, pp. 90–111. (Studies in Ancient and Medieval Combat).

Morell, M. 1989. *Studier i den svenska livsmedelskonsumtionens historia*. Studies in Economic History, 29. Uppsala Universitet. Uppsala.

Morris, I. 2007 Early Iron Age Greece. In W. Scheidel, I. Morris, and R. P. Saller (eds.) *The Cambridge Economic History of the Greco-Roman World*. Cambridge: Cambridge University Press, pp. 211–42.

Morris, I. et al 2001 Stanford University Excavations on the Acropolis of Monte Polizzo, Sicily, I: Preliminary Report on the 2000 season. *Memoirs of the American Academy in Rome* 46: 253–71.

Morris, I. et al 2002 Stanford University excavations on the acropolis of Monte Polizzo, Sicily, II: Preliminary report on the 2001 season. *Memoirs of the American Academy in Rome* 47: 153–98.

Morris I. et al 2003 Stanford University excavations on the acropolis of Monte Polizzo, Sicily, III: Preliminary report on the 2002 season. *Memoirs of the American Academy in Rome* 48(2003): 243–315.

Morris, I. et al 2004 Stanford University excavations on the acropolis of Monte Polizzo, Sicily, IV: Preliminary report on the 2003 season. *Memoirs of the American Academy in Rome* 49(2004): 197–279.

Mozsolics, A. 1967. *Bronzefunde des Karpatenbeckens. Depotfundhorizonte von Hajdúsámson und Kosziderpadlás*. Budapest: Akadémiai Kiadó.

Mühlenbock, C. 2008 *Fragments from a mountain society: Tradition, innovation and interaction at Archaic Monte Polizzo, Sicily*. GOTARC Series B. No 50. Gothenburg Archaeological Thesis. Göteborg: University of Gothenburg.

Mühlenbock, C., H. Påhlsson, and M. A. Hauge 2004 Field reports 2002–03. In C. Mühlenbock (ed.) *The Scandinavian Sicilian Archaeological Project. Archaeological excavations at Monte Polizzo Sicily. Reports 2002–2003*. GOTARC Serie C. No. 57. Göteborg: University of Gothenburg, pp. 19–56.

Mühlenbock, C. 2004 *The Scandinavian Archaeological Project – Archaeological excavations at Monte Polizzo, Sicily, Reports 2002–2003*. GOTARC Series C nr 57. Göteborg: University of Gothenburg, pp. 1–60.

Mühlenbock, C. and C. Prescott (eds.) 2004 *The Scandinavian Sicilian Archaeological Project. Archaeological excavations at Monte Polizzo Sicily. Reports 1998–2001*. GOTARC Serie C. No. 56. Göteborg: University of Gothenburg.

Mühlenbock, C. and C. Prescott 2004 Survey report 2000. In C. Mühlenbock and C. Prescott (eds.) *The Scandinavian Archaeological Project – Archaeological excavations at Monte Polizzo, Sicily, Reports 1998–2001*. GOTARC Series C nr 56. Göteborg: University of Gothenburg, pp. 139–70.

Mühlenbock, C. and C. Prescott 2004 Excavations at House 1, Monte Polizzo 1999–2000. In C. Mühlenbock and C. Prescott (eds.) *The Scandinavian Archaeological Project – Archaeological excavations at Monte Polizzo, Sicily, Reports 1998–2001*. GOTARC Series C nr 56. Göteborg: University of Gothenburg, pp. 83–122.

Mühlenbock, C. and C. Prescott 2004 Monte Polizzo House 1. Annual Report 2001. In C. Mühlenbock and C. Prescott (eds.) *The Scandinavian Archaeological Project – Archaeological excavations at Monte Polizzo, Sicily*,

Reports 1998–2001. GOTARC Series C nr 56. Göteborg: University of Gothenburg, pp. 171–82.

Müller, J. (ed.) 2002 *Vom Endneolithicum zur Frühbronzezeit: Muster sozialen Wandels?* Tagung Bamberg 14.–16. Juni 2001. UPA 90. Bonn.

Needham, S. 2009 Encompassing the Sea: 'Maritories' and Bronze Age maritime interactions. In P. Clark (ed.) *Bronze Age Connections. Cultural Contact in Prehistoric Europe*. Oxford: Oxbow Books, pp. 12–38.

Nenci, G. 1995 La ceramica indigena a decorazione geometrica incis ed impress. In G. Nenci (ed) *Entella I*, Scuola Normale Superiore Di Pisa, Pisa, pp. 77–162.

Netting, R. and R. Wilk 1984 Households: Comparative and historical studies of the domestic group. In R. Netting, R. Wilk, and E. J. Arnould (eds.) *Households: Comparative and Historical Studies of the Domestic Group*. Berkeley, CA: University of California Press, pp. 1–28.

Nevett, L. C. 1999 *House and Society in the Ancient Greek World. New Studies in Archaeology*. Cambridge: Cambridge University Press.

Nicholson, P. T. and W. Z. Wendrich 1994 *The Potters of Deir Mawas: A Village in Middle Egypt* (video).

Nielsen, B. H. and J.-H. Bech 2004 Bronzealderens kulthuse i Thy. *Anlæg med relation til gravkulten*. Kuml 2004, pp. 129–59.

Nielsen, P. O. 1999 Limensgård and Grødbygård. Settlements with house remains from the Early, Middle and Late Neolithic on Bornholm. In C. Fabech and J. Ringtved (eds.) *Settlement and Landscape*. Proceedings of a conference in Århus, Denmark May 4–7 1998, Århus: Moesgård Museum, pp. 149–65.

Nilsson, T. 1996 Store Tyrrestrup. En vendsysselsk storgård med bronzedepot fra ældre bronzealder. *Kuml* 1993: 147–54.

Nyegaard, G. 1983 Dyreknogler fra yngre bronzealderens boplatser i Sydskandinavien. Et studie over faunaökonomi samt bearbejdede genstander af ben og tak. Opubliceret specialafhandling ved Köbenhavns Universitet.

Nyegaard, G. 1996 *Faunalevn fra bronzealder. En zooarkaeologisk undersögelse af sydskandinaviske bopladsfund*. Zoologisk Museum. Köpenhamn.

Odgaard, B. V. 1994. The Holocene vegetation history of northern West Jutland, Denmark. *Opera Botanica* **123**.

Olausson, M. 1995 *Det inneslutna rummet – om kultiska hägnader, fornborgar och befästa gårdar i Uppland från 1300 f. Kr. till Kristi födelse*. Riksantikvarieämbetet. Arkeologiska undersökningar. Skrifter nr. 9. Stockholm.

Olesen, M. W. and B. V. Eriksen 2007 Krogstrup ved Snejbjerg. En bronzealderboplads med flintværktøj. In *Midtjyske fortællinger 2007*, Herning Museum, pp. 77–92.

Olsen, A-L. forthcoming a Bjerre Site 6. In J-H. Bech, B.V. Eriksen, and K. Kristiansen (eds.) *Bronze Age Settlement Structure and Land Use in Thy Northwest Denmark – primarily based on settlements from Bjerre Enge, Northern Thy*. Højbjerg: Jutland Archaeological Society.

Olsen, A.-L. forthcoming b Bjerre Site 7. In J-H. Bech, B.V. Eriksen, and K. Kristiansen (eds.) *Bronze Age Settlement Structure and Land Use in Thy Northwest Denmark – primarily based on settlements from Bjerre Enge, Northern Thy*. Højbjerg: Jutland Archaeological Society.

Oma, K. A. 2007 Human–animal relationships. Mutual becoming in Scandinavian and Sicilian households 900–500 BC. *Oslo Archaeological Series* **9**.

Osipowicz, G. 2007 Bone and Antler: Softening techniques in prehistory of the North Eastern part of the Polish lowlands in the light of experimental archaeology and micro trace analysis. *EuroREA*. **4**: 1-22.

Ottaway, B. S. 1994 *Prähistorische Archäometallurgie*. Espelkamp: Leidorf.

Otto, T., H. Thrane and H. Vandkilde (eds.) 2006 *Warfare and Society. Archaeological and Anthropological Perspectives*. Aarhus: Aarhus University Press.

Paine, Richard (ed.) 1997 *Integrating Archaeological Demography: Multidisciplinary Approaches to Prehistoric Population*. Carbondale: Southern Illinois University.

Palermo, D. 1996 Tradizione undigena e apporti greci nelle culture della Sicilia centro-meridionale; il caso di Sant' Angelo Muxaro. In R. Leighton (ed.) *Early Societies in Sicily. New Developments in Archaeological Research*. Accordia Specialist Studies on Italy 5. London. 147-54.

Påsse, T. 2001 *An Empirical Model of Glacio-isostatic Movements and Shore-level Displacement in Fennoscandia*. Stockholm: SKB.

Påsse, T. 2003 Strandlinjeförskjutning i norra Bohuslän under holocen. In P. Persson (ed.) *Strandlinjer och vegetationshistoria. Kvartärgeologiska undersökningar inom projektet kust till kust, 1998-2000*. GOTARC Serie C, nr 48. Göteborg: University of Gothenburg, pp. 31-64.

Petersson, M. 2006. *Djurhållning och betesdrift*. Riksantikvarieämbetet: Linköping.

Pető, A. et al 2002 Examination of stone implements of a Bronze Age earthwork in Hungary. *Archeometry 98. Proceedings of the 31st International Symposium Budapest, 1998*. BAR International Series 1043. Oxford: Archaeopress, pp. 783-93.

Pool, C. 2000 Why a kiln? Firing technology in the Sierra de los Tuxtlas, Veracruz (Mexico). *Archaeometry* **42**: 61-76.

Poroszlai, I. 1988 Preliminary report about the excavation at Nagykőrös-Földvár (Vatya culture): Stratigraphic data and settlement structure. *Communicationes Archaeologicae Hungariae* 1988: pp. 29-39.

Poroszlai I. 1996a Ásatások a százhalombattai bronzkori földvárban (1989-1993). Excavations in the Bronze Age earthwork in Százhalombatta between 1989 and 1993. In I. Poroszlai (ed.) *Ásatások Százhalombattán. Excavations at Százhalombatta 1989-1995*. Százhalombatta: Matrica Museum, pp. 5-15.

Poroszlai, I. 1996b *Excavations at Százhalombatta 1989-1995*. Százhalombatta: Matrica Museum.

Poroszlai, I. 1998 The Bronze Age. In I. Poroszlai and M. Vicze (eds.) *History of Százhalombatta. Guide to the Exhibition*. Százhalombatta: Matrica Museum.

Poroszlai, I. 2000a Excavation campaigns at the Bronze Age tell site at Százhalombatta-Földvár. In I. Poroszlai and M. Vicze (eds.) *Százhalombatta Archaeological Expedition Annual Report 1*. Százhalombatta: Archaeolingua, pp. 13-73.

Poroszlai, I. 2000b Die Grabungen in der Tell-Siedlung von Bölcske-Vörösgyűrű (Kom. Tolna) (1965-1967). *ActaArchHung* **51**: 111-45.

Poroszlai, I. 2003a The conservation and exhibition of archaeological remains: Archaeological parks and experimental archaeology. In Z. Visy (ed.) *Hungarian Archaeology at the Turn of the Millenium*. Budapest: Department of Monuments of the Ministry of Cultural Heritage, pp. 432-35.

Poroszlai, I. 2003b Fortified centres along the Danube. In Z. Visy (ed.) *Hungarian Archaeology at the Turn of the Millenium*. Budapest: Department of Monuments of the Ministry of Cultural Heritage, pp. 151–55.

Poroszlai, I. and M. Vicze 2004 *Százhalombatta Története a Bronzkortól Napjainkig. A Százhalombattai "Matrica" Múzeum Állandó Kiállításának Katalógusa*. Százhalombatta: Matrica Museum.

Poulsen, J. 1980 Om arealudnyttelsen i bronzealderen : nogle praktiske synspunkter og nogle synspunkter om praksis. In H. Thrane (ed.) *Bronzealderbebyggelse i Norden. Beretning fra det andet nordiske symposium for bronzealderforskning.* Skrifter fra Historisk Institut. Odense: Odense Universitet, pp. 142–64.

Prescott, C. 2004 Trial excavations at the stratigraphic section 1998. In C. Mühlenbock and C. Prescott (eds.) *The Scandinavian Sicilian Archaeological Project. Archaeological excavations at Monte Polizzo Sicily. Reports 1998–2001*. GOTARC Serie C. No. 56. Göteborg: University of Gothenburg, pp. 51–55.

Prescott, Christopher and E. Walderhaug 1995 The last frontier? Processes of Indo-Europeanization in Northern Europe: The Norwegian case. *The Journal of Indo-European Studies* **23**(3–4): 257–78.

Prescott, C. and C. Mühlenbock 2003 Mt. Polizzo, Sicily: Preliminary views on Elymians and ethnicity, landscape and identity. The Nordic TAG Conference, *Scandinavian Archaeological Practice in Theory: Proceedings from the 6th Nordic TAG, Oslo 2001*. Oslo: Institutt for arkeologi, kunsthistorie og konservering, Universitetet i Oslo, pp. 26–37.

Price, D. et al 2004 Strontium isotopes and prehistoric human migration: The Bell Beaker period in central Europe. *European Journal of Archaeology* **7**(1): 9–40.

Primas, M. 2008 *Bronzezeit zwischen Elbe und Po*. Strukturwandel in Zentraleuropa 2200–800 v. Chr. Universitätsforschungen zur prähistorischen Archäologie. Band 150. Bonn: Verlag Dr. Rudolf Habelt Gmbh.

Quillfeldt, I. Von 1995 *Die Vollgriffschwerter in Süddeutschland*. Prähistorische Bronzefunde, Abt. 4, Bd. 11. Stuttgart: Franz Steiner Verlag.

Rahmstorf, L. 2006 Zur Ausbreitung vorderasiatischer Innovationen in die frühbronzezeeeitliche Ägäis. *Praehistorische Zeitschrift* **81**(1): 49–96.

Randborg, K. 1974 Social stratification in Early Bronze Age Denmark: a study in the regulation of cultural systems. *Praehistorische Zeitschrift* **49**: 38–61.

Rasmussen, K. L. and J.-H. Bech in press. On the provenance of the ceramics from Bjerre. In J.-H. Bech, B. V. Eriksen, and K. Kristiansen (eds.) *Bronze Age Settlement Structure and Land Use in Thy Northwest Denmark – primarily based on settlements from Bjerre Enge, Northern Thy*. Højbjerg: Jutland Archaeological Society.

Rasmussen, M. 1993. Bopladskeramik i Ældre Bronzealder. *Jysk Arkæologisk Selskabs Skrifter* **XXIX**: 1–148.

Rasmussen, M. 1993 Gravhøje og Bopladser. En foreløbig Undersøgelse af Lokalisering og Sammenhænge. *Bronsålderens gravhögar. Report Series* **48**: 171–85. Lund: University of Lund. Institute of Archaeology.

Rasmussen, M. 1995 Settlement structure and economic variation in the Early Bronze Age. *Journal of Danish Archaeology* **11**: 87–107.

Rasmussen, M. 1999 Livestock without bones. The long-house as contributer to the interpretation of lifestock management in the Southern

Scandinavian Early Bronze. In C. Fabech and J. Ringtved (eds.) *Settlement and Landscape. Proceedings of a conference in Århus, Denmark, May 4–7 1998.* Aarhus: Jutland Archaeological Society, pp. 281–90.

Rasmussen, P. 1996 Pollenanalyser fra Gundsomagle So, Nordsjaelland. In Geobotanske Undersogelser af Kulturlandskabets Historie. Pollenanalyser fra gravhoje og soer i 1995. Udarbejet for Skov – og Naturstyrelsen. *GEUS Rapport* **8**: 27–46.

Renfrew, C. 1998 From here to ethnicity. In Jonathan Hall: Review feature: Ethnic identity in Greek antiquity. *Cambridge Archaeological Journal* **8**(2): 275–77.

Renfrew, C. 2001 Commodification and institutions in group-oriented and individualizing socieities. In W. G. Runciman (ed.) *The Origin of Human Social Institutions*. Oxford University Press, pp. 93–119.

Rice, P. 1984 Change and conservatism in pottery-producing systems. In S. E. van der Leeuw and A. C. Pritchard (eds.) *The Many Dimensions of Pottery. Ceramics in Archaeology and Anthropology*. Amsterdam: Universiteit van Amsterdam, pp. 231–88.

Riederer, J. 2004 Anhang: Ergebnisse metalanalytischer Undersuchungen von Bronzeschwertern. In H. Wüstemann *Die Schwerter in Ostdeutschland*. Stuttgart: Prähistorische Bronzefunde, Abteilung IV, Band 15.

Roland, Fletcher. 1986 Settlement archaeology: World-wide comparisons. *World Archaeology* **18**: 59–83.

Rønne, P. 1987 Stilvariationer i ældre bronzealder: Undersøgelser over lokalforskelle i brug af ornamenter og oldsager i ældre bronzealders anden periode. *Årbøger for Nordisk Oldkyndighed og Historie* 1986: 125–46.

Roymans, N. 1999 Man, cattle and the supernatural in the Northwest European plain. In C. Fabech and J. Ringtved (eds.) *Settlement and Landscape. Proceedings of a conference in Århus, Denmark May 4–7, 1998*: 291–300. Århus: Jutland Archaeological Society.

Roymans, N. and H. Fokkens 1991 Én overzicht van veertig Jaar nederzettingsonderzoek in de lage Landen. In H. Fokkens and N. Roymans (eds.) *Nederzettingen uit de bronstijd en de vroege Ijzertijd in de lage landen* Norwegian Archaeological Review **13**: 1–19

Rundin, J. 1996 A politics of eating: Feasting in early Greek Society. *American Journal of Philology* **117**(2): 179–215.

Rye, O. 1981 *Pottery Technology: Principles and reconstruction*. Washington: Taraxum.

Sahlins, M. 1958 *Social Stratification in Polynesia*. Washington University Press.

Sanders, William, J. Parsons and R. Santley 1979 *The Basin of Mexico: Ecological Processes in the Evolution of Civilization*. New York: Academic Press.

Sanjek, R. 1996 Household. In A. Barnard and J. Spencer (eds.) *Encyclopedia of Social and Cultural Anthropology*. London: Routledge, pp. 285–87.

Sarauw, T. 2006 Bejsebakken. *Late Neolithic Houses and Settlement Structure. Nordiske Fortidsminder. Serie C*, volume 4. Copenhagen: Det Kongelige Nordiske Old Skriftsselskab.

Sarauw, T. 2007a. On the outskirts of the European Bell Beaker phenomenon – the Danish case. *Offa*, www.jungsteinsite.de.

Sarauw, T. 2007b Male symbols or warrior identities. The "archery burials" of the danish Bell Beaker culture. *Journal of Anthropological Archaeology* **26**: 65–87.

Shanks, M. 1999 *Art and the Early Greek State. An Interpretative Archaeology*. Cambridge: Cambridge University Press.

Shennan, S. 1993 Commodities, transactions and growth in the central European Early Bronze Age. *Journal of European Archaeology* **1**(2): 59–72.

Sherratt, A. 1993 What would a Bronze-Age world system look like? Relations between temperate Europe and the Mediterranean in later prehistory. *Journal of European Archaeology* **1**(2): 1–58.

Sherratt, A. 1997 *Economy and Society in Prehistoric Europe. Changing Perspectives*. Edinburgh: Edinburgh University Press.

Shishlina, N. I. 2001 The seasonal cycle of grassland use in the Caspian Sea steppe: A new approach to an old problem. *European Journal of Archaeology* **4**: 323–46.

Sillar, B. 2000 Dung by preference: The choice of fuel as an example of how Andean pottery production is embedded within wider technical, social, and economic practices. *Archaeometry* **42**(1): 43–60.

Simon, L. (ed.) 2006 *Régészeti kutatások másfél millió négyzetméteren. Autópálya és gyorsforgalmi utak építését megelőző régészeti feltárások Pest Megyében 2001–2006*. Szentendre 2006.

Sofaer, J. 2006a *The Body as Material Culture. A Theoretical Osteoarchaeology*. Cambridge: Cambridge University Press.

Sofaer, J. R. 2006b Pots, houses and metal: Technological relations at the Bronze Age tell at Százhalombatta, Hungary. *Oxford Journal of Archaeology* **25**(2): 127–47.

Sofaer, J. and M. L. S. Sørensen 2002 Becoming cultural: Society and the incorporation of bronze. In B. Ottaway and E. C. Wager (eds.) *Metals and society: Papers from a session held at the European Association of Archaeologists sixth annual meeting in Lisbon 2000*. BAR International Series 1061. Oxford: Archaeopress, pp. 117–21.

Sofaer, J. and M. L. S. Sørensen, 2005 Technological change as social change: The introduction of metal in Europe. In M. Bartelheim and V. Heyd (eds.) *Continuity – Discountinuity: Transition Periods in European Prehistory. Forschungen zur Archäometrie und Altertumswissenschaft*. Rahden (Westf.): Verlag Marie Leidorf.

Somogyi, K. 2000 Előzetes jelentés a Kaposvár-61-es út elkerülő szakasz 1. számú lelőhelyén végzett feltárásról. (Preliminary report of the excavation of site No. 1 situated on the encircling section of Road 61 around Kaposvár.) *SMK* **14**: 245–49.

Somogyi, K. 2004 Előzetes jelentés a Kaposvár-61-es út elkerülő szakasz 29. számú lelőhelyén, Kaposújlak-Várdomb-dűlőben 2002-ben végzett megelőző feltárásról. *SMK* **16**: 167–178.

Sørensen, M. L. S. 1996 Women as/and metalworkers. In A. Devonshire and B. Wood (eds.) *Women in Industry and Technology from Prehistory to the Present Day*. London: Museum of London, pp. 45–51.

Sørensen, M. L. S. 2000 *Gender Archaeology*. Cambridge: Polity Press.

Sørensen, M. L. S. 2007. English and Danish Iron Ages – A comparison through houses, burials and hoards. In C. Haselgrove and Rachel Pope (eds.) *The Earlier Iron Age in Britain and the Near Continent*. Oxford: Oxbow Books, pp. 328–37.

Sørensen, M. L. S. and K. Rebay 2008. Interpreting the body: Burial practices at the Middle Bronze Age cemetery at Pitten. *Archaeologia Austriaca* **89**: 153–75.

Sørensen, M. L. S. and Rebay-Salisbury, K. 2009 Landscapes of the body: Burials of the middle Bronze Age in Hungary. *European Journal of Archaeology* **11** (1): 49–74.

Sørensen, M. L. S. and M. Vicze forthcoming In M. Mandella, G. Kovacs, and B. Kulcsarne-Berzsenyi (eds.) *Household*.

Sørensen, M. L. S. and M. Vicze in press. In I. Poroszlai and M. Vicze (eds.) *Százhalombatta Archaeological Expedition Report III*. Százhalombatta: Matrica Museum.

Spatafora, F. 1996 La ceramica indigena a decorazione impressa e incise nella Sicilia centro-occidentale: diffusione e pertinenza etnica. *Sicilia Archaeologica* **29**: 99–110.

Spatafora, F. 1997 Ricerche e prospezioni nel territorio di Corleone: insediamenti preistorici e centri indigeni. Seconde giornate internazionali di studi sull'area elima. *Atti Gibellina* 1994: 1273–1286. Pisa – Gibellina: Scuola normale superiore di Pisa.

Spatafora, F. 2003 *Monte Maranfusa. Un insediamento nella media Valle del Belice. L'abitato indigeno*. Palermo: Beni Culturi.

Spatafora, F. and G. Mannino 1992 Matreriali prehistorici dal territorio di Salemi: la Mokarta. *Giornate Internazionali do Studi sull'area elima Atti II*: pp. 567–75.

Sperber, L. 1999 Zu den Schwertgräbern im westlichen Kreis der Urnenfelderkultur: profane und religiöse Aspekte. In *Eliten der Bronzezeit*. Bonn: Römisch-Germanisches Zentralmuseum, Monografien Band 43.1. Rudolf Habelt, pp. 605–60.

Spriggs, M. 2008 Ethnographic parallels and the denial of history. *World Archaeology* **40**(4): 538–52.

Steinberg, John 1996 Ploughzone sampling in Denmark: Isolating and interpreting site signatures form disturbed contexts. *Antiquity* **70**: 368–92.

Steinberg, J. M 1997 *The Economic Prehistory of Thy, Denmark: A Study of the Changing Value of Flint Based on a Methodology of the Plowzone*. Unpublished Ph.D dissertation. Department of Anthropology, University of California, Los Angeles.

Stevanović, M. 2002 Burned houses in the Neolithic of south-east Europe. In D. Gheorghiu (ed.) *Fire in Archaeology*. Oxford: B.A.R, pp. 55–62.

Stika, H.-P. 2005 Preliminary Report on the Archaeobotanical Remains (2003 season) from Monte Polizzo (sixth–fourth century B.C. and twelfth century A.D.) and Salemi (fifth and fourth century B.C.) in Sicily. Appendix 6 (267–274). In I. Morris, et al Stanford University Excavations on the Acropolis of Monte Polizzo, Sicily, IV: Preliminary Report on the 2003 Season. *Memoirs American Academy Rome* **49**(2004): 197–279.

Stika, H.-P., A. G. Heiss, and B. Zach 2008 Plant remains from early Iron Age in Western Sicily – Differences in subsistence strategies of Greek and Elymian sites. *Vegetation History and Archaeobotany* **17** (Supplement 1): 139–148.

Stika, H.-P. and A. G. Heiss, in prep. a. Preliminary report on the investigations of archaeobotanical remains from Early Iron Age Monte Polizzo and Late Bronze Age Mokarta (campaign 2004). *Memoirs of the American Academy in Rome.*

Stika, H.-P. and A. G. Heiss, in prep. b. Analysis of plant macroremains from the Norwegian/Swedish excavations at Monte Polizzo, House 1.

Strahm, C. 2002 Tradition und Wandel der sozialen Strukturen vom 3. Zum 2. Vorchristlichen Jahrtausend. In J. Müller (ed.) *Vom Endneolithicum zur Frühbronzezeit: Muster sozialen Wandels?* Tagung Bamberg 14.-16. Juni 2001. UPA 90: 175–95.

Strathern, M. 1988 *The Gender of the Gift: Problems with Women and Problem with Society in Melanesia.* Berkley: University of California Press.

Streiffert Eikeland, K. 2006 *Indigenous Households. Transculturation of Sicily and Southern Italy in the Archaic Period.* GOTARC Series B, No. 44. Gothenburg Archaeological Thesis. Göteborg: University of Gothenburg.

Streiffert, J. 2004 Hus från bronsåldern och äldre järnåldern i Bohuslän. In P. Claesson and B. Munkenberg (eds.) *Landskap och bebyggelse.* Uddevalla: Bohusläns Museum, pp. 135–54.

Streiffert, J. 2004 Två rum och kök – spår av rumsbildning i halländska boningshus under bronsålder och äldre järnålder. In L. Carlie, E. Ryberg, J. Streiffert, and P. Wranning (eds.) *Hållplatser i det förgångna,* pp. 190–224.

Streiffert, J. 2005. *Gårdsstrukturer i Halland under bronsålder och alder järnålder.* Riksantikvarieämbetet. Arkeologiska undersökningar. Skrifter No 66 and GOTARC. Series B. Gothenburg Archaeological Theses No 39. Stockholm and Gothenburg.

Sumegi, P. 2008 'Pollen analyses of the lower Benta valley.' Unpublished report to the National Science Foundation.

Sumegi, P. and Bodor, E. 2006 Report on the findings of the geoarchaeological and archaeobotanical analyses carried in the valley of the Benta (Bekas) Creek. *The Sax Project,* Vol. 2. Százhalombatta: Matricia Museum.

Svedhage, K. 1997 *Tanumsslätten med omgivning.* Rapport 1997, 13. Uddevalla: Bohusläns Museum.

Szabó, G. 2003 The Expanding World: Masters of Bronzeworking in the Carpathian Basin. In Zs. Visy (ed.) *Hungarian Archeology in the Turn of the Millenium,* Ministry of National Cultural Heritage. Budapest, 163–67.

Szalontai, Cs. and K. Tóth 2003 Szeged-Kiskundorozsma-Nagyszék I, II, Szeged-Kiskundorozsma-Subasa. In Cs. Szalontai (ed.) *Úton útfélen! Múzeumi kutatások az M5 autópálya nyomvonalán* Szeged: Móra Ferenc Múzeum, 63–96.

Szathmári, I. 1992 Füzesabony-Öregdomb. In W. Meier-Arendt (ed.) *Bronzezeit in Ungarn. Forschungen in Tell-Siedlungen an Donau und Theiss.* Frankfurt: Pytheas, pp. 134–40.

Sz. Máthé, M. 1988 Bronze Age tells in the Berettyó valley. In T. Kovács and I. Stanczik (eds.) *Bronze Age tell settlements of the great Hungarian plain.* Budapest: Inventaria Praehistorica Hvngariae, pp. 27–122.

Tárnoki, J. 2003 The Expansion of the Hatvan Culture. In Z. B. Kiss (ed.) *Hungarian Archaeology at the Turn of the Millennium.* Ministry of National Cultural Heritage. Budapest, pp. 145–48.

Taylor, T. 2008 Materiality. In R. A. Bentley, H. D. G. Maschner and C. Chippingdale (eds.) *Handbook of Archaeological Theories*. New York: Alta Mira Press.

Tesch, S. 1993. *Houses, farmsteads and long-term change. A regional study of prehistoric settlements in the Köpinge area in Scania, southern Sweden*. Uppsala: Uppsala University.

Thrane, H. 1979 Malede vægge. *Skalk* **3**: 10–13.

Thrane, H. 1980 Nogle tanker om yngre bronzealders bebyggelse på Sydvestfyn. In H. Thrane (ed.) *Bronzealderbebyggelse i Norden. Beretning fra det andet nordiske symposium for bronzealderforskning*. Skrifter fra Historisk Institut. Odense Universitet **28**: 165–73.

Thrane, H. 1994 Centres of wealth in Northern Europe. In K. Kristiansen and J. Jensen (eds.) Europe in the first millennium B.C. *Sheffield Archaeological Monographs* **6**: 95–110.

Thrane, H. 1999a Bronze Age settlement in South Scandinavia – Territoriality and organisation. In A. F. Harding *Experiment and Design. Archaeological Studies in Honour of John Coles*. Oxford: Oxbow Monographs, pp. 123–32.

Thrane, H. 1999b Ridedyret. *Skalk* **1**: 12–14.

Thrane, H. 2003 Diachronic settlement studies in the south Scandinavian lowland zone – The Danish perspective. In H. Thrane (ed.) *Diachronic Settlement Studies in the Metal Ages. Report on the ESF workshop Moesgård, Denmark, 14–18 October 2000*. Aarhus: Jutland Archaeological Society / Aarhus University Press, pp. 13–27.

Tilley, C. 1999 *Metaphor and Material Culture*. Oxford: Blackwell Publishers.

Tilley, C. et al (eds.) 2006 *Handbook of Material Culture*. London: Sage.

Tinner W. et al in press. *Long-term interactions of Climate, Land-use, Fire, and Vegetation at Gorgo Basso, a Coastal Lake in Southern Sicily, Italy*.

Treherne, P. 1995 The warrior´s beauty: The masculine body and self-identity in Bronze-Age Europe. *Journal of European Archaeology* **3**(1).

Tringham, R. 2005 Weaving house life and death into places: A blueprint for a hypermedia narrative. D. Bailey, A. Whittle, and V. Cummings (eds.) *Unsettling the Neolithic*. Oxford: Oxbow, pp. 98–111.

Tusa, S. 1992 *La Sicilia nella Preistoria*. Palermo: Sellerio.

Tusa, S. 1998 Ethnic development and political formation in Sicily between II and I millennia BC. In M. Pearce and M. Tosi (eds.) *Papers from the EAA Third Annual Meeting at Ravenna 1997: Volume I: Pre- and Protohistory*, Oxford: British Archaeological Reports (International Series 717), pp. 284–89.

Tusa, S. 1999 Short-term cultural dynamics within the mediterranean cultural landscape. In R. H. Tykot, J. Morterand, J. E. Robb (eds.) *Social Dynamics of the Prehistoric Central Mediterranean*. Accordia Specialist Studies on the Mediterranean. London: Accordia Research Institute, University of London, pp. 149–83.

Tusa, S. 2000 Ethnic dynamics during pre- and proto-history of Sicily. *Journal of Cultural Heritage*. **1** (Supplement 2): 17–28.

Tusa, S. 2001 Mediterranean perspective and cultural integrity of Sicilian Bell Beakers. In F. Nicolis (ed.) *Bell Beakers today. Pottery, people, culture, symbols in prehistoric Europe*. Proceedings of the International Colloquium Riva del Garda (Trento, Italy) 11–16 May 1998. Volume I, pp. 173–186, Provincia Autonoma di Trento. Servizio Beni Culturali. Ufficio Benu Archeologici.

Tusa, S. and F. Nicoletti 2000 Gli Elimi. Giornate Internazionali do Studi sull'area elima *Atti elimi* **III**: 963–77.

Tusa, V. 1972 Monte Polizzo – scavo 1970. *Sicilia Archaeologica* **5**: 119–21.

Tylecote, R. F. 1987 *The Early History of Metallurgy.* London: Longman.

Uhnér, C. 2005 Tells and the tell-building tradition in the Carpathian basin during the Middle Bronze Age. In J. Goldhahn (ed.) *Mellan sten och järn. Rapport från det 9:e nordiska bronsålderssymposiet, Göteborg 2003–10–09/12. Del 2.* GOTARC Serie C. *Arkeologiska Skrifter* No 59. Göteborg: University of Gothenburg, pp. 745–53.

Ullen, I. 1994 The power of case studies. Interpretation of a late Bronze Age settlement in central Sweden. *Journal of European Archaeology* **2**(2): 249–62.

Ullén, I. 2003 Bronsåldersboplatsen vid Apalle i Uppland. Uppland, Övergrans sn, Apalle, RAÄ 260. Arkeologi på väg – undersökningar för E18. *Riksantikvarieämbetet UV Uppsala Rapport 1997*: 64.

Valamoti, S. 2002 Food remains from Bronze Age Archondiko and Mesimeriani Toumba in northern Greece. *Vegetation History and Archaeobotany* **11**: 17–22.

Van Der Leeuw, S. 1993 Giving the potter a choice. Conceptual aspects of pottery techniques. In P. Lemonnier (ed) *Technological Choices: Transformation in Material Cultures Since the Neolithic.* London: Routledge, pp. 238–88.

Vandkilde, H. 1996 *From Stone to Bronze. The Metalwork of the Late Neolithic and Earliest Bronze Age in Denmark.* Jutland Archaeological Society Publications XXXII. Aarhus: Aarhus University Press.

Vandkilde, H. 1999 Social distinction and ethnic reconstruction in the earliest Danish Bronze Age. In *Eliten der Bronzezeit*: 245–76. Römisch-Germanisches Zentralmuseum, Monografien Band 43.1. Bonn: Rudolf Habelt.

Vandkilde H. 2005 A biographical perspective on Ösenringe from the early Bronze Age. In T. L. Kienlin (ed.) *Die Dinge als Zeichen: Kulturelles Wissen und materielle Kultur: 263–81.* Universitätsforschungen zur prähistorichen Archäologie. Band 127. Bonn: Verlag Rudolf Habelt Gmbh.

Vandkilde, H. 2006 A review of the Early Late Neolithic Period in Denmark: Practice, identity and connectivity. *Offa*, www.jungsteinsite.de.

Vandkilde, H. 2006 Warriors and warrior institutions in Copper Age Europe. In T. Otto, H. Thrane, and H. Vandkilde (eds.) *Warfare and Society. Archaeological and Social Anthropological Perspectives.* Aarhus: Aarhus University Press.

Vandkilde, H. 2007 *Culture and Change in Central European Prehistory: 6th to 1st millennium BC.* Aarhus: Aarhus University Press.

Van Dommelen, P. 2006 Colonial matters: Material culture and postcolonial theory in colonial situations. In C. Tilley et al (eds.) *Handbook of Material Culture.* London: Sage, pp. 104–24.

Varberg, J. 2005a Flint og metal – mellem stenalder og bronzealder i Sydskandinavien. In J. Goldhahn (ed.) *Mellan sten och järn. Rapport från det 9:e nordiska bronsålderssymposiet, Göteborg 2003–10–09/12. Del 1.* GOTARC Serie C. *Arkeologiska Skrifter* No 59. Göteborg: University of Gothenburg, pp. 67–79.

Varberg, J. 2005b Oprindelsen til en ny tidsalder. Mellem stenalder og bronzealder i Sydskandinavien 2350–1700 BC. *Fornvännen* 2: 81–95.

Varga, A. 2000 Coring results at Százhalombatta-Földvár. In I. Poroszlai and M. Vicze (eds.) *Százhalombatta archaeological expedition, annual report 1*, pp. 75–81. Budapest: Matrica Museum.

Vassallo, S. (ed.) 1999 *Colle Madore: un caso di ellenizzazione in terra sicana*. Palermo.

Vecchio, P., M. Kolb, and G. Mammina 2003 Tracces di un insediamento del IV secolo a.C. a Salemi (TP). *Sicilia Archeologica* 101: 114–21.

Vianello, A. 2005 *Late Bronze Age Mycenaean and Italic Products in the West Mediterranean. A social and economic approach*. Oxford: BAR International Series 1439.

Vianello, A. 2008 Late Bronze Age Aegean trade routes in the western Mediterranean. In H. Whittaker (ed.) *The Aegean Bronze Age in relation to the wider European Context*. BAR International Series 1745. Oxford: Archaeopress, pp. 7–35.

Vickers, M. and D. Gill 1994 *Artful Crafts: Ancient Greek Silverware and Pottery*. Oxford: Clarendon Press.

Victor, H. 2002 Med graven som granne. *Om bronsålderns kulthus*. Aun 30. Uppsala: Uppsala universitet.

Vicze, M. 1992. Die Bestattungen der Vatya-kultur. In W. Meier-Arendt (ed.) *Bronzezeit in Ungarn. Forschungen in Tell-Siedlungen an Donau und Thiess*. Frankfurt am Main: Museum für Vor- und Frühgeschichte, Archaeologisches museum. pp. 92–95.

Vicze, M. 1993 Les pratiques funéraires de la culture de Vatya. In Le Bel Age du Bronze en Hongrie, *Mont-Beuvray* 1993: 92–95, 146–48.

Vicze, M. 2000 Background information to the field-survey. In I. Poroszlai and M. Vicze (eds.) *Százhalombatta archaeological expedition, annual report 1*. Budapest: Matrica Museum, pp. 119–25.

Vicze, M. 2001 Dunaújváros – Duna-dűlő. *The Early and Middle Bronze Age cemetery of Dunaújváros – Kosziderpadlás*. Unpublished PhD thesis. Eötvös Loránd University, Budapest.

Vicze, M. 2001 *Dunaújváros-Duna-dűlő. The Early and Middle Bronze Age cemetery of Dunaújváros-Kosziderpadlás*. Unpublished PhD dissertation, Budapest University.

Vicze, M. 2005 Excavation methods and some preliminary results of the SAX project. In I. Poroszlai and M. Vicze (eds.) *Százhalombatta archaeological expedition, annual report 2*. Budapest: Matrica Museum, pp. 65–80.

Vicze, M. 2008 Middle Bronze Age urn cemetery at Szigetszentszentmiklós-Ürgehegy. In M. Gyöngyössy (ed.) *Perspectives of the Past*. Szentendre: Pest Megyei Múzeumok Igazgatósága, pp. 43–44.

Vicze, M., Z. O. Czijlik, L. Timar, 2005 Aerial and topographical research of the Berta Valley. In I. Poroszlai and M. Vicze (eds.) *Százhalombatta archaeological Expedition, Report 2*. Budapest: Matrica Museum, pp. 251–54.

Vicze, M., T. Earle, and M. Artursson 2005 Bronze Age site gazetteer: Benta Valley, Hungary. In I. Poroszlai and M. Vicze (eds.) *Százhalombatta Archaeological Expedition, Report 2*. Százhalombatta: Matrica Museum, pp. 237–50.

Viklund, K. 1998 *Cereals, Weeds and Crop Processing. Methodological and Interpretative Aspects of Archaeobotanical Evidence* (Archaeology and Environment 14). Umeå: University of Umeå.

Vretemark, M. 1995. Stadsmiljöns livsbetingelser speglade i animalosteologiska material. In G. Dahlberg (ed.) Miljö och livskvalitet under vikingatid och medeltid. *Runica et Mediaevalia Opuscula* **3**: 99–123.

Vretemark, M. 2003 Djurbenen från Hus 1, Monte Polizzo, Sicilien. ANL Rapport 2003: 30. Göteborgs Universitet.

Vretemark, M. 2005 När rester av död blir glimtar av liv. In *Arkeologiska möten utmed väg 26 Borgunda-Skövde*. Skrifter från Västergötlands museum nr 33.

Vretemark, M. 2008 Osteologisk analys av benmaterial från Mörtlösa, Rystad sn utanför Linköping, Östergötland. *Rapport* Riksantikvarieämbetet UV Öst.

Vretemark, M. and S. Sten 2005 Diet and animal husbandry during the Bronze Age. In *Szazhalombatta Archaeological Expedition. Report 2*. Százhalombatta: Matrica Muzeum.

Vretemark, M. and S. Sten 2008 Skeletal manipulations of dogs at the Bronze Age site of Szahalombatta-Földvar in Hungary. In *Anthropological Approaches to Zooarchaeology. Proceeding of the ICAZ Conference of Archaeozoology in Mexico 2006*. Oxford: Oxbow Books.

Vretemark, M. and S. Sten, in prep. The faunal and human remains of Szazhalombatta Földvar.

Waterson, R. 1997 *The Living House. An Anthropology of Architecture in South-East Asia*. Oxford: Oxford University Press.

Webley, L. 2007. "Households and social change in Jutland 500 BC – AD 200. In C. Haselgrove and H. Moore (eds.) *The Later Iron Age in Britain and Beyond*. Oxford: Oxbow, pp. 454–67.

Weiner, A. B. 1992 *Inalienable Possessions: The Paradox of Keeping While Giving*. Berkeley: University of California Press.

White, K. D. 1970. Wheat-farming in Roman times. *Antiquity* **37**: 207–12.

Willcox, G. 2002 Charred plant remains from a late 10th century millennium kitchen at Jerf el Ahmar (Syria). *Vegetation History and Archaeobotany* **11**: 55–60.

Willis, K. J. 1997 The impact of early agriculture upon the Hungarian landscape. In J. C. Chapman and P. Dalukanov (eds.) *Landscapes in Flux: Central and Eastern Europe in Antiquity*, pp. 193–207.

Willis, K. J. et al 1998 Prehistoric land degradation in Hungary: Who, how and why? *Antiquity* **72**: 101–13.

Zimmerman, A. 1996 Zur Bevölkerungsdichte in der Urgeschichte Mitteleuropas. In I. Campen, J. Hahn and M. Uerpmann (eds.) *Festschrift Müller-Beck: Spuren der Jagd – Die Jagd nach Spuren*. Tübinger Monographien zur Urgeschichte 11: pp. 49–61.

Zimmermann, W. H. 1998 Pfosten, Ständer und Schwelle und der Übergang vom Pfosten – zum Ständerbau – Eine Studie zu Innovation und Beharrung im Hausbau. *Probleme der Küstenforschung im südlichen Nordseegebiet* **25**: 9–242.

Zohary, D. and M. Hopf 2000 *Domestication of Plants in the Old World. The Origin and Spread of Cultivated Plants in West Asia, Europe and the Nile Valley*. Oxford: Oxford University Press.

Zorn, Jeffrey 1994 Estimating the population size of ancient settlements: Methods, problems, solutions, and a case study. *Bulletin of the American Schools of Oriental Research* **295**: 31–48.

Index

Agency
  identity/ethnicity in, 8–9
  materiality in, 12–14
Almhov settlement structure, 91, 92f
Amber, 12, 19, 84, 133, 225, 227, 231, 234
Andersen, S. T., 36
Annales framework, application of, 2–3
Apalle
  domestic animal species distribution, 156, 157f
  settlement structure, 94, 95f
  subsistence strategies, 158
Arnoldussen, S., 244
Art and Agency (Gell), 8
Artemisia, 47, 48
Ås settlement, 96
Aurochs *(Bos primigenius)*, 169

Badger *(Meles meles)*, 159
Barley *(Hordeum vulgare* var. *nudum)*, 160, 162–164, 170–171, 177, 180–181
Barley *(Secale)*, 48
Batorliget (Hungary), 48
Battle Axe cultures, 16, 18
Bear *(Ursus arctos)*, 158, 169
Beaver *(Castor fiber)*, 158, 169
Bech, J.-H., 97
Becker, C. J., 31
Bedstraw species *(Galium* sp.), 173
Beech, 48
Beetroot *(Beta vulgaris)*, 162
Bejsebakken settlement structure, 90
Beklasket, 188
Belgium, settlement changes in, 62
Bell Beaker cultures, 18, 102–104, 198

Benta Valley (Hungary)
  Age settlements, 71
  agriculture in, 72, 78, 103
  animal husbandry, 45–48, 70, 103
  Bell Beaker cultures, 18, 102–104, 198
  Bia hillfort, 73, 76, 108, 113
  bronze working in, 103
  ceramics, 104, 105, 107, 113–114
  chiefdoms/political hierarchy in, 70, 72–77, 85–86, 101, 114, 120, 222, 245
  clay mining in, 104
  cremation urn cemeteries, 75–76
  cultivation, 46–49, 70
  described, 32, 70, 83t
  Dunakeszi, 110–111
  ecological succession in, 43–49
  Encrusted Ware culture, 109–110
  Érd, 72, 105
  fortifications, 73–74, 76, 77, 83t, 85, 101, 103, 107, 108
  landscape zones, 48–49
  Makó culture, 102–103
  as model, 69
  Nagyrév culture (*See* Nagyrév culture)
  palaeosols, 43–44
  paleo-environmental events generally, 53–56
  palynology, 45–49
  peat formation, 48
  population estimates, 71, 72, 74, 76, 83t, 101, 107, 113, 246
  research methodology, 70–71
  settlement pattern changes, 71–78
  settlement structure, organisation density, 101, 102t

Benta Valley (Hungary) (cont.)
    Early Bronze Age, 102–105
    Late Bronze Age, 102t, 110–114
    Middle Bronze Age, 102t, 105–110
    overview, 87, 100–102, 119–121
    proto-urban, 104, 108, 114
    social hierarchy development, 71–72, 140–142
    soil erosion, 47, 48
    Sóskút hillfort, 72, 73, 76, 105, 108, 113
    staple production, 74, 75
    subregional environmental sequences investigation, 35–36
    subsistence strategies in, 164
    Százhalombatta-Földvár (See Százhalombatta-Földvár)
    Tárnok, 72, 74–76, 105, 108–109, 113–114
    trade in, 70, 72, 74, 75, 84, 101, 102
    Tumulus culture, 110–111
    Urnfield settlements, 21f, 26, 76, 112–114, 120, 248
    Vatya culture (See Vatya culture)
    wealth, finance in, 74, 77–78
Bia hillfort (Hungary), 73, 76, 108, 113
Bifacial sickle manufacture, 189–191, 209–210, 219
Biography in objects, 9
Birds, 158–159, 169, 175
Bitter vetch (Vicia ervilia), 172, 178–179
Bjerre Enge (Denmark)
    agriculture in, 160, 161
    beklasket, 188
    Bjergene 1/2 barrows, 37
    Bjerre 7, 130, 132, 133, 187–190, 210
    ceramics, pottery in, 187, 188
    excavations, analysis of, 4
    households in, 133, 231–233
    metallurgy, 188–191, 210–211
    settlement patterns in, 64
    settlement structure, organisation, 96–98
    stone working, 188–191
    subsistence strategies, 156, 159–162
Blackberry (Rubus fruticosus agg.), 172
Black bindweed (Polygonum convolvulus), 172
Black medic (Medicago lupulina), 172, 173
Blanton, R. E., 245
Bohuslän (Sweden). See also Tanum (Sweden)
    agriculture in, 42, 180
    deforestation, heathland expansion, 40–42
    described, 24
    ecological succession in, 40–42
    fishing, 42
    grazing, 42
    political hierarchy in, 69
    rock art in, 42, 69, 98
    settlement analysis, 68–69, 83t
    settlement structure, organisation, 88, 98–100
    shore displacement, 40
Bornholm settlement structure, 90, 91
Bourdieu, P., 249–250
Brd Gram (Jutland), 132, 133
Bread wheat (Triticum aestivum), 160, 162, 170, 180f
Broomcorn millet (Panicum milliaceum), 170, 173
Built landscapes, 5
Bulgur, 182
Bulrush (Schoenoplectus cf. lacustris), 173
Burials/hoards. See also specific sites
    cremation urn cemeteries, 75–76
    distribution of, 234
    gender divisions in, 17, 239, 241
    identity identifications in, 18, 237, 247–248
    materiality in, 13, 252
    post-2000 BC, 19–21
    in Thy (Denmark), 66f, 67–68, 95, 96, 98, 186, 225
    tumulus, 17, 26, 248
    wealth disposition, analysis of, 7, 11
Bur-reed (Sparganium sp.), 173

Carex, 161
Caryopsis, 180f
Castillo, L. J., 8
Cats, 174
Cattle (cows), 157, 159f, 164–165, 182, 183, 199, 226
Chenopodium (goosefoot), 45
Chenopodium album, 163
Chenopodium bonus-henricus, 48
Chenopodium murale, 48
Chiefdoms. See Political economy; specific sites
Chuddia valley (Sicily)
    agriculture in, 79
    ecological succession in, 49–52
    geology, 50, 51f
    paleo-environmental events generally, 53–56
    population estimates, 79–80
Clover species (Trifolium sp.), 172, 173
Club wheat (T. compactum), 162

Corded Ware cultures, 16, 18
Coriander *(Coriandrum sativum)*, 177
Corn cockle *(Agrostemma githago)*, 173
Cornelian cherry *(Cornus mas)*, 172
Corn gromwell *(Lithospermum arvense)*, 173
Corn salad *(Valerianella dentata)*, 177
Cows (cattle), 157, 159f, 164–165, 182, 183, 199, 226
Craft activities. *See also specific sites*
  organisation of production, 209–212
  overview, 185–186, 217
  relationships, 213–217
Cresta di Gallo. *See* Mokarta (Sicily)

Deforestation, 37–42, 52–53
DeMarrais, E., 8
Denmark, 23
Dente di lupo, 205
Documentation system, 32
Dogs, 158, 164, 166, 174
The Domestication of Europe (Hodder), 4
Donkeys, 174
Dunakeszi, 110–111

Earle, T., 2, 8
Early Bronze Age, 22
The Early Mesoamerican Village (Flannery), 4
Economy. *See also* Trade; Wealth
  material basis of, 18
  political *(See* Political economy)
  post-2000 BC, 20
Einkorn *(T. monococcum)*, 162, 170, 171, 177
Elderberry *(Sambucus nigra, S. ebulus)*, 172
Elk *(Alces alces)*, 159
Elm *(Ulmus* spp.), 181f
Emmer *(Triticum dicoccum)*, 160–163, 170, 177, 180f
Encrusted Pottery culture, 194
Encrusted Ware culture, 109–110
Érd, 72, 105
Ermine *(Mustela erminea)*, 169
Ethelberg, P., 129

Faba bean *(V. faba)*, 172, 177, 178–179, 180f
Family, origins of, 16–19
Fat hen *(Chenopodium album)*, 161
Feudvar, 241
Field brome *(Bromus arvensis)*, 161, 173
Fig *(Ficus carica)*, 177

Filipendula, 45
Flax *(Linum usitatissimum)*, 163, 177
Fokkens, H., 123, 126
Fontijn, D., 244
Fortifications
  Bia hillfort, 73, 76, 108, 113
  Hungary, 73–74, 76, 77, 83t, 85, 101, 103, 107, 108
  Scandinavia (Southern), 92, 94
  Sóskút hillfort, 72, 73, 76, 105, 108, 113
  Százhalombatta-Földvár (Hungary), 254–255
Fox *(Vulpes vulpes)*, 158, 169
Fragtrup, 130, 132, 134

Gell, A., 8
Gender divisions, origins of, 16–19
Gerritsen, F., 123
Giving while keeping concept, 15
Goat, 174
Gold of pleasure *(Camelina sativa)*, 133, 160, 163, 172
Grapevine *(Vitis vinifera)*, 177, 180f
Grog, 194, 202
Gustafsson, S., 163
Gyulavarsand, 194

Haddenham (England), 126
Halstatt, 21f
Hare *(Lepus timidus)*, 158, 169, 175
Hawthorn *(Hippophae rhamnoides)*, 161
Hazel *(Corylus avellana)*, 162
Heather *(Caluna vulgaris, Erica tetralix)*, 161
Helmets, 234
Hicks, D., 6
Hjelle, K., 51
Højgård settlement structure, 92, 93f
Holland, settlement changes in, 62
Hooked/green bristlegrass *(Setaria verticillata/viridis)*, 172, 173
Horse harness, 235, 236f
Horses, 158, 164, 166, 174, 226, 234
Households. *See also specific sites*
  charioteer's, 233–234
  composition of, 125–126
  concepts of, 123–124
  elements of, 124t
  merchant's, 235–236, 237f, 243f
  overview, 122–123, 151–154
  research design, 31–33, 124
  size estimates, 125–126
  trends, long-term, 251–254
  warrior's, 231–233

Hungary
   Benta Valley (*See* Benta Valley [Hungary])
   Bronze Age periods in, 22
   consumption patterns in, 223–225
   described, 24–26
   environment, impact of exploitation of, 250–251
   households in, 123, 126, 127*t*, 151–154, 233–234
   identity in, 239–242
   international trade in, 84
   research design, 30–31
   settlement analysis, 69–71, 83*t*
   settlement structure, organisation, 87, 100–114, 119–121, 220–223, 246
   subregional environmental sequences investigation, 35–36
   subsistence strategies in, 164
   Százhalombatta (*See* Százhalombatta-Földvár [Hungary])
   trade in, 225, 230
   trends, long-term, 251–255

Identity/ethnicity
   agency in, 8–9
   context in, 6
   development of, 236–243
   fluid *vs.* stable, 5–6, 7*f*
   in Hungary, 239–242
   materiality in, 12–14, 243
   Nagyrév culture (*See* Nagyrév culture)
   in Scandinavia (Southern), 237–239
   in Sicily, 242
   swords in (*See* Swords)
   Vatya (*See* Vatya culture)
Institutions
   materialisation (agency) in, 8–9
   overview, 7–8
   political (*See* Political economy)
   power, symbolic meaning in, 12, 13

Juglans (walnut), 46

Kis-Mohos To (Hungary), 48
Klostergaard, 189, 190
Kristiansen, K., 11, 12, 38, 86
Krogstrup, 189, 210

Lago di Pergusa (Sicily), 49
Larsson, T. B., 11, 12
Late Bronze Age, 22
La Tène, 21*f*
Late Neolithic (Dagger Period), 22
Legård
   agriculture in, 161–162
   households in, 130–131, 231–233, 251–252
   settlement patterns in, 65–67
   settlement structure, organisation, 97, 98
   subsistence strategies, 159–162
Leighton, R., 145
Lentil (*Lens culinaris*), 172, 178–179
Limensgård settlement structure, 91
Linseed (*Linum usitatissimum*), 172
Little hodgeweed (*Portulaca oleracea*), 173
Little Ice Age, 50
Long-distance exchange networks, 5. *See also* Trade

Marten (*Martes martes*), 159
Materiality, 10–14
Metallurgy, 19–22, 185. *See also* Wealth; specific sites
Metaphor and Material Culture (Tilley), 13
Millet (*Panicum miliaceum*), 162, 163
Mokarta (Sicily)
   chiefdom/political hierarchy in, 82
   described, 28
   ecological succession in, 49–52
   households in, 146
   population estimates, 79
   settlement analysis, 78–82, 83*t*
   settlement structure, organisation, 116–117
Montagne Grande (Sicily)
   chiefdom/political hierarchy in, 82
   ecological succession in, 50
   population estimates, 81
   settlement analysis, 78–82, 83*t*
Monte Polizzo (Sicily)
   agriculture, 52, 177–178, 180*f*, 181*f*
   analysis of, 4
   animal husbandry, 174–176
   capeduncula, 150, 151
   ceramics, 149, 150, 202–205, 208*t*, 209, 220
   chiefdom/political hierarchy in, 82, 85–86, 118, 120, 230
   craft relationships, 213, 215*t*, 216–217
   described, 26–28, 32, 80
   domestic animal species distributions, 174–176
   drinking, feasting in, 226, 235
   ecological succession in, 49–52

food preparation, processing, 149, 177–178, 183
households in, 146–151, 206–207, 208t
human occupation of, 50
hunting in, 174–175
organisation of production, 210t, 212
population estimates, 81
ritual, spirituality, 150, 151, 235
settlement analysis, 78–82, 83t
settlement structure, organisation, 117–118
site methodology, 176–177
stone working, 205, 208t
storage, 150
subregional environmental sequences investigation, 35–36
subsistence strategies, 173–174, 183–184
trade in, 176, 178–179, 183, 224, 226, 235–236
trends, long-term, 255
weaving, 149, 151, 225–226
Monte Rosa. *See* Salemi (Sicily)

Naesbyholm Storskov (Zealand, Denmark), 39
Nagyrév culture
 house construction, 202
 identity in, 103
 settlement analysis, 72
 settlement structure, organisation, 102–103, 120
 stone working, 195–196
Naked barley (*H. vulgare* var. *nudum*), 170
Nizna Mysl'a, 234
Nordic culture, 23
Nuts (*Amygdalus communis*), 177

Oak, 178, 181f, 191
Oats (*Avena* sp.), 162, 163, 177
Objects in social relations, 8–9 *See also* Swords
Olive tree (*Olea*), 50, 181f
Olsen, A-L Haack, 97
Omaha kinship, 16
Opium poppy (*Papaver somniferum*), 172, 177
Otomani, 21f
Otter (*Lutra lutra*), 158
Outline of a Theory of Practice (Bourdieu), 249–250
Oxen, 157

Palaeo-environments, 34–36
Pea (*Pisum sativum*), 172
Pearlweed (*Sagina*), 47
Persicaria lapathifolium, 163
Persicarias (*Persicaria* spp.), 161
Pigs, 157–158, 164, 166, 174, 182
Pigweed (*Polygonum*), 47
Plantago lanceolata (ribwort), 45
Plantago major/media (plantain), 45, 46
Poa arvensis (grasses), 45
Poggio Roccione. *See* Montagne Grande (Sicily)
Polecat (*Mustela putoris*), 159, 169
Political economy. *See also* Social organization; *specific sites*
 centralised *vs.* decentralised, 246f, 247–249
 household size in, 125
 institutional mechanisms of, 15, 16f
 materialism in, 10–12
 overview, 6–8, 58, 85–86, 243–249
 power, symbolic meaning in, 12–14, 249–250
 study methodology, 1–3
 trade in, 222–231
 trends, long-term, 249–256
Polynesia, political economies/ social stratification in, 2
Poplars (*Populus* sp.), 161
Princes's feather (*Amaranthus*), 47, 48
Property divisions, origins of, 16–19
Prostrate knotweed (*Polygonum aviculare* agg.), 173
Pulses, 172, 177, 178, 183

Red deer (*Cervus elaphus*), 158, 169, 174–176
Reduction firing, 195, 204
Reed (*Phragmites australis*), 173
Religion, post-2000 BC, 19–20
Renfrew, C., 11, 245
Research design overview, 29–33
Rethinking Materiality: the Engagement of Mind with the Material World (Renfrew et al), 13
Rib-grass (*Plantago lanceolata*), 47
Rock art
 in Bohuslän (Sweden), 42, 69, 98
 in Scandinavia (Southern), 225
 in Tanum (Sweden), 68, 98
 trade depiction, 228f, 229f
Roe deer (*Capreolus capreolus*), 158, 169
Rumex acetosella, 163
Rye (*Secale cereale*), 170

Rye brome *(Bromus* cf. *secalinus)*, 162, 163

Safflower *(Carthamus tinctoria)*, 172
Sahlins, M., 2
Salemi (Sicily). *See also* Monte Polizzo (Sicily)
   agriculture, 116
   animal husbandry, 116
   chiefdoms/political hierarchy in, 245
   colonisation of, 116
   international trade in, 84–85
   proto-urban, urban centres, 115, 117–118, 223
   settlement analysis, 78–82, 83*t*
   settlement structure, organisation, 87, 114–118
   trade in, 82, 115
Sarret (Hungary), 48
Sawgrass *(Cladium mariscus)*, 173
Scandinavia (Southern). *See also* Tanum (Sweden); Thy (Denmark)
   Almhov settlement structure, 91, 92*f*
   Ångdala, 156–159
   Apalle *(See* Apalle)
   Bejsebakken settlement structure, 90
   Bornholm settlement structure, 90, 91
   Bulbjerg, 156, 157*f*
   chiefdoms/political hierarchy in, 90–94, 99, 222–231
   consumption patterns in, 223–225
   deforestation in, 39
   described, 22–24
   domestic animals species distribution, 156–159
   environment, impact of exploitation of, 250–251
   farm densities, 61
   fortifications in, 92, 94
   Hasmark, 156, 157*f*
   Højgård settlement structure, 92, 93*f*
   households
      activities, workings, 130–135
      architectural form of, 129–130
      construction of, 191–192
      overview, 122–123, 126–129, 151–154
   identity in, 237–239
   Kirkebjerg, 156–159
   Kolby, 156, 157*f*
   Limensgård settlement structure, 91
   metallurgy, 132–133, 185–186, 223–225
   research design, 30–31
   ritual chiefs in, 237–239
   rock art in, 225
   settlement analysis, 31, 60–61
   settlement structure, organisation, 87–94, 119–121, 220–223, 246
   subregional environmental sequences investigation, 35–36
   subsistence strategies, 156–159, 179–181
   trade in, 84, 89, 91, 159, 225
   Voldtofte, 156, 157*f*, 192, 226
   warrior chiefs in, 90–91, 237–239
Scania
   barrows in, 23
   farm densities, 61
   households in, 128
   metallurgy in, 211
   settlement hierarchy, 68, 69
   settlement structure, organisation, 88, 92*f*, 99
Scleranthus annuus, 163
Sedges *(Carex* spp.), 162
Selinunte (Mazaro del Vallo, Sicily)
   agriculture in, 178–179
   ecological succession in, 52
   trade in, 226, 236
Settlement pattern analysis. *See also specific sites*
   agricultural productivity, 83
   area density estimates, 59
   dwelling-based method, 59
   international trade, 83–85
   openness/closure dynamics, 5
   overview, 4–5, 5*f*, 57–59, 82–86
   population estimates, 59–60
   post-2000 BC, 20–21
   problem formulation, 60
   research design, 31
   structure and organisation of, 87, 119–121
Sheep, 157, 164–166, 174, 182, 183, 223–225
Shennan, S., 11
Sicily
   analysis methodology, 78–79
   Bronze Age periods in, 22
   Chuddia valley *(See* Chuddia valley [Sicily])
   consumption patterns in, 223–225
   described, 26–28
   environment, impact of exploitation of, 251
   households in, 123, 126, 127*t*, 145–154, 235–236, 237*f*, 243*f*
   identity in, 242
   Mokarta *(See* Mokarta [Sicily])

Montagne Grande (*See* Montagne Grande [Sicily])
Monte Polizzo (*See* Monte Polizzo [Sicily])
   research design, 30–31
   settlement analysis, 78–82, 83*t*
   settlement structure, organisation, 87, 114–121, 220–223
   subregional environmental sequences investigation, 35–36
   subsistence strategies, 173–179
   Thapsos, 145
   trade in, 230
   trends, long-term, 255
Sickle (bifacial) manufacture, 189–191, 209–210, 219
Single Grave cultures, 18
Sloe (*Prunus spinosa*), 180*f*
Social organization. *See also* Political economy
   households, Hungary, 71–72, 140–142
   integrative, material approach to, 3–9
   objects in, 8–9 (*See also* Swords)
   Polynesia, 2
   post-2000 BC, 19, 21
   power, symbolic meaning in, 12–14
   Thy (Denmark), 67–68
Solanum nigrum, 163
Sørensen, M. L. S., 214
Sóskút hillfort (Hungary), 72, 73, 76, 105, 108, 113
Spelt (*Triticum spelta*), 160, 161, 162, 170
Spergula arvensis, 163
Stellaria media, 163
Streiffert, J., 123
Subsistence strategies, 155–156, 179–184. *See also specific sites*
Swords
   biographical life, analysis of, 11–12, 234
   burial methods, 14–15
   identity, as symbolic of, 10, 14, 237–242
Symbols in Action (Hodder), 12
Százhalombatta-Földvár (Hungary)
   agriculture in, 165, 170–173, 182–183
   analysis of, 4
   animal husbandry, 144–145, 164–166, 181–182
   bone working, 185, 198–200, 208*t*, 211–212, 219
   burials, 239–241
   ceramics, 144, 192–196, 208*t*, 211, 219–220

   craft relationships, 213–216
   described, 26
   domestic animal species distribution, 164–167
   ecological succession in, 43–49
   Encrusted Pottery culture, 194
   food processing, 142–144, 169, 224
   fortifications, 254–255
   fruits found in, 172
   Füzesabony, 135
   gender distinctions, 216
   Gyulavarsand, 194
   House 3076, 139
   House 3136, 139
   House 3147, 139
   House 3181, 139, 142, 143
   House 3497, 139, 142
   House 4043, 139, 142
   households
      activities, workings, 143–145
      additions, remodeling, 138–140
      architectural character of, 138–140
      artefacts, 138
      authority, ownership, 138
      charioteer's, 233–234
      construction of, 200–202, 208*t*, 212
      hearths, fireplaces, 140–143, 224
      overview, 135–138
      social differences, 71–72, 140–142
   hunting in, 166–167
   identity in, 239–242
   material culture investment, 208
   metallurgy, 144, 195, 197, 199–200, 223–225
   organisation of production, 210*t*, 211–212
   palaeosols, 43–44
   palynology, 45–49
   population estimates, 72, 246
   settlement analysis, 72–76
   settlement structure, organisation, 104, 107–108, 112–113
   site methodology, 170
   stone working, 144, 196–198, 208*t*, 211
   subregional environmental sequences investigation, 35–36
   subsistence requirements in, 168
   subsistence strategies in, 164, 181–183
   Tiszaug-Kéeménytet, 135
   tool making, 144
   trade, 167–169, 182, 197, 225, 230
   woodworking, 195, 196, 212
   wool production, 144, 166, 168, 223–225

Tanum (Sweden)
  agriculture in, 162–164
  animal husbandry in, 158
  artefacts generally, 69, 99
  burial monuments in, 69
  chiefdoms/political hierarchy in, 90, 99, 222, 227
  ecological succession in, 40–42
  fishing in, 158
  house structure in, 128
  international trade in, 98–99
  maritime economy in, 99
  overview, 24, 32–33
  paleo-environmental events generally, 53–56
  population estimates, 100, 246
  rock art in, 68, 98
  settlement analysis, 68–69, 83t
  settlement structure, organisation, 88, 98–100, 119–121
  shore displacement, 40, 41f
  subregional environmental sequences investigation, 35–36
  subsistence strategies, 156, 162–164
  Uddevalla, 99
Tárnok, 72, 74–76, 105, 108–109, 113–114
Technology. *See also specific sites*
  ceramics, 219–220
  post-2000 BC, 20
  tools, 218–219
Tell societies (Hungary). *See also* Benta Valley (Hungary)
  economy of, 102
  giving while keeping in, 15
  overview, 24–26
  settlement structure, organisation, 222–223
  Százhalombatta-Földvár (*See* Százhalombatta-Földvár)
Thisted Museum, 95
Thlaspi arvense, 163
Thy (Denmark)
  agriculture in, 133, 160–162, 180–181
  analysis methodology, 62
  animal husbandry in, 61–62, 130–132, 180
  arrowhead finds in, 96
  artefacts generally, 62, 95, 98
  Ås settlement, 96
  Bjerre Enge (*See* Bjerre Enge [Denmark])
  burial patterns in, 66f, 67–68, 95, 96, 98, 186, 225

ceramics, 131, 133–134, 186–188, 208t, 209, 219
chiefdoms/political hierarchy in, 65, 68, 85–86, 90, 95–98, 207–208, 222–225, 227, 245
craft relationships, 213–214, 215t
cultivation, 38, 39
Damsgard barrow, 37
deforestation, 37–40
described, 61
ecological crises in, 34
farm densities, 61, 63, 64f, 97
food processing, storage in, 133, 160
Fragtrup, 130, 132, 134
grazing/pasture, 38, 39
Hassing Huse Mose profile, 37f
heath vegetation, 38–40
herbs, open-ground, 38
households
  activities, workings, 130–135
  construction of, 191–192, 208t, 251–252
  distributions, 63–65
  structure, 128–130, 181
  warrior's, 231–233
Klostergaard, 189, 190
Krogstrup, 189, 210
Legård (*See* Legård)
lithics, 207, 209–210
material culture investment, 207–208
organisation of production, 209–211
paleo-environmental events generally, 53–56
pollen diagrams, 37f
population estimates, 65, 246
pottery, 131, 133–134, 186–188
settlement analysis, 61–68, 83t
settlement structure, organisation, 88, 95–98, 119–121
social hierarchy in, 67–68
soil degradation, 39–40
stone working, 96, 132–133, 189–191, 207, 209–210, 219
subregional environmental sequences investigation, 35–36
subsistence strategies, 156, 159–162, 179–181
textile production, 133
tool production in, 65–67
trade in, 84, 135
tree succession (natural) in, 36–37
Vilhøj, 132
Visby barrow, 37

Thy Archaeological Project, 23, 32–33, 62, 95, 160, 189
Timopheev's wheat *(Triticum timopheevi Zhuk,* new type glume wheat), 171–172, 182
Trade. *See also* Wealth; *specific sites*
  as control mechanism, 76, 244–246
  in Hungary, 225, 230
  overview, 19–22, 222, 226–231
  in Scandinavia (Southern), 84, 89, 91, 159, 225
  in Sicily, 230
  warrior's control over, 11, 15, 75, 224, 226–231
Troina valley (Sicily), 52–56
Tumulus culture, 21f, 110–111

Urnfield settlements, 21f, 26, 76, 112–114, 120, 248

Vatya culture
  bone working, 198
  ceramics, 192–196
  chiefdoms/political hierarchy in, 72–73
  household activities, 135–136
  identity/ethnicity, 106, 242
  settlement analysis, 71–73, 76
  settlement structure, organisation, 105–109, 120
  stone working, 197
  trade in, 230
Voldtofte (Scandinavia), 156, 157f, 192, 226
Vroue (Scandinavia), 39

Wall germander *(Teucrium* cf. *chamaedrys),* 173

Warfare, post-2000 BC, 20
Warrior aristocracies. *See also* Political economy; Swords
  alliances in, 226–231
  barrows of, 15, 18
  horses and, 166
  households of, 231–233
  overview, 19–22
  Scandinavia (Southern), 90–91, 237–239
  staple production, control over, 74
  trade, control over, 11, 15, 75, 224, 226–231
Wealth. *See also* Trade
  alliance in, 226–231
  as control mechanism, 11, 76, 244–246
  disposition, analysis of, 7, 11
  in Hungary, 74, 77–78
  transmission of, 16–17
Webley, L., 128
Weeds, 163, 172–173
Weiner, A. B., 15
Wheat *(Triticum aestivum),* 162, 163, 170–171, 173, 177
White goosefoot *(Chenopodium album),* 172
Wild apple *(Malus sylvestris),* 172
Wild boar *(Sus scrofa),* 169
Wild cat *(Felis silvestris),* 158, 169
Wild strawberry *(Fragaria vesca),* 172
Willow *(Salix* sp.), 161
Wolf *(Canis lupus),* 158, 169, 175
Wool production, 144, 166, 168, 223–225

Yamna cultures, 16

Zubrow, E. B., 126

Made in the USA
Lexington, KY
20 January 2019